# Elizabeth

## GRAND DUCHESS
## OF RUSSIA

D1025276

# *Elizabeth*

## GRAND DUCHESS
## OF RUSSIA

## *Hugo Mager*

CARROLL & GRAF PUBLISHERS, INC.
NEW YORK

Copyright © 1998 by Hugo Mager

All rights reserved

First Carroll & Graf edition 1998
 Second printing September, 1998

Carroll & Graf Publishers, Inc.
19 West 21st Street,
New York, NY 10010-6805

Library of Congress Cataloging-in-Publication data is available
ISBN: 0-7867-0509-4

Manufactured in the United States of America

# *Acknowledgments*

I gratefully acknowledge the gracious permission of Her Majesty Queen Elizabeth II to examine material and reproduce photographs from the Royal Archives at Windsor Castle. The expert assistance of the Registrar, Lady de Bellaigue, and the curator of the Photograph Collection, Miss Frances Dimond, has been invaluable.

I am also indebted to the late H.R.H. Princess Margaret of Hesse and by the Rhine, who kindly gave me permission to visit the Hessian Grand Ducal Archives and generously verified the accuracy of the manuscript. Professor E.G. Franz and the staff of the Hessisches Staatsarchiv were punctilious and helpful in supplying material. Fräulein Birgit Aschenbrenner spent several hours transliterating texts in German Gothic script.

Lord Brabourne and the Trustees of the Broadlands Archives Settlement have generously given permission to examine the Broadlands Archives and reproduce photographs from them. Mrs. Chalk, the Librarian at Broadlands, and Dr. Christopher Woolgar and the archivists of the Hartley Library, Southampton University, have provided courteous and painstaking assistance.

I should also like to thank Dame Ann Warburton for helping me secure access to Cambridge University Library, and the librarians there for efficient answers to my requests.

Thanks to the exhaustive editing efforts of Ms. Frances Kuffel of the Jean V. Naggar Literary Agency, and Mr. Kent Carroll and Ms. Martine Bellen of Carroll & Graf Publishers, the manuscript has been transformed into smooth, coherent text in this volume.

Without the invaluable loan by Mr. and Mrs. Anthony Robertson of a word processor, this book could never have been finished.

Above all, I am indebted to Mr. David Duff. Not only has he allowed me to use material and quote from the new edition of *Queen Victoria's Highland Journals,* from *Albert and Victoria,* and from *Hessian Tapestry* (an essential foundation for any serious study of the Hessian and Romanov dynasties), but he and Mrs. Duff have provided advice, encouragement, and criticism at every stage of the work. Without their help, and the resources of their private library on European royalty, this book would not even have been begun, let alone finished.

*v*

# Family Tree

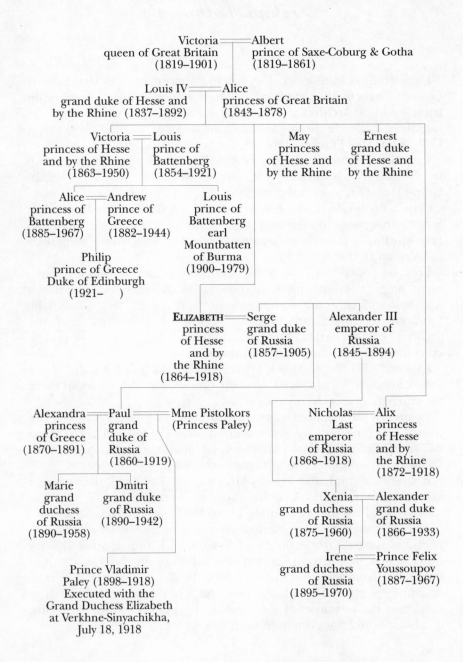

Victoria
queen of Great Britain
(1819–1901)
═══
Albert
prince of Saxe-Coburg & Gotha
(1819–1861)

Louis IV
grand duke of Hesse and
by the Rhine (1837–1892)
═══
Alice
princess of Great Britain
(1843–1878)

Victoria
princess of Hesse
and by the Rhine
(1863–1950)
═══
Louis
prince of
Battenberg
(1854–1921)

May
princess
of Hesse and
by the Rhine

Ernest
grand duke
of Hesse and
by the Rhine

Alice
princess of
Battenberg
(1885–1967)
═══
Andrew
prince of
Greece
(1882–1944)

Louis
prince of
Battenberg
earl
Mountbatten
of Burma
(1900–1979)

Philip
prince of Greece
Duke of Edinburgh
(1921–   )

**ELIZABETH**
princess
of Hesse
and by
the Rhine
(1864–1918)
═══
Serge
grand duke
of Russia
(1857–1905)

Alexander III
emperor of
Russia
(1845–1894)

Alexandra
princess
of Greece
(1870–1891)
═══
Paul
grand
duke of
Russia
(1860–1919)
═══
Mme Pistolkors
(Princess Paley)

Nicholas
Last
emperor
of Russia
(1868–1918)
═══
Alix
princess
of Hesse
and by
the Rhine
(1872–1918)

Marie
grand
duchess
of Russia
(1890–1958)

Dmitri
grand duke
of Russia
(1890–1942)

Xenia
grand duchess
of Russia
(1875–1960)
═══
Alexander
grand duke
of Russia
(1866–1933)

Prince Vladimir
Paley (1898–1918)
Executed with the
Grand Duchess Elizabeth
at Verkhne-Sinyachikha,
July 18, 1918

Irene
grand duchess
of Russia
(1895–1970)
═══
Prince Felix
Youssoupov
(1887–1967)

# Contents

# Elizabeth

## GRAND DUCHESS
## OF RUSSIA

# Prologue

On the crowded, dusty platform at Moscow station, I looked ahead at the gleaming rails stretching into the distance. Here an English princess had begun her final journey under armed guard three-quarters of a century before. A thousand miles to the east in the Ural mountains, her Bolshevik captors had subjected her to a torturous death in a lonely mine shaft that I intended to find. She was the Grand Duchess Elizabeth, a favorite granddaughter of Queen Victoria and a great-aunt of Prince Philip. Considered the most beautiful princess in Europe, she had rejected the suit of the future emperor William II of Germany to marry a Russian grand duke. After her husband's death from an assassin's bomb in the Kremlin, she showed remarkable courage and compassion in founding a convent and caring for the poor and sick in the most squalid quarters of Moscow. She firmly opposed the friendship of her sister, Empress Alexandra, with Rasputin and supported his assassins' decision to murder him. After the Russian Revolution she was sent, on Lenin's orders, into exile in a schoolroom one hundred miles north of Yekaterinburg. Two months later, she was thrown down a nearby mine shaft.

In search of the mine shaft, I boarded the Trans-Siberian Express for the Urals. I soon passed the magnificent blue-and-golden domes of the cathedrals of Sergiev Posad; the sight of this ancient citadel of Russian Orthodoxy had, no doubt, revived Elizabeth's faith as she traveled eastward. The train crossed the shimmering gray waters of the Volga, and rolled on over the immense flat expanse of Russia. For hours I looked out at a dense forest of birch and pine, and in a clearing I sometimes glimpsed a remote peasant village of wooden cabins. Where the train stopped elderly peasant women, wrapped in head scarves, sat selling strings of onions, and peddlers strolled about, offering food to add to the watery soup and black bread served in the train restaurant. After a day's journey, the train climbed through the pine-clad foothills of the Urals, passed a stone obelisk at the eastern border of Europe, and drew into the sprawling, industrial, Asian city of Yekaterinburg.

A chill autumn wind was blowing down the main street as I walked past the grim statue of the Bolshevik commissar Sverdlov. I noticed that someone had daubed its granite plinth with red paint symbolizing the blood of the Romanovs, whose execution he had ordered. In a side street, I came to my destination, a patch of waste ground opposite a massive onion-domed church. Two crosses had been put up amid the weeds and rubble, and some flowers had been laid at their feet. Beside them stood a small wooden chapel decked with a golden roof. In this place, Sverdlov's gruesome orders had been carried out. The day before Elizabeth's death, also on his orders, her sister Alexandra and Emperor Nicholas II had been murdered here, where the Ipatiev House had once stood. Awed by the enormity of these crimes, I entered the chapel. Inside, on the altar, surrounded by lighted candles, was an icon of a beautiful woman dressed in a nun's habit. A bearded Russian appeared and told me that the Moscow patriarch had recently canonized the martyr-saint Elizabeth, as she became known, and built this chapel in her honor. She had briefly been imprisoned in a nearby monastery in May 1918, before being taken to Alapayevsk.

The following day, I headed north in a Russian taxi driver. The driver said I was the first Englishman in seventy years to visit Alapayevsk. The sun rose and the morning mists cleared as I jolted along a pot-holed and almost deserted road through a virgin forest of birch and pine. We drove into a wide plateau dotted with mineral workings and industrial railways and, outside a gray concrete mining town, a policeman called me to a halt. He asked me the purpose of my journey, expressed astonishment that an Englishman should visit this lonely place and, after the payment of a suitable bribe, waved me on. I carried on over a bleak mountain landscape of shallow valleys and bare grassy meadows, passed a field full of peasants harvesting turnips, and saw ahead a sign in rusting letters, ten feet high, "Alapayevsk."

The taxi wound through several rutted, unpaved streets and drew up beside the drab one-storied red-brick building where Elizabeth, her companion Sister Barbara, and some distant relatives had spent the last two months of their lives. The Napolnaya School, as it was called, had changed little in seven decades of Communist rule. The small room in which Elizabeth and Sister Barbara had slept on bare wooden beds was now crammed with classroom desks. The yard outside, once a garden enclosed by a high wall where they had all tended vegetables under the eyes of the Red Guards, had become a plot of bare earth strewn with weeds. Here they had lived a monotonous day-to-day existence, being treated ever more strictly by their captors and becoming increasingly anxious about their fate. On the night of July 17, as the White armies drew near, they had been spirited away in darkness to be executed at Vorkhne-Sinyachikha.

Among the small crowd that had gathered out of curiosity at the sight of a foreigner in their town, I found an old woman who could show me the way to the mine shaft. A few miles farther north, in a pine copse at the center of a rolling grassy plain, I found a small brick chapel topped by a gleaming silvery cupola. Beside the chapel, in front of a shallow pit, stood a tall wooden cross. Beneath it had once stretched a deep mine shaft.

This was the shaft toward which Elizabeth had walked, followed by a guard with a rifle at her back. This was the edge where she knelt and prayed: "Father, forgive them, for they know not what they do." The guard swung the butt of his rifle on to her head and threw her, unconscious, sixty feet down, into the depths of the pit. One by one, her fellow prisoners went after her. Sister Barbara, who had kept company with her all the way from Moscow, her nephew Vladimir Paley, not yet twenty-one, a highly gifted dramatist and poet, and the three young sons of Grand Duke Constantine, who had played in her garden as children, passed over the edge. Grand Duke Serge Mikhailovich, an unhappy and taciturn old soldier, protested at this treatment and was shot in the head. A hand grenade was thrown down after them, and its explosion buried them all under a mass of earth and stones.

Later that night, the faint singing of hymns could be heard above the mine shaft. The prior of the Monastery of Alapayevsk, Father Seraphim, was one of those allowed near there by the Red Sentinels. When the White armies took over the area in September, Father Seraphim knew where to begin the excavation of the corpses. As he dug into the shaft, he was overwhelmed by what he saw. All but one of the victims had evidently survived the fall; the wounds and fractures of Prince John Constantinovich had been bandaged with strips of clothing, Elizabeth's last act before she died. We are told that when her body, the last to be recovered, was raised to the surface, it was found to be uncorrupt, and the fingers of her right hand were stiffened in the sign of the cross.

This sight made Father Seraphim, a devotee of the grand duchess, take the body of Elizabeth and those of the other prisoners eastward to a chapel of God outside the domain of the Bolsheviks. He set out with their coffins over the wide steppes of Siberia. Word had spread that Elizabeth was a saint, and people gathered by the wayside to pray at her bier. He was caught up in a wave of half-starving, destitute refugees in retreat from the Red terror. He crossed the mountains by Lake Baikal into China, and after nine months he reached Beijing.

In the autumn of 1920, Elizabeth's sister Victoria received a newspaper photograph of an Orthodox shrine in Bejing. This, she believed, must be the place where Elizabeth was buried. Victoria made inquiries, and the truth was confirmed. Knowing that Elizabeth had wished to be buried in the sacred soil of Jerusalem, she arranged for her coffin to be transferred there for a funeral in the Russian church beneath the Mount of Olives. A vast crowd of mourners, Russian peasant pilgrims and royal relatives, gathered outside the church as she was entombed in an elaborate mausoleum. She lay for seventy years, watched over by Father Seraphim for the rest of his life, until the Patriarch of Moscow hallowed her memory with the name of "Martyr-Saint Elizabeth." So ended the story of heroism which had begun more than a century earlier as Elizabeth's grandfather lay dying at Windsor Castle.

# Chapter 1

*I would like to shelter you in my arms, to protect you from all future anxiety, to still your aching longing! My own sweet Mama, you know I would give my life to you, could I alter what you have to bear!*

—LETTER FROM PRINCESS ALICE TO QUEEN VICTORIA, 23 AUGUST 1862, AFTER THE DEATH OF PRINCE ALBERT

On a gray wintry afternoon, December 8, 1861, Prince Albert, deathly pale from typhoid fever, lay watching the clouds sail past his bedroom window at Windsor Castle. Princess Alice, his third child, was playing his favorite hymns. Alice looked around and saw that her father's eyes were closed and his hands folded as if in prayer. After a while he looked up and smiled, and she asked if he had been asleep. "No," he replied, "only I have such sweet thoughts." To Alice it was clear that Albert was serenely resigned to the inevitable advance of the disease. Three days later he asked her if she had written to her sister, the crown princess of Prussia. "Yes," she said, "I told her that you were very ill." "You should have told her that I am dying. Yes, I am dying."[1]

Princess Alice became his chief nurse. She moved her bed into the room next door and was constantly by her father's side. Risking infection, she would play the piano or read to him. There were times when she found his pathetic groans almost unbearable, and she would leave for her room when she felt in danger of breaking down. She would emerge, recovered, a little later, pale but tranquil. Unlike Queen Victoria, she managed to appear calm and cheerful, and kept up her own private battle against despair. She warned her mother, who refused to acknowl-edge it, of the coming end, and took it on herself to send for the Prince of Wales. She saw many of the anxious callers at the Castle, including the duke of Cambridge, at 7:15 A.M.[2]

On December 14, it was clear that all would be over within twenty-four hours. The dying prince repeatedly asked for his daughter, and Queen Victoria was continually in and out of the room. At around ten in the evening, Alice was comforting her sis-ter Helena, who had given way to tears. She saw the unmistakable signs, and calmly whispered to a lady-in-waiting: "That is the death-rattle." Alice called in her mother. They knelt by the bed, and the queen clasped a hand from which life ebbed away.[3]

After his death, it was the eighteen-year-old Alice who was in charge, and her mother whose strength was sapped by grief. Alice moved her bed into her mother's room and for the next three nights underwent an intense ordeal. She heard the loud sobs of the queen, who lay clasping her husband's nightshirt and dressing gown. They only managed a fitful sleep from sheer exhaustion. "It is no exaggeration," Gerard Noel has written, "to say that the soundness of the queen's mind was balanced on a needle point." Through Alice's devoted attention, the queen recovered from her despair. The strain was so great that Alice wondered how she bore it.[4]

For months afterward, Alice was by her mother's side at Windsor and Osborne. She shared her outbursts of grief and became her representative to the outside world. She saw the ministers, and it was through her that all the messages to the sovereign were sent. Visitors noticed the change in her. She had become thin and worn, prone to frequent headaches, and her character was trans-formed. Lord Clarendon wrote: ". . . there is not such a girl in a thousand. I never met one who at her age had such sound princi-ples, so great judgement and such knowledge of the world. . . ." Alice had now acquired a stern will, and great fortitude and under-standing.[5]

Few could now recognize Alice as the forgotten child of the

royal family, the shy, thoughtful, and sentimental young girl with a sad face and deep set dark eyes. In her childhood she had been overshadowed by her more forward brothers and sisters. She always gave place to the eldest, Victoria, "Vicky," the Princess Royal, a precocious child, fluent in French by the age of three. She was the closest friend of the next oldest, Albert Edward, the Prince of Wales, a boy made lazy and rebellious by the spartan regime of gymnastics and forced learning that his father had imposed. A bond of understanding grew up between them, and only Alice could soothe away "Bertie's" tantrums. She grew up with a pronounced sensitivity to the sufferings of others.

In her sheltered childhood there were incidents which helped form the strength of will which she showed on her father's death. In 1849, at the age of six, she was with the queen when an Irishman fired a blank round from a homemade pistol at the carriage. The following year, she saw Robert Pate, a deranged ex-Hussar, leap at her mother's carriage. He struck the queen a violent blow on the head with a cane. Alice and the other children screamed, and the crowd seized and roughly handled the attacker. The Crimean War gave her a foretaste of a sight to become more familiar. With the queen and the Princess Royal she toured the hospitals and spoke to the wounded soldiers, retired from the war.[6]

In 1858, at fifteen, she endured the absence of the Princess Royal on her marriage to Prince Frederick, the eventual heir to the throne of Prussia. Vicky and Alice shared a bedroom for the last time. The following day, after the ceremony, Alice threw herself into her mother's arms and heaved with sobs.[7] In the following year, she went through her confirmation, which involved the ordeal of an examination by the archbishop of Canterbury. Her father tutored her according to the Lutheran Coburg ritual, and encouraged her to make serious and independent reflections on religion.

Alice, however, soon turned into a pert and forward young woman, full of larks. It was being said that she would be off to

Germany of her own accord to be married. In time the queen thought of finding Alice a husband from one of the pocket-states that made up the geographical expression "Germany."[8]

In choosing marriage partners from Germany, Queen Victoria was engaging in geopolitics as well as arranging domestic harmony. For Germany had long been the battlefield of Europe, and was now becoming the fulcrum of its power balances. For centuries it had been disunited, a loose assembly of autonomous kingdoms, electorates, free cities, grand duchies, and principalities that had once formed the entity known as the Holy Roman Empire. This itself was descended from the empire founded by Charlemagne in the ninth century, which claimed a misty continuity from ancient Rome. In the seventeenth century the ravages of the Thirty Years' War had destroyed the emperor's authority, reducing his domains to a rabble of minuscule territories. Out of the ruins of the Holy Roman Empire two powers had risen to preeminence. To the east the Hohenzollern dynasty had scythed out a swath of territory for the Kingdom of Prussia from Berlin to the eastern Baltic Sea. Further south, the Hapsburg dynasty ruled over a diverse array of Germans, Hungarians, Croats, Slovenes, Czechs, Slovaks, Poles, Ruthenians, and Romanians that was sometimes called the Austrian Empire. Their ruler had held the imperial crown for four centuries until in 1807 Francis II had abandoned the meaningless title of Holy Roman Emperor. The defeat of France in the Napoleonic Wars had brought the Prussian territory over northern Germany right up to the Rhine. It had also allowed the German states to assemble in the German Confederation, a hollow expression of the growing desire for national unity whose only concrete achievement was a powerless parliament. Its boundaries included almost all of Prussia and the German-speaking part of the Austrian Empire. Austria was the paramount power in the Confederation, but Prussia was soon to vie for supremacy with the appointment of Count Otto von Bismarck, a diplomatic genius, as its Minister-President. The crucial question was whether the sovereign of a future united

Germany would be the king of Prussia or the emperor of Austria. If the Austrian emperor took the crown, he would be ruler not only of all the German states and his own German-speaking territories, but also his peoples outside the Confederation, making him the most powerful man in continental Europe. If the Prussian king was made sovereign, the Austrian emperor's territories would be wholly excluded from his domains, for no Hapsburg would ever submit to being a vassal of the upstart Hohenzollerns.

Few were more aware of the potential for discord than Prince Albert, himself a German prince from Coburg. He regarded a smaller, Prussian-dominated Germany as the best guarantee of European stability. With deliberate intent he had arranged Vicky's marriage to Prince Frederick. Having carefully tutored her in his political views, he hoped for an English queen of Prussia at the head of a united, liberal, and progressive Germany in a peaceful Europe.[9] He looked to a future united Germany as a bulwark against the aggressive designs of Russia and France.

Alice's marriage was less significant. Queen Victoria wanted her husband to be from a small state, with obligations light enough for Alice to return and stay beside her. The queen's attention was drawn to Darmstadt, an antiquated town lying on the flat plain of the Rhine. It was the capital of Hesse-Darmstadt, a pocket-state whose ruler was Grand Duke Louis III of Hesse and by the Rhine. His sister Marie had married in 1841 Tsarevitch Alexander of Russia, who was now Emperor Alexander II. His younger brother Alexander had been a military adventurer of a high order. Grand Duke Louis had no children, and his other brother, Charles, was the heir to the grand duchy. It was Charles's eldest son, Louis, that the queen chose for Alice.[10]

In June 1860 Louis arrived in London. He proved to be a good-natured, agreeable young man, a soldier serving in the Prussian army. The queen liked him immensely. Alice met him at Buckingham Palace to the serenade of the Yorkshire Choral

Union, and lost her heart to him in the pouring rain at Ascot races. Before he left, Prince Louis asked the queen for Alice's photograph.

In November he returned to Windsor, and on the thirtieth the prince consort told him that he would have a chance of speaking to Alice. That evening the queen left him and Alice by the fireside, and retreated to a corner of the Red Room. After an interval she rose and received a whispered message from the couple that they were engaged. Louis was too overwrought for coherent speech. Alice, quiet but agitated, retired to her mother's room. Under the gaze of her parents she and Louis exchanged their first kiss. During a bitterly cold winter, their sad parting came on December 28. They gave each other tear-stained handkerchiefs, and he left her with his portrait on a locket. She wore it around her neck and caressed it so often that its durability was in doubt.

The new year opened in deep gloom. On January 1, 1861, the king of Prussia was dead, and Vicky was now crown princess. The queen's mother, the duchess of Kent, was suffering from cancer. Her eyesight failed her, and her hands stiffened. Almost every day Alice crossed the frost-ridden Home Park at Windsor to play the piano or read to her.

On March 15, the news came that she was dying. The family was at Buckingham Palace, and Alice and her parents rushed to be at her bedside. They found the duchess so far gone that she could not recognize her own daughter. The following morning, Prince Albert and Princess Alice were called in to join the queen, who had kept watch for most of the night. For half an hour they knelt by the bedside, then saw the end come. Prince Albert half-carried his wife to a sofa, and turned to Alice with the words: "Comfort Mama."[11] It was Alice, "full of intense feeling, tenderness and distress,"[12] who consoled the weeping queen and accompanied her on her daily pilgrimages to her mother's mausoleum.

Later in the year, Alice was wild with delight to learn that her Louis could join the family at the Highland paradise at Balmoral.

That summer she could roam freely with him through the glens. His good humor greatly enlivened the great expeditions the family took for miles over the green and rocky hills. They trekked along misty valleys, past a ruined castle, and a well of pure water, through narrow rocky defiles, and climbed up to a remote spot from which they could see mountains miles away in the soft evening glow.

As autumn approached and the evening shadows lengthened, the end came for the happiest time in Alice's life. Louis said good-bye to the family and to Alice, and drove away. As she and the queen took leave of John Brown, the Highland retainer, he expressed the hope that they would all remain well through the winter and return safe to Scotland, "and above all that you may have no deaths in the family."[13]

At this time Prince Albert said to his wife: "I do not cling to life. You do; but I set no store by it. If I knew that those I love were well cared for, I should be quite ready to die tomorrow. . . . I am sure, if I had a severe illness, I should give up at once."[14]

He was now a graying man. The heavy burdens of the past five years and the strain of comforting the queen after her mother's death had taken their toll. After the family's return to Windsor, more shocks were to follow. Family worries piled up.[15] The Princess Royal caught a severe cold and retired to bed; she took a long time to recover. News leaked out that the Prince of Wales had spent an intimate evening with an Irish actress. Albert's cousin, the king of Portugal, died from typhoid. King Pedro had been from the branch of the Coburg family* on whom a Hungarian monk had pronounced a terrible curse.[16] At midnight in a churchyard, surrounded by lighted candles, one Brother Emericus had intoned: "Then verily shall I pray to the Lord Almighty to visit the sins of the fathers upon the children to the third and fourth generation of the Coburg line." Now it seemed as if the curse had descended on Albert.

Albert struggled on. He was now beset with rheumatic pains, insomnia, and exhaustion. Complete rest was required, but he ploughed on with his official duties; one of the last was to inject a more conciliatory tone into a dispatch sent to the American government over the battleship *Trent*,† helping to avert a possible war. He was so tired, he told the queen, that he could hardly lift his pen. By the beginning of December he could eat nothing, and barely slept. On the seventh, he was confined to bed with what later turned out to be typhoid fever. The queen, herself always in robust health, refusing to accept the worst, believed that he would recover. Albert knew that he was going to die. It was to his capable, self-effacing daughter who had borne up so well on her grandmother's death, that he turned. Alice was the only person he could tell.

After her father's death Alice proved to be worthy of his confidence. She was resolved to carry out his principles of progress, social welfare, and education. Her maturity was grounded in a deep religious preoccupation. The inquiring mind her father had instilled in her now began to show itself. Her earnest reading of the chief Victorian theologians, F. W. Robertson's *Sermons* and Professor Jowett's *Essays and Reviews,* widened her spiritual outlook. She conversed with the leading churchmen, who were among the few visitors to the queen, and began to take a delight in discussing obscure questions with men of different denominations. She peered beneath the veil of the conventional religion in which she had been brought up, and questioned the many inconsistencies she found, feeling she must be sincere in her faith. As religion became her guide and support, she in turn came to feel that its doctrines must be embraced wholeheartedly, or not at all.[17]

On his visits to England, Prince Louis hardly recognized Alice as the carefree and high-spirited girl he had courted. Their wedding, set for July by the queen, who now followed her late husband's plans in everything, was far from the joyous celebration of young love he had anticipated. Instead it was to take place, with as little ceremony as possible, in the dining room at the seaside mansion of Osborne on the Isle of Wight. The house itself was still heavily laden with the prince consort's presence. His clothes were laid out in his dressing room, and his hat and cloak hung up in the hall as if he had just returned from a walk. When Alice came over for the wedding, she was accorded little of the privacy normally given to young brides. She was bound to remain constantly by her mother's side.[18]

The wedding day, 1 July 1862, dawned gray and windy. The distant sea was whipped into white-flecked rollers. Alice awoke and went over to her mother in the bed beside her. She smiled down at her and kissed her. The queen gave Alice her blessing and a prayer book. Sometime before one o'clock, Alice was dressed in a trousseau partly of black; by some portentous coincidence all four of her daughters were also to marry in mourning. The guests were dressed in half-mourning; among them were Prince and Princess Charles of Hesse, Louis's parents. The wedding ceremony, conducted by the archbishop of York, seemed to the queen more like a funeral.[19]

Afterward the queen clasped in her arms her son, Prince Alfred, who had been crying throughout the service, and broke into tears herself. "The bridegroom's parents were admitted and told the Queen how deeply they felt for her, and tears rolled down the Archbishop's cheeks."[20] The guests departed from the saddest wedding that any of them had ever known.

A four-horse brougham took the couple away for their honeymoon. It lasted three days and was spent at the nearby castle of St. Claire.

Alice and Louis then set off for the continent, and made a leisurely journey through the Low Countries before their triumphant entry into the Grand Duchy of Hesse. From Bingen, on the Hessian border, the crowds began to gather as they traveled down the steep and dense-wooded Rhine Valley. At the station before Darmstadt, the old Grand Duke Louis III, Prince Alexander of Battenberg and his wife, and Louis's parents, Prince and Princess Charles, boarded their special train. As they alighted at Darmstadt, a guard of honor awaited them. Alice and

Louis drove away in a six-horse carriage, a mounted escort following behind. The bells were ringing, the bands played, and the population gave a deafening roar of welcome. Throughout the long straight Rheinstrasse, decked with flags and triumphal arches, they were packed in rows of townsmen and schoolchildren who showered the couple with flowers. The welcome reached its climax as they drove through the main square past the statue of Louis I on a giant Doric column and the old baroque sandstone castle in the distance. They entered the house of Louis's parents, and that evening, the dense crowds called them out time and time again to welcome them with thunderous cheers.[21]

Alice still felt the pull of home as she settled in. There were pangs of guilt at deserting the bereaved queen. Alice poured out encouragement and support in her letters: "Take courage, dear Mama, and feel strong in the thought that you require all your moral and physical strength to continue the journey which brings you nearer to *Home* and to *Him*. I know how weary you feel, how you long to rest your head on his dear shoulder, to have him soothe your aching heart."[22] Alice knew that she would be expected to spend much time in her mother's company. The queen was slowly emerging from the anguish of bereavement and, as David Duff has written, she

> had no intention, or desire, to go mad. She had a job to do, and a man's memory to immortalise. She possessed what she termed "pluck," inherited from her mother and her father, whom George III had called "the bravest of my sons". She herself admitted that it was through lack of pluck that her husband had died. She badly needed, for company's sake, a married daughter and her husband about the house, but under the surface she had no intention of being dependent on anybody.[23]

Alice was that married daughter, and she knew that she would be expected to fill the post for some years. For a long time the queen would remain in the seclusion of mourning, much to the resentment of her subjects, but gradually her black clothes and her appearance as a grieving widow became more a habitual indulgence than a genuine expression of sorrow. In the meantime, Alice must be ready to return for two or three months of the year to Windsor and Balmoral. There would have to be a visit for the anniversary of her father's death. Alice was soon to be expecting a child, and the queen wanted it to be delivered at Windsor.

The nineteen-year-old Alice was also facing the novelty of life with a husband whose character was the opposite of her own. She was earnest, religious, and intellectually-minded; Louis was a bluff, good-natured soldier, fond of the outdoors, shooting, sherry, and horses. Nonetheless they were devoted to each other. They spoke and wrote their endearments partly in English, partly in German, Alice having learned the latter language from her father (though Queen Victoria used English with her children). On their visits to Windsor, Louis, often sporting a Norfolk jacket, liked to pose as an English gentleman, but his thick Germanic accent and limited vocabulary gave him away. A fellow dinner guest wrote satirically: "Louis' English and whole conversation consists in: 'You have in your country a—a what you call—ah—so. Like what you call—Alice! Alice! Was herst ein wohlengeblandersuhe? Fog. Ah so, yes. A fog, which makes what you call—ah—Alice! Was ist geblandesbend? Dark, yes, dark.'"24

In her husband's strange country, not yet emerged from the eighteenth century, Alice was like a new girl at school. She was obliged to meet people with no idea of polite conversation and to eat the customary gargantuan dinner every day at four. Her new home was worlds away from the grandeur of Windsor, a cramped house in a narrow cobbled street along which carts continually rumbled past. At night, the church bells could be heard tolling their melodious peals as they had done for centuries before.[25] Life in the town pursued a leisured course; the bands played in beer gardens, and the burghers strolled sedately through the chestnut avenues. In the surrounding half-timbered villages, peasant girls would drop curtsies to passing carriages.[26]

The grand ducal family's castles and their inhabitants were set in the same antiquated mold. Louis took her to Kranichstein, a magnificent old hunting lodge adorned with stags' antlers. Inside, by the ancient winding staircase, hung a life-sized picture of a stag on the spot where one had sought refuge from the pursuit of a medieval prince of Hesse.[27] In the surrounding oak woods, where wild boar and deer roamed, Alice could escape to ride. This, they decided, would be their summer home.

They saw the castle of Heiligenberg, set in the hills above the valley of the Rhine. It consisted of a pair of farm buildings, the "Front House" and "Back House," and some outbuildings grouped around a central courtyard, with a fountain. This was the summer home of Louis's uncle, Prince Alexander of Hesse, a military adventurer whose valor in battle had won him the highest military decorations of Austria, Prussia, Russia, and Electoral Hesse. In 1851, becoming infatuated with Julie von Hauke, a pretty Polish lady-in-waiting at the Russian court, he had eloped with her to Warsaw and married her at Breslau. His morganatic wife was created countess, and later princess, of Battenberg, the name of a ruined castle of the north of Hesse-Darmstadt. He eventually retired to Heiligenberg. He had four sons, Louis, Alexander, Henry, and Francis Joseph and a daughter, Marie, who all bore the name of Battenberg.

At the center of Darmstadt stood the old castle, a jumble of medieval courtyards surrounded by a baroque sandstone facade. On market days, the cries of traders drifted up to the first-floor rooms from the square outside. There lived another uncle of Prince Louis, the old grand duke, Louis III, who on their first visit took Alice to dinner on his arm. The grand duke was immensely tall and almost bald. He was a widower, and an eccentric, old-fashioned recluse. His chief interests were a collection of watches in his study, which all struck the hour at the same time, and a vast hoard of cigar holders to which more were added on his birthday and at Christmas. He carried no handkerchief, but would ring for one to be brought on a salver when necessary. Every letter he received, however trivial, was registered and filed away. In his bearing he resembled an eighteenth-century grand seigneur. He would address the lower orders in the third person, "er," and would make his frequent journeys to his other homes in a barouche with postilions and outriders. As an honest, constitutional sovereign, he was respected by his people.[28]

A source of pride for the grand duke was a row of pink sandstone statues in the castle courtyard. These were his forebears, the old princes of Hesse from a dynasty of a thousand years;‡ by comparison the Hohenzollern rulers of Prussia were parvenus. One prince, George of Hesse-Darmstadt, had commanded the British forces in the war of the Spanish succession and captured Gibraltar. Another, Prince Frederick, had led the galleys of the Knights of Malta to a victory over Turkey and become their captain-general. Further in the past, Philip the Magnanimous had brought the Protestant reformation to Hesse and founded the University at Marburg, the town where his medieval ancestors lay buried. It was at Marburg that the foundress of the Hessian dynasty, the legendary Saint Elizabeth of Hungary, had lived and died in the thirteenth century.

Alice was able to visit Marburg soon after the birth of her first child, Victoria, in 1863. In the stifling August heat, she and Louis traveled north through the dense forests to the old town lying in a fold of the hills beneath a gothic castle.[29] In the Elizabeth Church, they saw the tombs of Hessian rulers covered by their stone effigies. In a corner, decked with jewels, stood the gilded shrine of Saint Elizabeth. An inscription ran:

> *Glory of Germany, jewel of virtue, source of wisdom, ornament of the church, flower of the faith, ideal of the young, curer of illness, hope of the guilty, bow thy heart to the wishes of thy servants, O Elizabeth, thou who rulest in Heaven after thou hast*

*conquered the Jebusites by healing us in this mausoleum with thy holy body.*

The tale of this suffering princess had moved Alice; she had read Kingsley's *Saint's Tragedy* as a child. Her life in Hesse was to follow the saint's example in helping the poor and sick, and suffering without complaint. A long line of Hessian women had done so before her.

In 1220, Saint Elizabeth had married Ludwig, heir to the county of Thuringia. She became torn between her love for her husband and a religious compassion toward the poor. One winter, on her way to a banquet, she gave her gilded cloak to a shivering beggar. Legend has it that once she saw a leper in the street, took him home, bathed him, gave him food and drink, and placed him in her marital bed. Her infuriated husband ran into the bedroom and tore back the sheets. By a miracle he saw, not the beggar, but a picture of the crucified Christ, and was converted to her good works.§

Ludwig died on a crusade in 1227. Thereafter Elizabeth refused to eat any food that had been extorted from the peasants from a territory defeated in war. Her shocked relatives banished her from the Thuringian court, and she lived in the castle at Marburg. She gave away her worldly goods to the poor, and founded hospitals where she personally nursed and fed the poor and sick. She entered the order of St. Francis, and spent the remaining four years of her life struggling against failing health and doing works of charity.

When Alice gave birth to her second daughter, on November 1, 1864, she decided to name her after Saint Elizabeth. She and her husband were disappointed that the child was a girl.[30] They could have no idea how closely this infant was to follow in the footsteps of her saintly ancestress. She also was to marry a foreign prince, to enter a holy order after his death, dedicate herself to nursing and charity, give away her riches to the poor, to found hospitals, and be revered by the people and mocked at court. She, in her turn, was to become a saint.

## Notes to Chapter 1

*King Pedro of Portugal was a grandson of Prince Albert's great-uncle, Prince Ferdinand of Coburg (1785–1851). Prince Ferdinand had married Antoinette de Kohary, only child of Prince Joseph Kohar, chancellor of the Austrian Empire and one of the richest men in Hungary. Prince Joseph persuaded the emperor to sign a filiation order giving Antoinette the legal status of a man, and allowing her to inherit his estate, which was normally entailed in favor of the male line. Brother Emericus was one of her male relatives outraged at losing their inheritance.

The curse struck not only King Pedro of Portugal but his successor, King Carlos of Portugal, and his son Luis, who were assassinated in 1908 in Lisbon. Prince Philip of Coburg married Princess Louise of Belgium, but his bestiality so ruined her health that he had her certified as mad. "The climax of the curse," David Duff has written, "came upon Philip's son Leopold, of the third generation. On 17th October 1915 a volley of shots rang from a first-floor flat in Vienna. The police fetched a locksmith to force the door. The Hussar uniform of Leopold had been ripped by revolver bullets. There was a hole where an eye had been. The flesh on his face had been eaten away to the bone. Camilla Rybika, his mistress, had fired five shots at him and then smashed a bottle of vitriol in his face. And yet he breathed and screamed. The last bullet she had kept for herself. She lay, half-naked, shot through the heart."

As we shall see, in later years the curse also seemed to fall on Princess Alice and her children.

†American antagonism toward Britain had been aroused by the sympathy of the British upper class for the Confederate side in the Civil War. When the U.S. Navy arrested Confederate agents onboard a British ship, the *Trent*, the British inserted a clause enabling the federal government without loss of honor to declare the arrest unauthorized. Remarking, "One war at a time," President Lincoln eventually agreed to release the arrested man.

‡In his highly detailed, privately published work, *The Mountbatten Lineage*, Earl Mountbatten of Burma traced the Hessian pedigree back to the fourth century. The source only becomes well documented, however, in the ninth century, when the Holy Roman emperor Charlemagne emerges as an ancestor.

§Another version of the story has it that Elizabeth met her husband while taking food to the poor. He asked what she was carrying in her basket, and received the reply: "Only roses, my lord." He opened her basket and, by a miracle, the food was turned into roses.

# Chapter 2

*Impossible. I have the key in my pocket.*

—GRAND DUKE LOUIS III,
ON BEING TOLD THAT THE INVADING PRUSSIANS
HAD ENTERED THE HESSIAN TREASURY, JULY 1866

For the first nineteen months, there was nothing in the trivial events of this baby's life to set her on the path of her famous ancestress. She was a fat and heavy child, bearing a thin growth of chestnut hair. She was baptized Elizabeth Alexandra Louise Alice and called "Ella" in the nursery. Elizabeth screamed throughout the christening while her maternal grandmother, Princess Charles, patiently held her in her arms. Her elder sister, Victoria, kept kneeling down and tumbling over a footstool.[1]

Victoria and Ella, their mother wrote, were "so dear together" and became devoted to each other. They shared a bedroom, Elizabeth sleeping in her bath and Victoria in a wicker cradle lined with chintz. Alice hoped that a nearby stove would keep the cold away during the harsh winter of 1865. But the snow piled up several feet deep, the two girls caught severe coughs, and Elizabeth's was the most violent.[2]

Alice found Elizabeth "too funny, and by no means easy to manage." "Ella is civil to all strangers," she wrote, "—excepting to my mother-in-law, or to old ladies. It is too tiresome." It was fortunate that she was civil to Louis's aunt, the grieving Empress Marie of Russia, when she came to Heiligenberg the following

23

summer. Marie's married life had been made miserable by her poor health and the repeated infidelities of her husband, the Emperor Alexander II. Her eldest and favorite son, Nicholas, to whom she had devoted her life to prepare him for the throne, had recently died of meningitis. She was pale and worn when Alice introduced her two children. While Victoria romped with Marie's two sons, Serge and Paul, Marie held the infant Elizabeth on her knee. She was able to distract herself by playing with the baby for half an hour, and found her "particularly sociable and amiable." The child seemed to enjoy her attentions.[3]

Elizabeth also exercised her charm on Queen Victoria, who arrived in August 1865, partly to see her new granddaughter. The short and stout queen-empress, still dressed in mourning, bearing her usual imperious air, did not intimidate the child, who made no protest when the queen took her in her arms.

The queen, however, was shocked to hear that Alice was feeding Ella herself. To her the practice was newfangled and unladylike. She fumed that Alice was making a cow of herself, and was soon to name a black heifer at Balmoral "Princess Alice." This represented the parting of the ways for the queen and her daughter. When Alice took her family to Balmoral that autumn, she found that the queen no longer needed her presence. She had acquired a personal servant in the form of John Brown, her Highland retainer. She now had a man to lean on, who filled the place previously held by Prince Albert and Lord Melbourne, and ceased to demand that a married daughter be about the house.[4]

Now Alice could dedicate herself to her children and her life in Darmstadt. In March 1866, she at last moved her family out of the cramped house in the Wilhelminenstrasse: the New Palace, an expensive building in the style of a Piccadilly mansion, was now fit to be occupied. Alice decorated the rooms in the light, airy English Regency style she remembered from her childhood. Bright chintzes were laid round the windows, and on the walls she hung portraits of King George III and her parents, and treasured sketches of Windsor, Balmoral, and Osborne.[5]

Here the infant Elizabeth grew up surrounded by English domestic habits and learned to appreciate her mother's country. English was the language she first knew, which she spoke to her mother and sister, and all her life she was to consider herself chiefly English. Soon a Mrs. Mary Anne Orchard, nicknamed "Orchie," was to come and enforce a strict regimen on her and Victoria in the large plain nursery rooms. "She was the ideal head nurse," Baroness Buxhoeveden later wrote, "quiet, enforcing obedience, not disdaining punishment, but kind though firm."[6] Each night she would put the two girls to sleep in their bedroom, which they were to share until Victoria's marriage. They were affectionate and intimate friends, sharing each other's joys, sorrows and secrets.[7]

But for an accident of history, the young Elizabeth might have enjoyed this secure and carefree childhood right up to her marriage, and never set out on the long road to her sainthood. She could have lived the existence common to so many German princesses, married in dutiful obedience to a princeling from a neighboring state, dedicated to her children and dying in obscurity. But before the age of two she faced the upheaval of a war which in turn would set into motion events leading to a greater war and further trials for Elizabeth and her mother. The mental strain on her mother would leave a permanent mark on Elizabeth's religious character.

Sandwiched between Germany and Denmark were the largely German-speaking duchies of Schleswig and Holstein. In 1863 the childless King Frederick of Denmark had died, leaving his kingdom to Prince Christian, a relative by female descent. According to the Treaty of London of 1852, Christian was also entitled to inherit the two duchies, hereditary possessions of the Danish crown, and to incorporate them into the Danish Kingdom. By the Salic law of the duchies their rightful heir was the duke of Augustenburg, a German prince and a relative of King Frederick by male descent.

When King Christian signed a constitution incorporating

Schleswig into the Danish Kingdom, a storm of nationalist protest was aroused in Germany. The army of the German Confederation, which included Hessian troops, occupied Holstein in support of the claims of the duke of Augustenburg. The Prussians and Austrians then defeated the Danes in battle and occupied Schleswig.

At this point a difference of opinion arose. Austria, Hesse, and the other German states wanted the duke of Augustenburg to rule the duchies; the King of Prussia, persuaded by his wily chief minister, Bismarck, maintained that they belonged to Prussia and Austria by right of conquest. Beneath this trivial dispute was a struggle for the mastery of Germany. A growing spirit of nationalism sought to unite the German Confederation in a single nation, and the two great German powers, Austria—half in and half out of Germany—and Prussia—with the greatest army—were vying to lead it. Bismarck's aim was to provoke a quarrel with Austria, secure the duchies for Prussia, and exclude Austria from any say in German affairs, by war if necessary. Austria sought an alliance of the smaller states against Prussia.

Relations between the two powers steadily deteriorated. In the face of the Prussian menace, the armies of the smaller states were obliged to evacuate Holstein. On June 1, 1866, Austria entrusted the future of the duchies to the parliament of the German Confederation. Prussian troops took over Holstein from the Austrians. The federal parliament, alarmed at Prussia's aggression, voted at Austria's suggestion to mobilize against Prussia. On June 15 Prussia delivered ultimata to its neighbors Hanover, Saxony, and Electoral Hesse,* threatening hostilities if they did not take Prussia's side. On the 16th, without a declaration of war, the Prussians occupied these states, and were fifty miles from Darmstadt.[8] The Seven Weeks' War had begun.

Hesse-Darmstadt was now in a ferment of agitation. The grand ducal family was caught up in the heat of war. Prince Louis took command of the Hessian cavalry brigade. His brother, Prince William, joined the staff of their uncle, Prince Alexander, who commanded an entire army corps.[9] The Darmstadt streets were crowded with soldiers and shouting citizens. An insurrection was feared.

To Alice, it seemed that the safety of her two small daughters was in peril. On June 17, a fierce cold wind blew up, gathering strength by the hour; the trains were still running, and Alice managed to get Elizabeth and Victoria to the station, where a lady-in-waiting received them to take off by train and boat to Windsor.[10] By noon that day a hurricane was sweeping the streets of Darmstadt. In the surrounding countryside trees were bent, cracked or entirely blown over. In the nearby castle of Heiligenburg the occupants were not even able to push the main door shut.[11]

Elizabeth and Victoria, in the care of Queen Victoria, spent a lonely time in the gray stone castle at Windsor. The war ended after seven homesick weeks, and the two girls returned to Darmstadt. After the first great upheaval in her life, Elizabeth was delighted to see her mother again. "Ella won't leave me when I come into the room," Alice wrote, "she keeps kissing me and putting her fat arms round my neck. There is such a scene when I go away. She is so affectionate. . . ." A little later, she was to cry when her parents left to visit friends for a few days, and would try to join them on the train.[12]

Much had changed in the few weeks of her absence. She now had a new baby sister to play with, who was soon to be christened Irene (the Greek word for "peace"). Alice had fallen ill with rheumatism and neuralgia, and it was a wonder that she had not caught the cholera and smallpox now raging in Hesse. The Darmstadt hospitals were filled up with wounded soldiers. Worse, the town was overrun by Prussian troops, appropriating meat and common luxuries and looting the barracks and arsenal. They billeted themselves on the citizens and extorted millions of thalers.† In the neighboring Free City of Frankfurt the Prussian officers were hiring cabs and buying jewelry, leaving the city to foot the bill; the burgomaster had hanged himself in despair.[13]

Prussia had defeated Austria at the bloody battle of Königgrätz and wrested the leadership of Germany from her; the German Confederation was dissolved and replaced by the North German Confederation dominated by Prussia. The southern German states and Austria were excluded from this new arrangement; henceforth Austria would play no part in the new Germany. Prussia had won the war and was exacting onerous terms of peace. Besides Schleswig-Holstein, she swallowed up Hanover, Nassau, Frankfurt, and Electoral Hesse. Grand Duke Louis III was forced to give up his northern territory of Upper Hesse; it was only through the intervention of his brother-in-law, the Russian emperor, that he kept Hesse-Darmstadt. The Hessian railway, telegraph, and postal revenues were taken over, and an indemnity in the Hessian currency of three million florins was imposed. The Prussian demands had emptied out the Hessian treasury.

This result of the war was to deny Elizabeth the wealthy and leisured life of so many other German princesses. For Alice had dug deep into her dowry to pay for the New Palace; there was now nothing left, and she had to live very frugally. She could take her children only to the cheapest seaside resorts, and had to sew their clothes herself. From that time on Elizabeth was brought up in stern austerity. Her homemade dresses were of the plainest kind, and she would always bear memories of the endless succession of rice puddings and baked apples served in the nursery. Soon she was to be taught a housemaid's duties, and would learn how to make her bed, bake cakes, lay the fires, and sweep and dust the rooms. She would quickly adapt to plain living and for the rest of her life consider luxury trivial.[14]

Elizabeth was brought up by her mother to take no pride in being a princess. Instead Alice instilled in her "the double duty of living for others and of being an example—good and modest."[15] During Christmas of 1866 she made sure that Elizabeth appreciated her good fortune. It was a bleak time for Darmstadt. Few gifts could be found in the shops, and the hospitals were still filled with the wounded. Alice reminded Elizabeth that others lived harsher lives. She made her give away some of her presents to the poorer children and taught Elizabeth to become adept at sewing; the following year Elizabeth eagerly sewed together a Christmas present for Queen Victoria with her own hands. "She is so very good, my grandmama," she said.[16]

Alice also set an example of an earnest concern for the poor and sick. She was applying her father's progressive ideas to Hesse, and transforming the primitive medicine, hygiene, and public welfare of this antiquated grand duchy into models for the rest of Germany. As patroness of a society assisting pregnant women, she gave help to the poorest of expectant mothers. Once she went unrecognized to cook, clean, and nurse in the house of a poor woman with four children and a baby. She founded a lunatic asylum with the proceeds of a bazaar she held in her own home. In addition, she set up societies training women for nursing, needlework, and even paid employment; fought for public hygiene and a drainage system in Darmstadt; and laid down a revolutionary principle that help should be given by right to those who needed it and the costs paid out of the public purse. These reforms were astonishing in a society where one respected citizen opposed improved hygiene on the grounds that he had never had a bath in his life.[17] This atmosphere impressed Elizabeth as she grew up. Years later, her mother's example was to be a primary influence.

Nonetheless, Elizabeth was a merry, high-spirited child, with a ready smile and the prettiest face of the three girls. She was far less tractable than her elder sister Victoria. Alice wrote to Queen Victoria of her contrariness: "Ella, who was breakfasting with me just now, saw me dip my Bretzel in my coffee, and said: 'Oh Mama, you must not! Do you allow yourself to do that?' because I don't allow her to do it."[18]

Elizabeth had many diversions from the serious routine of the adult world. At Christmas there was a huge fir tree set up for the children, its branches laden with candles, apples, gilt nuts, pink quince sausages, and small treasures. The whole family would sit down to a dinner of the traditional German goose, with mince pies and plum pudding sent over from England.[19]

Almost every year Elizabeth had a chance to see a brilliant assembly of the Russian court when Louis's aunt, Empress Marie, brought her younger children to come and stay with her brother, Prince Alexander. Alexander's castle, at Heiligenberg nearby, was set in a fold of the beech-wooded hills above the flat plain of the Rhine. From the shade of the lime trees on the terrace, the river could be seen far below in a bluish haze. Before the recent war, Alexander had rebuilt the castle as a splendid Italianate mansion with two turrets stretching above the trees. Even so, its sixty rooms could not house the vast Romanov retinue of courtiers and servants, many of whom would be lodged in the village beneath. Marie's husband, Emperor Alexander II, would join her after taking the waters at a nearby spa with one of his eldest sons, Vladimir, or his newly married heir, Alexander, both in their twenties.

Vladimir and Alexander were too old to join Elizabeth and her sisters in their childish games or when they were running about the woods and picking the wildflowers Elizabeth adored. Instead the girls had the two youngest Russians for their playmates, Serge and Paul, who were a few years older. The young Grand Duke Serge, the older of the two, soon became Elizabeth's childhood sweetheart. "Serge," recalled the daughter of a British diplomat stationed in Darmstadt, ". . . often left his games with the other boys, to lead her gently by the hand, guiding her uncertain footsteps down the steep garden paths."[20]

Another diversion came with the birth of a baby on November 25, 1868. The boom of a saluting gun startled Elizabeth as she played in the nursery. Fifty guns in all were fired: "That," the nursemaid told her, "is for a brother." Elizabeth, dressed in red and white and holding a bouquet, saw him being christened Ernst, or Ernest in English.[21] "The girls are delighted with their brother," Alice wrote.[22] He became the pet of the girls, and Elizabeth was to be his trusted friend and the most sympathetic of his sisters.

It was not long, however, before dark clouds overshadowed the carefree childhood of four-year-old Elizabeth. Early in January 1869 a minor earthquake shook Darmstadt and scared Elizabeth with its eerie dull rumbling. "It seemed as if the house rocked," Alice wrote, "and at the same time the unearthly noise."[23] A few weeks later, Elizabeth was the victim of a short but severe asthma attack. Her mother wrote to Queen Victoria: "Two nights ago she could not speak—barely breathe—and was so uncomfortable, poor child."[24]

These two small shocks foreshadowed the far greater trauma of another war, the end result of the chain of events that had been detonated by the Schleswig-Holstein storm of 1864. In Berlin, diplomatic maneuvers that would set off the conflict were already taking place. In the summer young Elizabeth had a foretaste of the Prussian dynasty's armed might, when Alice and Louis took their children to Potsdam, a kind of Prussian Versailles situated outside Berlin. It was an elegant little town of palaces, canals, statues, lime trees, and an imposing domed and pillared church. They stayed with the crown princess, Alice's sister "Vicky." Vicky had endured a harsh and lonely life at the Prussian court. Her marriage to Crown Prince Frederick had turned out to be a painful contrast to Prince Albert's high-minded political intentions. Vicky had found that militaristic chauvinism reigned in Berlin, with her being expected to become a submissive German wife. The resultant strain had so lowered her health that her first son, William, barely survived his birth in 1859 and emerged with a withered left arm.‡[25]

This deformity had turned Prince William, now eleven, into a restless character, determined to prove that he was as fit and agile as anyone else. As the eldest child and ultimate heir to the Prussian throne, he took charge of the children's indoor games during the cold and wet June. Elizabeth and Victoria found themselves under his thumb, and along with his brother and sister, Henry and Charlotte, they meekly complied with his orders.

Elizabeth also found the atmosphere cold, formal, and militaristic. Wherever she walked about the baroque stone palace or the clipped lawns and chestnut trees in the grounds, she was followed by a liveried footman. She stood in awe of William's tutor, Dr. Hinzpeter, a stern, fearsome man. From a nearby parade ground she could hear the bark of orders as recruits were constantly drilled. She and Victoria saw the imposing First Guards Regiment march past in perfect order.[26] Prince William took part, dressed as a lieutenant in a uniform specially tailored to conceal his withered arm.[27] The pace was too quick for him, and a tall sergeant dragged him along by his good hand to keep him in step.

While Elizabeth was watching this display of the Prussian royal house's armed might, rumors were flying around the chancelleries of Europe that an offer was being made to a relative of King William of Prussia, an offer that was to embroil all Germany in another war. The previous year a revolution had driven the queen of Spain from her throne. The revolutionary government sought as her successor a prince more amenable to their liberal ideas. After several rejected offers, their choice fell on Prince Leopold of Hohenzollern-Sigmaringen, from the Catholic branch of the Prussian dynasty.

It was in February 1870 that the Spanish government actually pressed Leopold to accept the throne. Now the consequences of the wars of Schleswig-Holstein began to show themselves. Bismarck and the Prussian generals had learned several lessons; the war of 1866 had served as a useful trial run, and they had planned ahead for more aggressive military expansion. They were keenly aware that the British had refused to come to Denmark's aid in 1864 and would be convinced until 1914 that Britain would give them a free hand in conquering other parts of Europe as well. Bismarck now sensed the opportunity to unite Germany by a victorious war with France. The south German states of Bavaria, Württemberg, and Baden were solidly opposed to any union with the Prussian-dominated North German Confederation; left to itself, German unification would take decades. Here was a chance, with the threat of a German on the Spanish throne, to goad the French into belligerence and to impress on the south Germans the need for a union to prevent their seizure by France. If Germany presented a united front, Austria would be cowed into rejecting an alliance with France. Bismarck secretly persuaded Leopold to accept the Spanish offer and King William to approve.

As the French grew more hostile over the next few months, Bismarck schemed so adroitly that it was left to them to fire the first shot and bear the aggressor's blame. As he foresaw, all German states rallied to the defense of the fatherland. On 15 July 1870 the Franco-Prussian war began.

Back in Darmstadt, Elizabeth could sense the tense atmosphere at the opening of the war. From the Hessian hills the battle of Strasbourg could be seen, and an invasion was thought imminent. Alexander of Hesse's carriage horses were let loose in the woods lest the French should commandeer them. His servants prepared to bury his silver and jewels. Elizabeth and the other children were now escorted by an armed gendarme on their rides; it was feared that Gypsies and camp followers might attack them. For a while no letters or telegrams could be sent; the military took over the post and railways, and an endless succession of troop trains passed through Darmstadt to the front. The children's Prussian governess taught them to sing patriotic songs.[28] On July 25 their father buckled on his sword and marched off to take charge of the Hessian troops.[29]

Elizabeth and the other children, living out of town at Kranichstein, could see their mother growing ever more weary and nervous under the strain of nursing the wounded. Although she was expecting another child, she drove into Darmstadt every morning. She organized the running of three military hospitals and arranged supplies for the front. Risking infection, she comforted and spoke to the hundreds of wounded and sometimes mutilated soldiers who poured in by each train from the front. Every evening Elizabeth would see her mother return more exhausted and suffering from constant headaches. She was unable to sleep from her anxiety for her husband's safety. As she neared her confinement she was stricken with fever and neuralgia. Her eyes became so inflamed she was forbidden to read or write. To make matters worse, her doctor contracted a dangerous infection and dared not treat her; a replacement was rushed out from England. On October 6, Frederick William, her fifth child, was born prematurely. He was a hemophiliac.

That year a bitterly cold winter set in early. In the beech woods around Kranichstein Elizabeth and Victoria gathered up the frozen swallows that had not had time to migrate, and brought them indoors. Their nurse Orchie warmed them in the nursery. Soon afterward the family moved to the New Palace in Darmstadt. There Elizabeth saw for the first time the grim reality of war. The poor lined up outside soup kitchens for a meager meal. The squares were crammed with wounded soldiers and prisoners of war living in huts. Nowhere were the children free from the danger of infection. At the bottom of the garden, one thousand two hundred Frenchmen, many wounded, were crowded into a barracks. In the house Alice had put up two wounded soldiers. One lay close to death with typhoid for six weeks; Alice's attentions, said the doctors, saved his life. The other showed Elizabeth and her sisters the fragments of his shattered leg he kept in a pillbox. Daily they heard the march of a dead soldier's funeral in the street outside.[30]

In November the doctors decreed that Alice had had enough. She spent three weeks with her sister in Berlin, where she recovered from the enormous nervous strain of the past four months, a strain that was to have momentous results for Elizabeth's future life and the history of Europe. The girls were handed over to their grandparents at the Luisenplatz.

"We grown-up ones of the family have given up keeping Christmas for ourselves," Alice wrote to Queen Victoria.[31] On Christmas Day it was five months since Louis had marched off to war, and the family held a gloomy celebration in his absence. The snow lay thick outside as they gathered around the Christmas tree. With them were the two wounded soldiers and the servant children whose fathers were at the front. Elizabeth, pale and thin, was now a child with an experience of bloodshed and suffering rare in the life of any princess; she tried to be good and comfort her mother. Together with Victoria she wrote thank-you letters in a clumsy hand for the presents Queen Victoria had sent.[32]

In the new year of 1871, the outlook brightened. The two soldiers were recovering, and on crutches attended the christening of Elizabeth's baby brother Fredrick William.[33] In the snow-covered streets children were playing with kepis given away by French prisoners. It now had become clear that Germany was winning the war. The captured French emperor, Napoleon III, was imprisoned nearby in Cassel, and was paraded in the public park like a circus animal.[34] His empire had fallen, his army had surrendered, and the Germans were bombarding Paris with the aim of starving the besieged city into surrender.

Not far from the desperate fighting in Paris, an equally tumultuous event had taken place. At Versailles the conquering Germans proclaimed King William of Prussia to be their Emperor. It was the culmination of years of diplomacy by Bismarck, and the end of a process stretching back to the Napoleonic Wars. By a combination of bribes, concessions, and bullying, Bismarck had ensured that underneath a semblance of equality with the smaller states, Prussia was all-powerful in the united Germany with its new federal constitution. The sovereign pretensions of the petty German princes, whose territories were often smaller than the land owned by an English duke or an American millionaire, were swept away at a stroke. The formidable Prussian army made the new Germany the dominant power on the continent. That power lay largely with the King of Prussia, whose right to rule, or appoint a dictatorial chancellor such as Bismarck, was little fettered by the ineffectual parliament of the new nation. It was a far cry from Prince Albert's dream of a liberal Germany in a peaceful Europe.

## Notes to Chapter 2

*Electoral Hesse, also called Hesse-Cassel, was adjacent to Grand Duke Louis III's territory of Hesse and the Rhine. Until the Prussian invasion it was ruled by a relative of Louis.

†A north German currency, equivalent to three marks in the unified Germany.

‡The birth had been fraught with complications. The child was delivered with a pair of forceps, and at first could not breathe. By continuous rubbing, slapping, and dousing in hot baths he was persuaded to take his first breath. Controversy has arisen over whether this caused his physical deformities; the most probable explanation is that they were the result of cerebral palsy brought on by a lack of oxygen in his mother's womb. This in turn may have been caused by the pressure exerted on the crown princess by Queen Victoria and the hostile atmosphere she met with at the Prussian court.

From his earliest moments William was surrounded by militarism. A field marshal, hearing of his birth, broke a palace window and shouted to the guards outside: "Lads! It's a fine recruit!"

# Chapter 3

*Each year brings us nearer to the reunion with the dead, though it is sad to think how one's hourglass is running out and how little good goes with it.*

—LETTER FROM PRINCESS ALICE TO PRINCESS VICTORIA,
DECEMBER 1865

The war was now over. On March 6, 1871, the whole town of Darmstadt was illuminated in a blaze of color at the news that a peace treaty was signed. Elizabeth anxiously watched a housemaid clamber precariously through an upper window of the New Palace to light a candle on the ledge outside. With Victoria and her mother she went out into the streets, and marveled at the brilliant glow from candles set in every window.[1]

An even greater spectacle was the return of the Hessian army. Garlands and flags covered the streets, lined by cheering crowds. The pouring rain was no deterrent to the children, who were allowed to join the procession in their mother's coach. Elizabeth was filled with pride as her father rode at the head of his troops, wearing Prussia's highest medal for his bravery in battle. The bands played rousing tunes as the soldiers marched with oak leaves in their helmets. Plumed horses drew captured cannon surrounded by shields inscribed with the names of battles. The children later saw two of these cannon, bearing Napoleon III's monogram, placed on the terrace of the New Palace.[2] "It is a thing for them never to forget," wrote Alice in a prophetic sentence, "this great and glorious, though too horrid, war."[3]

The family could now relax at Seeheim, a pretty country seat in the hills above the Rhine. "The children," Alice wrote, "are beside themselves with pleasure." Elizabeth ran without a care through the fine woods and the grassy valleys dotted with rocks and splashing brooks. She took delight in seeking out wildflowers and learning their names. She went over to play at Heiligenberg, where the Empress Marie of Russia was staying with her children.[4]

In August, Elizabeth saw the seaside for the first time. The family stayed at Blankenberghe, a chilly resort on the Belgian coast that was all they could afford. They put up in cramped, untidy rooms in a hotel beside the treeless beach where they sat all day. The seashore was crowded and open to all, and many turned and stared at the unexpected royal visitors. Elizabeth, oblivious to this attention, played happily in the sand and mingled with others of her own age. Her particular delight was to take rides on the donkeys. She and the other girls bumped and rocked into the sea in a horse-drawn bathing machine. The family was to return to this bleak, unpromising North Sea place for years to come.[5]

Queen Victoria had asked the family to Scotland, and on the way north they moved from the cheap Belgian hotel to the grandeur of Buckingham Palace. Alice took Elizabeth and Victoria to the Great Exhibition. "What impressed Ella most," she wrote, "was a policeman, who was, as she said, 'so very kind' in keeping the crowd off."[6]

On September 13, 1871, the family arrived at Balmoral, where they found the queen ill and depressed. She was recovering from a grave throat infection and an abscess on her arm. Four days later she succumbed to a painful bout of rheumatoid arthritis, and, unable to walk, was confined to a sofa. Alice brought her nursing experience to bear as she sat by her mother playing the piano, just as she had done during her father's final illness. The children came to the queen's side and tried to amuse her.

It was not only overwork* during the continental wars that had sapped the queen's strength. The fall of the French Empire had brought on a wave of republicanism in Britain. Gladstone's government was widening popular education, reforming the army, universities, and civil service on meritocratic lines, and everywhere sweeping away vested interests. Sir Charles Dilke led a growing movement which contended that the royal family was one such expensive anachronism. Writers, artists, poets, and the populist section of the press gave him their support. There was talk of abdication, and bitter criticism of the Prince of Wales, whom one journalist called a "louse." The queen's reclusiveness and the generous financial provisions for her children were greatly resented. The long mid-Victorian boom was coming to an end, and the conviction grew among the working classes that abolishing the monarchy would improve their standard of living. "In London and the great cities the bulk of the working classes are republican by conviction, unless where they are not perfectly indifferent," wrote a journalist. "There are a score of towns in the north and center where the republican feeling is at fever heat. . . ." The throne was in greater danger than at any subsequent time.

The queen's spirits were barely raised by her slow recovery, for others in her family fell ill. The Prince of Wales, traveling down to Sandringham for his birthday, was struck down with typhoid. Alice stayed with her brother to nurse him while Louis rejoined the army in Germany.

Meanwhile Elizabeth and her brother and sisters, and the Prince of Wales's children, with whom they played, had caught whooping cough. They were all sent to Buckingham Palace, and spent a bleak, gray November recovering in the attics. They explored the nurseries on the same floor, where Alice, her brother Bertie, the Prince of Wales, and all the queen's children had played years before. There was a curious mechanical lion which swallowed a figure of a soldier when its crank was turned. They raced along the corridor on bicycles adorned with horses' heads and tails which their uncles had once owned.

To convalesce they were moved to Windsor Castle, where the

queen was now back at work. Amid the gray stone battlements and rooms decked with suits of armor, muskets, and swords, they played hide-and-seek and romped with wild abandon. For their daring games Elizabeth and Victoria joined forces with the two elder Wales cousins, "Eddy" and George, who later became the duke of Clarence and King George V. Unseen, they would steal sugar lumps from the nursery and hold them over lighted candles. Their aim was to make caramel, but the result was burnt fingers and a bad smell. Hiding in dark corners, they would creep up to the queen's room and steal biscuits from the tray placed outside. They would run up and down the great corridor with their aunt Beatrice, then thirteen. When their shrieks grew too hard to bear, a page would be sent by the queen with an order for less noise.[7]

The children were too young to understand the anxiety the queen was feeling for her son. For at Sandringham Alice was now nursing the Prince of Wales through a crisis. With the prince's wife, Alexandra, "Alix," she kept a constant vigil by his bed. On November 29 the queen herself came and saw him gasping for breath in his half-lit room. Soon he became delirious. "For thirty-six hours he talked incessantly in many languages, sang, swore, whistled and poured out the secrets of his sexual ecstasies." He asked his equerry to bring a glass of water and kneel down, "it was always done in former days." He did not recognize his wife, calling her "my good boy." With manic strength he would throw the pillows about the bedroom; on one occasion Alexandra came in on all fours to dodge his missiles. On the evening of December 13, he was at the nadir of his illness. Alice and the queen saw him clutching at the bedclothes "seeming to feel for things that were not there." Alice said: "There can be no hope. It is the death-rattle—I have heard it before."

In desperation one of the doctors rubbed the prince all over with champagne brandy. There was a slight return of animation, and at 4 A.M. the prince fell asleep. Awaking at eight, he drank two glasses of ale, and slept. A slow recovery had now begun.[8]

It was not lost on the press that on the same day eleven years earlier Prince Albert had died. They had followed the drama of the prince's illness with all the feverish attention due to a good story. The public had reacted with a keen sympathy. Hearing of Bertie's recovery, the nation now rejoiced. All talk of a republic suddenly died off. The queen and her son were to meet with a triumphant reception from a vast crowd when they attended a thanksgiving service in St. Paul's.[9]

Late in January 1872 Alice came to Windsor to take her children home. To Elizabeth she looked pale and emotionally drained. She had saved her brother and helped the British throne, but her faith and fortitude were undermined. Hearing her brother's recovery ascribed to Providence, she had burst out: "Providence, there is no Providence, no nothing, and I can't think how anyone can talk such rubbish."[10] For now the effects of the mental strain caused by the Franco-Prussian War had become noticeable in Alice. During the war Alice, though outwardly calm and collected, had moved from an earnest reflection on religion to an intense spiritual anxiety.

This religious crisis, though triggered by the war, had its source in her earlier life. In her childhood and youth she had thought of life as a pilgrimage through an uncertain land to the bliss of eternity and reunion with the dead of the family. Slowly she began to feel that to be sincere, the beliefs she held emotionally must also be intellectually sound. After 1869 she was wondering if the supernatural elements of Christianity were not wholly mythical, and only the scientifically valid parts were true. It was in that year that she came to know David Strauss.

Strauss was a radical theologian, and his work had aroused a storm of bitter criticism. His appointment to a professorship at Zurich University had caused such an uproar that he was pensioned off before taking his chair. A restless, passionate man, he had married a beautiful opera singer, Agnes Scherbst, left her on discovering her infidelity, and thereafter wandered throughout the German universities in his studies before turning up in

Darmstadt.[11] As a soured, weary old man he met Princess Alice. Until then she had found no one in Darmstadt who could share and discuss her religious preoccupations, which were too sophisticated for her husband, a bluff, unintellectual soldier. When Strauss arrived she found a mind equal to her own. He became a frequent visitor to the New Palace, and a close but purely intellectual friendship developed. In January 1870, she asked him to give a series of lectures on Voltaire. A bout of smallpox in the palace had put off the intended audience of friends, and, risking infection, he read them to Alice alone. At her insistence he dedicated the published book of the lectures to her, to the consternation of Queen Victoria and the German empress, who called her "a complete atheist."

Alice became an eager disciple of Strauss's doctrine. He had set out in his *Life of Jesus* the view that what was scientifically impossible was untrue. The life of Christ had a historical basis, but the supernatural elements, including the miracles and the Resurrection, were mythical; the moral teachings of the founder of Christianity were alone important.[12]

In the normal routine of life at Darmstadt, these ideas might have remained little more than intellectual speculation. But during the Franco-Prussian War Alice was in a state of acute nervous strain as she nursed the mutilated and gangrenous bodies of German soldiers and carried her unborn child. She might otherwise have borne the sight of her brother in a raving delirium without permanent mental upset, but it now compounded her emotional trauma. As a result, the correspondence she kept up with Strauss in this period exercised a dangerous influence. At this time she most needed the consolation of faith; the table in her study was littered with a mass of religious books in many languages. Yet she found that Strauss's skepticism put faith out of her reach. From denying the supernatural elements in the life of Christ it was a short step to denying the possibility of His omniscient Father. Alice began to doubt the existence of God.

In later years her spiritual struggles were profoundly to affect her daughters. Victoria was to inherit her inquiring mind, and acquire a progressive, even Socialist outlook and a skepticism toward religion. It was on Elizabeth that Alice's spiritual turmoil was to have the greatest effect. It set her on the road to the intense religious faith of her later life. This was not apparent during her childhood, but a latent conviction was planted in her that the undemanding conventional homilies of Victorian religion were not enough to be a good Christian. A Christian must show complete sincerity in professing the faith; the truth must be sought out and followed to the letter. To become closer to God one must seek to carry out His will.

Just as her mother was now wrestling with her faith and intellect, Elizabeth was to endure soul-searching doubts in her efforts to find the right path; she also was to study the works of religious authorities in great depth. Like her mother, she was to become determined to accept without complaint the duties and burdens of her conscience. This was the seed that her mother's religious strife had planted in her. It was many years before it bore fruit.

During this period, on 6 June 1872, Alice's fourth daughter, Alix,† was born. Empress Marie of Russia and her children were staying at Heiligenberg, and her son Alexander, heir to the Russian throne, became Alix's godfather. On a visit to the castle, Alice held the baby on her knee and said, half in jest, to a Russian lady: "Look at this child with great respect. She will be your future empress."‡

"It has been suggested," David Duff has written, "that the mysticism of the future Empress of Russia was due to her being conceived at a time when her mother was in a state of tension over her religious convictions."[13] Whatever the cause, Alix was to inherit an intense religiosity which slowly emerged in her adult life. As with her mother, religious anxieties would come to the fore in her at times of crisis. She was also to feel that religion must be embraced wholeheartedly or not at all. When much later she became Orthodox, she immersed herself fervently in

Orthodoxy's doctrines and rituals in an effort to draw nearer to her Maker. But unlike Elizabeth, she never founded her faith on an intellectual study of Christian doctrine. She acquired a blind faith in Orthodoxy, Holy Russia and its monarchical traditions and peasantry as a true religion, and dogmatically maintained it until she died. It was this difference in the religious makeup of Alix and Elizabeth that was in some measure the source of their quarrels in later life.

For the moment, however, little of their future characters could be discerned in the young Ella and the infant "Alicky." At that time Elizabeth's religion probably contained only the sentimental piety inculcated in every Victorian nursery. But at an impressionable age her character had been indelibly marked by the experience of the Franco-Prussian War. The anguish of her mother and the obvious torments of the wounded soldiers had opened up a sensitivity to the sufferings of others. Almost four decades later she was to write, without vanity, "it seems to me often that already as a child there was longing to help those that suffer."[14] Elizabeth was becoming the most sympathetic of the Hessian children, as Baroness Buxhoeveden wrote:

> She was the personification of unselfishness, always ready to do anything in order to give pleasure to others. She was cheerful, with a strong sense of humour, and as a child always the peacemaker in the nursery and schoolroom, a favourite with all her sisters and brothers, and a link between them.[15]

Elizabeth had developed a pensive, artistic streak, and delighted in making sketches of flowers, easily acquiring a fine sense of line and color. She took a childish pleasure in simple things, and was enraptured by a basket of ivy filled with wildflowers. "I should have liked to send it to you," she wrote to Queen Victoria, "but it would not have kept fresh for so long."[16]

This thoughtfulness and compassion were soon to be intensified and became more noticeable by another tragedy in her family. The cause was the hemophiliac gene that was to play a fateful part in both her sister Alix's life and Russia's history. Hemophilia, an ancient disease, found its way into the British royal family through a genetic mutation in one of Queen Victoria's parents; through the queen[§] it had descended to Alice. The disease is transmitted by females but affects only males. The youngest boy of the family, Frederick William, "Frittie," was its victim. Its symptoms are an inability of the blood to clot as well as severe pain and swellings resulting from cuts and bruises. They were first noticed in Frittie in February 1873. He cut his ear, and blood flowed for three days. At times it seeped through the bandage and covered his head and neck.[17]

In May 1873, Alice returned from a journey to Rome. On the 28th the family spent a carefree afternoon on the Glasberg, the children chasing each other through the meadows and gathering lilies of the valley.

The day after began with a beautiful spring morning. Elizabeth, Victoria, and Irene were already at their lessons while Alice, still reviving from her travels, lay late in bed. Ernest and Frittie were playing by her bedside. For a game Ernest ran around to appear at a window of a room set at right angles to Alice's bedroom, from which he could be seen. Alice ran after Ernest to pull him away from the window. In her absence Frittie climbed onto a chair to see his brother better. The chair tipped over, and Frittie fell forward through the window and down twenty feet to the balustrade below.[18]

The senseless boy was picked up and taken to bed. The doctors diagnosed an effusion of blood into the brain; by the evening he was dead. Elizabeth saw her mother shed a flood of tears, so distraught she could not contain herself. On June 1 the family all followed the small coffin to the funeral at the Rosenhöhe, the family mausoleum. Alice would repeatedly take the children there over the next few months; she could never pass a flower by the roadside without wishing to lay it on Frittie's grave. She never entirely recovered from the tragedy, and her body and mind remained weary and weak. From then on she wrote letters of pitiful sadness to her mother, and anniversaries of trivial events in Frittie's life would bring on fresh bouts of melancholy. That the accident could so easily have been prevented, and that she had been within yards of the boy at the time, added a layer of guilt onto her grief.[19]

Ernest, a highly sensitive boy who had deeply loved his brother, suffered acutely in silence. Henceforth he bore a lifelong fear of death; one day he sobbed out to his mother: "When I die, you must die too, and all the others. Why can't we all die together? I don't want to die alone, like Frittie."[20]

The blow fell less heavily on Elizabeth and Victoria, who were already old beyond their years. It helped them acquire a resilience and mental strength unusual in such a sheltered upbringing. It was the first time Elizabeth had experienced a tragedy so close to home, and she was never to forget it. She knew how her brother and mother must feel, and did her best to comfort them and cheer them up. Of all the girls, she was the closest to Ernest, and understood him as few sisters could.

But for Alice, the shock and grief had flooded out her religious doubts, which "crumbled away like dust." She could only cope with her present burdens by being convinced of a consolation in the next world. She ceased to correspond with David Strauss, who died soon after. Alice turned to prayer again, and took delight in singing hymns with her children.[21]

For the next few years Alice was to give Elizabeth a secure, tranquil, and pleasant childhood. Though alert to the dangers of becoming an excessively doting mother ("baby-worship," as she called it), she was devoted to the children. The family, to which a new daughter, Marie, or "May," was added in 1873, was very close.

Grand Duke Louis was an equally attentive parent. His generosity, his bluff, easygoing nature and his love of their childish amusements made him an ideal father. While trying to work at his desk he would let them sit around him, playing, painting, working or chattering at their ease. On his birthday they would recite to him poems of their own making.[22]

Louis, an enthusiastic sportsman, passed on to Elizabeth a great love of animals. He and Alice filled up Kranichstein with a varied menagerie on which Elizabeth and the others doted. There was a fox that soon smelled inordinately, a baby wild boar that became dangerous as it grew and had to be released, a sheep with a pitiful cough that the children dragged along by a string tied around its neck, and an ever growing colony of white rabbits and guinea pigs.[23] Elizabeth was much distressed when Alice's "poor little bullfinch, who piped beautifully," was killed by an owl which Louis had placed in the same room.[24] Alice's brave bull terrier, Boxer, also suffered when he lost a fight with a wild boar. His entire left flank had to be stitched up while a footman held him down on the operating table.

It was Boxer, suddenly darting off to chase wild boar, who would follow the children in their rides around the woods at Kranichstein. There they learned to ride on Shetland ponies given them by Queen Victoria. After her tenth birthday, when the queen gave her the useful present of a saddle and bridle,[25] Elizabeth was allowed to ride out with her elder sister. Soon she and the elder girls could be seen making long treks in the wild and solitary glens at Balmoral.

The family's holidays in Scotland and England were some of the high points of the year. Elizabeth soon became so at home at Windsor, Osborne, and Balmoral that she made friends among the royal retainers. She played with the Prince of Wales's children when the family stayed at Marlborough House. Queen Victoria became her adored grandmother who doted on her without the strictness with which she had treated her own children. At Balmoral the children would never miss going to a nearby shop run by two old sisters, "the merchants." They would buy sweets and notepaper, and return laden with purchases. The two women taught them the art of baking scones, which they remembered all their lives.[26] Years later, as an adult, Elizabeth would ask her aunt Beatrice to send the same sweet pear drops that she had bought there as a child.

The other great family occasion was Christmas. A huge fir tree, laden with small presents, was set up for the children, and the whole family would gather for a lavish dinner. Alice, however, took care to remind Elizabeth that it was a time for giving, and made her hand out presents to the servants and their children. One year Alice arranged a party for ninety-one of the servants' children, and Elizabeth had to wait at their table. Alice would also take the children to her hospitals, where they would sing hymns, give presents to the patients, and listen to the chaplain's sermons. In winter their regular Saturday duty was to arrange flowers and deliver them to the wards.[27] At a very early age Elizabeth learned to treat the sick without shyness.

A concern for the poor and sick was only part of Alice's efforts to make Elizabeth "unselfish, unspoiled and contented"[28] and give her other goals in life besides marriage. This aim in mind, she prescribed a rigorous daily routine. Elizabeth and the elder girls, later joined by the other children, would rise soon after six, in freezing darkness in winter. Then began an hour and a half of lessons, which Elizabeth, who was no scholar, hated, for the printed word bored her and sums made her cry. Only at eight-thirty could she have breakfast with her mother. Having worked up an appetite, she would fall eagerly on the porridge, sausage, and cold meat. There followed an hour out of doors, whatever the weather, in which the children would ride in the oaks and beeches around Kranichstein or walk in the Darmstadt parks. After a mid-morning "little lunch" of milk and cookies, another lesson had to be endured, and at 1 P.M. Alice would tutor one of the older girls in French reading. Lunch at two with their parents was a solid, plain meal with only sugar lumps to sweeten it. The children were free afterward until their early bedtime.[29] On Sundays, their one day off, they must appear, beautifully turned out, before the eccentric old Grand Duke Louis III at the family dinner in the castle. He gave them finger biscuits, Alice having forbidden sweets, and terrified them with a series of grimaces intended for their amusement.[30] This stern upbringing gave Elizabeth self-discipline and dedication to duty. It was to prove valuable in the European courts, where poise and a willingness to shine at dreary social functions were essential.

But Elizabeth still kept her buoyant cheerfulness, and the tragedies of the past few years could not repress her love of fun and childish games. When freed from discipline, she and the other children gave rein to boisterous high spirits. Acting became a favorite pursuit. They would play at being characters from history books or fairy tales, or put on a play for their parents. They would ransack Alice's wardrobe for old clothes, and would strut up and down the long corridors like great ladies in crinolines or Indian shawls.[31] Another great game was to stage mock battles in a private park, the Prince Emil Garden. With the children of the visiting princes and family doctors or secretaries, they would devise ways of defending or attacking a sham ruin. The sheltered Darmstadt girls would soon become as wild as the Hessians, but cried if they were hurt, for which the tougher grand ducal family heartily despised them. As Elizabeth and the others grew into adolescence and traveled around the courts of Europe, they became notorious for their riotous daredevilry.

At first it was Victoria, as the eldest, who led the children's wild horseplay and ruled them all "with a rod of iron." She was becoming a tomboy, reveling in physical games and competition. She loved to tell and hear heroic stories, Arthurian and Homeric legends. Elizabeth, on the other hand, preferred "nice little girl stories" and the dolls and girlish things that Victoria loathed. She was more feminine and becoming prettier than her elder sister, though less practical or clever. But as she grew she began to rebel against Victoria's iron rule. One day Victoria gave in and agreed to share her authority with Elizabeth. Underneath her docile front Elizabeth had gained a character at least as strong as her sister's and tougher than those of the younger ones.[32]

Their joint authority was extended after two deaths in the family in 1877. On March 20 Elizabeth heard that her paternal grandfather, Prince Charles, had died of erysipelas, an infectious disease involving inflammation of the skin. On the twenty-fourth she followed his coffin to the Rosenhöhe mausoleum with the rest of the family and the distraught widow, Princess Charles. A few weeks later, the old grand duke fell ill at Seeheim. Early in June his temperature became feverish. On the thirteenth, hearing that he was failing fast, Alice and Louis rushed over to Seeheim. Soon after arriving they sent Queen Victoria a telegram: "Dear Uncle Louis is no more. We arrived too late."[33]

Elizabeth and the others saw their great-uncle's corpse exposed as he lay in state and hundreds of his mourning subjects filed past. They bore up through the long funeral and interment in the Rosenhöhe. Their parents were now grand duke and duchess of Hesse, and were burdened by the weight of state business. Alice's health, already frail, declined further as she took on the duty of being "Landesmutter," "Mother of the Realm," and both she and Louis feared she would not recover. Elizabeth and Victoria, still in adolescence, were obliged to take on more responsibility for the younger ones. They had already grown up fast, and now were called on to set a parental example.

Elizabeth had acquired an unhealthy pallor during the mild upsets the family had received, and it was a relief when they could take a seaside holiday. As grand duke, Louis could now afford to take them to the more comfortable French resort of Houlgate. They all revived, and Elizabeth got back her color and her spirits. They faced a triumphant welcome on their return; the whole town of Darmstadt waited to see their carriage. Schoolgirls, given a holiday, turned out dressed in white. The flags were out, the bells were ringing, and a shower of nosegays was thrown down on the grand ducal carriage. In the evening, choirs came and serenaded under the palace windows. It brought home to Elizabeth that she was now the daughter of a reigning sovereign.[34]

At the same time, another change was taking place in Elizabeth. She was turning into a young woman and beginning to attract many admirers. A Colonel Williamson had set up an Army Cramming School in Darmstadt, and soon dozens of fit and healthy young Englishmen began to mix with the grand ducal family. Of the Hessian girls it was Elizabeth they noticed most. The seventeen-year-old Lord Charles Montagu was probably the first young man to attract her. He was the son of the duchess of Manchester, Alice's friend, there to study German. Soon he developed an adolescent passion for Elizabeth. Joining in their mock battles in the Prince Emil Garden, he fought by her side as protector.[35] Years later his chivalry was to remain a fond memory in a letter she wrote to Ernest: "If you see Charlie Montague give many kind messages from his old friend, that I remember our games of lawn tennis and other romps when we were children."[36] Elizabeth's cousin, Prince William of Prussia, became a student at Bonn University. Vicky had asked Alice to keep an eye on him, and he spent many weekends in Darmstadt.[37] His eyes were fixed on Elizabeth, and would only be silent when she was speaking.

Another young prince was attracted to her and Victoria in London in the summer of 1878. While the family stayed with the Prince and princess of Wales at Marlborough House, their cousin Prince Louis of Battenberg, now a naval lieutenant, was on leave. The two girls found him to be gallant, handsome, and debonair. For a long time they had both wanted to row on the lake at Buckingham Palace, but their old nurse Orchie had insisted, "only if you have an experienced person to look after you." They both appealed to the strong, experienced sailor, and Prince Louis, dressed in his best morning coat, launched the boat. To the delight of both, especially Victoria, he rowed them around the picturesque lake.

That summer also gave Elizabeth her first glimpse of London society. She attended a big garden party given by the Prince of Wales, for which the queen was persuaded to come up from

Windsor. It was held at the prince's London home, Marlborough House, a red-brick mansion facing the mall near Buckingham Palace.[38] A military band played marches as dukes and duchesses, earls and countesses, officers in full dress, and notables in morning coats talked and took tea on the immaculate green lawn. They bowed and curtsied as they were presented to Elizabeth; she strained her mind to find a few polite words to say to each. She saw her grandmother again when Alice took the family to lunch in the lodge at Frogmore near Windsor. She and Victoria were also taken on a round of "improving" visits to London institutions. Learned professors gave them private tours of Kew Gardens and the Natural History Museum, and the gentleman usher of the Black Rod, a duke's illegitimate son, showed them the House of Lords.[39]

Away from the capital, the family took a happy holiday on the south coast at Eastbourne. Alice, never losing her reforming zeal in spite of poor health, visited hospitals and met reformed prostitutes in their refuge. Elizabeth and the others learned tennis or played games on the beach with the children of their mother's friends. Without a care they bathed, built sand castles, and fished for crabs. For Elizabeth, the summer was to be a particularly vivid memory, for it was the last the whole family spent together; it was to be her final holiday that she spent with the lightheartedness of a child.[40]

Shortly before their return to Darmstadt, news came of a terrible accident on the Thames. The pleasure steamer *Princess Alice,* filled with seven hundred passengers, cheering, laughing, and playing accordions, was run down by another boat in the murky darkness off Woolwich pier. Six hundred people drowned, their cries echoing from the shore as they struggled in the fast currents. Princess Alice was one of the first to send sympathy and money to the bereaved.[41]

On the evening of November 5, the family was gathered as usual in the New Palace. Victoria told her mother that she had a stiff neck, and her mother thought it might be mumps; it would be very comical, she said, if all the family caught it. Victoria sat on the sofa reading *Alice in Wonderland* to the younger children spread out on the floor around her. Alice was talking to Katie Macbean, an old friend who was standing in for a lady-in-waiting. Little May begged her mother for some more cake, and the others asked Miss Macbean to play them the piano. They danced energetically for half an hour, and went to bed tired and flushed but happy.

The next morning, the family physician, Dr. Eigenbrodt, announced that Victoria had diphtheria, an infectious disease capable of paralyzing, or suffocating, its victims.[42]

## Notes to Chapter 3

*The continental upheavals entailed a voluminous correspondence. The queen sometimes wrote five thousand words in a single day.

†Christened Victoria Alix Helena Louise Beatrice.

‡The remark was made in French: see chapter 8.

§The queen had also transmitted it to her daughter Beatrice and her youngest son, Leopold, Duke of Albany.

# Chapter 4

### THE KISS OF DEATH

*It became her lot to break to her son, quite a youth, the death
of his youngest sister, to whom he was devotedly attached. The
boy was so overcome with misery that the agitated mother to
console him clasped him in her arms—and thus received a kiss
of death.*

—BENJAMIN DISRAELI (LORD BEACONSFIELD),
ADDRESS OF CONDOLENCE TO THE HOUSE OF LORDS
AFTER PRINCESS ALICE'S DEATH

No one was allowed to visit the palace.[1] From her nursing experience Alice had a horror of diphtheria. She dreaded the
thought of her other children being infected and moved
Elizabeth into Irene's room. She took charge of the nursing,
assisted by the staff of her hospital. For five days she watched over
Victoria; to her immense relief her critical condition improved
by November 10.

At three in the morning of the twelfth, Alice was awakened to
hear that Alix was feverish with a bad throat. An inspection
revealed white spots and a white membrane already covering
the sides of the throat. Alice immediately got the child a steam
inhaler, and averted a catastrophe. The doctor pronounced her
a severe case, and she was sent upstairs away from the others.
That same morning, four-year-old May clambered onto her
mother's bed and kissed her. By midday the grim white spots
had appeared on her tiny throat. Alice was almost in despair at
the thought of losing her. Her fever was still high the next day,
when Irene became infected. The day after, Louis and Ernest
had fallen sick. It was clear that Elizabeth would be the next,

and that day Alice sent her and the governess, Miss Jackson, to her grandmother's house at the other end of the Wilhelminen-strasse.

For the next month Elizabeth was cut off from her family. She had a lonely time, taking brisk walks with Miss Jackson and writing cheering letters to her brother and sisters.[2] With growing anxiety she heard news of the tragedy that was being played out a few hundred yards away. Early on the morning of the sixteenth, the doctor roused Alice to tell her that the fatal white membrane had appeared on May's throat. She rushed to the nursery and saw that her favorite child had choked to death. All Alice could do was sit beside the corpse and kiss the face and hands in a fit of distraction. She steeled herself to tell her husband, and watched from upstairs as the small coffin covered in white was wheeled away to the family mausoleum. Then she faced the anguish of hiding the news from the sick children when they repeatedly asked after May and tried to send her their toys. By the beginning of December they were far enough out of danger to be told. Ernest at first refused to believe it, then, overcome with tears, talked at length about her. Alice broke her rigid rule of nursing, put her arms around him, and kissed him.

On the evening of December 7 Alice recognized in herself the symptoms that had appeared in all but one of her children. She went to bed and tried to sort out her affairs during a high fever exacerbated by weeks of tension and sleeplessness. On Friday, December 13, her husband came to see her in the evening. "Good night," he said, "I'll see you in the morning." The next day was exactly seventeen years after the death of Prince Albert and four weeks after the death of Princess May.

That morning Elizabeth heard that her mother had died at half-past eight with the words, "From Friday to Saturday—four weeks—May—dear Papa."

At last Elizabeth could see the family. "It was a terribly sad meeting," she wrote, "—no-one daring to speak of what was uppermost in their thoughts. Poor Papa looked dreadfully miserable—Ernie very pale, but otherwise calm, he does not realise it, as we none of us can do yet. It seems like a horrible dream—would that it were." [3]

There was some comfort in a distraught letter from Queen Victoria, who had followed the drama in anguish in a stream of letters and telegrams sent to Windsor. She promised to act as their mother:

*Dec 14 1878*

*Darling Victoria,*

*Poor dear children, for I write this for you all — You have all had the most terrible blow which can befall Children — you have lost your precious, dear, devoted Mother who loved you & your dear Papa! That horrible disease which carried off sweet little May & from which you & the others recovered has taken her away from you & poor old Grandmama, who with your other kind Grandmama will try & be a Mother to you! Oh! dear children, dearest beloved Mama is gone to join dear Grandpapa & your other dear Grandpapa & Frittie & sweet little May where there is no more sorrow or tears or separation.*

*I long to hear every detail! Poor dear Ernie, he will feel it so dreadfully! May he & dear Papa not suffer from this dreadful blow. Try & do everything to comfort & help dear Papa! God's will be done! May he support and help you all.*

*From your devoted & most unhappy Grandmama*

*VRI*

*let Ella see this letter.* [4]

Elizabeth knew how acutely the queen must have suffered on that terrible anniversary, and she wrote: "Dearest Grandmama, I have no words to express what I feel for you & poor Papa. May God help us all to be a comfort to you both." [5] She also wrote a note to Ernest, who was still in the grip of the disease:

"You must ask GOD to help you bear the pain & I am sure He will help you if you ask him, dear Erny . . . ."[6]

On the evening of the seventeenth, Elizabeth joined the family in the New Palace for a service over her mother's coffin, draped in the British flag, as she had wished. A procession bore it by torchlight to the chapel of the castle. Thousands of Hessians, who had first resented Alice's efforts for their welfare, now lined the route in silent grief at the loss of their benefactress. The next day they came in crowds to file past her coffin. In the evening, the funeral proper took place in the family mausoleum, the Rosenhöhe. Among the mourners, the Prince of Wales could not be recognized as the jovial, ebullient figure of the past. Princess Alice was laid to rest alongside May's little coffin. A statue was to be placed on the tomb of the mother holding the child in her arms.

In a state of numbed grief the family gathered for Christmas in the cold castle, where years before they had sat at Sunday dinners with the old grand duke. They were still convalescing and passively trying to come to terms with their irreparable loss. Ernest's throat was half paralyzed and he could only speak with difficulty.[7] It was a break with the past to move away from the New Palace, where their mother's room was kept untouched. Another change was that the children could not distract themselves with their toys, for they had all been burnt.[8] They could only admire the lockets that Queen Victoria had given them, and look forward to seeing her at Osborne in the new year. Already showing the consideration of an adult, Elizabeth wrote to the queen:

> We all wish you, dearest Grandmama, a happier
> New Year than this has been and that you may take
> comfort in the thought that dear Mama is happy
> at last. It has been said that death is a dark lattice
> that lets in a bright day, and may that comfort you,
> as it did poor Mama in thinking of little May . . . .[9]

Late in January 1879 they left for two months at Osborne and Windsor. The salt sea air of the Isle of Wight revived them, and once more the children could play games. Alice's brother Leopold, a scholarly and cultured man, was on hand to cheer them and join in their pranks. The hemophilia he had inherited from the queen caused him agonizing pain, and produced a keen sympathy for the sufferings of others. He gamely bore his illness with cheerful indifference, and was adored by all the children. He was to return with them to Darmstadt and, later on, to guide their manners and artistic tastes.

The queen bore the loss of her daughter with unprecedented stoicism. She took control of the details of the children's lives. Henceforth she would see regular reports on their education, and approve the patterns for the girls' frocks before they were made. Photographs of the children were to be sent to her. The family was to come every year to Britain, usually to Balmoral in the autumn to allow Grand Duke Louis to enjoy the shooting. The British cousins would make frequent calls on them at Darmstadt. Victoria and Elizabeth, the queen decided, were to be prepared for confirmation.

In March the children returned home to the routine of lessons and daily walks amid the bare beeches and snow of the nearby park of the Herrengarten.[10] But their old pattern of life could not be entirely resumed. They were now living in the castle, and it would be more than a year before their return to the scene of the tragedy at the New Palace. Beside the palace, a stone column was built, "dedicated by the women and maidens of Hesse to the unforgettable grand duchess of Hesse and the Rhine."

Grand Duke Louis closed Kranichstein, and with it the memories of the cheerful holidays there. Occasionally some stroller in the woods thought he saw the face of Alice at the windows, and heard her happy voice calling in the children from play. Some years later an English girl, Meriel Buchanan, passed the abandoned house: "The old gray castle itself seemed to me like the enchanted palace of the Sleeping Beauty, its walls and battlements reflected in the waters of the lake, deserted, silent. . . ."[11]

It was the girls' governess "Madgie," Miss Margaret Jackson, who helped the children adjust to life without Mama. She had their trust and affection, and possessed a strong character and forward-looking mind. She went a long way toward molding their moral sense. It was Alix who was the most severely upset and who most needed her guidance. She was lost without little May, who had been her constant playmate, or her mother who had doted on her two youngest girls. Having been "Sunny," the merriest child, she was now becoming sorrowful, silent, and shy. Her cousin, Princess Marie Louise* was to say to her: "Alix, you always play at being sorrowful: one day the Almighty will send you some real crushing sorrows and then what are you going to do?"[12] It was clear to Elizabeth that Alix could not experience the carefree and secure childhood of her older sisters: "Alix will never know what we have known," she said.[13]

Ernest was a frail, tender child. His mother's death denied him the childish wish he had expressed on Frittie's death, that he should die with her. It added to his fear of death, which would haunt him all his life. A mother and child had rarely understood each other as he and Alice had, and without her he was prone to sleepless nights and a lasting melancholy.

To Elizabeth, soon to be confirmed, it seemed that her childhood had come to an end. Never again could she play and run riot without thought of responsibility. Her resilient spirits gave her the strength to take on new burdens. She remembered the queen's admonition: "Do everything to comfort and help dear Papa!" Victoria and she were constantly by his side in their mother's place. They now bore the task of being the "mother" to the others, and the solicitude Elizabeth had shown them during their illness became a confirmed habit. She followed the queen's exhortation to imitate Alice, "to become really *worthy* of her, to walk in her footsteps—to be unselfish, truthful, humble-minded, *simple*—and to try to do all you can for *others,* as she did!"[14]

In the spring they moved to a new summer home at

Wolfsgarten, an old hunting lodge deep in the woods north of Darmstadt. As a remnant of the wild animals that had provided quarry for the chase, two wolves were kept in a cage by the gate. The graveled avenues led straight through the beech and pine trees up to a baroque mansion in a grassy park. Behind the mansion lay a garden courtyard fronted by the stables and some low sandstone houses. In these houses were the rooms of the two elder girls.[15] Elizabeth could look out onto a fountain and pergola, and breathe in the scent of roses.

Here she could rest and ponder, and look toward an uncertain future without the mother who had been her guiding spirit. She prepared for life as a young woman for whom men were beginning to show a keen admiration.

## Notes to Chapter 4

*Princess of Schleswig-Holstein-Sonderburg-Augustenburg, daughter of Queen Victoria's fifth child, Princess Helena.

# Chapter 5

*Russia I could not wish for any of you.*

—LETTER FROM QUEEN VICTORIA TO HER GRAND-
DAUGHTER PRINCESS VICTORIA OF HESSE, 1882.

At fourteen, Elizabeth was now becoming a dazzling beauty. A
chance combination of the genes of her ancestors had produced
a face with features of exceptional purity, and a tall, elegant figure. Photographs of the time rarely did her justice. They showed
a well-proportioned face, but could not depict her fairish hair or
that she "had eyes of a grey-blue, on one of which was a spot of
brown, and the effect of her glance was unusual."[1] The strained
expression caused by the long exposure meant that they never
showed the charm of her smile.

No princess in Europe was said to be more beautiful. Those
who saw her recorded their impression in phrases that sound
almost hyperbolic. Years later the queen of Romania wrote down
her childish memory:

> . . . her purity was absolute; one could never
> take one's eyes off her, and when parting from her
> in the evening one longed for the hour when one
> would behold her again the next day. . . . Eyes that
> have never beheld her will never be able to con-
> ceive what she was then.
>
> Here she comes! With that divine smile curving

her perfect lips, with a blush on her cheeks only comparable to almond blossom and an almost bashful look in her long-shaped, sky-pure eyes. . . .[2]

Henry Wilson, a young Englishman then in Darmstadt, later a distinguished soldier, wrote simply: "She was the most beautiful creature of God I have ever seen."[3]

Inevitably the young princes of Europe sought her hand. They found her to be unlike any of the other young noblewomen they knew. For Elizabeth was not the typical German princess. To her, marriage was more than wifely submissiveness, motherly devotion, unthinking attendance at church, and rigid support for a husband's dynasty. Her docile feminine front concealed a strong, intelligent character and an independent mind. War, bereavement, nursing, an austere upbringing, and her mother's religious wanderings had given her an adult's outlook while still a girl. She had gained an acute sympathy for human suffering and an awareness of natural beauty and art. In the depths of her mind she searched for religious truth and spiritual certainties. These rare qualities were enough to deter her from the philistine, swaggering German soldier-princelings who thronged the courts of her relatives. Her mother's mental isolation in a marriage to an intellectual inferior served as an additional warning. Instead, even if she had no clear picture of her ideal husband, she vaguely sought a man set apart from the rest, a thoughtful, sensitive mind on the same plane as her own.

She could therefore find little to admire in her cousin, Prince William of Prussia, who soon resumed his weekend visits from Bonn. He was an unattractive choice. His painful self-consciousness of his withered left arm had not made him more stoical or mature, as his parents had tried to compensate by making sure that he always won at games. A few years before he had shot his first roebuck; half-tame beasts were provided, but he missed four times.[4] He was forever trying to prove that he could ride, shoot, or row as well as, if not better than, anyone else. William had a priggish streak in him and had become convinced that God had personally chosen him for the German throne, reasoning that this divine favor must mean that he possessed some special qualities.[5]

William had a dimple on his chin, a sign, according to phys-iognomists, of a desire to attract the opposite sex. He also had a compulsive wish to kiss feminine hands. "In later years," David Duff has written, "he would have the lady of his choice brought to him, veiled. Then, impatiently, he would carry out his little strip-tease act. He would order her to take off her veil and coat. He himself would carefully withdraw the glove, then passionately kiss the hand and the little finger."[6] When he became emperor, his clique of effeminate courtiers would pick up the embarrass-ing habit of kissing his hand at every opportunity.[7]

Early in 1879 Elizabeth endured the attentions of this head-strong, conceited young man on his weekend visits. As the future German emperor he appointed himself leader among the young people. Elizabeth and her brother and sisters would suffer his decreeing a ride in the woods, then by a sudden change in plan they would all have to go for a row on the lake. Or he would throw down his tennis racquet during a game and order them all to listen to him reading the Bible.[8]

Throughout, his attention was on Elizabeth. Her beauty entranced him; he had fallen in love, and followed her every movement with his eyes, only falling silent when she was speak-ing so that he could hear her voice.[9] He always wanted her to play with him, sit beside him, and listen to him. One summer day he had the chance of getting her attention. Elizabeth had stepped on a soap dish and cut her foot. While she lay immobi-lized on the sofa, William sat beside her reading Captain Marryat's *Midshipman Easy*.[10] She also had to put up with the love poetry that he regularly sent from Bonn, but in her opinion, the bombast and vanity that characterized William's manners made his verses fit only for wastepaper.[11]

His efforts were in vain. He had no attraction for her, and the idea of being German empress had little appeal. The militarism and cold formality of the Berlin court had repelled her on her visit in 1869. The sad life her aunt Vicky led as crown princess, who was treated with hostility because she was English, was a warning to her. When William came she spent time with him as with others, but politely ignored his advances.

Soon afterward William, intensely frustrated, gave up his studies at Bonn without taking a degree, and left permanently for Berlin. He kept a photograph of Elizabeth on his desk. Four months later he became engaged to the plump Princess Augusta Victoria of Schleswig-Holstein-Augustenburg.* Thereafter he refused to meet Elizabeth at state occasions and kept his distance from her.[12]

It is tempting to regard his failed romance with Elizabeth as a great lost opportunity of history. Elizabeth had inherited through her mother not only a close identity with Britain but a strong belief in Prince Albert's liberal views. "She favoured the spread of liberal ideas as the best antidote to violence," Gerard Noel has written, "as well as for their own intrinsic value."[13] Had she married William, she might well have exercised, with the support and guidance of Queen Victoria, a powerful influence on his political views. Her aunt Vicky, even while she was treated with scorn at the Prussian court, had had a similar effect on William's father, the German crown prince. William was an insecure, restless man, with an enormous sense of his own physical inadequacy. He adored Elizabeth, and her strong, intelligent mind could have shaped a character that lacked self-confidence. On his accession to the German throne William might have turned Germany into a constitutional monarchy on the British model, instead of the semiabsolutist regime that it eventually became. In place of the arrogant, blustering foreign policy (that mirrored William's own character) with its aggressive naval expansion, Germany could have aligned itself closer to Britain and promoted the balance of power. Prince Albert's dream of a progressive Germany at the center of a stable, peaceful Europe might have been realized, and the horrors of the Great War avoided.

The point was not lost on Queen Victoria, who was keen to arrange dynastic marriages for her children and maintain close links among the courts of Europe. Herself the product of an Anglo-German marriage, she had already arranged the marriage of her daughter Vicky for precisely these reasons, hoping to cement these ties further in the next generation. In building a network of marital alliances she had paired off her eldest son Bertie, the Prince of Wales, to Princess Alexandra of Denmark, adding another piece to a complex jigsaw of interrelations. For Alexandra's sister Marie† was the wife of the heir to the Russian throne and daughter-in-law to Emperor Alexander II. Alexander II's wife was Princess Marie of Hesse, who was Grand Duke Louis IV's aunt. In 1874 Alexander II's daughter had married Queen Victoria's son Alfred, Duke of Saxe-Coburg and Gotha, who had burst into tears at Alice's wedding. Queen Victoria would look on approvingly when Alfred's children added yet further links to this matrix. In 1893 his beautiful eldest daughter Missy would become the wife of the crown prince of Romania. Their second daughter Victoria Melita, "Ducky," would marry Elizabeth's brother Ernest in 1894.

The queen was confident that the peace of Europe would be secure if the crowned heads could meet at their frequent family reunions. As a relative and the most influential sovereign, she could always fire off a dictatorial letter if she thought that one of the family members stepped out of line. Arguably her policy was sound; it would not be until 1914 that another general European war broke out.

She therefore deeply regretted the failed romance between Elizabeth and William, and later wrote: "I could not but think with regret what might have been. But I will say no more of that painful past."[14] Indeed, had Elizabeth been Victoria's own daughter, she might well have been forced to marry William. But Grand Duke Louis was determined that his daughters should choose their own husbands. Unlike their mother's generation, they would marry for love or not at all.

William's hasty departure from Bonn may have been caused by the knowledge that he had a rival. In September 1879, Grand Duke Louis's aunt, Empress Marie of Russia, weak from a terminal illness that gave her headaches and made breathing difficult, came to rest at Heiligenberg. Her two younger sons, Serge and Paul, now grown men, followed on a few days later.[15] It was Grand Duke Serge, once Elizabeth's childhood sweetheart, who was now attracted to her.

Of all the sons of Alexander II, he was the oddest. His eldest brother, Alexander, heir to the Russian throne, was a plain-spoken phlegmatic soldier. His younger brothers, Vladimir and Paul, were boisterous, pleasure-loving men-about-town. Serge was the odd one out, a solitary figure who had often left his brothers in their childhood games to wander off on his own. He was deeply religious and had an artistic mind. His manners were cold and stiff, his thoughts inscrutable beneath his haughty manner. His letters were written in convoluted formal French and a spidery handwriting. He had a habit of clasping his hands together in front and toying with one of his rings. Serge was tall and had a handsome face with green eyes and a close-cropped beard.[16]

The Russian grand duke saw Elizabeth as a young woman for the first time when she and Victoria came over to Jugenheim for picnics and tea.[17] He became strongly attracted to her. But being haughty and reserved, he and Paul made a poor impression on their cousins. Victoria wrote to her grandmother:

> . . . they have such odd manners & say such odd things to each other and even once about the English that it made one quite angry, they seem to think themselves perfect too. . . . The cousins are very tall and lazy & never seem to know how to amuse themselves, they talk very little & don't seem to know what to say, so that after we have talked about the weather & the roads, they generally are silent or talk among themselves. . . .[18]

Elizabeth's head was not turned by her monosyllabic cousin. In

October the Russians returned home. The empress, a little recovered, gave the girls brooches as farewell presents.[19]

By now Elizabeth was receiving a stern instruction for her confirmation from the Hessian divine, Dr. Sell. This learned man impressed on her the force of Lutheran doctrine. In particular he emphasized the search for truth, which Elizabeth interpreted as an injunction to be sincere in matters of religion. Dr Sell's teaching, adding to her mother's example, deepened her religious consciousness. Yet it was only later in her life that she began to strive to obey the letter of religious commandments. She made efforts to behave considerately, amiably, and respectfully, like a true Victorian daughter. Elizabeth made clothes for the Darmstadt hospitals and carried on the charitable works of her mother, but her buoyant spirits, with her ready smile that endeared her to the people of Darmstadt, kept her from priggishness or an earnest absorption in religion.

In the spring of 1880 Queen Victoria arrived for her granddaughters' confirmation ceremony in mournful spirits. The family accompanied her on a pilgrimage to the Rosenhöhe. As they knelt beside Alice's tomb and the two small coffins containing her children, she was "terribly shaken" with grief. Afterward she went up to Alice's room, unlocked the door, and observed its contents, unchanged since the death of the occupant.[20] It was in an appropriately solemn mood that Elizabeth and Victoria, dressed in white, knelt down, recited the catechismal responses, and felt the press of the bishop's hand on their heads.

According to the custom of the German courts, they had "come out" of the schoolroom and were now young women fit to mix in society. Grand Duke Louis gradually initiated them into their role as adult members of the Hessian ruling house. He took them to the theater and the opera, and prepared them to receive his subjects. Their first trial came at a grand dinner for sixty-seven people at the castle. To save money, they wore their old confirmation dresses, slightly lower-cut. Elizabeth managed to smile graciously and express polite interest as she stood beside her ailing widowed grandmother, Princess Charles, and the Hessian subjects filed in and paid their respects. A little later, wearing the same dresses, she and Victoria repeated the procedure at a concert given in the castle. They were taught how to dance without mistakes, and their first test came at a "thé dansant," an afternoon dance with tea and a few friends. To round off their education, after the celebration was over, Elizabeth and the elder girls toured Switzerland and northern Italy. At the marketplace in Venice several Italians were struck by her beauty, and murmured to one another: "O che la bella!"[21]

Queen Victoria lived up to her promise of acting as second mother. Every summer she asked Elizabeth and Victoria to Windsor and Balmoral, where they learned to dance Scottish reels. The queen gave them a mass of advice on how to conduct themselves, and intimate knowledge that was normally only passed on by a mother to a daughter. She warned them not to take false pride in their position, like so many German princesses.[22]

After this extensive preparation Elizabeth, at the age of eighteen, was ready to search for a husband. The queen, who thought her "very sweet, sensible"[23] kept a close watch on the men who courted her, and expected to have a say in her decision.

Meanwhile, events in the life of the Grand Duke Serge were afoot that were to settle Elizabeth's future. At that time in Russia his family was living in a climate of fear. His father, the Emperor Alexander II, had freed the peasantry from serfdom and established an impartial system of justice; a band of Nihilist terrorists, the self-appointed "Will of the People," set about trying to frighten his government into further reforms by assassinating its officials. Within the past few years scores of governors had been murdered, and several attempts made on the life of the emperor.

On one winter's evening, on March 1, 1880, Serge's mother,

Empress Marie, lay upstairs in the Winter Palace in St. Petersburg. She was pale and thin, and firmly in the grip of nervous exhaustion. Herself naturally frail, her vitality had been drained by the rigorous demands of the Romanov court and the Russian winter. Her husband's repeated infidelities and the fear of assassination brought on a fatal decline. Downstairs, Emperor Alexander II was walking along one of the immense corridors of the palace toward the luncheon room. With him were Prince Alexander of Hesse (Grand Duke Louis's uncle) and Prince Alexander's two sons, Alexander ("Sandro") and Louis. The previous year, at the age of only twenty-two, Sandro had been elected sovereign prince of the newly formed state of Bulgaria. After the Russo-Turkish war, Bulgaria had been wrested from the Turkish Empire, and the prince wanted his country to be fully independent. His many Russian generals and advisors and a large Pan-Slavist faction wanted to turn the country into the Russian satellite that it eventually became after 1945. Sandro was now in Russia to try and bring the emperor around to his point of view. His father and brother had arrived that evening to assist in the negotiations. Their train was late, much to the emperor's annoyance; had it been on time, the party would now have been seated at the table.

At that moment a thunderous explosion was heard in the luncheon room. "Everything was enveloped in a thick cloud of smoke and dust," Prince Alexander wrote. "The floor shook under our feet, the gas jets flared high for a moment and then all was covered in darkness." Shrieks and groans were heard everywhere, and eleven courtiers and servants were killed. Large craters had opened up in the luncheon room and two salons. The emperor's first thought was for his mistress, Princess Dolgoruki. He ran upstairs to her rooms, shouting "Katya, my dearest Katya!" and found her unhurt. Prince Alexander of Hesse, meanwhile, ran up to his sister's bedroom. The empress too was unharmed; she was so ill that she had not even noticed the explosion.[24]

Her health continued to wither until she was little more than an emaciated skeleton, barely conscious of her surroundings. When she died on June 3 no one was present at her bedside. Within a few weeks the emperor married Princess Dolgoruki.[25]

His happiness was brief. Less than a year later the terrorists were successful. On March 13, 1881, Alexander was returning home to the Winter Palace after inspecting the marine corps. Beside the Summer Garden a Nihilist threw a bomb directly at his carriage. By some chance it missed the emperor but blew off the back of his carriage and wounded a cossack in his escort. The emperor called a halt and alighted to see after the cossack. He then turned and faced the assassin, whom a soldier held tight by the arms. He ordered him to be removed, and turned back to his carriage.

At that point a young man strode forward and threw another bomb at Alexander's feet. The explosion was so great that it was heard all over St. Petersburg. When the smoke cleared, the emperor was found lying in a pool of blood. His face was disfigured and his right hand lacerated. His abdomen was torn open, one leg was severed at the knee, and the other shattered to the top of the thigh, held to the body only by a few strands of flesh. Lifted onto a sleigh, Alexander managed to murmur to his brother Michael, "Quick home, carry to the Palace, there die."

At the palace the emperor was laid on a couch, and a priest recited the prayers for the dying. His family knelt at his side, and at half-past three the emperor took his last breath.[26]

His eldest son became the Emperor Alexander III. "A strange change had already come over him," his cousin, Grand Duke Alexander, recalled. "In less than five minutes he had acquired a new personality."[27] The new emperor became inflexibly determined to yield nothing to the Nihilists who had murdered his father. That very morning, the old emperor had signed a decree for a consultative national assembly to assist in Russia's government. A few days later, his son was still toying with the idea of implementing it when he received a letter from the revolutionaries‡ demanding a host of liberal and Socialist concessions; instead the emperor embarked on a policy of repression and moved Russia closer to being a full-blown police state.[28]

The effect on his brother, Grand Duke Serge, was even more marked. He was in Italy at the time of his father's murder, and was spared the gruesome sight of his death.[29] But losing both his parents within a few months was still a severe blow. To him it was monstrous that anyone should lay hands on the sacred person of the emperor; it seemed that the foundations of his life were torn away. At the funeral he faced another ordeal. By the Russian custom he had to go up to the coffin containing the dismembered corpse and kiss what remained of the face. Serge had adored his father, and to him the sight was an atrocity.

He was filled with an intense hatred for the liberal progressives whom he imagined the terrorists represented. This turned him into an unthinking reactionary, determined to defend the autocratic power of the imperial dynasty. A streak of cruelty entered his character; photographs from this time showed a hard look and a stern mouth. He took over the command of the Preobrazhensky Regiment from his brother Alexander and imposed a ruthless discipline on the troops.

Some peculiar vices were common among his brother officers. "The Guards," a Russian historian has written, "a closed male fraternity, encouraged paederasty and heavy drinking." One of their strange pastimes was to strip naked, run into the midnight snow and, howling like wolves, sip champagne from an enormous vat.[30] In this environment, it seems that Serge, emotionally crippled by his parents' deaths, had somehow lost his manhood. Grand Duke Alexander wrote:

> The generals visiting the messroom of the Preobrazhensky Regiment listened with stupefaction to the chorus of officers singing a favourite song of the Grand Duke Serge, with its refrain consisting of the words—"and peace, and love and bliss." The august commander himself illustrated

those not very soldier-like words by throwing his body back and registering a tortured rapture in his features.[31]

Serge's cousin, Prince Nicholas of Greece, later wrote that he had "something indefinably effeminate in his general appearance."[32] No firm evidence is available, but at this time Serge probably became, or emerged as, a homosexual.

In some strange way he also became set on marrying Elizabeth. Whatever passion he had felt for her had faded, but he sought a substitute for his parents in his childhood sweetheart. Possibly he imagined her as an ideal of beauty and purity that satisfied his religious feelings. The fear of another assassination attempt gave his courting an extra urgency. Late in 1882, with his brother Paul, he arrived in Hesse,[33] an odd combination of guilt at unnatural inclinations, intense religiosity, high artistic feelings, reactionary bigotry, and cold arrogance.

Elizabeth, knowing little of her cousin's private life, saw him in a new light. His father's assassination had been a profound shock. She had faced the same trauma on her mother's death, and her sympathy was strongly aroused. Elizabeth had always given her support and affection to the weaklings of her family, Alix and Ernest. Now she was inclined to give them to a man who, it seemed, was cultured, sensitive, suffering, and sincerely religious.

When they met, they had much to talk about. Serge had been in the same towns in Italy as she had. Shedding his natural taciturnity, he showed off his wide knowledge of Italian art, an interest Elizabeth eagerly shared. The high value he attached to religion also matched her own convictions. Soon she began to envisage this tall, handsome, and habitually gruff grand duke as a kind of Russian Mr. Darcy. She imagined a noble, deeply religious soul beneath his haughty facade, and hoped that she might soften his extreme political opinions. In the few days that she saw him, her thoughts turned to love and marriage. At eighteen, she had no idea of how hollow such a marriage would be.

Queen Victoria, however, had deep-seated fears for her grand-daughter's future life as a Russian grand duchess. She remembered the unhappy married life of Elizabeth's great-aunt Marie in Russia, and she loathed the country, for good reasons. A few years before, British India had been threatened by the arrival of a Russian diplomatic mission in Afghanistan. After an unsuccessful British invasion of the country, a new Emir, Abdur Rahman, exiled for years in Russia, had arrived wearing a Russian uniform, and assumed power. Worse, the new reign of Alexander III had outraged British public opinion with its repugnant persecution of the Jews. Hundreds of thousands had been driven out of their homes by a wave of pogroms. In May 1882, the emperor had forbidden Jews to own landed property or settle outside a ghetto in southwest Russia. Violent public protests had been aroused in London.[34] To the queen, it seemed that Russia was Britain's most dangerous enemy and the opponent of all that she stood for. Reversing her usual policy of creating dynastic alliances, she preferred to isolate Russia from the other European powers.

She was relieved to hear of another suitor, an agreeable, steady young man far more to her taste. Early in January 1883, Frederick, the son of the grand duke of Baden, arrived at the New Palace. His sole purpose, which he communicated to Grand Duke Louis, was to see Elizabeth. Though glad to arouse a young man's interest, Elizabeth was not attracted. She received him amiably, said he was good-natured, and laughed at his oddities. Her elder sister sent a report to the queen:

> You ask me about Ella and Fritz of Baden—he was here the other day but said nothing according to Papa's wish. Ella and I never talk about those sort of things—but she seems neither to like or dislike Fritz in any way. . . . I do not think she cares at all for him yet—though I think Papa told her that he came here because of her. . . .[35]

The German empress, Frederick's grandmother, now tried her hand at matchmaking. With her daughter, the grand duchess of Baden, she contrived to bring the two parties together. The silver wedding of her son, the crown prince, and Elizabeth's aunt Vicky was to be celebrated in February. As well as inviting Frederick and his parents, she asked Elizabeth and her elder sister Victoria to Berlin. The stage was set for a proposal to be made.[36]

It was a very grand setting, and the Prince of Wales and royalty from all of Europe arrived. A brilliant costume pageant in the Berlin castle was planned to represent the union of England and Germany. Elizabeth and Victoria attended the extensive rehearsals in some attractive costumes. Princes and princesses prepared to take part in processions representing the courts of Queen Elizabeth and Frederick III and dance ancient quadrilles. A few days later the British ambassador was to hold a grand dinner and ball. At this ball Empress Augusta planned to announce the engagement.

Her plans, however, went awry when Elizabeth departed from her prepared script. Some time during the celebrations Frederick proposed to Elizabeth. But she knew her own mind and resolutely remained true to her Russian grand duke. Unable to submit to a loveless marriage made for dynastic convenience, she refused Frederick. The empress was shocked and furious. When the grand pageant came, she absented herself on the grounds of illness. In ignorance of her anger, Elizabeth and Victoria attended and enjoyed themselves, attracting admiring glances. But at the British ambassador's ball they suffered a humiliation. The empress came and refused to speak to them.[37]

Queen Victoria, also shocked, wrote a distraught letter to her granddaughter Victoria:

Oh! Dear! How very unfortunate it is of Ella to
refuse good Fritz of Baden so good & steady, with

such a safe and happy position, & *for a Russian.* I
do deeply regret it.

Ella's health will *never* stand the climate which
killed your poor Aunt & has ruined the healths of
almost all the German Princesses who went there.[38]

Meanwhile, Elizabeth had noticed that her sister Victoria was
falling in love. Her cousin, Prince Louis of Battenberg, the son
of Prince Alexander of Hesse, had come to stay in Darmstadt for
Christmas while on leave from his duties in the British Royal
Navy. The bronzed and fit sailor, who had just sailed around most
of the world, charmed Victoria with his exotic tales of faraway
lands. He appealed to the adventurous, tomboyish spirit in her.
She was fresh, lively, and clever, unlike the other girls he had
known; he soon fell in love with her.

Elizabeth was alert to their attachment as they danced together at the frequent balls that winter. Louis left in mid-March,
intending to return in June after attending the coronation of the
new Russian emperor. Soon afterward Queen Victoria invited
Elizabeth and Victoria to spend the summer as usual at Balmoral.
With a sister's intuition Elizabeth told her father: "If Victoria
does not go with me to Scotland she will become engaged to
Louis Battenberg." She was right, and that May she traveled
north without her sister.[39]

It was a trying time in the Highlands for Elizabeth. Her grandmother was in poor spirits. She had not entirely recovered from
spraining her ankle a few weeks before. She was in mourning, for
her faithful John Brown who had died the previous month. At a
loss without her old servant, she took Elizabeth and her aunt
Beatrice to church and out on gloomy carriage drives.

The queen's somber mood made the thorny question concerning Grand Duke Serge all the more awkward. The prospect
of marriage was in the air, and Elizabeth was of two minds. She
loved him, but quailed at living in a harsh climate and bowing to

alien customs inimical to her upbringing. She told her grand-mother that she hated the Russians and had no wish to live in their country. The queen was quick to point out the hazards. She recalled the unhappy lives of the Hessian princesses who had married into the Romanov family. She insisted that provision must be made for Elizabeth to spend most of her time out of Russia. Elizabeth said there was no hurry, and the queen declared that girls should not marry before the age of twenty.[40]

In July they moved down to Windsor, and then to Osborne. There was some comic relief when Grand Duke Louis joined them. He was trying to learn to play the bagpipes, but could only produce a gruesome squeal. As he and Elizabeth left, the queen was still hoping that she would reconsider and marry Prince Charles of Sweden instead.[41] She would not put up with a Russian staying with her for long on one of Elizabeth's visits to England. "Politics or no politics," she wrote, "the Russians are *totally* antagonistic to England."[42]

Back in Darmstadt, Elizabeth's doubts grew as she pondered the queen's advice. She knew also that the Prussian court in Berlin would deplore her accepting a Russian where two of their own candidates had failed. She would have to spend most of her time thousands of miles away from Germany and England, the sites of her friends, family, and childhood memories.

Late in September, as she wrestled with her doubts, Serge arrived in person. During a stay of a few days he spent time with her. They had intimate talks in some secluded drawing room or during strolls through the beech woods of Wolfsgarten as they caught glimpses of retreating deer. She still saw only his hand-some, dignified exterior and imagined him as a high-minded, cultured grand seigneur. To her he appeared to be the ideal sen-sitive man set apart from others. Yet fearing the pressure on her from Windsor and Berlin, in the short time available she could not settle her mind enough to come to a decision. He proposed to her, and she refused.[43]

However, in his absence she rallied her spirits and decided to accept a man whom she had known for only a few days during the past four years. She spent some time composing a defiant and almost "modern" letter to Queen Victoria:

*Darmstadt*
*October 13th 1883.*

*Dearest Grandmama,*

*I am afraid this letter will not give you as much pleasure as I should wish, but as it concerns my happiness & you have always been so kind to me, I wish you to know what I think about Serge.*

*Those few days I saw him last month have convinced me that I shall be happy with him. We have the same tastes for things & although he may have opinions you do not like, do you not think, dear Grandmama that I might do him good?*

*Mama always liked him so & we both have had that great sorrow of losing one we loved so dearly, that it draws us closer together & we feel for each other more. As to Russia, it will be easily arranged that we should spend a great part of the time out of that country & I shall try to keep in the right path & will always keep those I love in my mind & follow their good example.*

*I am afraid you will think me very changeable but I think I know what I am doing & if I am unhappy, which I am sure will never be, it will be all my doing as you know. Please forgive me if you are vexed with what I shall do, & although I will have to begin a new life, I will always cling to those who have been dearer to me than I can say.*

*Ella* [44]

## Notes to Chapter 5

*Daughter of the duke of Augustenburg, who had claimed the throne of Schleswig and Holstein in 1864.

†She was born Princess Dagmar of Denmark, but took the name Marie when converting to Russian Orthodoxy on her marriage.

‡His father, Alexander II, had begun this process by allowing terrorist acts to be tried by special courts-martial and granting powers to the police to exile even those merely suspected of political crimes. Alexander III, however, was the first ruler of Russia to grant its police powers normally associated with totalitarian regimes. He introduced certain "temporary" regulations, never repealed, which put Moscow, St. Petersburg, and eight other provinces under "reinforced safeguard." At the whim of the police, anyone could be expelled, fined, or imprisoned for up to three months, all public or private gatherings could be forbidden and any public employees dismissed. A vast range of activities had to be approved by the police, making it, as one observant American, George Kennan, noted, "a sort of incompetent bureaucratic substitute for divine providence." One police chief declared that Alexander's decrees caused the fate of the "entire population of Russia to become dependent on the personal opinions of the functionaries of the political police."

However, these enormous powers were used with remarkable leniency. During Alexander's repressive reign only four thousand persons, out of a population of nearly a hundred million, were detained or interrogated in connection with political offenses; only forty-four, all assassins or potential assassins, were executed for political crimes. The right to travel abroad and property rights, even those of expatriate revolutionaries, were scrupulously respected. The vast majority of criminals were tried fairly, by jury. Censorship was little more than a nuisance: between 1867 and 1894 only 158 books, not including Marx's *Capital,* were forbidden to circulate in Russia. Compared with its Soviet successor, Alexander III's empire was a remarkably free country.

# *Chapter 6*

*I hate marriages*

—Letter from Queen Victoria to her daughter
Vicky, Crown Princess of Prussia.

The queen reacted with severe shock. She had never known any of her children or grandchildren to show such an independent mind and accept a suitor against her will. In great confusion she wrote to her granddaughter Victoria:

> I have got Ella's letter but I *really* do *not* feel *quite* able to answer her *yet*—as I do feel this prospect *so very deeply.* . . . Dear Ella, she really is so changeable and *unaccountable;* she told me how she hated the Russians, she refused Serge 3 weeks ago & now she takes him & forgets *all!*[1]

In a similar mood the queen wrote to her daughter Vicky in Berlin: "It is a real sorrow to me and the less I say about it the better."[2] In the Prussian court, where obedience was counted as a supreme virtue, Vicky had to face the outrage of Empress Augusta, her mother-in-law. It was bad enough that Elizabeth had rejected the suit of Prince William. William, who hated Serge,[3] had lost no time in portraying him to his grandmother in the worst possible light. The empress had never really forgiven Elizabeth for refusing to accept her planned engagement to Fritz of Baden. That a princess from one of Germany's smallest courts should again defy the wish of the imperial Hohenzollern dynasty was another insult. It was a long time before her antagonism was to subside.*4

Unbowed, Elizabeth ignored this storm of protest. She spent part of the winter in bed with influenza and a bad cough, buoyed up as she looked forward to the announcement of her engagement in the following year.5 When it was made on February 26, 1884, she was reunited to her joy with Serge. The Russian emperor and empress were present to load her with the riches of the Russian court.6 They bestowed on her the Order of St. Catherine and a diamond and sapphire brooch, the most valuable present she had ever received. Serge gave her a "most beautiful jewel," an Indian shawl and a bracelet which her great-aunt Marie, Serge's mother, had received on her engagement. For the occasion a dance, trivial by the grand standards of the Russian court, was held for one hundred and thirty guests.

The matrimonial details were soon settled. Grand Duke Louis insisted that his daughter should keep her Lutheran faith. The wedding was to be in June in the Winter Palace in St. Petersburg. Queen Victoria, now glumly resigned to the match, gave her blessing in a letter which pleased her granddaughter. As the Russians left, Elizabeth looked forward to years of married bliss, and her sister Victoria eagerly prepared for her own wedding to Prince Louis of Battenberg on April 30.

Their bright prospects were overshadowed by some unforeseen family complications. On March 28 their uncle Leopold, Queen Victoria's youngest son, met with the death long threatened by his hemophilia. At Cannes he fell downstairs; an infusion of blood led to an epileptic convulsion.7 Elizabeth lost a favorite uncle whose sympathy had been a valuable support after her mother's death. She and Victoria, like their mother before them, would now be marrying in mourning.

To add to this gloom, their father formed an emotional attachment which was to bring a diplomatic scandal to Hesse and some inadvertent shame to Elizabeth. Grand Duke Louis was already feeling abandoned at the thought of losing his two favorite daughters. Since Alice's death he had leaned heavily on their support, and the loneliness he faced seemed almost unbearable. Some years before, the Prince of Wales had anticipated that Louis would need a new wife. He hoped that Louis might marry Princess Beatrice, Queen Victoria's youngest daughter. He exerted all his influence to annul the law against marriage to a deceased wife's sister, but the bishops threw his bill out of the House of Lords.

Instead, an ambitious, beautiful, and accomplished woman had entered Grand Duke Louis's life. The thirty-year-old Madame Alexandrine von Kolemine, who had already divorced the Russian chargé d'affaires, was now entangling Louis with the help of Prince Isenburg, a Hessian nobleman, and his wife. Elizabeth and Victoria knew about the friendship and sometimes accompanied the couple on their walks. They liked Mme. Kolemine, who expressed kind attentions to them, and were glad to think that their father would have company when they were married. Victoria thought that the lady's low rank and her divorced status ruled out any marriage, and declared: "Dear Papa will never marry." But Louis went ahead and proposed.[8]

Early in April the news of his engagement shocked his daughters into momentary silence at the breakfast table. It was at this point that Elizabeth made an uncharacteristic blunder. She had promised to keep the secret of her father's affair. But she was in the habit of writing intimate letters to her aunt, Princess Beatrice, Queen Victoria's youngest daughter. In one letter she offered a hint about Mme. Kolemine. Louis learned of the indiscretion and sent an admonitory telegram from one of his country residences. Pained at causing him embarrassment, Elizabeth wrote a contrite reply.

*Victoria read me your telegramme this morning and V. was very unhappy about it so I write to explain to you what I did so as to show you what I wrote. . . .*

*As I have been always writing and saying my inner thoughts to Aunt I thought it would not be breaking my promise if I said I knew there was somebody you admired very much — of course I did not mention names — I am <u>very very sorrow</u> [sic] indeed if I have caused you any trouble with the relations [sic] but my great love for you made me act imprudently — I see my greatest fault is I ought to have told you and Victoria I was going to write and have asked your permission. Please forgive me and tell me if in any way I can make good what I have done.*

*Ever your loving*
*child*
*Ella*[9]

Fortunately Beatrice kept the news from Queen Victoria and spared Elizabeth further shame. But the family had a difficult task of concealment when the queen traveled to Darmstadt two weeks before the wedding of Victoria and Louis of Battenberg. Her spirits were at odds with the customary glee of wedding festivities. Her eyes still reflected sadness at the loss of the two men who were dear to her. "I am a poor desolate old woman," she wrote, "and my cup of sorrow overflows!"[10] Grand Duke Louis, Elizabeth, and all the Hessian family received her at Darmstadt with a minimum of ceremony. One morning before breakfast the queen ordered the grand duke to take her to Alice's suite. It was kept exactly as on the moment of her death, the clothes still lying on the floor. A little later, the queen was to take the family on an obligatory visit to Alice's tomb at the Rosenhöhe.[11]

Besides fearing her grandmother's anger if she discovered her father's affair, Elizabeth was in trepidation as the time came for her fiancé's arrival for the wedding. She dreaded that the queen would meet Serge with an icy hauteur. Earlier she had prepared the encounter in a letter: "I am so glad you will see Serge when you come next month and *hope* he will make a favourable impression on you, all who know him like him and say he has such a true and noble character. . . ."[12]

Serge duly arrived, and was in despair on hearing of Grand Duke Louis's entanglement, but kept his promise of secrecy. As he nervously strode in to be introduced to the queen, Elizabeth waited anxiously. Fortunately her fears were not realized. The queen received him courteously and noted down her good impression: "very tall, and gentlemanlike, but very thin, pale and delicate-looking."[13]

At the same time, Elizabeth's sister Victoria had cause for disquiet in addition to her approaching wedding. Her father asked her to tell the queen about his engagement. Some five days before the ceremony she steeled herself to break the news. The queen was outraged. To her it was deplorable that a prince should place his private marital pleasure above the interests of his country or international diplomacy. In a note the next day she fulminated against the marriage.

> . . . his marrying such a person—a divorced Russian lady—would lower him so much. . . . He cannot say that this intended union is for the sake of Children or for his Country—it would be the very reverse of *both,* it can only be for what *he thinks,* (and I am afraid he is much mistaken) will be for his *own* personal happiness. It will do him immense harm in his own Country—in England he will lose the position he held and enjoyed and I could *not* defend such a choice. . . . I do *most earnestly* ask him to *pause* and put off at least for a time—and to think, that the difficulty of doing so—or even of breaking off such an engagement is *infinitely less* than the *pain* and *suffering* of hurting all those he loves best and offending his best friends and subjects by such a marriage which would be the inevitable result.[14]

In ignorance of the impending scandal guests were pouring in from England and Germany for Victoria's wedding. The Prussian crown prince and princess came from Berlin, and Alexander of Hesse's two sons, Alexander (Sandro) and Henry (Liko), turned up to cheer their brother. Only the Prince of Wales was in the know, and he feared the developments of the next few days.[15]

Grand Duke Louis, full of jokes and compliments, seemed in indecently high spirits as he met his guests on the station platform. His subjects echoed his mood, and turned out in crowds to see a gaudy array of royalty and their entourages that few could remember in Darmstadt. The festivities that followed were elaborate and many. On a single day, there was a royal confirmation in the morning, attended in full uniform, then a two-hour banquet, in the afternoon the christening of a royal baby, again in full uniform, and in the evening a "Punch" and a heavy dinner, after which a Russian colonel "played beautifully on the pianoforte."

The wedding took place on a clear, fine day. For the last time Elizabeth shared a bedroom with Victoria. With her sisters, all dressed in white, she descended to meet the queen. The bride emerged a little later, pale but radiant in her mother's wedding dress. Vast crowds lustily cheered the sovereigns and one of their favorite princesses. A gun salute followed the ceremony, and then a banquet in the Kaisersaal. In a bittersweet mood Elizabeth looked forward to saying farewell to her closest friend and favorite sister.

Few people noticed that the grand duke had deserted his guests for a while. He slipped away to a room in the castle where a beautiful woman and three men awaited him. They were Madame von Kolemine, her brother, the Hessian prime minister, Starck, and Prince Isenburg. Without delay the prime minister conducted the second marriage of that day. Everything was veiled in secrecy, and the bride stayed that night elsewhere. She was never to spend one with her new husband.

Grand Duke Louis had hoped that this furtive ceremony would protect him from the intervention of his relatives. He had little idea how much his personal freedom was curtailed by his family ties to the ruling houses of Russia, Germany, and Great Britain. His secrecy was in vain. Vicky got wind of the news and told the Prince of Wales. Lady Ely was given the unwelcome task of telling the queen. In private the queen was furious and sent for her eldest son. She ordered him to interview Alexandrine von Kolemine and somehow annul the marriage. A telegram was despatched to the already infuriated Empress Augusta. At her command her son and his wife ate a hasty dinner and caught a train to Berlin on the evening of May 2. Courtiers developed diplomatic colds, and ministers suddenly found urgent business elsewhere. Outside the deserted palace the bunting hung limp in empty streets.

Soon the story appeared in the press, and consternation arose in London. Gladstone declared that the grand duke's conduct was an unjustifiable slight to the queen. Her cousin, the duke of Cambridge,† once entangled in a similar situation, now vehemently expressed the view that "when a man, through some unfortunate accident, makes a great mistake he must abide by it."

Slowly the marriage was untangled. In June 1884 Hermann Sahl, formerly the queen's German secretary, who had retired to Darmstadt, reported to Sir Henry Ponsonby:

> You will be glad that *substantially* the untieing of the morganatic knot is now accomplished, and by degrees the *formal* severance will be pronounced by a Court of Law convened for this purpose. Diplomatists and Lawyers are never embarrassed about finding a suitable *form*—as soon as they have secured a convergence of views and aims in *substance.*

Unfortunately the bride proved less cooperative. Mme. von Kolemine fled to Russia with the grand duke's love letters. Later there were rumors of blackmail threats, but these ceased after the sum of 500,000 marks had been handed over.[16] The marriage was dissolved on July 9.

In the meantime, Elizabeth had gone back to Windsor with the British royal party. It was a relief to be away from her broken-hearted father. The queen wanted to be alone with her grand-daughter before the wedding. She gave plenty of unsolicited advice and warnings about married life in Russia. Soon, however, Grand Duke Louis was invited to Windsor by the queen as a gesture of reconciliation. He was, the queen wrote, "in *such* a state of distress and grief that it is pitiful to see."[17] But his fellow guests considered his plight ridiculous, his flouting of propriety an unmanly weakness. With cruel English mockery they jokingly urged him to forget his old love and marry at once. When he returned to Darmstadt with Elizabeth, she and her sisters tried to take their mother's place and console him as well as they could.

Elizabeth sadly realized that she had made the last of her annual visits to the queen. It would be some years before she was to set foot in England again. She was losing the advice and support of a grandmother who had always had her own interests at heart, even though her dictatorial attitude had frustrated Elizabeth's independent spirit. She wrote: "I cannot say how sad we were leaving you & how all your kindness touched us & will never be forgotten. Leaving Windsor was to me so painful—just like going away from my home. . . ."[18] All her thoughts were centered on her unpredictable future in a foreign country whose language she could not understand. Shortly before her departure for Russia, she expressed the hope to Queen Victoria that she would remain true to the ideals which her mother had set her: "I hope that when you see me again you won't find any change in my character for the worse, as I long to be simple in manners and as good as Mama would have wished me to be."[19]

## *Notes to Chapter 6*

*The empress's anger was still heated in the following summer. Queen Victoria, whose antipathy by then had cooled toward Elizabeth, warned a diplomat not to provoke the empress:

> "The Queen writes to Sir Howard to *warn* him *not* to enter with the Empress *on* the *subject* of the *Grand Duke* of Hesse and his daughter, against whom she is filled with spite and unchristian feelings. Please cut it short; say you know nothing. . . ."

†George, second Duke of Cambridge (1819–1904), was the son of Prince Adolphus, the first duke, and a grandson of King George III.

# Chapter 7

*Russia is a whole separate world, submissive to the will, caprice, fantasy of a single man, whether his name be Peter or Ivan, no matter.*

—PETER CHAADAYEV

At half-past six on a June evening in 1884, the Hessian and Battenberg families were gathered on the platform of Darmstadt station. Standing beside their father, Grand Duke Louis's children looked forward to the thousand-mile journey to Russia. It was an adventure for twelve-year-old Alix; for Ernest, at fifteen, it provided a chance to wear the uniform of the Hessian guard regiment, and Irene, two years older, who had just "come out," eagerly awaited the parties and receptions. Victoria was to meet her dashing sailor-husband Prince Louis at St. Petersburg, where he was due to arrive on Queen Victoria's yacht, the *Osborne*. Also in the party, Louis's parents, Prince Alexander of Hesse and Princess Julie of Battenberg, could remember their passionate elopement from the Russian capital thirty-three years earlier, Emperor Nicholas I having forbidden their marriage. But for Elizabeth, excited as she was, this was the last time in many months that she was to stand on her native soil. She had already made her sad farewells to old friends and servants. Although she had been popular in Hesse, few of her father's subjects were present to see her depart. The citizens of Darmstadt had left the grand ducal family alone in the shame of the Kolemine affair.[1]

The train drew in, and Elizabeth took leave of her beloved Darmstadt. She and her family then began a tiring journey of three days and two nights over most of Europe. They stayed overnight in Berlin, and in switching to the imperial train at the Russian border they first encountered the splendid luxury of the Romanovs. The nine vestibuled cars of this palace on wheels measured more than a thousand feet and contained individual sleeping quarters for every passenger. Serge had decorated it throughout with flowers of white, her favorite color. Their journey took them across Poland and the endless pine forests and clear streams of the flat Russian plain, past wooden peasant villages and walled towns with gold-domed churches. Whenever the train was scheduled to stop for water, the couple were greeted by frock-coated dignitaries and bearded bishops clad in shining vestments. Crowds would gather to see the most beautiful princess in Europe. They gave high praise to her gracious dignity and charming smile.[2]

A few miles outside St. Petersburg, at Peterhof on the shore of the Baltic Sea, the train came to a halt. Grand Duke Serge, his brother the emperor Alexander and the entire imperial family greeted them on the station platform. They were driven to a scene of gilded magnificence that far outstripped the muted grandeur of Windsor or Potsdam. Their carriages drew up outside the huge baroque Grand Palace. Beside it was a gold-plated statue of Samson killing a lion; from the lion's mouth a jet of water spurted up higher than the palace roof. Beneath it a canal lined by alternate fountains and pine trees stretched for miles down to the sea. Inside the palace were vast halls and a rabbit warren of rooms and corridors, a pervading smell of sunflower oil and leather and cigarettes. A small army of servants and ladies-in-waiting overawed Elizabeth and her sisters. One evening the family was shown around the vast gardens, waterfalls, and elaborate flower beds by the brilliant glow of the aurora borealis.

For a week their host was Emperor Alexander III, a simple,

straightforward bearded giant, very much in love with his wife Marie, a strong-willed Danish princess. He was ever keen to show off his strength, said to be sufficient to break a horseshoe in half, and his love of jokes kept the party in high spirits. There were reunions with relatives from all over Europe. Marie's family came over from Denmark, Prince Alfred, Queen Victoria's second son, arrived with his wife Marie, Serge's sister, and there were numerous German cousins. All the imperial family, Elizabeth wrote to Queen Victoria, "are most kind to me,"[3] and Serge was full of "little attentions" to his bride. Twelve-year-old Alix forgot her shyness and joined in the laughter with glee. She formed a friendship with the sixteen-year-old tsarevitch Nicholas, eldest son of the emperor and heir to the throne. With a stone set in Alix's ring they carved their names together on a window of the palace. Nicholas gave her a diamond brooch but Alix, feeling it improper to accept the gift, pressed it back into his hand the following day. They played hide-and-seek, and her shrieks of delight echoed as they ran up and down the corridors.[4]

On June 14, a clear and bright day, the wedding festivities began in earnest. The royal party and numerous guests took a train to St. Petersburg. At the station Elizabeth followed Empress Marie into a gilt coach built for Catherine the Great. Eight white horses decked with red plumes were led forward by servants in gold livery; the other guests followed in lesser carriages. For the first time Elizabeth saw the city built by Peter the Great on nineteen islands, the "Venice of the North." For hours the procession crawled through the broad straight avenues, past pillared palaces and the red, white, and gold Engineers' College, over intricate arching bridges across the winding canals. Everywhere vast crowds gave lusty cheers to the nineteen-year-old princess, who was the center of attention. The cavalcade drew up outside the huge Winter Palace, the largest in Europe.[5] Here in 1880 Elizabeth's great-uncle, Prince Alexander of Hesse, arriving late from Germany, had inadvertently saved the emperor Alexander II from a terrorist bomb. Here, a few months later, the emperor's mutilated body had been brought in after a second bomb, and he had died with his family. But these gruesome deeds were forgotten as Elizabeth was led up a grand marble staircase, past halls the size of churches decorated with French furniture, Gobelin tapestries, and intricately carved chandeliers. She was shown into an immense bedroom with four windows overlooking the broad Neva river. On the far bank she could see the Fortress of St. Peter and St. Paul, its gilded needle spire gleaming against the sky. Nearby stood the Academy of Sciences, its cream facade fronted by eight pedimented columns, and mansions of classical elegance stretching into the distance. That summer night darkness never fell on what was the finest view Elizabeth had ever known.

She was awakened early the next morning to be dressed according to a complicated eighteenth-century tradition,[6] with the empress on hand to direct the proceedings. Marie handed over the hairpins to the court coiffeur who curled Elizabeth's hair in front of a gold-framed mirror that had belonged to Empress Anne, an eighteenth-century ruler of Russia. A long train of silver cloth was pinned onto the shoulders of Elizabeth's heavy gown of the same material, so thick that it seemed made of cardboard.

The bridal jewels of Catherine the Great were brought in on cushions by the ladies of the household. A diadem with a brilliant pink diamond was hung on a thread around her neck; over it was placed a necklace of diamonds. The earrings, in the shape of cherries, were so heavy that they were hung by a wire over her ears and slowly dug into the flesh. On her head were placed a lace veil and the crimson crown, adorned with a cross and covered with diamonds. A great mantle of red velvet and ermine was then fastened around her neck with a massive silver buckle.

Hours after she had sat down before the gilt mirror, Elizabeth rose and found that walking under the weight of this heavy finery took an immense effort. A ten-ruble coin, placed earlier into her right shoe for luck, now dug into her toes. She passed through rooms scented with roses, orchids, and lilies of the valley and adorned with columns of marble, malachite, and jasper. At ten o'clock she entered the white-and-gold chapel on her father's arm, six pages bearing her train behind her. As Princess Eugenie Golitsina later recalled, "She looked the most beautiful bride ever to make her way to the palace chapel."

Elizabeth made her way up the aisle beneath a gilded ceiling painted blue to represent the skies of heaven and dotted with floating cherubs. In front of the jeweled altar screen she took her place beside Serge, who was wearing a military uniform. The lengthy Orthodox service began. The bridesmen took turns to hold the heavy golden crowns over their heads as the choir sang soaring, polyphonous chants. The bride and groom exchanged rings three times in a sign of the Holy Trinity. At her father's insistence, a Lutheran marriage followed in the Blue Drawing Room. The bride then emerged with the man she loved, bearing the new name of Grand Duchess Elizabeth.

Soon afterward an elaborate and extended banquet was held in the concert hall in the presence of hundreds of guests. Behind the chair of each royal guest a courtier, dressed in heavy gold braid, stood ready to hand a glass of wine on a gold plate. At length a carriage took the bride and groom a mile down the long straight Nevsky Prospect to Serge's palace, the Sergievskaya. Here the emperor and empress, taking the place of Serge's parents, welcomed them with the traditional gifts of bread and salt.

Throughout the ceremonies, Elizabeth had cheerfully borne the oppressive weight of her clothing. Now she could thankfully retire, exhausted but delighted to be alone with her husband. "She breathed happiness," as all the wedding guests had concurred. The new grand duchess was exhilarated by the prospect of a private and intimate honeymoon. These thoughts consoled her as the time drew near for the parting from her family and she went through yet more formal receptions. For hours she stood beside Serge to be presented to the diplomatic corps, clad in dark gold-leaved uniforms, and managed to say a few gracious words in French to each as they bowed to her. She repeated the procedure at a "drawing-room" for the numerous aristocratic wedding guests.[7]

The farewells to her family were wrenching. "Beloved Papa," she wrote a little later, "I cannot tell you how terribly I miss you and the others."[8] It was hardest for Louis, as he was losing the daughter who had bound his family together and he would return home deprived of the woman he had loved. Elizabeth wrote afterward to Queen Victoria of "dear Papa who writes to me so sadly that it is dreadful to think of."[9] She was to write numerous letters to him, expressing her homesickness, her love, and sympathy. She had now irrevocably left behind her family from whom she drew her strength, her friends, her native home, her old habits. Victoria had given her a final warning from the queen to send private letters only by the British diplomatic couriers.*[10,11] It was an unhappy portent for her new life in an exotic country of whose religion, customs, and language she knew almost nothing.

Traveling beyond the westernized city of Peter the Great, Serge gave his bride her first contact with the true "Holy Russia" in the ancient capital of Moscow. On the Sunday she entered the city, hundreds of church bells sounded out a rich melodic peal. The golden cupolas of the "forty times forty" churches gleamed over the roofs of the columned mansions of princes and millionaire merchants and the humble wooden lodgings of artisans. At the center, the couple drove over the cobbles of the vast Red Square† and past the many-colored onion domes of St. Basil's Cathedral. Through a gate in a high brick wall, they entered the citadel of Moscow, the Kremlin. In one of its palaces they stayed for a few days of sight-seeing.

Serge showed his new wife the Kremlin churches and rooms that had represented the glory of Russia's church, and the might of her rulers, ever since they had thrown off the yoke of the Tartars in the fourteenth century. She saw the frescoed medieval hall, where coronation banquets had been held for centuries, and a room set aside for the descendants of men who had saved the lives of past tsars. In the Cathedral of the Assumption, where Serge's ancestors had been crowned, lay sacred icons that they had taken with them to war. Beside the cathedral stood the massive bell tower of Ivan the Great which the troops of Napoleon's invading army had failed to demolish.

Outside the city, they visited the ancient monasteries that were the heart of Russian Orthodoxy. Elizabeth saw humble peasants praying with fervor, but found the reverence shown to the icons difficult to reconcile with her Lutheran faith: "Of course there were holy pictures," she wrote to Queen Victoria, "but where Serge knelt and kissed them I made a very low curtsy, in that way it does not shock the people so much and yet I do not think that I go too far. I only kiss the cross when held out to me and as it is the custom to kiss the priest's hand when he kisses one's own I do it too—it is a mark of politeness."[12] Everywhere the Muscovites shouted with wild enthusiasm on seeing the two members of their imperial family. Some seemed to worship them; on one occasion Elizabeth found that she was held fast by the feet by an old woman on her knees. A policeman had to drive her away.

One evening they attended a banquet in the Kremlin, and watched a dancing and singing troupe of Gypsies. They were "very smartly dressed," Elizabeth wrote, "fantastic costumes with much colour—they sing Russian and Bohemian songs— very melancholy and at times so wild that they shriek in between. If one hears them out of doors they dance and tremble with one shoulder whilst hopping about in a most extraordinary way. . . ."[13]

For their honeymoon they traveled ten miles out of Moscow to an estate which Serge had inherited from his mother. As their carriage emerged from a pine forest onto a vast green meadow, they saw, in the distance, the roof of the house hidden among a wide belt of trees. They crossed the smooth, broad Moscow river on a wooden pontoon bridge, and passed through the village of wooden cabins and a green-roofed church: Ilinskoe. There the peasant inhabitants were gathered for a glimpse of their new lady. The coach turned into the wide wooden gates and drove up a magnificent avenue between four rows of lime trees. At its end was a square, two-storied eighteenth-century house of old oak, its classical facade lined by white pedimented windows. Underneath the pillared portico, white-liveried servants were awaiting their arrival. Here they were to retire every summer for a holiday.[14]

At Ilinskoe Elizabeth settled in to a life of idle tranquility. She would breakfast with her husband in the shade of a broad balcony that ran around the second floor of the house. They would take a short stroll, braving the intense heat and a plague of flies, and she would then spend an hour and a half learning Russian from her tutor, Mlle. Schneider. When talking to her, their entourage would use the words she had learned in their conversation.[15] After lunch Serge, whose English was poor, would read to her from a French novel, *Le Roman d'un jeune homme pauvre*. (Later he introduced her to Russian stories as she began to know the language.) Then, sometimes taking a picnic, they would wander about the vast estate.‡ In the birch woods they searched for mushrooms, which the peasants had often furtively stolen, even under the threat of strict punishment. Sometimes they saw the distant figure of a peasant woman gathering up her skirts as she ran away. In the meadows, where Serge's prize herd of Holstein cattle roamed, Elizabeth gathered flowers to scent the rooms of the house. When the heat was broken up by a heavy thunderstorm, they would settle down in the library and read bound volumes of the *Illustrated London News*. After tea and supper, they would descend the steep winding path to the Moscow River where two sailors kept charge of several boats moored by the bank. They would row alone on the river in the cool evening twilight, the only sound coming from the paddles in the water. They would retire to the house, and Elizabeth would play the piano. If their entourage were present, they would listen to them playing waltzes or operettas. Sometimes Serge's brother Paul and some neighbors would visit, and they would play at spirited charades.[16]

While appearing peacefully content to those around her, Elizabeth was coping alone with a grave shock. Her doubts about her husband had, perhaps, been aroused on finding that he wore bone corsets to preserve his slim figure. Serge revealed himself to be a man without physical interest in women who was unlikely ever to sire her children. In the accounts of the time and Elizabeth's letters a discreet veil was drawn over their private life. Outwardly at least their marriage seemed normal. Throughout their life together she and Serge would always share a large marital bed. But it soon became clear that, in the unlikely event that he attempted procreation, he found it a duty rather than a pleasure and soon abandoned it. Her marriage would remain little more than a sexually empty formality.§

The experience in childhood of bearing up under adversity now served her well. Too proud to complain of her disappointment, she resolved to live her life as happily as she could. She was determined to fulfill the vows she had made to love, honor, and obey her husband. Although he began to treat her as a child, and would often reprimand her in public, she never contradicted his will. She remained loyal to him, and loved him for what he was. Given her sheltered Victorian upbringing, she probably had no idea that Serge could have any other sexual desires. His intense religiosity prevented him from exercising them outside his marriage, and instead caused him torments of guilt. Just as she had looked after Alix and Ernest in her childhood, Elizabeth now felt a strong protective streak of pity for one of nature's victims. She still admired his religious piety and artistic sensibility. Appreciating the conflict of a tormented conscience, she could still partly see in him the ideal sensitive character she had always sought. She praised the gentler side that she found beneath his cold, inflexible exterior, as his niece Marie later described him: "introspective, essentially diffident, his true spirit imprisoned within him, he hid private impulses of extreme sensitiveness and acted according to rigid conventions. . . ."[17] In return Serge abandoned his cold arrogance and treated her in private with consideration and affection. Elizabeth wrote on July 14 to her father:

> Serge is a person, of whom the more one sees and the more one is with him, the more love one has for him, and he has also a calmness in his character which I like so much. He thinks so much of me that I do not feel homesickness so much, and he often speaks of you all with such feeling that it does me good.[18]

If discovering her husband's true nature was one unwelcome surprise, Elizabeth found another in the life of the rural Russians that lagged centuries behind the West. Soon after her arrival at Ilinskoe she saw a religious procession passing through the village in memory of an epidemic that had afflicted the area in the previous year.[19] It was composed largely of bearded, unkempt peasants clad in drab, coarse clothing, paying reverence to the icons borne by the priests. It was one of her first glimpses of a backwardness that she had never seen before. On venturing to the village past the gates of her house, Elizabeth found the people living in squalor in wooden log cabins, the men getting drunk at every opportunity in the village tavern. In the summer they would toil all day long in the fields; in August they worked around the clock to reap the harvest. Their agriculture was nothing like the careful husbandry of the neat and prosperous farms that Elizabeth had seen in southern Germany and England. They had no idea of the threshing machines and seed drills that were common in the West. Ignorant of crop rotation, they still left a third of their fields fallow each year. Their land was divided into a medieval‖ system of strips, and their primitive wooden ploughs barely broke its surface. Unlike the contented farm laborers of Hesse, the poverty made the Russian peasants grasping of their possessions and callous toward their children. If a child died, many a mother was grateful for having one less mouth to feed. Medicine consisted of a hut manned by a poorly trained orderly; a doctor might visit once a fortnight. Shocked at the infant mortality, Elizabeth managed to induce Serge to install a trained midwife in the village.[20]

But in spite of their downtrodden existence, the peasants were forever cheerful and good-natured. They seldom complained of their misfortunes, considering them to be the will of God. They could show generosity and compassion to convicted criminals and beggars, people even more unfortunate than themselves. Ignorant of the Bible or Orthodox doctrine but profoundly aware of the blessings of poverty and humility, they believed in a genuine primitive Christianity. In their religion they regarded the emperor, their father-tsar, almost as a god. They saw him as their protector who would do them justice, and the landlords as their oppressors. The land they considered as their own by right. They believed that government officials had concealed the decree of Alexander II to grant it to them when he had abolished serfdom in 1861. One day, they were convinced, the benevolent tsar would drive away the landed gentry and restore the land to them.

As a relative of the tsar, Elizabeth found herself treated with a deep reverence. In her turn, she was obliged to play the role of a lady bountiful when the day of her patron saint arrived in September. That day she and Serge were rowed across the Moscow River to a meadow where hundreds of peasants were gathered. The fete began after an anthem in honor of St. Elizabeth. Elizabeth handed out small presents, some handkerchiefs, teapots, samovars, portraits of the imperial family, and bags of boiled sweets for the children. The boys took part in sack races, and the adults danced and sang for Elizabeth. Some tea was served, but the peasants had brought along their own supplies of vodka. By the time Elizabeth and Serge were rowed back across the river, most of the men, in true Russian fashion, had got exceedingly drunk.[21]

Elizabeth's own social sphere, the gilded Russian aristocracy, was a world apart. She first entered it outside St. Petersburg late in July at a dance at the nearby estate of Archangelskoe. She was dressed in a medieval Russian court costume, "red with little white stars," she wrote to her father, "a pinafore in chequered pattern, a red handkerchief tied on the head and my hair fastened with multicoloured bands."[22] With Serge she drove a few miles, passed through vast parks and gardens, and drew up at a columned eighteenth-century palace, a kind of Russian Versailles surrounded by clipped lawns, fountains, and Olympian statues. Here lived the Youssoupovs, the richest family in Russia, richer even than the emperor. Their immense estate at Archangelskoe, virtually a small town with hundreds of servants, a private theater and zoo, numerous greenhouses, and a porcelain factory, was only a small part of their wealth. They owned four palaces in St. Petersburg and three in Moscow, one of which, built for Ivan the Terrible, had a secret tunnel stretching for miles to the Kremlin. Their property encompassed thirty-seven estates throughout Russia, and factories, mills, collieries, iron mines, and oilfields. One estate ran for one hundred and twenty-five miles along the Caspian Sea, and its oil was so abundant that peasants used it to grease their cart wheels.[23]

The owners of this fortune, Prince Felix Youssoupov and his wife Princess Zenaide, proved to be generous and attentive hosts. Elizabeth got on well with the princess, an attractive and intelligent woman with luminous, intense gray eyes and a ready smile. She was to become one of her closest friends in Russia and an ally in her future political struggles.

Elizabeth also became acquainted with another nearby aristocratic family, the Golitsyns, one of the oldest families in Russia, who held the rank of prince, and could trace their descent from the legendary founder of the nation, Rurik Sviatoslavich.# Since the ninth century they had served Russia in important posts. Prince Paul Golitsyn was a retired diplomat, and his wife, who had borne him many children, was a very dignified elderly figure. At their country house she was to be found sitting in an armchair on the terrace, wearing an expensive scent and formal dresses with priceless lace. She also was to become Elizabeth's friend.[24]

Even with her new friends, Elizabeth found that, as autumn approached with a plague of flies, she felt homesick for her old life with her family. "How I wish I could see you all," she wrote to her father, "for the autumn weather here makes me think of the homely evenings of Wolfsgarten, where we all sat around the lamp and read. I very much hope we shall come together there next autumn."[25] One morning she looked out and saw the ground covered in snow. The time had come for Serge to resume his regimental duties in St. Petersburg. She now faced a glittering and entirely unfamiliar life in the high society of the capital.

## *Notes to Chapter 7*

*At that time the British diplomatic bag was virtually the only one in Europe to reach its destination with its contents unexamined. Such was its reputation for probity that the brothers Cambon, French ambassadors in Berlin and St. Petersburg, used it in preference to their own national carrier.

†Called "Red Square" (Krasnaya Ploshchad) not from any association with Communism, but from another meaning of the word krasny, "beautiful" or "brilliant." The gaudy St. Basil's Cathedral so impressed Tsar Ivan IV ("the Terrible") that he reputedly had the architects eyes put out so that they should never produce a building of equal merit.

‡At 2,400 acres, however, it was small by the standards of the Russian aristocracy.

§There is, of course, no proof of Serge's homosexuality, but the amount of circumstantial evidence makes it probable. The fact that married women on both sides of Elizabeth's family for at least two generations all bore children makes it very unlikely that her childlessness was due to a hereditary defect on her part. On the other hand, in the Romanov family one can find an example of homosexuality in Serge's first cousin, Grand Duke Constantine Constantinovich (proven from his recently published diaries).

That said, it is still possible that Serge may have merely become impotent after the emotional devastation of his parents' deaths. Yet, as we have seen, his reserved, haughty, and defensive character and cold, stiff manners point to a rigid self-repression of unwanted impulses. His handwriting was spidery (and difficult to read), and his characteristic gesture was to clasp both hands in front of him while toying with one of his rings. In photographs he is often shown with one leg twined round the other while glowering at the camera in a hollow attempt at ferocity. All these traits suggest, as Prince Nicholas of Greece wrote, that he was forever trying to "counteract something indefinably effeminate in his general appearance."

||As an illustration of the backwardness of Russian agriculture, it can be pointed out that Russia only abandoned the prehistoric "slash-burn" system (burning down a patch of forest, clearing away the trees, cultivating the land, then repeating the process in another area of virgin forest) in the sixteenth century. By that time the system of strip-farming the Russian peasants moved on to was already being abandoned in western Europe in favor of the enclosed fields that were normal in the nineteenth century. Similarly, serfdom was only imposed in Russia toward the end of the sixteenth century, when it had ceased to exist in parts of western Europe.

#Most of the Russian aristocracy, like some of the English, were of Norman descent. Rurik Sviatoslavich was a Viking chief who had conquered Russia in the ninth century, and his descendants (or those of rulers of territories conquered by Russia) claimed the rank of prince. However, as the title was inherited by every child of the family, princely rank was ceasing to be exclusive, and some princes were even paupers. The grander princely families tended to look down on the imperial family, whose line stretched back only to the foundation of the Romanov dynasty in 1613. The imperial princes' title "grand duke" is really a mistranslation of veliky knyazh, "grand prince," the name originally given to the supreme prince of Rurik's dynasty in ancient, Kievan Russia.

# Chapter 8

*. . . she herself not knowing why*
*in Russian winters thrilled at seeing*
*the cold perfection of the sky,*
*hoar-frost and sun in freezing weather,*
*sledges, and tardy dawns together*
*with the pink glow the snows assume. . . .*

—ALEXANDER PUSHKIN, *EVGENI ONEGIN*

After a spartan life in an impoverished German pocket-state, Elizabeth had become the most beautiful princess and one of the richest women in the grandest court in the world. The New Palace of Darmstadt seemed cramped and provincial when she and Serge moved into the magnificent eighteenth-century Sergievskaya Palace.* Its grand stucco facade adorned with giant statues stretched for fifty yards along the smartest avenue in St. Petersburg, the Nevsky Prospect. Inside were a ballroom, a private chapel, and numerous rooms filled with gilt furniture and carved white paneling by the finest French artists from the reign of Catherine the Great. Among the paintings were portraits by Boucher of voluptuous women from the court of Louis XV. One English visitor, Lady Randolph Churchill,† considered it the finest house she saw in Russia.[1]

On her birthday, where previously she had been content with small trinkets, the imperial family gave Elizabeth glistening jewels. Serge's present was "two half moons in diamonds with a long ruby, uncut, in the middle and a fan in beaten gold with flowers in stones . . . and a grey silver tiffany looking-glass and some charming embroidered Japanese things. . . ."[2] Over the years he was to adorn his bride with many other heirlooms from a vast store.

This was only a foretaste of a world of extravagant luxury that Elizabeth encountered in the new year of 1885 when the St. Petersburg "season" began. From the Sergievskaya Palace she could look out at the bridge surmounted by statues of rearing horses over the frozen Fontanka Canal. Here she could watch the beau monde dressed in furs passing in three-horse sleighs. She was to meet this elegant crowd in person at the Imperial Ballet at the Maryinsky Theatre. With Serge and the emperor and empress she would arrive at the imperial box, draped with blue and gold curtains. A luxuriant scent arose from the leather and wood furnishings, cigarette smoke, and the flowers that decorated the corridors. Around her she could see the white-and-gold boxes, so highly prized that most were booked permanently and passed on from father to son.[3] The entire audience would look up at the gorgeous new imperial princess, dressed in the most expensive gown and commanding the admiration of the men and the envy of their wives. Among the girls in elegant gowns she would often look the finest.

Still greater was the spectacle of the Imperial State Ball that awaited her in January 1885 when her sleigh drew up in the snow and bitter cold outside the floodlit Winter Palace. She and Serge strode through the long corridors past the Chevalier Gardes standing stiffly at attention in white uniforms with polished breastplates and silver helmets decked with the imperial eagle. Some three thousand guests were gathered in the immense galleries lined with columns of jasper, marble, and malachite, underneath massive crystal-and-gold chandeliers. Women in low-cut dresses and flashing jewels, court officials in black gold-trimmed uniforms, and hussar officers in full dress with tight elfskin breeches bowed and curtsied as they passed. Elizabeth's training in dancing served her well in the polonaises, quadrilles, and mazurkas. At dinner, she and the other grand duchesses were seated next to the foreign ambassadors around a long semicircular table. After the meal she and Serge circulated among the other guests.[4] The practice in manners and conversation that she had received from Queen Victoria gave her a self-confidence that helped overcome her youthful shyness.

Far from being overawed by the social elite of St. Petersburg, nineteen-year-old Elizabeth was adapting with polished ease. Soon she was receiving aristocrats, princes, ambassadors, government ministers and their wives at her own palace. As E. M. Almedingen wrote, she "promised fair to become the most brilliant hostess in the capital. Her taste in clothes was impeccable, her dancing exquisite, her conversation and her laughter enchanting."[5] She began to host balls at the Sergievskaya Palace, where her looks and finery made her the center of attention. Prince Christopher of Greece was to write: "At State balls she outshone every other woman in the splendour of her gowns and jewels. When the ball was at her own house she had a habit of disappearing at midnight to change into a new dress and another set of jewels, then she would return to the ballroom more resplendent than before."[6]

Yet in spite of the attention she received and wealth of her possessions, Elizabeth kept the modest simplicity that her mother had instilled in her as a child. Very quickly she endeared herself to the imperial family and the court. She became a favorite of Empress Marie. While Serge was absorbed in commanding the Preobrazhensky Regiment, Elizabeth took to making frequent visits to the empress and Emperor Alexander at their palace in Gatchina, south of the capital. The palace had once been the home of the mad emperor Paul; after his murder by his courtiers, his bloodstained camp bed had been brought there and was shut up in one of the towers, and his ghost was said to haunt the place.[7] The imperial couple, however, had made the house a snug family home where they lived a simple life in the smallest rooms. Here Elizabeth would sit with Marie and play with her children. Outside she would join the two eldest sons, Tsarevich Nicholas and Grand Duke George, in the snow at their game of sliding down an ice hill. She was to develop a warm friendship with Nicholas, a shy, modest teenager who affectionately called her "little aunt Ella." She would refer to the emperor and empress by their nicknames of "Sasha" and "Minnie." When they lived in St. Petersburg in the winter months, she would join them at the Anichkov Palace, almost opposite her own on the Nevsky Prospect.

She was equally liked by the rest of the imperial family. Grand Duke Alexander Mikhailovich, son of the emperor's uncle, Grand Duke Michael, recalled in admiration:

> Ravishing beauty, rare intelligence, delightful sense of humor, infinite patience, hospitality of thought, generous heart, all gifts were hers. It was cruel and unjust that a woman of her caliber should have tied up her existence to a man like uncle Sergei. Everybody fell in love with "Aunt Ella" the very first moment she arrived in St. Petersburg from her native Hesse-Darmstadt.[8]

Yet she soon discovered that Serge's haughty taciturnity had earned him the dislike of everyone but his own brothers. Grand Duke Alexander and his brothers were united in their loathing for him. "I despised the condescending grimace of her husband," Alexander wrote, "when exaggerating his St. Petersburg drawl he would address 'Aunt Ella' as 'my child.'"[9] Such was Serge's reputation that by December 1884 a rumor had spread around the courts of Europe that Elizabeth was miserably unhappy and was seeking a divorce. It could not have been further from the truth. Even after the physical reality of Serge's nature had been revealed, she still loved him and found his absence a trial. "Being away from him ever so short [sic]," she wrote to her brother Ernest, "makes me long for him, he is so dear and good and really all to me."[10] She compensated by making herself at home in St. Petersburg. "This new country," she wrote to Queen Victoria, "of course is getting very dear to me."[11] She abandoned all plans of spending several months of the year out of Russia, as her grandmother had insisted. The queen's fear that the severe Russian winter would ruin her health was proved to be groundless. She wrote to her father that she delighted in the cold and felt extraordinarily well. Even Queen Victoria was forced to admit that rumors of her unhappiness were untrue. "It is too absurd about Ella," she wrote. "She is quite happy."[12] It was not until April 1885 that she returned to Darmstadt with her husband.[13] Glad as she was to see her family and the scenes of her childhood, she realized that her life and destiny now lay in Russia.

Her routine in St. Petersburg became well established. When she was not with the imperial couple or at a glittering social gathering, she was receiving at home or beginning a new pastime: she was learning to sing, draw, and ride. The couple had an ample stable that included two black horses, two bays, and four chestnuts, even if she soon found riding tedious. In winter Elizabeth could skate at the Tauride Gardens. She stuck to her Russian lessons with Mlle. Schneider, and after two years was to be complimented on her proficiency by the imperial family. "You should hear me speak it now," she wrote to her brother. ". . . they say I have a very good accent. . . . The Emperor says that if the English speak Russian well, they are those who have not the least foreign accent and one cannot distinguish them from a Russian."[14] Elizabeth began speaking the language with her household and her husband. She began to sample Russian novels, although English books were her favorites, French literature being in her opinion too frivolous.

Every summer, when the heat grew too much for town life, she and Serge boarded the imperial train for a ten-hour journey to Moscow, and took their carriage to Ilinskoe. There, as on their honeymoon, they could relax away from the formality of St. Petersburg. Elizabeth, like her mother before her, imported chintzes and furniture from England and arranged the house in the style of her childhood home. She painted the doors of her sitting room with pink and white flowers. Friends and relatives would arrive and enliven their holiday. Serge's favorite brother, Paul, now a Hussar officer, would join them while on leave. Their other brother, Vladimir, an anglophobe who had objected to Serge's marrying Elizabeth, also came with his wife, Marie, "Miechen," and now reversed his hostility, joining with relish in their entertainments.[15] With gusto and laughter the party would act out some comic plays or perform charades. Once Elizabeth dressed up as Robinson Crusoe, another time as her distinguished ancestress St. Elizabeth of Hungary.[16]

Alongside her life of amusement, Elizabeth was introduced to the burden of state ceremonies. At first they proved a strain with her limited Russian. In 1885 she faced the trial of meeting and making polite conversation with a score of diplomats. "It was fearfully shy work," she wrote to her brother Ernest, especially with those who spoke no French: ". . . think only with the Chinese I spoke a little Russian and that was 'le comble' and I felt as if the earth would swallow me up."[17] She felt more at ease on a visit to Helsinki, the capital of Finland, then a part of the Russian Empire. She and Serge attended a church service on the battleship *Peter the Great,* visited a bank, picture gallery, and "an enormous establishment for experiments and vivisection." In the evening they attended a ball, and Elizabeth, dressed in white and wearing diamonds, danced with skill and grace with the chief Finnish dignitaries.[18]

A state duty of far greater importance came in 1887, when she attended Queen Victoria's golden jubilee celebrations in London. With Serge she dined at the duke of Cambridge's London house, fellow guests including the king and queen of Belgium and the kings of Denmark and Greece. She was seated in a carriage in a magnificent procession to Westminster Abbey; Serge was among the thirty-two princes who rode in the cavalcade. A service followed in the vaulted, Gothic church, where the kings and queens of England had been crowned and entombed for a thousand years. An anthem was sung in thanksgiving, and all the queen's family knelt to pray for the long life of the small woman, still dressed in widow's black, who sat on a gilded chair at the center.[19]

For Elizabeth it was like returning to her old home, to Buckingham Palace, where she had played at the age of six, and to her grandmother, who had so often dispensed advice. Much as she now appreciated the wisdom of the queen's warnings about Russia, she had few regrets. She was reunited with her family, who all arrived from Darmstadt. She had remained close to her brothers and sisters, and taken a keen interest in a continual correspondence in their affairs.

In the years that had elapsed since her marriage she had often made the journey to Darmstadt, and recaptured her childhood memories in holidays at Wolfsgarten. In 1886 it had been a keen pleasure to have her father and her sister Irene stay in St. Petersburg. They entered into an unending round of entertainment. They sleighed, skated, saw the fine collection of Sèvres porcelain in the Winter Palace, and danced to the point of exhaustion. "We all danced like mad," Irene wrote, "and got fearfully hot in consequence—everyone dances so terribly fast here and so ceaselessly."[20] Some months later, Elizabeth had the further happiness of hearing that Irene had become engaged to Prince Henry of Prussia, William's younger brother, who was pursuing a career in the German Navy. The wedding was set for Berlin in May 1888. It was to be a small incident in a clash between two generations of the Hohenzollern dynasty that would be decisive for the history of Europe. Elizabeth would play a minor part in this episode.

Early in May Elizabeth and Serge arrived for the wedding ceremony. By now the Prussian court had forgiven her for refusing Prince Frederick of Baden, and she was welcomed courteously by Empress Augusta. The Prince of Wales had come from England.

The wedding took place in the private chapel of the Charlottenburg Palace on May 24. It was clear to Elizabeth that her sister was in love, and the sight pleased her.

What impressed the congregation most, however, was the presence of the new German emperor, Frederick III. On the death of his father, William I, in March, he had succeeded to the throne in a grave state of health. He had severe pain in his throat from a cancerous growth. Its discovery had been delayed by a mistaken diagnosis by a British specialist whom Queen Victoria had recommended, Dr. Morell Mackensie. A tube had been inserted into the emperor's throat to allow him to breathe; on the wedding day, unable to speak, he somehow found strength to appear in a general's uniform. Beside him was his widowed mother, dressed in black, shaking with palsy in a wheelchair. "As the organ played Handel's 'Largo'," David Duff has written, "he walked from the chapel. It was his last, unaided exit." Field Marshal Moltke, the hero of many battles, admired the emperor: "I have seen many brave men, but none as brave as the emperor has shown himself today."[21]

A more savage remark was made by Herbert Bismarck, the son of the German chancellor. He said to the Prince of Wales, who barely suppressed his anger, that a sovereign who could not speak should not be allowed to reign.

The German chancellor, Otto von Bismarck, had already begun to interfere in the ailing emperor's court. He distrusted Frederick and his wife, for they represented a threat to the reactionary and repressive policies he had pursued under the old emperor. Bismarck had harassed the Social Democratic and Socialist parties. Their newspapers, associations, and any gatherings had all been banned, their activists arrested or expelled from the cities, and the trade union movement virtually killed off. The slightest criticism of the emperor had been met with draconian punishments.‡ In the parliamentary elections of 1884 Bismarck had employed tactics of intimidation against the "Progressive Party," and he was privately keen to disband the parliament and set up a "Staatsreich," or rule by decree. Venomous newspaper attacks on the Jews had appeared.[22]

By contrast, the sick emperor Frederick was the center of liberal hopes. For Germany he favored a parliamentary monarchy on the British model, with freedom of speech and equality before the law. His wife Vicky, Empress Victoria, had done Prince Albert's work in instilling in him her father's plans for a liberal Germany at the center of a peaceful Europe. From the start of his reign he had known he would face stiff opposition. He had awarded honors to brilliant men of Jewish extraction; right-wing extremists had caused placards and grafitti to be put up in Berlin: "The Emperor of the Hebrews, Frederick III, alias Cohen" and "Cohen I, King of the Jews."[23]

It was over Sandro, Prince Alexander of Battenberg, that the enmity between the emperor and Bismarck showed itself most deeply. Sandro had suffered several vicissitudes as sovereign prince of Bulgaria. Emperor Alexander III of Russia had opposed his vision of a Bulgaria strong in resources, civilization, and military power, preferring a weak satellite of Russia. When the territory of Eastern Rumelia was incorporated into Bulgaria, Sandro incurred the lasting hatred of the emperor. Sandro was kidnapped by a squad of discontented Bulgarian soldiers under Russian officials and abducted to Austria. To avoid a war with Russia he renounced his throne.[24]

Now Vicky, the German Empress Victoria, dearly hoped that her daughter, also called Victoria, might marry Sandro. Supported by her mother, Queen Victoria, Vicky persuaded Frederick to give his consent. Hoping to isolate the emperor, Bismarck opposed the marriage and threatened to resign if it went ahead. On his side was Crown Prince William who had courted Elizabeth in his student days in Darmstadt, whom Bismarck had adroitly flattered. William wrote to Sandro threatening never to speak to him if he married his sister.[25]

Sandro agreed to give up his suit and turned his attention to the opera singer Johanna Loisinger. The emperor was never informed. It was at this point that Elizabeth became involved. Some time after Irene's wedding William, already behaving as if he were emperor, had a talk with her and Serge. He did not use his habitual blustering and arrogant tone on the woman he had once loved and still greatly admired, but assumed a moderate, reasonable approach, explaining the question from both sides. William managed to convince Elizabeth that Sandro, having renounced his suit, could not honorably resume his suit. He painted his sister's character in the worst colors, and persuaded Elizabeth that Victoria was a spoiled child who would ruin Sandro. As a result Elizabeth wrote to her father endorsing William's views and asking him as the head of the House of Hesse, to prevent the marriage.[26] Sandro soon proposed to Johanna Loisinger.

On June 15, 1888, Emperor Frederick died, and with him Prince Albert's enlightened hopes for Germany. As the new emperor, William's first act was to cordon off the palace where his dead father lay, while he went through his father's papers. After a brief liberal phase he embarked on ruling as much like an absolute monarch as he could, refusing to devolve any power to parliament, which he called "a troop of monkeys and a collection of blockheads and sleepwalkers." He resented Queen Victoria's support for his mother in the quarrel over Sandro's engagement. Dr. Mackensie's mistaken diagnosis of the late emperor's cancer seemed to him, and much of the German press, as an English conspiracy to shorten his father's life. With these feelings he began to develop an inferiority complex toward Britain. This was one cause of William's increasingly aggressive, blustering foreign policy and vast expansion of his army and navy, which ultimately brought Germany to a catastrophic war and greater horrors for all of Europe.

As well as proving a crucial year in the history of Europe, 1888 was to mark a change of course for Elizabeth's own life. For by now the glamour and grandeur of the Russian court and the endless frivolous amusements of St. Petersburg had begun to pall. Her popularity and the spectacle she made at balls could not hide the lack of purpose in her life. Four years after her wedding, she was beginning to despair of bearing a child to which she could dedicate herself. Her marriage was now little more than a hollow formality. In his own rigid, condescending way, Serge still showed her affection, but more as an indulgent father than a husband. He continued to adorn her with jewels, and she could order as many of the finest dresses as she chose. The adoration she had felt for him at the outset of their marriage was withering away into a settled fondness. She took pride in his soldiering, and loved him as she had loved her father and brother in her childhood. Beyond this, passion never intruded.

In every matter she must submit to his will. On her engagement she had written to Queen Victoria: ". . . although he may have opinions you do not like, do you not think dear Grandmama, that I might do him good?"[27] Now Serge became ever more haughty and unbending. His inflexible political views had been irrevocably molded by his father's gruesome death. Elizabeth was unable to exercise the influence she might have had on the mercurial Prince William of Prussia. Her hopes of softening her husband's character were disappearing.

Her twenty-fourth year was a painful contrast with her life before her marriage, an existence that most girls of her time could only dream of. From being the center of attention at magnificent court balls with the pick of Europe's princely bachelors, she was stuck in a hollow marriage in an alien country.

Yet Elizabeth had a tougher fiber than most women. It took a continuous effort of self-discipline to appear at court ceremonies with a smiling face, always polite, without a hint of irritation. With the rigid Victorian sense of duty and the resilience gained from her childhood trials Elizabeth managed to keep up a cheerful, gracious facade. She was sustained by the underlying religious faith she had inherited from her mother. The energy and passion that she suppressed were gradually channeled into a striving for spiritual certainty, which was outwardly expressed as conventional Victorian piety. On Sundays in St. Petersburg she would attend a Lutheran service or listen to Dr. Watson's ponderous, erudite Anglican sermons, returning to the Sergievskaya Palace to read from the Bible in German or English. At Ilinskoe she would play some of her mother's favorite hymns at the piano, *Oh God, Our Help in Ages Past, All People That on Earth Do Dwell, I Heard the Voice of Jesus Say*.[28] Underneath she was seeking a tangible goal in her now aimless life, and it was gradually dawning on her that it lay in drawing closer to her Maker and carrying out His will. This desire might well have remained buried in her monotonous St. Petersburg social routine of balls, soirees, and opera and rigid court ceremonies or her placid married life at Ilinskoe, where she sketched, played tiddledywinks or arranged flowers. It was a voyage to Jerusalem that took her further toward embracing Christianity without reservation.

A large Russian Orthodox church had been built at the foot of the Mount of Olives as a memorial to Empress Marie, Serge's mother and Elizabeth's great-aunt. Emperor Alexander appointed Serge and Paul to represent him at the consecration. Late in September 1888 Elizabeth joined them as they set off for the Holy Land.[29]

En route they stayed in Kiev, the ancient capital of Russia and the cradle of Russian Orthodoxy. From their Baroque blue-and-white palace, high on the hills above the Dnieper River, they could see a mass of golden-roofed churches and cathedrals. A few hundred yards away was the site of a stream where Prince Vladimir had led his people to be baptized exactly nine hundred years before. Nearby, in an ancient monastery, a damp, malodorous underground labyrinth concealed the mummified bodies of Orthodox saints.

They endured a choppy voyage over the Black Sea, and saw glorious views as they sailed up the Bosporus into Constantinople. In one of his palaces, the sultan of Turkey received them with lavish oriental generosity. "He is overwhelming," Elizabeth wrote to her father, "in his amiable manners and with his rich presents." Elizabeth received "a magnificent pendant in diamonds—quite beautiful." At his harem he presented his mother but only one of his four wives, fearing that more might shock them. His three daughters were laden with diamonds and pearls but were plain in appearance. They visited a raucous, crowded bazaar and found St. Sophia's, the historic mosque, imposing and very beautiful.

They sailed on to Beirut, where the heat was intense. But Elizabeth bore it well as she rode on horseback for hours along dusty roads through the bare rocky landscape of the Biblical lands. She recalled the Scriptures she had learned as a child with religious awe. "You cannot think how joyful it is," she wrote to her brother, "to see all these holy places, to go on the same roads where our Lord walked and lived." From Nazareth they journeyed to Jerusalem, where Elizabeth was awed by the places of the Gospel stories. She saw the pool of Siloam, to which Christ had sent the blind man to be cured, and toured the site where the high priest Caiaphas had condemned Him to death and where Peter had disowned Him. The place of the Crucifixion and Resurrection overawed her. She wrote to Ernest: "You cannot imagine what a profound impression it makes on entering the Holy Sepulchre." Here she knelt and prayed wholeheartedly for all her family. She prayed that by some miracle she might bear a child.

With Serge and Paul she visited the Church of the Nativity at Bethlehem, and returned for the consecration of the Church of St. Mary Magdalene. It took place at the foot of the Mount of Olives, from the summit of which Christ had ascended into Heaven; nearby was the Garden of Gethsemane where His disciples had gathered with their leader. In this sacred place the soaring and emotive chants of the Orthodox service made her wonder if the Russian religion was not the only true one.

She returned to St. Petersburg with her character transformed. The whole visit had been like a dream, she wrote to Queen

Victoria, and an intense comfort to her.[30] Henceforth she was to turn to religion as a guide and a consolation.

## Notes to Chapter 8

*Also called the Belosseilsky-Belosseivsky Palace.

†Daughter of Leonard Jerome, born in Brooklyn, New York, mother of Sir Winston Churchill.

‡In an extreme example, a woman had been imprisoned for eighteen months for remarking, after an assassination attempt on Emperor William: "At least, the emperor is not poor; he can have himself cared for."

# Chapter 9

*. . . the flower-like pallor of the maiden,*
*her look, so sweetly sorrow-laden,*
*all plunged his soul deep into the stream*
*of a delicious, guiltless dream. . . .*

—PUSHKIN, *EVGENI ONEGIN*

The emptiness in Elizabeth's life that religion partly filled also made her yearn to have a member of her own family with her in Russia. An opportunity came in the autumn of 1888, when she and Serge traveled to Darmstadt for her sister Alix's first ball. The sixteen-year-old "Alicky" had become a debutante after her confirmation the previous June. The instruction she had received from Dr. Sell, the Hessian divine, had reinforced her shy, sad, and serious character. His emphasis on the search for truth had made her introspective, self-critical, and determined to set her ideals high.[1]

It was therefore fortunate that Elizabeth was on hand to guide her sister through the intricacies of etiquette and procedure. She saw to every detail of Alix's appearance, and with Mrs. Orchard she helped her dress for the grand night at the New Palace. There was a motive behind her assistance. Alix was now tall and thin with an elegant long neck, a pale complexion, luminous blue-gray eyes, and luxuriant golden hair, which fell to her waist when uncoiled. Her features were more severe and solemn than Elizabeth's, but could attract the interest of many young men. Elizabeth wondered if she still retained the affection for Tsarevich

Nicholas she had shown at Peterhof in 1884. She wished above all to have her sister with her in Russia. From long experience of caring for the weaklings of her family, Elizabeth feared that this naive and vulnerable schoolgirl could easily make a disastrous decision in the marriage game.

Queen Victoria, however, wanted Alix to marry her first cousin, Albert Victor, Duke of Clarence and eldest son of the Prince of Wales. She hoped that Alix might steady the unintelligent, listless and sensual Eddy, the eventual heir to the throne after his father. Dark rumors surrounded the duke. It was said, without foundation, that he suffered from syphilis of the brain. That summer a notorious murderer, who called himself Jack the Ripper, had strangled and disemboweled five London prostitutes; it was alleged that Eddy was that man. The story collapses when considering that Eddy was undoubtedly out of London at the time of three of the five murders;[2] its value lies in the light it sheds on his unsuitability as a potential husband. Elizabeth, from experience of her own marriage, found the idea abhorrent. She had written to Ernest: ". . . about Eddy, I find the idea of his marrying Alix quite dreadful . . . he is not over strong and is too stupid—you would see that clever girl turn into a flirt. . . . I am sure you understand that she would really not be happy. . . ."[3] Instead she aimed to turn her sister's head in favor of Nicholas. She made her father promise that he would bring Alix to stay in St. Petersburg for the "season" of 1889.

In arranging this visit, Elizabeth may unknowingly have tipped the scales of history. For she was beginning a discreet contest with her grandmother, to be conducted in letters to relatives, private talks, and invitations, over whether Alix should ultimately be empress of Russia or queen of England. It was an enormous choice for a teenage girl. On the one hand she would reign over a land that was the second home of her childhood, with the same Protestant faith and the liberal, constitutional ideas in which her mother had believed. On the other she would be the consort of an autocrat with unfettered powers over a backward country, alien in its language, religion, and culture. Her decision might even decide the downfall of a dynasty. Alix's visit to Russia would cause her to dream of marriage to Nicholas. No one could imagine that this marriage would ultimately lead to the birth of the hemophiliac Alexis and to Alexandra's blind faith in the false "holy man," Rasputin.

But if Queen Victoria's will had prevailed, as it had with her own children, and Alix had married the duke of Clarence, Great Britain might have been the victim of the hemophiliac gene that she bore. The combination of his degeneracy* and her genes would probably have produced a physical weakling with subnormal intelligence to inherit the British throne.

Elizabeth, ignorant of these momentous consequences of her plans, watched her sister dancing gaily at the ball, greatly admired by the men present. She had high hopes.

But even while this cheerful party was in swing, her pleasure was marred by the knowledge of the approaching death of her great-uncle. Nearby, Prince Alexander of Hesse was in the grip of a stomach cancer which condemned him to slow starvation. Elizabeth and Serge and the other relatives came frequently to call at his house on the Luisenplatz. Every day Serge prayed that the soul of his mother, Alexander's sister, might be allowed to appear and comfort the dying man.

One December day Elizabeth and Serge were waiting in the next room while Alexander's daughter, Princess Marie of Battenberg, sat by his bedside. Marie emerged, and in tears she told them that Alexander had just had a vision of his sister. He had whispered to Marie, "My sister tells me she is there, and she says she is happy, and that I, too, shall be happy." Hearing this, Serge "fell on his knees, and raising his folded hands to heaven, cried, 'Oh my God! I thank Thee, Thou hast heard my prayer!'"

On December 15, Prince Alexander died. The family followed his coffin to its resting place in the Rosenhöhe. His widow, Princess Julie of Battenberg, sat many hours beside it. Her health gravely deteriorated, and she eventually retired for some years to a nunnery.[4]

Elizabeth and Serge, meanwhile, left Darmstadt to spend Christmas at Kiel on the German Baltic coast with Irene and Prince Henry of Prussia before returning home to prepare for the Hessian visit.

As Alix and her family traveled to St. Petersburg in January, the young man of twenty who Elizabeth hoped would attract her had his mind on far more frivolous pursuits. Nicholas was now serving in the Guards, and cared only for balls, Gypsy singers, shooting, and heavy drinking. "Yesterday," he wrote in his diary after a spree with fellow officers, "we drank 125 bottles of champagne." The following morning he "woke up and felt as if a squadron had spent the night in my mouth."[5] His only intellectual achievements were a good command of French, English, and German. He was as ignorant of the world as the average Guards officer. Emperor Alexander, believing there was no hurry, had not yet introduced his son to state affairs. Yet Elizabeth was confident that this polite, good-natured, but diffident and vacuous figure would interest her earnest, high-minded sister. Many others shared her opinion, for the newspapers were predicting that Alix and Nicholas would become engaged when she arrived with her father and brother in St. Petersburg.[6]

All society and the entire court were therefore expectant when the Hessian family appeared in public. Unfortunately Alix was so intimidated by the brilliance of the social functions that she was reluctant to appear. At the first ball Elizabeth arrived in all her finery with her father, but had to say that her sister was ill.[7] A few days later Elizabeth was at the Maryinsky Theatre with the imperial family, but again her sister was absent.[8] When Alix did participate, Elizabeth had a hard task in shepherding her. She was shy, spoke chiefly to Elizabeth in English or to others in clumsy schoolgirl French. Society thought her awkward and ungracious.

She held herself rigidly erect, looking, it was said, as though she had swallowed a ruler. But all admired her beauty; only Elizabeth was more beautiful, but Alix's features seemed more expressive. One nobleman thought her so stunning that her engagement to the tsarevich must be going smoothly.[9]

Undeterred by her sister's poor performance, Elizabeth contrived in private to bring the two together. The Sergievskaya Palace, where all her family were staying with her, was almost opposite the Anichkov Palace, where Nicholas lived with the imperial couple. There were ample opportunities for him to slip across the Nevsky Prospect and join them for tea or tobogganing. Elizabeth wrote him notes inviting him to accompany them on their diversions.[10] When he went skating, she would join him with Alix beside her. She invited him to lunch at her palace, placing him opposite Alix at the table. Her final effort was to hold a ball where, Nicholas wrote, "we danced till we dropped and had a wonderful time." Elizabeth made sure that he was seated next to Alix, and that they danced the interminable mazurka together.[11]

The Hessian visit was so agreeable that the family stayed until Lent. The grand duke's family remained together until the last moment, and there was a frenzied rush to prepare to leave. Though sad to see them go, Elizabeth was highly satisfied as she bid farewell. She gave Nicholas a framed photograph of herself, Alix, and Ernest, around whose border she had painted scenes from their visit.[12] The modest, diffident young Guards officer and heir to the throne had attracted her sister. She, her future lady-in-waiting, Baroness Buxhoeveden, wrote, "had quickly fallen in love with the Cesarevitch. She hid it carefully, and at first, indeed, did not realise it herself."[13] Nicholas had set his heart on her, and dreamed of marriage. He pasted her photograph in his album.

Empress Marie, however, it was said at court, disliked Alix's awkward shyness. Bearing in mind Elizabeth's unfortunate marriage, she argued that Alix would be equally unlucky with the tsarevich. The emperor could not agree to a marriage that would dilute the growing rapprochement with France, soon to evolve into a full alliance, with German-British blood. He quietly persuaded his son to forget the idea.

As the March snow continued to fall and the cold remained intense, Elizabeth wrote to her brother: ". . . how dreadfully I miss you—the house is so awfully empty and sad—you cannot think how very happy your nice long stay made us." She had a diversion from loneliness in the form of a bear-shooting expedition with the imperial family. They drove for miles on sleighs deep into the woods near Gatchina, and ate a lunch in dense cover after Tsarevich Nicholas had bagged two small bears.[14]

Elizabeth was also pleased that another romance in which she had taken a close interest had come to fruition. She had grown fond of Serge's brother Grand Duke Paul, who had been her childhood playmate at Heiligenberg and a convivial guest at Ilinskoe. A few years earlier Paul had stayed with the Greek royal family at Athens. At the time she had hoped that Paul would become engaged to Alexandra, the radiant daughter of the Greek king. Now she had accepted him, and the marriage was held in July 1889 in St. Petersburg. For their honeymoon the couple stayed at a cottage on the estate at Ilinskoe. With Elizabeth, Serge and the bride's brother, Prince Nicholas of Greece, they had a cheerful time together with charades and amateur tableaux.

Alexandra charmed her in-laws. As Prince Nicholas later wrote, she "had one of those sweet and lovable natures that endeared her to everybody who came in touch with her. She looked young and beautiful, and ever since she was a child, life looked as if it had nothing but joy and happiness in store for her."[15] Elizabeth became Alexandra's closest friend. When the wedding guests had left, she joined her in painting and sketching the scenery. After the return to St. Petersburg, they helped each other nurse their husbands back to health during an epidemic of influenza.

"What a darling your sister is," Elizabeth wrote to Prince Nicholas. "I love her daily more and more & not only I but all who see her."[16]

Elizabeth was also attracted to Prince Nicholas, a handsome dilettante youth. Over the next few months she wrote him several affectionate letters, using florid expressions that seemed more appropriate between husband and wife. She would begin, "My darling Nicky," and write that she missed him. She had posed with him for a tableau representing a scene from *King Lear,* he dressed as Lear, she as Lear's daughter Cordelia: "Poor Cordelia is very sad without her Papa. . . . Saying goodbye was a nasty moment and she was so stiff and calm to keep back her tears—really I miss you awfully." She would sign "your loving Cordelia." Her intentions were innocent, and she never went beyond flirtation. It was probably the nearest she ever came to an adulterous love affair.[17]

Meanwhile, maneuvers were afoot over Alix's future husband. In June, Nicholas had had a long conversation with Elizabeth, and had poured out his feelings for Alix. This spurred Elizabeth on to continue her role as go-between; the following day she had written a note of encouragement to Nicholas, promising to act as an intermediary between him and Alix:

> . . . I prayed so deeply for you both to bring you
> together in love for each other—I wrote today to
> Alix and told her we had a long chat yesterday and
> also about her and that you recall with such *plea-*
> *sure* the visit of this winter and the pleasure of hav-
> ing seen *her* and might I give you kind messages
> from her. More distinctively, I dared not say, you
> will do that once—God grant all will go well. . . .[18]

Over the next few years, Elizabeth would keep the romance alive, conveying secret messages between the two.

Queen Victoria, however, kept trying to thwart Elizabeth's hopes. She was still determined that Alix should marry the duke of Clarence. The queen feared greatly that his sensual appetites could one day cause enormous damage when he ascended to the throne. He had been greatly attracted by his cousin Alix on his occasional visits to Darmstadt, but the queen was set firm against her granddaughter marrying into Russia, a country that she still found abhorrent. In August 1889 she summoned Alix and Ernest to Balmoral. The stage was set for Eddy to begin his courting.[19]

Elizabeth was well aware of the queen's intentions, and was keen on subverting them. She wrote to Ernest, asking him to intercede for the tsarevich Nicholas. Evidently fearing the attentions of the Russian secret police, she resorted to the code name "Pelly" for Nicholas:

> . . . Alix is sure to speak to you about a certain person and tell you all I wrote to her. Give her courage and be yourself very careful in what you say in your conversations with Grandmama. It would be much better not to speak about Pelly or, if she does, tell her there had been nothing whatever between Alix and Pelly and that you have of course no voice in the question. As you know there were no advances whatever made but, if she wishes to know frankly your opinion about Pelly, say what a perfect creature in every way and that he is adored by all and deserves this loving being in every way that is noble and pure.—Give an idea of the happy family life so that Grandmama's prejudices may be lessened; that will be a great step and help when once the deciding moment arrives. Through all the idiotic trash in the newspapers she gets impossible untrue views and founds all her arguments on facts which probably never existed.—Do you know what Mama once said at Jugenheim to Mlle. Pillas (she told me that once at Petersburg) when she had Alix a Baby on her lap: "Regardez cette enfante avec beaucoup de respect. Elle sera votre future Imperatrice."†—

It may have been said as fun yet God grant will once come true[sic]. I assure you that if Eddy were Georgy or a clever bright fellow of course a better match could not be dreamt of, but as it is, I assure you without love or respect no good could come of such a marriage.—Put it off; the voyage to India‡ won't be short and she can say she would reflect seriously during that time.—I had a letter from Pelly always longing for news and feeling very lovesick and lost. . . .

a good hug from Serge and Ella [20]

Whatever Ernest said to Queen Victoria, he did little to shake off her distrust of Russia. But the danger was past for Alix; her cousin's clumsy advances repelled her. She was still interested only in the heir to the Russian throne. Like her elder sisters, she was determined to choose her own husband.

Elizabeth was confident that Nicholas had his heart set on Alix. That winter she saw much of him when she arranged an amateur performance of *Evgeni Onegin*. She played the heroine, Tatiana, and he acted as Evgeni. He often walked across the Nevsky Prospect to her palace for tea, and she continued to encourage his hopes.[21] She looked forward to new developments in the summer of 1890, when her father took Alix and Victoria to stay at Ilinskoe.

Queen Victoria, however, was equally well aware that Alix would meet Nicholas again, and she was just as keen as Elizabeth to prevent Alix from becoming entangled with the wrong man. As head of the British royal house,§ the queen mistakenly assumed that she could dictate who that man would be. ". . . *tell* Ella," she wrote to her granddaughter Victoria, "that no marriage for *Alicky in Russia* would be allowed."[22] She was becoming increasingly irritated with Elizabeth's matchmaking, and a little later angrily wrote: "in spite of *all your objections* and still more contrary to the *positive* wish of *his* parents . . . well in spite of all this behind *all* your backs, Ella and Serge do *all they can* to bring it *about,* encouraging and even urging the Boy to do it."[23] But no lasting damage to their relations was done. Elizabeth still remained a favorite granddaughter, and continued to write sympathetic letters beginning with the words "My dearest Grandmama."

More importantly, Nicholas was forbidden by his father to meet Alix. He was detained in St. Petersburg, and wrote in his diary: "Lord! Am dying to go to Ilinskoe. . . . Otherwise, if not now then I might have to wait an entire year to see her, and that is hard!!!"[24] In his absence, Elizabeth showed her sister the Russian countryside at its most agreeable, as Baroness Buxhoeveden wrote:

> She taught her sister to feel the peculiar charm of the Russian country atmosphere. The Grand Duchess took her guests on informal surprise visits to her neighbours. They also visited every village fair in the place, to the whole party's great enjoyment. It was all so different from anything they had ever seen. Even Princess Alix lost her shyness. She felt at ease with her sister's guests at the simple meals from which etiquette was banished, and got to love the good-natured peasants, who welcomed "their" Grand Duchess's young sister, with low bows and the language of signs.[25]

Elizabeth also talked of the Orthodox religion, and hinted to Alix that converting to that religion, an obligatory step for the bride of the tsarevich, was not such a great obstacle. When the family left, she knew that Alix would look forward to seeing Russia again. In England, her family was certain of her resolve to bring her sister back as a bride. "Uncle Bertie," the queen wrote to her granddaughter Victoria, of the Prince of Wales, "says he knows Ella will move Heaven and Earth to get her to marry a Grand Duke."[26]

## Notes to Chapter 9

*Several other children and grandchildren of the Prince and Princess of Wales (later King Edward VII and Queen Alexandra) seemed to have had some form of physical weakness. Their second son, the duke of York (later King George V), was bowlegged; his own children had learning disabilities; the lastborn, John, was epileptic and unstable, and died in childhood. It has been suggested that both Queen Alexandra and her sister, Dagmar, Empress Marie of Russia, were in the rare blood group of Rhesus negative, a factor which may have likewise caused the indecisiveness and diffidence of Marie's son, Tsarevich Nicholas. In the British royal family, the introduction of the Bowes-Lyon strain (from Queen Elizabeth, the Queen Mother, now a nonagenarian) seems to have restored strength, and that of the ebullient Mountbattens appears to have wiped away the frailty altogether.

†Look at this child with great respect. She will be your future empress.

‡By the duke of Clarence.

§Under the Royal Marriages Act of 1772, members of the British royal family in the line of succession to the throne had to secure the sovereign's approval if they wished to marry before the age of twenty-five. Alix, then eighteen, was distantly in line to succeed to the British throne, but the law did not apply to Hesse-Darmstadt. It is still in force in Great Britain.

# *Chapter 10*

*When microbes have to be destroyed, we do not pause to enquire how microbes like the process.*

—PRINCE MECHERSKY, on the Jews of Russia

The future husband of Alix was not the only matter that weighed on the mind of Grand Duchess Elizabeth. For some years she, like her mother before her, had been enduring a torturous spiritual conflict. Since her arrival in Russia she had admired the brilliant and dazzling ceremonies of the Orthodox Church. In the St. Petersburg cathedrals she had heard the polyphonous chants of its choirs and their vast range of pitch that expressed intense religious feelings, "successsively transports of prayer, sighs of despair, appeals for mercy, cries of distress, screams of fear, the anguished voice of repentance, the fervour of regret, the grief of self-abasement, flickers of hope, outpourings of love, transport of holy ecstacy, the splendours of glory and bliss."[1] She had witnessed these emotions at their extreme in a midnight Easter service, the high point of the Orthodox calendar. In a darkness punctuated by thousands of candles and the glimmering golden vestments of the priests, the congregation, almost giddy from fasting, stood throughout for hours on end. Crossing themselves with fervor, they sang the responses in growing exultation, culminating in triumphant shouts of "Christ is risen! Truly He is risen!"

Slowly Elizabeth had come to understand more of the church's doctrines. The Russian Church set far greater store by faith and enthusiasm than the sober theology of the western churches. Instead of the prescribed penances and absolutions of the Roman Church or the austere morality of Protestantism, it put forth a vision of a constant battle of the spirit for salvation. It preached a patient acceptance of one's fate and silent suffering. Inherent in its character was the idea that through sin and suffering and redemption one could come closer to God. Its theologians claimed that the Orthodox belief in the power of prayer and its simple faith were truer to the original spirit of primitive Christianity. They held that the only surviving citadel of true religion was Moscow. The city was the "Third Rome": the corrupted Rome of St. Peter had fallen to the Goths in the fifth century, and Constantinople, the source of the Orthodox faith, had been seized by the Turks in the fifteenth. The profound faith of the Russian peasants, their humility, charity, and compassion seemed a more genuine Christianity than the conventional platitudes of Victorian religion Elizabeth had known in the West. It pained her that her Lutheran faith made her a foreigner in the eyes of many Russians and barred her from taking part in the religion of the country she now loved. She had written to Queen Victoria soon after her arrival that her new country was "very dear to me." Since then she had so absorbed herself in learning Russian and reading the country's literature, in the social life of St. Petersburg, and the fetes at Ilinskoe, that she considered the country as her own.

On her way to Jerusalem, she had seen the site in Kiev where Prince Vladimir and his people had been baptized nine hundred years earlier.* The holy places of Jerusalem, the sites of the miracles and the consecration of the Russian church on the Mount of Olives had given her some small sense of the divine that she had not known before. Like her mother before her, she began to feel the need to draw closer to her Maker. Gradually it seemed to her that Orthodoxy was the highest form of religion and offered the most direct approach to God. An urge grew in her to be at one with the people around her, to share their religion and pray beside them. "I adore . . . my new country," she was to write to Ernest, "and so have learnt to love their religion."[2]

In drawing closer to Orthodoxy, she gained a new intimacy with her husband. It had begun on the same summer day in June 1889 that she had held a long talk with the tsarevich Nicholas about Alix. Serge had spoken to her about Orthodoxy, and she had replied that she wished to know more about it.[3] Over the next eighteen months, during the quiet evenings at Ilinskoe while the rain beat down outside, they would sit together reading works on Orthodoxy, just as years earlier her mother had pored over religious books in search of truth. Serge would patiently explain the finer points of doctrine to her. He showed her a new sympathy that she cherished. He was anxious for her to convert, but made no effort to influence her, instead warning her of the "dukh prelest," the evil spirit of enchantment, in changing without conviction.[4] "I felt how Serge longed for this . . . ," she wrote to her brother, "and I often knew that he must suffer in consequence. He was a real angel of kindness."[5] She began to wonder whether to convert, and with Serge beside her would kneel and pray to be shown the right course.

Slowly she came to consider herself an Orthodox, to pray and feel like one. Just as her mother had striven to be sincere and intellectually honest in her faith, so Elizabeth felt she could only be wholehearted as an Orthodox. To convert would be a righteous act in God's eyes and the only possible course; to remain in her old religion would be a deceit. It would be "simply lying before God and man," she wrote to Ernest, "—it would be hateful, despicable. . . ."[6]

Elizabeth agonized about the shock her family would feel. To prepare them she dropped hints on their visit to Ilinskoe. Finally "God gave me courage,"[7] as she wrote to Queen Victoria. She made up her mind to convert, and was "intensely happy." She felt sure of God's blessing and relieved at no longer living out a falsehood. On January 1, 1891, she wrote to her family. To her father she made an emotional plea for understanding:

> . . . now dearest Papa there is something I want to tell you, beg you for *your blessings*—you must have remarked what deep reverence I have for the religion here when you came last—since over a year and a half I have been thinking and praying to God to show the right way and have come to the conclusion that only in their religion I can find all the true and strong faith one must have in God to be a good Christian. . . . I would have done it so even before, only it hurts me to give you pain and that many of my dear relations will *not understand* me, you do, don't you? Dearest Papa—you know me so well you must see that it is with such *profound faith* I only decide an inch a step that I feel that before God I must stand with a pure and believing heart . . . forgive your child if she hurts you, but is not belief in God and faith one of the *most* comforting things in this world?—please do just telegraph one line when you receive this letter only *God bless you*, it will be such a comfort because I know there will be many *painful moments* and all won't *understand* this step. . . .

Her father, however, gravely shocked, wrote a bitter reply:

> . . . it greatly taxed my strength for several nights . . . and it struck me like a blow to the head. . . . One expects only the heathen to forsake their old beliefs. . . . But what have you done? Do you know exactly, and do you find no surprise? . . . It is the first disgrace that any of you [children] has inflicted on me. My God, what would Mama say! I cannot think of it in peace. It so grieves me that I want to shut it away. God protect and forgive you if you are doing wrong. . . .[9]

This letter pained Elizabeth, and it saddened her to know the shock had come to him while he was already in poor health. From then on his condition took a downward path. Irene was also horrified. It seemed to her and Grand Duke Louis that Elizabeth was betraying her country and the dynasty in deserting the faith of her ancestors. "I cried terribly over it," she wrote to her father "It comes to me like a bad dream."[10]

Elizabeth also had to bear the sneers of many in society and at court. Emperor William of Germany spread the rumor that Serge had forced her into it.[11] It did the rounds in St. Petersburg. It was also said that the grand duchess, in despair at having no children, had sought the advice of Father John of Kronstadt, a revered priest of the church. The rumors had it that she had resorted to prayer on his advice and, finding herself pregnant, had turned to Orthodoxy in gratitude.[12] None of these snide comments discouraged her.

But from England she also received some sympathetic letters. Her sister Victoria and the queen both understood her decision, and she wrote to her grandmother: "You *cannot* think how intensely and deeply touched I was by all you say.—I was so afraid you would not understand the step and the comforting joy your dear lines gave me I shall never forget. . . ."[13]

Early in 1891, she pledged herself to Orthodoxy. She knelt before a priest and went through a simple service for which she had carefully learned the responses. She now bore the title of the truly believing Grand Duchess Elizabeth Feodorovna, and could take communion beside her husband.

The emperor and empress, and her friends, were overjoyed. The peasants at Ilinskoe were delighted to see their lady worshiping beside them.[14] People noticed the change in her character. She practiced her new devotions with zeal, and acquired a lofty spirituality. "After her conversion," Prince Nicholas of Greece wrote, "there was in her character a certain mixture of idealism and mystery added to her natural charm, which made her adored by all with whom she came into contact."[15]

The compassion and charitable duties enjoined by her new faith were soon to be put into use. At this time, Emperor Alexander appointed his brother Serge to be governor-general of Moscow. Elizabeth made her farewell to the brilliant world of St. Petersburg and moved to the ancient capital, which was to be her home for the rest of her life. It was a delight to visit some of the sixteen hundred churches and see the glories of the Kremlin. She and her husband took up residence in the governor's palace on Tverskaya Street, a broad avenue which was the beginning of the road to Tver and beyond to St. Petersburg. At Christmas and the new year they would retreat to the Crown Palace of Neskuchnoe on the banks of the Moscow River. In its quiet and spacious gardens, sealed off from the surrounding factory suburbs, they could feel themselves in the country.

Alexander had made his brother governor of Moscow because he regarded the city as a hotbed of subversive radicalism. The city's university, the oldest in Russia, had long produced many intellectuals devoted (with as much ardor as Elizabeth found in her new faith) to Nihilist, Socialist, and Marxist doctrines. Some of these had joined groups of earnest propagandists who tried to persuade the peasants to rise up against their masters.† Others had tried to preach the doctrines of Karl Marx to the workers who, however, were more interested in wage hikes. Others had turned to terrorism, and Alexander could never forget the sight of his father's body, dismembered and still half alive, brought into the Winter Palace after being hit by an assassin's bomb. Rather than relieve the hardship among the Moscow students that had partly caused their radicalism, he preferred a policy of repression. Recently there had been more trouble in the student body, and he thought Serge the right man to sort it out.[16]

Like his brother, Serge was a pupil of Pobedonotsev, an influential reactionary propagandist. Pobedonotsev was the procurator of the Holy Synod, or governor of the Church, and the architect of Alexander III's repressive system of government. From him Serge had acquired a firm distrust of progressive western political ideas and a belief that Russia could only be governed by an autocratic tsar; democracy, Pobedonotsev wrote, was "the biggest lie of our time."[17] Orthodoxy was Russia's only true religion, and all the non-Orthodox must be disloyal. Serge was led to believe that one religious group, which included many terrorists and revolutionaries among its brethren, was the worst enemy of Russia, and so he hated the Jews.

Serge and Elizabeth had hardly settled in when he began to exercise his prejudice in the most brutal manner. During Passover he decreed that all the city's twenty thousand Jews be expelled. They were to be given a few months' grace to settle their affairs. As a result, hundreds of their businesses had to be sold at bargain prices. Those who had no residence permit were brutally and immediately exiled. Many could be seen in the streets, departing in carts laden with all their possessions, to wander until they found some ghetto in southwest Russia in which to live. One contemporary historian wrote that Serge amassed a fortune in bribes from rich Jews who tried to evade his edict, but declared to one of their deputations that "all Jews ought to be crucified." He also made an exception of Jewish stable-lads and young Jewish girls if they registered themselves as prostitutes. He made it a criminal offense for Jews to adopt Christian first names.

By a similar heavy-handedness he offended many others in the city. He founded the Orthodox Palestine Society to enable some peasants to afford to travel to the Holy Land. It was soon said that donations to this charity were exacted compulsorily and that many went into his own pocket.[18] His hauteur and illiberal attitudes irritated the rich merchants, and one refused to meet him when he called at his mansion.[19] He imposed stringent restrictions on the students and professors of the university. By these means Serge was to make a vast number of enemies and reverse Alexander's idea of suppressing subversion by causing many conservative citizens to sympathize with the revolutionaries.

To Elizabeth this came as a profound shock. Serge had never discussed politics with her, and she had never seen the ruthlessness that he had exercised in command of the Preobrazhensky Regiment. Having regarded him as a compassionate Christian who treated her with gentle sensitivity during her conversion, she now found him an arrogant, dictatorial ruler and a cruel bigot with an obsessive hatred of a defenseless minority. She had been brought up in the liberal tradition that Alice had inherited from her parents, and in the Germany of her childhood Jews had been tolerated. For once she may have abandoned her unquestioning obedience and argued with her husband. But she could have no influence on Serge. He would refuse even to discuss his affairs with her, let alone listen to her advice. The hope she had expressed to Queen Victoria on her engagement, that she might reform his character, was gone forever. On discovering his streak of cruelty, she could never again picture him as the ideal character who had courted her.

The intimacy they had enjoyed during her conversion withered to a strained fondness. Elizabeth had long ceased to expect any children from her marriage; she now gave up hope of drawing much emotional strength from it, regarding it more as a domestic arrangement that had to be endured. Serge had always treated her like a child, and often contradicted her in public. His attitude became that of an aloof, haughty father. He forbade her to read *Anna Karenina,* perhaps seeing Tolstoy's portrayal of the failing marriage of a beautiful, vivacious woman to a pompous, unfeeling bureaucrat as a caricature of his own position. But for Elizabeth there was no Vronsky whom she might love, and no Seriozha on whom she could lavish maternal affection.

A distance grew between her and Serge, and he avoided being alone with her. Instead he surrounded himself with a crowd of eccentrics, stemming perhaps from his desire to set off his own rigid stuffiness with flamboyant characters. One was Princess Vassilshikova, who, Felix Youssoupov later wrote, "was as tall as a drum-major, weighed over four hundred pounds, and in her stentorian voice used the language of the guard room." Her favorite amusement was showing off her physical strength. "Anyone within her reach risked being snatched up as easily as a new-born baby." Another was Count Olsufiev, whose wife was to become Elizabeth's mistress of the robes and a trusted friend. He, however, was fat, rude, and deaf. His irreverence at church services acutely embarrassed Elizabeth. He would speak loudly to all present, and walk around the church kissing the icons and blowing kisses to those out of reach.[20]

Elizabeth not only endured the company of these eccentrics but in moving to Moscow bade her farewell to many good friends, including the imperial family, who rarely visited the city. Only in the summer months would she meet Princess Zenaide Youssoupova when she and her husband took their holiday at Archangelskoe. Life there was far less stimulating than in St. Petersburg. There was little "society," apart from a handful of nobles with whom she could associate, and a coterie of rich mer- chants whose commercial spirit ruled the city. Instead of being the center of attention at glittering court balls, her task now was to take on the wearying official duties of entertaining the civic dignitaries. Sometimes she was so fatigued that she suffered from attacks of migraine.[21] Loneliness, a failed marriage, and the bur- den of making polite conversation for hours on end were a con- tinuous, compounded nervous strain.

To many women these trials might have been a crushing blow. In the modern liberal era of free love and easy divorce it is hard to appreciate the rigid demands made on royal brides by the closed marriages of nineteenth-century Europe. Even princesses with fulfilled and fully consummated marriages found it hard to cope. Princess Alice had buckled under the combined pressures of wartime nursing and childbirth. Elizabeth's contemporary and namesake, Empress Elizabeth of Austria, stuck in an even more demanding marriage to the Emperor Francis Joseph, had been unable to endure the pyschological strain. She had suffered several nervous breakdowns, become obsessed with her health, developed what modern physicans would call anorexia nervosa, and taken to excessive dieting, a punishing regime of exercise, reckless riding, and endless travel.

Elizabeth was not entirely immune from a minor fixation with her looks. Her niece, Grand Duchess Marie, was later to describe how "even in the country my aunt gave a great deal of time and attention to her appearance." She would sketch and design her own dresses. When dressing for dinner each evening, "she made a veritable ceremony and one that required much time." After a bath several maids would step forward to dress her while she regarded herself "attentively, usually with pleasure, in a high triple mirror, so arranged that she saw herself from all sides."[22]

Yet with her usual resilience, Elizabeth was not downcast or embittered. In her new faith she found a refuge and a source of strength that most other women lacked. Her mother had likewise turned to religion in a crisis, but for Elizabeth there was none of the spiritual conflict that Alice had endured; that stage had already been passed during her conversion. Unlike Alice, she had no need for a man to support and guide her. She accepted that her conscience gave her no choice but to keep her marriage vows and remain loyal to her husband.

To compensate for her failed marriage, she sought to find an outlet for her energies in works of charity. But for her it was more than a distraction from her present despondent existence. It was rather a yearning to involve herself in a faith that had gradually grown inside her. She was later to write that religion gave her "in all my life *so much joy* in my *sorrows* so much *unboundless* [sic] comfort. . . . I long to thank and thank every minute for all God gave me and long to bring Him my feeble *gratitude* by *serving Him* and [His] *suffering children*. Oh this is not a *new feeling*, this is an *old one* which *always* was in me."[23]

It was at this time, in 1891, that Russia was gripped by one of the worst famines in its history. All over the empire the harvest had been meager. Moscow was spared from hunger, but in many country places peasants were struck down with dysentery and ate bread made from weeds. Stories spread that the winter grain had failed in all the eastern provinces, that all the children of some villages had died. The government's efforts at relief were managed with gross incompetence. Serge did little, and many of the aristocracy did nothing, regarding the peasants as innately idle, spendthrift drunkards who deserved their plight. The Marxist revolutionaries, such as one Vladimir Ulyanov—who later was to become known as Lenin—then a university student, thought the famine would be useful in arousing revolutionary discontent.

But Elizabeth put to use the compassion and charity that her new faith demanded of her, and raised money for the starving. She at once formed a committee with some wealthy ladies and appealed to the rich of Moscow. They held a bazaar which raised 10,000 rubles, and by the end of the year she had amassed the phenomenal sum of 400,000 rubles. On one occasion she traveled to the Tambov province to see that the money was well spent.[24]

She also became aware of the misery, crime, and disease that lurked in the poorer quarters of the city. Beggars and cripples were an unavoidable sight on the streets, and Elizabeth, following her mother's example, made a few tentative steps toward easing their plight. She visited the wards of the Lefortovo Hospital, and on Trinity Sunday she handed out the traditional gifts of sausage, pies, and pickled cucumber to the inmates of the Butyrka Prison.[25] She visited an orphanage, and conceived an idea far ahead of her time, of building a refuge for mothers of illegitimate children.[26] It proved too advanced to be achieved, but her effort brought attention to the misery of such women and the city's other unfortunates, who remained in her thoughts.

Soon she became popular, and did much to erode the discontent her husband aroused in the citizens. From her modest works of charity, merchants' wives called her an angel. One visitor, a wealthy young woman from Kursk, wrote: ". . . She is adored by everybody here. . . . Her dignity does not freeze you at all."[27]

There was soon another test for Elizabeth's new faith. Serge's brother, Grand Duke Paul, his wife Alexandra and their infant daughter Marie came to stay at Ilinskoe during the hot summer of 1891. There were cheerful picnics, and spirited dances and receptions in Moscow. Alexandra was pleased to be expecting her second child.

One July morning Alexandra walked down the hill from the house to the Moscow River. A boat was moored by the river. Instead of climbing in from the jetty, she jumped into it as usual, inadvertently upsetting her unborn child. At a ball the following evening she was suddenly gripped by labor pains, and fainted. She was hastily carried to her room.[28] There was no doctor for miles around, and only the old midwife from Ilinskoe could attend. When at length the doctors arrived, Alexandra was in a coma. For six days she remained unconscious while Elizabeth, Serge, and Paul watched over her in a state of acute anxiety. Still unconscious, she died giving birth to a son two months premature. The family were so distraught at losing her that they paid little attention to the frail, undersized infant who no one believed would survive. He was wrapped haphazardly in some blankets and put to one side on a chair.[29]

The peasants gathered in a vast crowd, and bore Alexandra's coffin shoulder-high to the railway station. The eight miles of road were strewn with flowers. The coffin was taken to St. Petersburg covered in a gold cloth, with a priest who continually recited prayers. All along the route peasants gathered by the tracks, knelt, bared their heads, and prayed fervently.[30]

A long funeral followed at the Fortress of St. Peter and St. Paul. Alexandra's corpse lay revealed with crossed hands, on which an icon leaned. Russian custom decreed that at the end of the ceremony the relatives must come up in turn to kiss the icon. This was too much for Paul to bear. Queen Marie of Romania, then a young girl, recalled, "I remember the tears running down his cheeks and how Uncle Serge, his favourite brother, took him in his arms when he made a desperate gesture of protest when at last they laid the coffin lid over the sweet face he loved." Emperor Alexander was also in tears, and exclaimed: "Why should this angel be taken from us, and we old ones remain?"[31]

Elizabeth was also heartbroken, for she had been Alexandra's closest friend. Serge ordered Alexandra's room at Ilinskoe to be locked and kept exactly as it was when she died. To preserve the site of a death was a habit of nineteenth-century royalty, for the Romanovs as well as for Queen Victoria. The key had been irrevocably turned and furniture gathered dust in many a room at Tsarskoe Selo or Windsor or Osborne.

Elizabeth reconciled herself to her loss as she and Serge looked after the two children at Ilinskoe. Serge gave the frail newborn baby the baths prescribed by the doctors. The boy, wrapped in cotton wool and kept in a cradle heated by hot water bottles, slowly recovered and began to thrive.[32] Soon Elizabeth was able to write to Queen Victoria: ". . . he is a sweet little fat boy with a merry character."[33] In November he was christened Dmitri Pavlovich.

Paul then took his children away to St. Petersburg. "It is heartrending," Elizabeth wrote, "to see him so resigned but so utterly broken down . . . poor motherless darlings, it is too sad."[34] Each Christmas, the two children would be brought to Moscow to stay with Elizabeth and Serge.

In January 1892 news came that the duke of Clarence had died. He had stood shivering at the graveside in freezing wind at the funeral of a cousin, caught pneumonia, and died raving, his mother holding his hand.[35] Alix was now free from Queen Victoria's scheming.

Two months later, Elizabeth heard that her father had had a paralytic stroke and was close to death. Without delay, she and Serge sped to Darmstadt.

## *Notes to Chapter 10*

*According to legend, it was the brilliant Orthodox ritual that made Vladimir adopt that religion. He had sent emissaries to inquire into Islam, the Roman Church and the Greek Orthodox Church at Constantinople. On their return they told him, as The Tale of Past Years relates: ". . . the Greeks led us into the edifices where they worship their God, and we knew not whether we were in heaven or earth. For in earth there is no such splendour or such beauty, and we are at a loss to describe it. We know only that God dwells there among men. . . ."

†The efforts of these "populists" to "go to the people" were spectacularly unsuccessful. The peasants, suspicious of all outsiders, ignored them or turned them over to the police.

# Chapter 11

*Poor Tanya's bloom begins to languish,*
*and pale, and fade without a word!*
*There's nothing can employ her anguish,*
*no sound by which her soul is stirred.*
*Neighbours in whispered tones are taking*
*council, and with profound head-shaking*
*conclude that it's high time she wed.*

—PUSHKIN, *EVGENI ONEGIN*

At Frankfurt Irene met them with the news that Louis had deteriorated further.[1] They traveled to the New Palace. All the grand duke's children had already arrived, and the family went in together to see him. Speechless and half paralyzed, the grand duke was lying in the dark with a nurse beside him. Victoria wrote:

> . . . the light was switched on and Ella leant over the bed & took Papa's hand. I said "Papa, Papa, Ella ist da" . . . Then he suddenly opened his eyes in a dazed sort of way, looked puzzled from her to Serge, and then a pleased look came over his face. He murmured "Jeh, jeh, jeh!" raised his whole head off the pillow, put out his hand and stroked Ella's face still murmuring. Then as the breathless pause came and he closed his eyes we turned out the light, but in a moment he opened them and looked for her, so we brought a candle and he kept his eyes on her a minute or two longer. Ella soothed him gently and when he was again quiet we left the room. . . .[2]

The grand duke was so pleased to see his second daughter that his health seemed to improve, far more than Dr. Eigenbrodt had dared hope. That night his breathing was calmer.

But after a day he began to sink once more. On the evening of March 12 he lost consciousness. Relatives and ministers were summoned to the palace. Alix was "brokenhearted," and Ernest, only twenty-four, was in despair at the thought of becoming grand duke. When Princess Marie of Battenberg came to his father's bedside, he broke down, threw his arms round her neck and cried, "God help me, do not forsake me!"[3]

Louis passed his final hours in the company of his family.[4] His pulse grew more feeble by the hour. His face appeared calm and still, and remained so. A little after one A.M. his breathing became rapid and heavy, then ceased.

Elizabeth and her sisters dressed his corpse in the uniform of his favorite regiment, the Leib-Garde, and the cloak he had worn in two wars. They pinned onto his chest the Hessian star and the decorations he had won for bravery in battle. Around his tunic they fitted the blue Garter ribbon, and they placed his sword between his hands. They covered the bed and pillow with violets, and draped the bier in black.[5]

For three days the Hessians streamed in to pay their respects to the grand duke who had fought for their country and reigned as an honest and fair constitutional sovereign. Throughout the state he was universally and sincerely mourned. The family followed his coffin to the Rosenhöhe to lay him to rest beside Alice, May, Frittie, and his ancestors. The cortege was so long that when its head had reached the mausoleum, its rear had not yet left the New Palace three miles behind.[6]

Elizabeth stayed behind for a few weeks to look after Alix and Ernest. She did her best to fortify her brother in his new role as grand duke, for which he was completely unprepared. She consoled Alix, whose natural melancholy had been intensified by the loss of her father. "For years she could not speak of him," Baroness Buxhoeveden wrote, "and long after, when she was in

Russia, anything that would remind her of him would bring her to the verge of tears."[7] Elizabeth tried to help Alix become the "Landesmutter" of Hesse, and perhaps reminded her that she need not remain in Darmstadt forever.

Returning to Moscow, Elizabeth received from Queen Victoria a brooch containing a miniature portrait of her father. She placed in it a lock of his hair, and wore it constantly. It still seemed impossible, she wrote to the queen, that she would never see him again.[8] Having lost in her father the last person who might act as a trusted counselor, and feeling some guilt at the thought that her own conversion may have hastened his death, she turned further to her religion as a refuge. She longed even more to have her sister with her in Russia.

For the next few months Grand Duchess Elizabeth was absorbed in her duties as the Moscow governor's wife. She and Serge managed to find time for a journey down the Volga.[9] They slowly cruised the wide river with the flat Russian plain dotted with birch and pine woods on its banks, and saw the ancient towns of Yaroslavl, Rostov, and Anglich. The German artist Kaulbach was commissioned to paint her portrait; after several sketches he said, almost in despair: "She is the most difficult subject I have ever painted. An artist can never entirely capture such perfection."[10]

Elizabeth began to suffer from rheumatism, and in October 1892 she and Serge went to Italy for a cure. Somewhat recovered, she went with her husband on another visit to Windsor and Darmstadt, returning to Russia late in December.

Sometime during her visit to Darmstadt she must have heard from Alix that she still loved Tsarevich Nicholas. Alix was still unable to bring herself to convert to Russian Orthodoxy, an obligatory step for the wife of the heir to the Russian throne. During Elizabeth's own conversion Alix had written her numerous letters describing her own tormented conscience; without success Elizabeth had sent her the books on Orthodoxy that she had read.[11] Nonetheless Elizabeth was encouraged, and when she returned to Russia she continued to act as a go-between. At this time Nicholas was enjoying a flirtation with a star of the Imperial Ballet with wide luminous eyes, Matilde Kschessinka. Elizabeth was keen to remind him of his old flame. She passed on news of Alix and confided to Nicholas that Alix loved him.[12]

In the fall of 1893, another opportunity came to advance the romance. By now Emperor Alexander III and his wife Marie were resigning themselves to the idea of Nicholas and Alix getting married. Elizabeth hoped to square Queen Victoria's opposition when she, Serge, and Paul stayed at Balmoral in September. There Elizabeth had a chance to talk to the queen. The queen had seen Tsarevich Nicholas in July at the wedding of the Duke of York,* and her antipathy toward the Russian marriage was slowly declining. Elizabeth did her best to present Nicholas in an attractive light.

In October they went on to Hesse, where Elizabeth found that Alix was still wrestling with her conscience over her religion. She sensed that a critical point had arrived. It was now imperative for her to step in as matchmaker. She knew that any direct attempt to persuade her headstrong younger sister would be futile. Instead she repeated in several private conversations that Nicholas longed to see Alix and plead with her. She managed to wring a promise from her sister to let him come. On November 1, 1893, she dashed off a confused and conspiratorial letter to Nicholas to arrange a meeting, using code names and partly altering the genders:

> . . . well dear much hope there is not and he [Alix] begs me to tell you not to *misunderstand* him [her] but my idea is that *seeing Pelly II* [Nicholas] *talking with her* [Alix] perhaps God will give him [Alix] the courage to do a thing for love which now seems to him [her] impossible. . . .
>
> If *Pelly II consents* telegraph to me *all right* then

> *Sergei* will *write* to the person who invited for Easter
> and we [the Hessian family] would go together to
> pay a visit and meet Pelly II there. You must answer
> *directly*. . . . May I now say my opinion this is her
> [Nicholas's] *last and only chance* she [Nicholas]
> must come now or it is a finished thing forever
> whereas if they meet who knows it is so difficult to
> refuse accepting the only being you love since
> years. . . . Pelly I [Alix] said said he [she] would
> die for his [her] love and if they speak perhaps the
> only real barrier which has kept them apart will
> melt before the words of love from Pelly II. . . .[13]

But Nicholas lacked the will to take the decisive step; he
ignored Elizabeth's pleas and remained in Russia. Her hopes
dashed, Elizabeth returned crestfallen to St. Petersburg bearing
a photograph and a letter from her sister. Alix was still adamant
that: "It would be acting a lie to you, your religion and your God.
. . . I can *never* change my confession." Nicholas was overwhelmed. ". . . all my hopes," he wrote in his diary, "are shattered by this implacable obstacle, my best dreams and my most
cherished hopes for the future. . . . All day I went about in a daze.
. . ."[14]

Nonetheless Elizabeth persevered, sensing that Alix might yet
change her mind if given the tranquility to think out her future.
From afar she tried to ensure that the conditions were right. She
wrote Alix a sympathetic letter, and on November 20, 1893, she
wrote to Ernest, offering to come if her presence would be of any
help:

> . . . may God give strength is all we can pray—I
> so perfectly understand all she must be going
> through and trust in your tender heart to help
> her. If ever she takes this step, it will be a fearful
> battle with her heart and soul and if you find my
> presence necessary as of course I can easiest help,

then do send for me and if only possible I shall arrive directly even if it should be for a few days, Serge is sure to let me go. . . .[15]

On the same day she wrote to Queen Victoria, urging her to leave Alix alone but support her when she had made up her mind:

> Now about Alix—I touched the subject—all is as before and if any decision is taken which entirely settles this affair I shall of course write directly. The best is of course to leave her alone as of course it is a very sore heart . . . all is in God's hands and, dearest Grandmama, if ever she accepts, your motherly love will be what she longs for most—alas the world is so spiteful and, not knowing how long and deep this affection on both sides has been, the spiteful tongues will call it ambition. What fools; as if to mount this throne was enviable. Only love pure and intense can give strength to such a serious step—will it ever be I wonder? . . . I like the boy, his parents lead a model family life, all heart and religion which gives them strength in the difficult moments of life and brings them nearer to God—it will be a rough school, but one that prepares for a future life and thank God much is exaggerated—are not our lives always in His hands and may we not all die suddenly? "L'homme propose et Dieu dispose". . . .[16]

Yet in spite of Elizabeth's machinations, Alix showed no sign of wavering. Elizabeth was not required to come to her side at Darmstadt. She was instead extremely busy in Moscow. "I am very much occupied all morning, people to receive and different, more serious affairs about my charity societies," she wrote. She saw Kate Marsden, an amazingly adventurous English nurse who was searching for a cure for lepers in eastern Siberia. She helped

Miss Marsden with her journey, which was to take her 3,000 miles by boat and 2,000 miles riding across insect-infected swamps and a fiery plain to a colony at Viliusk. "What a remarkable woman she is," Elizabeth wrote to Queen Victoria.[17]

Elizabeth's eyes were now set on another romance. Her brother Ernest had fallen in love with their first cousin, "Ducky," Princess Victoria Melita of Coburg. Ducky was a restless, mercurial character, fond of the social whirl, and a superb and reckless horsewoman. Ernest was artistic, sensitive, high-strung, and averse to riding, which sometimes scared him. Late in 1893 Ducky accepted his proposal without ever having got to know him properly. The wedding was set for April 1894 at Coburg.

This shed a new light on Alix's marriage plans, and once more raised Elizabeth's hopes. For Alix would soon be supplanted in her role as *Landesmutter* of Hesse, and the idea of life with the beautiful, regal, overbearing Ducky was unattractive. It provided another powerful reason for her to marry. Alix was still deaf to Elizabeth's pleas: "I know Ella will begin again," she wrote to Nicholas's sister Xenia, "but what is the good of it . . . ."[18] Yet Elizabeth continued to hope that Nicholas's presence might be a decisive influence. The wedding at Coburg was an ideal opportunity for him to see her. Elizabeth encouraged him to go, and so on April 12 he boarded the imperial train bound for Coburg, along with Elizabeth, Serge, Paul, and Grand Duke and Duchess Vladimir, who represented the emperor.

Two days later the train drew into the medieval town where Prince Albert had grown up. On the platform a guard of honor and a large family gathering awaited the Russians. The host was Prince Alfred, one of Queen Victoria's less favored sons, who had inherited the dukedom of Saxe-Coburg and Gotha from Prince Albert's lecherous elder brother Ernest. Beside him was his wife Marie, a stout and eccentric woman, who had her boots made to fit either foot. Imperious and devoutly Orthodox, she never forgot that she was a daughter of Emperor Alexander II. Also present were their daughters Marie, "Missy," now crown princess of

Romania, and Ducky with Ernest in tow. Next to Ernest was Alix, and Nicholas, now twenty-five, saw her for the first time in years. The party drove through the cobbled streets, lined with cheering crowds, past the ten-foot-high statue of Prince Albert, to Ehrenburg Castle.

The following morning Nicholas began to press his suit. Elizabeth was talking to Alix in her rooms when Nicholas appeared. Pleased, Elizabeth withdrew to allow them an intimate talk. That afternoon, Nicholas accompanied her and Serge on a carriage drive. He had been closeted for two hours with Alix, and as he wrote in his diary, "the talk took place for which I longed so long and so much." The twenty-one-year-old Alix had cried a good deal, but her religious conscience still overrode her love.[19]

Meanwhile, an extraordinary number of royal wedding guests were converging on Coburg. A British courtier remarked that he had never seen so many. All but Queen Victoria expected that an engagement would be announced with far-reaching consequences for European diplomacy. Elizabeth's sisters, Irene of Prussia and Victoria of Battenberg, came with their husbands. The duke of Connaught and the Prince of Wales traveled from England. Among the German royalty Emperor William and his mother, Vicky, the dowager Empress Frederick, were conspicuous. William, his sword clanking, was wearing a military uniform; as he did not wear civilian clothes, all the male royalty had to dine in uniform. Having dismissed Bismarck, William came to oversee Alix's engagement as part of his own personal diplomacy. He believed that her marriage to Nicholas would strengthen Russo-German ties, and break up the Franco-Russian alliance. It was to be one of his many diplomatic blunders; in the end the marriage helped Great Britain to join the Franco-Russian entente.

The one guest who was ignorant of these machinations was Queen Victoria. As her train approached, she was absorbed in happy memories of the times she had spent in Coburg with Prince Albert. She looked forward to the wedding between two of his grandchildren that she had done much to arrange. On the platform a guard of her Prussian regiment was at attention, a typically theatrical gesture of Emperor William. As she drove through the gaily decorated streets, two girls dressed in white dropped flowers on her carriage as it passed under a triumphal arch.[20]

After a round of plays, operas, and convivial dinners, the wedding took place on April 19. The bride, the Empress Frederick thought, "looked charming and very distinguée," wearing a diadem of emeralds and sprig of orange blossom stuck in her hair.[21] Ernest was deeply in love. During the service, Nicholas yearned to look into Alix's soul.[22] The bride's father, exhausted by an overindulgent dinner, dozed off and dropped his cane with a clatter.

The next morning saw the scene everyone was waiting for. Elizabeth, Emperor William, and most of the family were gathered in the drawing room. Next door, Nicholas was pleading his suit. For two hours he repeated his arguments, and she cried and whispered, "No, I cannot." He left her with a letter from his mother about a Danish princess who had converted happily to Orthodoxy, and joined the company in the next room. The letter decided Alix. She came in and agreed at once.[23]

Weeping like joyful children, Nicholas and Alix accepted the company's congratulations. Elizabeth was scarcely less moved. In great agitation she ran to Queen Victoria and surprised her at breakfast. The queen was, as she wrote in her diary, "thunderstruck" on hearing the news. Elizabeth begged that the couple might come in and receive her blessing. Hurriedly composing herself and facing the inevitable, the queen agreed, and kissed them both while Elizabeth looked on in triumph. "She is much too good for me," Nicky said, and the queen made him agree to make his bride's conversion an easy one.[24] Then the company went over to Duchess Marie, "where in their joy," Nicholas wrote in his diary, "the family indulged in an orgy of kissing."

The summer of 1894 was to be one of the happiest Elizabeth had known. She returned to Russia delighted that her sister was soon to be joining her. "It does one's heart good," she wrote to Queen Victoria, "to know Nicky and Alix at last happy and I am sure God will bless this union in which such deep feelings of religion are."[25] She foresaw her sister enjoying many years of contented marriage; Emperor Alexander, a man of immense strength and robust health, was only forty-nine, and Nicholas would have years in which to learn his responsibilities. She busied herself preparing for the wedding, and opened up the Sergievskaya Palace in St. Petersburg to receive a complement of guests.

At the end of July the festivities began for the wedding of the emperor's daughter, Grand Duchess Xenia, to Grand Duke Alexander Mikhailovich. So full of abandon were the celebrations that at one point the bride and groom were thrown from their coach into a river, emerging laughing and covered in mud.[26] Elizabeth and Serge then spent a carefree holiday at Ilinskoe. As they rowed a boat on the lake, fished, rode about the estate or sketched the scenery, Elizabeth dreamed of arranging another marriage between two of her German cousins, Prince Peter of Oldenburg and Princess Victoria of Schleswig-Holstein-Sonderburg-Augustenburg.[27]

Meanwhile, Emperor Alexander had fallen ill. Six years earlier, in 1888, he had saved his family from a railway accident by holding up the roof of the wrecked carriage until help arrived. The resultant strain on his constitution had gone unnoticed. After his daughter's wedding an illness compelled him to rest with his wife at his shooting lodge at Belovezh. He slept little, his appetite faded, and soon food even became distasteful to him. His boots began to feel too tight, the first symptom of the gathering of a watery fluid in the body's cavities, known as dropsy or edema. A specialist diagnosed an acute form of Bright's disease, an inflammation of the kidneys now known as nephritis. He advised a change of climate, and in the fall Alexander moved to his palace at Livadia on the Crimean coast.[28]

Elizabeth heard the news without too much concern, but knew her sister must be anxious. "Poor Alix," she wrote, "must be very worried about Sasha. We have news and the doctors say if he has one warm winter and is careful he may be entirely cured." Believing the emperor to be in no immediate danger, she and Serge began plans to spend five weeks in Paris and Darmstadt.[29]

At Livadia, however, Alexander's appetite deteriorated until the sight of food made him ill. By October, it seemed that he had only a few weeks to live. On the seventeenth, Elizabeth prepared to travel to his side, and sent a despairing telegram to Queen Victoria:

Leaving tonight for Crimea, news bad, too awfully sad,
God grant health, fear worst.
Ella.[30]

## Notes to Chapter 11

*Later King George V, to Princess May of Teck. His looks so resembled the Tsarevitch's that people confused the two princes. Courtiers reminded the duke of York that he must on no account be late for the wedding, and afterward came up to congratulate the tsarevich on his good fortune.

# Chapter 12

*A coffin now lies on the table*
*Where once the board was festive and gay.*

—DERZHAVIN,
ODE ON THE DEATH OF PRINCE MESHCHERSKY

 

The emperor was a pitiful sight when Elizabeth arrived at Livadia. The man who had been a model of strength now wore an expression of wistful weariness. His eyes were glazed and his cheeks sunken. "It was like seeing a magnificent building crumbling,"[1] wrote Prince Nicholas of Greece. Empress Marie, worn out from fear and sleeplessness, nursed her husband day and night. An eminent doctor, Zacharin, crept in and out of the tsar's bedroom. The doctor was short of breath and could only take a few steps before sitting down; chairs had been placed along the corridor outside.[2] Courtiers and ministers hurried about with a silent tread and conferred in anxious hushed voices. The sudden end of a long reign was a crisis for which they were unprepared. Father John of Kronstadt, a priest revered throughout Russia, came to pray for the emperor. He was thought capable of working miracles. Countless diseased Russians had begged him for his prayers, believing, if they recovered, that it was through his intercession. It was hoped that the man of God might have a chance where the doctors had seemingly failed.

Elizabeth had hardly arrived before it was decided that she should bring Alix from the German frontier to Livadia. A

German specialist had told Alexander that he still had a fort-night to live. Alexander had begged that Alix be sent for, who was now hurrying from Darmstadt, traveling as an ordinary passen-ger as there was no time to organize a special train. At Alexandrov, on the Polish-German border, Elizabeth met Alix, accompanied by Victoria and their old nurse, Mrs. Orchard, who was to continue with them to the Crimea.[3] She prepared to usher her shy and gauche younger sister, barely out of the schoolroom, into the funereal gloom of Livadia and her awesome responsi-bilities as the future empress. In circumstances grimly different from those she had imagined, she was fulfilling her dream of wel-coming Alix as a bride to Russia.

The three sisters consulted together, and it was decided that Alix should adopt the religion of her new country as soon as pos-sible. A telegram was despatched to Livadia to that effect. Another was sent Queen Victoria about the emperor's health.[4] Bidding farewell to Victoria, Elizabeth and Alix prepared to enter the imperial train. A guard of honor was arrayed outside, and a courtier stepped forward with flowers and a few words of welcome. Alix was crippled by her shyness, a portent of her later ordeals at the ceremonies of the Russian court. She was at a loss; she accepted the flowers but hardly knew what to say. It was a relief to be safely inside the train.[5]

The next day, at Alushta on the Crimean coast, Nicholas, to his joy, was reunited with his bride-to-be. They drove to Livadia, Elizabeth and Serge, who had arrived from Moscow, following in a second carriage.[6] Peasants gathered by the wayside with flowers and respectfully proffered bread and salt as a gift of welcome. Alix and Nicholas saw the emperor that evening; he was so pleased to meet her that he insisted on a full dress uniform for the occasion and gave her his blessing.[7] Elizabeth was too tired to accompany her. She had traveled almost three thousand miles in less than a week.

By October 29, it was clear that Alexander had only a few more days left. The empress despatched an urgent telegram to her sister, the Princess of Wales, begging her to come at once. The prince and princess set out without delay. A service was held on the same day to celebrate Alexander's survival from the train accident at Borki six years earlier.

The emperor spent the night of the thirtieth sitting in an armchair, unable to lie down. Marie was by his side and continually went to the window to see if dawn had broken.[8] That morning the household rose unusually early. Alexander remembered that it was Elizabeth's birthday, called her and Serge, and congratulated her. He "had a clear voice and all his head," Elizabeth wrote, "but we saw the look of death already in his eyes." Marie called in all the family and kissed them in turn. The empress, her children, and Alix knelt round the emperor. Elizabeth and the rest withdrew to the next room. Through the open door they saw Alexander asking them for their prayers. All knelt as his confessor came to give him communion. Father John of Kronstadt entered, and the doors were shut. As Elizabeth heard later, Father John pressed his hand to the emperor's forehead; Alexander said: "I feel so well." Father John anointed him with holy oil, and the emperor's pulse became stronger. It weakened after a few minutes, and the doors were opened. The empress was by his side, her right arm passed across his shoulders, his head resting against her cheek. "We all knelt down to hear his last quiet breath," Elizabeth wrote to Queen Victoria, "no agony whatever, and that pure soul went to heaven. To die like that makes one feel God's presence and that from this world we are called to real life. If you knew the comfort, the calm it gave our souls while our hearts were breaking. God bless him, never had He a truer or nobler servant."[9]

A little later, the youth of twenty-six, who was now tsar, left the room and broke down in tears. "Sandro, what am I going to do?" he asked his brother-in-law, Grand Duke Alexander. "What is going to happen to me, to you, to Xenia, to Alix, to Mother, to all of Russia? I am not prepared to be a tsar. I never wanted to become one. I know nothing of the business of ruling. I have no idea of even how to talk to the ministers."[10]

Outside, the imperial standard was lowered to half-mast. The warships in the bay began to thunder out a salute to the dead emperor. At four o'clock the grand dukes, courtiers, ministers, and servants swore allegiance to the new emperor, Tsar Nicholas II.[11]

The next morning, as a wild storm raged over the Black Sea, Elizabeth and Alix, dressed in white as Orthodox custom decreed, entered the chapel. In a ceremony "so simple and touching that it went straight to all our hearts," Alix was received into the Orthodox Church. She pronounced the responses in a clear and unfaltering voice. "She was calm and heart and soul belonging to what she said," Elizabeth wrote, "there was not a word which could hurt her old belief."[12] She now became "the truly believing Grand Duchess Alexandra Feodorovna." Directly afterward she, Elizabeth, Nicholas, and Marie knelt and took communion. "It gave us all strength for the sad times to go through."

On November 6, Nicholas and his brothers lifted their father's body from his deathbed into the coffin. That evening, all the family followed the coffin, borne by Cossacks, in a torchlit procession to the cathedral of Livadia. A few days later, Elizabeth and Serge left behind Nicholas, Alexandra, as she was now named, and the family, and traveled ahead to Moscow to prepare for another exhausting round of ceremonies. There the sleet cut into their faces and low clouds scudded across a gray sky as they met the funeral train from the Crimea. After two more days, the cortege reached St. Petersburg. An immense silent crowd filled the square outside the Nicholas railway station. The drizzle turned the snow into yellow slush as it fell from a leaden sky. Elizabeth and Alexandra were separated once more. Alexandra was placed in a carriage with Marie; Elizabeth rode further behind. For four hours they crawled down the Nevsky Prospect, across the ice-bound Neva and into the Fortress Cathedral of St. Peter and St. Paul, where every tsar since Peter the Great had been buried except Peter III. Alexander, his hand resting on the coffin's side, was placed on a dais screened by curtains of silver and gold.[13]

Afterward, Elizabeth, Serge, and Alexandra returned to Serge's palace. On the other side of the Nevsky Prospect, at the Anichkov Palace, another pair of mourning sisters, the dowager Empress Marie and the princess of Wales, together with the prince and the new emperor Nicholas, had taken up residence. Marie, now thin and pale, was stoical in her grief: "she prays with such fervour it is beautiful and touching to see."[14] Nicholas visited his fiancée several times during the week that elapsed before the burial. Irene and Ernest were also staying at Sergievskaya Palace. Visits had to be paid to all the foreign guests, and twice-daily services attended in the cathedral. "I rarely have a moment's rest," Elizabeth complained.[15]

Alexander's interment lasted two and a half hours. The congregation knelt with unlit candles in their hands. Burning tapers were passed silently among them, and the cathedral was slowly filled with light as the service progressed: the old reign was over, and a new one began. At the end Nicholas made a last farewell to his father. He rose and kissed his face and hands. His mother, Elizabeth, Serge, Alexandra, all the grand dukes and duchesses, and three kings and seventeen princes from abroad, followed in their turn.[16]

A week after this final dirge came Alexandra's wedding. Nicholas, supported by his mother, wanted to marry as soon as possible; he needed a wife's support. His bride would rather have returned to Darmstadt. The date chosen was November 26, Marie's birthday, on which mourning was relaxed for a single day. The memory of Elizabeth's wedding was only too prominent in the minds of both sisters. She had entered St. Petersburg in a golden coach, watched by cheering crowds. The sun had shone all day and hardly set in the evening. Their father had cheerfully given her away, and Tsar Alexander had given his blessing. Twelve-year-old Alix had run up and down the corridors with Nicholas, squealing with delight, and they had carved their names together with a diamond ring on a window at Peterhof. Their romance now came to fruition on a gray November day with barely five hours of light, and both fathers dead. ". . . our fathers were missing—that was dreadful—no kiss, no blessing from either. . . . One day in deepest mourning, the next in smartest clothes being married," Alexandra wrote.[17]

Everything had been arranged in a hurry, and there were many mishaps. Elizabeth helped her sister dress, just as she had done five years earlier at Alix's first ball. A crisis occurred; the famous coiffeur, Delcroix, who was to dress the bride's hair was nowhere to be found. Inquiries were made but yielded no result. It was thought that he had been kidnapped by Nihilists. The situation became desperate as the last of the guests arrived at the Winter Palace. Alexandra was now in a state of collapse, Elizabeth almost in tears. At that point the dowager empress arrived to take the bride to the palace. They both rushed toward her and explained the situation in an excited gabble. She calmly suggested that some mistake in the security arrangements had sent the coiffeur to the wrong place. Servants were sent running everywhere. The bewildered hairdresser was discovered in the guardroom of the Sergievskaya Palace. A suspicious sergeant had found something wrong with his pass. The bride's hair was quickly dressed, and she put on the veil Princess Alice had worn at her wedding at Osborne.[18] She was rushed to the Malachite Room at the Winter Palace to be robed, as Elizabeth had been ten years earlier, in the jewels of Catherine the Great. After passing through several enormous rooms filled with staring courtiers and nobles, Marie on her arm, and Elizabeth following behind, Alexandra entered the chapel late.

The ceremony over, the guests were presented to Alexandra. She spoke no Russian, and answered their compliments with a slight smile, a stiff nod or some schoolgirl French. At one point she almost fainted under the weight of her train, and Ernest ordered two chamberlains to hold it up. This was against custom, as it was felt a Russian empress had to bear such weight. To her relief there was no customary banquet afterward. Instead, Elizabeth joined the bride and groom for a simple tea.[19]

Alexandra was at a loss as she began to reign as empress. She was so shy during court ceremonies that she admitted to hoping that the floor would open and swallow her up. She would redden and her French would desert her. That she was only beginning to learn Russian was another handicap, which was worsened by her ignorance of the rigid court protocol. Her ladies-in-waiting, chosen by her mother-in-law, were of little help. Elizabeth's friend, old Princess Golitsyna, too well established to be removed from her post of honor, frightened Alexandra. She told her nothing about those to be presented to her, or what she should say to them. In her old-fashioned frame of mind it was honor enough simply for the empress to receive her guests.[20]

Worse, the dowager Empress Marie turned out to be an unusually awkward mother-in-law. She resented losing her son immediately after the death of her husband. Having been born a Danish princess, she looked down on Alexandra as an upstart from a minor German state. She ignored the custom that a widowed empress should retire from public life. Still endowed with good and vitality, she prepared to host brilliant balls after the end of court mourning, but barely helped Alexandra with her own festivities. She had some trivial disputes with her daughter-in-law over precedence and the ownership of jewels.[21]

Elizabeth did what she could to help. She was a friend of Marie, and tried to smooth over her quarrels with Alexandra. She and Serge stayed on in the capital while the guests departed. Elizabeth spent much time with her sister and brother-in-law. She joined them for games of sliding down an ice hill at the Anichkov Palace, and they would cross the Nevsky Prospect for tea with her and Serge. Elizabeth drew plans for the decorations in their rooms in the Winter Palace, discussed them with the imperial couple, and found that her ideas agreed exactly with their own.[22]

As the governor's wife, Elizabeth was tied by her duties to Moscow, but she traveled north every few weeks to offer advice and support. In October 1895, she came to be beside her sister as the time drew near for the birth of her first child. She sat painting or doing needlework with Alexandra, and accompanied her on carriage drives. She looked after her sister, and made sure that she took proper exercise. When the birth came, on November 15, it was particularly painful as the child was so large. Elizabeth arrived several hours before, and it was said that Empress Marie was praying on her knees while Nicholas was crying in the next room.[23] Elizabeth and Marie "gently rubbed her back and legs which relieved her," she wrote to Queen Victoria a little later.[24]

But try as she might to help, Elizabeth found that her efforts brought sneers on her sister from society. She angrily wrote to Queen Victoria:

> You know how spiteful people are, and the affection of two sisters will never be taken simply. Either they will say I am intriguing and ambitious, two things I loathe, or that Alix can do nothing without my advice, which also does not do. She has her husband and mother-in-law and if I can help her of course I will do my best, but they are her nearest here and I do not wish to seem to come between them.[25]

It did nothing to help Alix's popularity that the child which so delighted her was a disappointment to Russia. As the salute boomed out from the Fortress of St. Peter and St. Paul, the citizens listened to count the number of guns. The salute stopped short at one hundred and one, not three hundred; the child was a girl, and hopes of a boy to succeed to the throne were dashed. The child was christened Olga Nikolayevna.

Worse, Alexandra, fatigued from nursing her baby, made a poor impression at court balls in the "season" in 1896, the first after the end of court mourning. Elizabeth reveled in being the center of attention, but Alexandra, E. M. Almedingen wrote, was rigid from stage fright:

> . . . she seemed a piece of sculpture. The smile, which had endeared her to so many, never appeared. Her lips were pursed, her eyes cold. She had the air of someone anxious to get away at the first chance. What few words she spoke were shorn of all graciousness.[26]

Society unanimously condemned her, comparing her unfavorably with the gracious Empress Marie.[27] Many grand dukes and duchesses, particularly Serge's brother Vladimir and his wife, disliked her English origins. Her foreign upbringing was seen as another shortcoming. Alexandra spoke only English to her husband, and later to her children, who would use Russian only with their father. She gradually learned Russian and spoke it fluently, but it was said with contempt that only English was spoken at court.*[28] To the French- or Russian-speaking aristocracy this was taken as an alien imposition.

Alexandra was hurt, and began to feel reluctant to entertain outsiders. Soon even grand duchesses had to make an appointment through a lady-in-waiting before seeing her. Nicholas, devoted to his wife, agreed to her arrangements. Over the years, the couple were slowly to retreat into a world of their own.

Nicholas's inexperience in state affairs was also a handicap in the new reign. Some outside observers hoped that this very lack of fixed ideas of government might make him amenable to liberal and progressive principles. But Nicholas had been tutored, like his late father, by Pobedonotsev to regard these principles as anathema. He was under the sway of his uncles, Serge in particular. Serge enjoyed discussing politics with his nephew, and convinced him that any projects of reform would be disastrous for Russia.[29] Nicholas soon made his views clear. Some representatives from the strongly liberal *zemstvo,* or local council, in the province of Tver stressed that public opinion must be listened to.† In a speech at a reception for local officials, Nicholas was to give them a stern rebuff:

> I am informed that recently in some zemstvo assemblies, voices have made themselves heard from people carried away by senseless dreams about participation by representatives of the zemstvo in the affairs of internal government. Let all know that I, devoting all my strength to the welfare of the people, will uphold the principle of autocracy as firmly and as unflinchingly as my late, unforgettable father.[30]

It was in this atmosphere that Serge oversaw preparations for the coronation of the new tsar in Moscow. He explained all the details to Alexandra, and impressed her with their deep religious significance. He and Elizabeth were absorbed in preparing for the grand ceremonies and receiving numerous foreign guests. ". . . the town is topsy-turvy with the preparations," Elizabeth wrote to Nicholas, "dust, noise and Sergei works hard daily with all the affairs."[31] For months in advance the Kremlin was swarming with workmen putting up decorations. As the date drew near, the city was covered with banners, flags, bunting and electric lights. Vast crowds surged in from all over Russia; due to the growth of the railways, they were far larger than at any previous coronation.

As governor, Serge had an onerous responsibility in handling this influx. Bearing in mind his past treatment of the Muscovites, there were many who prayed earnestly that his management would not cause suffering or discontent.

## Notes to Chapter 12

*Indeed, by 1907, English had become the fashionable language in St. Petersburg. Russians who knew only French spoke it with an English accent. Among royalty, it was becoming the lingua franca. The emperors Nicholas II and Wilhelm II of Germany corresponded in it in preference to their native tongues, and Nicholas always used it with his wife.

†They fared better than their predecessors. In 1862 thirteen noblemen from Tver Province, calling for an elected popular assembly, had been incarcerated in the Fortress of St. Peter and St. Paul in St. Petersburg.

# Chapter 13

*Here stands, with shady park surrounded,*
*Petrovsky Castle; and the fame*
*in which so lately it abounded*
*rings proudly in that sombre name.*
*Napoleon here, intoxicated*
*with recent fortune, vainly waited*
*till Moscow, meekly on its knees,*
*gave up the ancient Kremlin-keys . . .*

—PUSHKIN, *EVGENI ONEGIN*

Emperor Nicholas's idea of maintaining his father's principle of autocracy was grandly symbolized in his coronation. The ceremony in Moscow was the greatest display to the world of the tsar's sovereign might. It represented the belief that Nicholas was anointed by the church and entrusted by God with the responsibility of governing hundreds of millions of peoples. The ceremony was an expression of the ancient traditions of Holy Russia, the belief in a union of church and state under a single ruler. It was a link with a past stretching back to the foundation of Kievan Russia more than a millennium before. The coronation was to be one of the last times Russians felt themselves to be heirs to this tradition.

In May 1896, a vast concourse of foreign royalty was assembled in Moscow. Elizabeth was detailed to meet many of them and spent long wearying hours in receptions. Her sister Irene and Prince Henry of Prussia came, and her brother Ernest with his new wife, Ducky. Her other sister Victoria and Prince Louis of Battenberg arrived from England and stayed with Elizabeth at the governor's palace on the Tverskaya.[1]

The grand spectacles began with the solemn entry of the tsar

169

and tsarina into Moscow.[2] By tradition, the uncrowned tsar did not enter the city until shortly before the coronation. Nicholas and Alexandra went into retreat at the Petrovsky Palace outside the city. In the romantic castle, built by Catherine the Great with Gothic windows and turrets, they fasted and prayed. On May 21, Elizabeth, Serge, all the grand dukes and duchesses and foreign princes gathered there for the ceremonial procession.

The sun gleamed on the golden domes of the countless Moscow churches as they set off. Nicholas rode alone at the head, followed by the grand dukes and foreign princes on horseback. Cossacks in long red robes and black fur caps and hussars and lancers flanked them on both sides. In gilded state coaches, driven by footmen in powdered wigs and golden liveries, the dowager Empress Marie, already crowned, and behind her the uncrowned Alexandra, followed on. Elizabeth and the other grand duchesses were seated in state coaches further behind. In their silver court dresses and jewels they all attracted admiration.

Throughout the route lined by a triple row of troops, the people were packed in a dense mass. On every building garlands and flags hung brightly in the sunshine, and the windows and balconies were black with spectators. The church bells chimed out a sonorous peal, and the bands played the national anthem. They could barely be heard above the echoing cheers of the crowd. "Side by side with well-dressed ladies were peasants in their Sunday clothes," Baroness Buxhoeveden wrote, "and the enthusiasm of all was indescribable, all crossing themselves in emotion as the procession passed." After several hours the procession passed through the narrow Nicholas Gate in the Kremlin, "and then vanished from the sight of the people, who stood gazing spellbound after it, as if hoping that the brilliant vision would appear again."[3]

On May 25, after a few days in the quiet of the Neskuchnoe Palace, the sovereigns drove to the Kremlin in another procession. Not long before the procession started there was a minor catastrophe in the governor's palace. A mysterious fire suddenly broke out in Serge's private chapel. Serge, dressed in full uniform, burst into the Battenbergs' rooms and saved their clothes. The culprit was never found; had the fire occurred half an hour later, when all eyes were occupied with the procession, the palace would have been destroyed.[4]

The following day, heralds in medieval dress handed out a proclamation in the Moscow streets announcing "to the good people of Our first capital" that the coronation was to be held on May 26 in the Cathedral of the Assumption. Elizabeth, robed as on her wedding day in a heavy silver court dress and wearing a set of emeralds that had become famous, took her place with the imperial family and foreign princes. At a quarter to nine, the old Empress Marie, crowned and robed with a train held by a dozen pages, led the procession out of the Granovitaya Palace down the Red Staircase. They crossed the square outside on a red carpet, beside which countless spectators from all classes were gathered.

The interior of the cathedral glowed with light from hundreds of candles, reflected on the gilded frescoes that covered every inch of the walls and pillars. The iconostasis before the altar glittered with gold and silver and a mass of jewels. In front of it Empress Marie took her place on a throne, "alone, pale and serious-looking, with sad eyes, that reminded the onlookers that her own coronation had been not many years before."[5] All then turned to see the entrance of the imperial couple. Nicholas, in miltary uniform, and Alexandra, wearing a silver court dress, sat down on two thrones, the throne of Tsar Alexis, covered in hundreds of diamonds, and the Ivory Throne, brought as a dowry centuries earlier from Byzantium.

For hours the choir sung the stirring chants as the bishops held a high mass amid the heady smell of incense. Throughout the ceremony, Alexandra never tired in the least, as Elizabeth noted later, for "everything was so beautiful. It seemed to her to be a kind of mystic marriage to Russia. She became one with Russia, sealed forever a Russian in heart and soul."[6] The tsar and tsaritsa were robed, and Nicholas knelt alone and prayed to God "to direct, counsel and guide him in his high service as Tsar and judge of of the Russian Empire, to keep his heart in the will of God, to help him so to order all to the good of his people and the glory of God, that at the day of Judgement he may answer without shame."[7] He was anointed and swore to rule Russia and uphold its autocracy. Then he stepped up to the altar and took the communion in his own hands, the only occasion on which, as head of the Orthodox Church, he was allowed to do so. These mystical rites reinforced his conviction that God had entrusted him with an inalienable responsibility for Russia's fate, and that he was a vehicle for the divine will. But by chance as he stepped up to the altar the chain of the order of St. Andrew, Russia's patron saint, slipped from his shoulders and fell to the ground. This seemed an ill omen, and all who saw it were sworn to secrecy.

Tsar Nicholas then took the crown from the metropolitan and placed it on his head with his own hands.* His wife knelt before him, and he removed the crown and touched it gently on her forehead. He placed a second crown on her head, and they sat on their thrones to receive the homage of the imperial family. When Elizabeth's turn came, she noticed that some malicious onlookers were waiting to see if she would kiss her sister's hand. "Why, it was a real joy," she later wrote to Queen Victoria.[8]

At the end of the service the tsar and tsaritsa, crowned and robed, headed a procession of the imperial family and the foreign princes to the Kremlin Palace. As she emerged from the cathedral, Elizabeth saw a vast crowd gathered in the Kremlin square. Nicholas, his mother, and Alexandra, underneath ornate canopies held by court chamberlains, ascended to the head of the Red Staircase. They turned and solemnly bowed three times in greeting to their subjects. From all sides and in the streets beyond the crowd erupted into a deafening cheer. Above the din the bells rang out from hundreds of churches, and cannon roared in salute. Nicholas had no doubt that his people acclaimed him truly as their father-tsar and autocrat.

There followed a coronation banquet in a form unchanged for

centuries. The imperial family and thousands of guests were gathered in Granovitaya Palace. At each table on a parchment the menu was written in illuminated medieval Cyrillic script. In one room were gathered several humble Russians in plain peasant dress. They were the descendants, present by hereditary right, of those who had saved the lives of past tsars. The most renowned of these had been an old servant who had refused under torture to tell the Poles where the first Romanov tsar was hidden. All the guests could look down from balconies into another room, richly decorated with medieval frescoes, where a scene worthy of a historical play was being enacted. Under a gilded canopy, Nicholas and Alexandra, still crowned and robed, dined alone on golden plates, waited on by the highest court officials.[9]

Just after dusk, the whole of Moscow was lit up in fairy-tale manner. Elizabeth's brother and all her sisters were present on the terrace of the Kremlin overlooking Red Square for the inauguration of the illuminations. So were two of the daughters of Queen Victoria's son Prince Alfred, Missy, the crown princess of Romania, and Ducky, Ernest's wife, brilliantly dressed in cloth of gold. Elizabeth stole much of the attention, "looking especially magnificent," Baroness Buxhoeveden wrote, "in a Court dress of cream velvet embroidered with gold fuchsias."[10] Alexandra stepped forward and pressed a button hidden in a bunch of roses. At that moment the entire Kremlin was lit up in a blaze of thousands of bulbs in different colors, and floodlights threw beams into the sky. The population gazed up in awe.

A ball which exceeded even those of St. Petersburg in splendor was held in the Kremlin that night. "There were tiaras," Robert Massie has written, "necklaces, bracelets, rings and earrings, some with stones as big as robins' eggs." Elizabeth, covered in emeralds, attracted many admiring glances. Other women wore masses of sapphires and rubies. Around her waist Alexandra wore a thick girdle studded with diamonds. Nicholas had an immense collar of diamond clusters reaching down to his chest.

Even on such a resplendent day, the jewels aroused astonishment.[11]

There was another cause for celebration. The prince of Naples, heir to the Italian throne, had met Princess Helena of Montenegro at the governor's palace. The two had become engaged under Elizabeth's roof. That night the grand duchess retired to bed exhausted but content.

Four days later, on the morning of May 30, Elizabeth looked out and saw a seemingly endless procession of carts bearing dead and wounded bodies along Tverskaya Street. These were the victims of a disaster at Khodinsky Field on the outskirts of Moscow. On this wide plain, normally a parade ground, plays, dancing, and the coronation fête were to be held that day. From a row of wooden booths the tsar's traditional gifts of sweets and cups, each embossed with the imperial eagle, were to be distributed to the population. During the night thousands of peasants had arrived from all over Russia to encamp on the plain. By dawn they numbered more than half a million, and the Muscovites streamed in toward the booths by a rough track leading from the city.

At that point a rumor spread that the gifts were being handed out and that the Muscovites would take the lot. The crowd surged forward; there were few police and no barriers to control them. The officials hastily began to hand out the gifts. Noticing this, those at the edge pressed further forward, and hundreds were squashed together in the middle. Panic-stricken screams could be heard. Masses were trampled underfoot in the crush around the booths. Troops were called in, but had to cut through the crowd to get at the center. Thousands were killed from suffocation, and far more wounded by the soldiers. Sir Donald Mackensie saw the scene the following morning and said, "it was a sight more terrible than a battlefield."[12]

"The Emperor and Empress," a London journalist wrote, "were

terribly distressed by the news of the awful catastrophe, but subsequently took their places in the Imperial pavilion, and the fête proceeded to its end, for the sake of the survivors and in the interests of public order, even while the works of removing the injured and the dead was still going on."[13]

It was a shock for the imperial family. The emperor's impulse was to retreat into a monastery and pray. Elizabeth was grieved by the oppressive sight of the bodies being carted past the governor's palace. "Aunt Ella was in despair," said her cousin Missy, Crown Princess of Romania.[14] Elizabeth made every effort to help. She steeled herself to tour the hospitals and try to console the injured victims. She and Serge visited the wounded every day. They gave generous provisions for the families of the dead.[15]

Elizabeth had to face the fact that the husband she still half-loved was blamed for the disaster. His numerous Moscow enemies were quick to condemn him, and dubbed him "Duke of Khodinka."[16] It was said that he had ordered the police away from the plain, allowing the riot to occur. Grand Duke Alexander Mikhailovich and his three brothers, long united in their hatred for their cousin, accused him of negligence. Serge offered the new emperor his resignation, which was refused. An inquiry was set up, and Serge's brothers, Vladimir and Paul, declared that they would leave the court if Serge suffered in any way. Instead, Serge was exonerated, and the chief of police, Colonel Vlasovsky, was found to have failed to carry out his orders and was dismissed.†[17]

One event strongly established the image in court circles of Serge's cruelty. The night after the disaster, a grand ball was to be held by the French ambassador in the emperor's honor. Nicholas felt that it would be an act of appalling callousness to be dancing so soon after the disaster at Khodinka. It was expected that the ball would be called off. But Serge and his brothers prevailed on the emperor and empress to attend, in order not to offend Russia's greatest ally. The imperial couple, sick at heart, did so with the greatest reluctance.[18]

The tragedy was taken by thousands of Russians as an omen that the new reign would be unhappy. Elizabeth was never to forget that day. In public she loyally supported her husband. "Dieu merci Sergei n'a rien à faire dans tout cela!"‡ she told Nicholas's sister Xenia.[19] In private she could never be entirely free from the thought that Serge could have prevented the tragedy. She had seen for herself signs of his callous indifference. On the day of the disaster he had arranged for a group photograph with some officers of the Preobrazhensky Regiment who were staying with him. The officers had dispersed, feeling that photography would be inappropriate. Serge had called them back, and the session had gone ahead in the courtyard of the governor's palace. On the same day he had refused to visit Khodinka.[20]

With some mental strain she kept up a front of polite amiability during the remaining receptions, balls, and reviews. It was a relief when the foreign princes left on June 7. She was now able to retire to Ilinskoe with the imperial family and her sisters and her brother. The Hessian family was reunited on a rural estate much like Wolfsgarten. Elizabeth was able to take her family to visit again the neighbors they had met in 1890.

Although they had all arrived "under a cloud of sadness and premonition" after the tragedy, they tried to forget it and assume a holiday mood. The more callow of the younger guests let their high spirits roam free. Missy challenged a young officer to a daredevil ride in the woods, and during a prank had to be saved by her brother from drowning in the river. Her sister Ducky flirted with Grand Duke Cyril. "Amusement followed amusement," Missy later wrote, "it was a period of buoyant, almost mad gaiety, a giddy whirl of enjoyment."[21] Serge, wanting his guests to celebrate, insisted on providing theatricals and concerts. Next door, at Archangelskoe, the Youssoupovs held entertainments of still greater opulence. At one the Italian Opera performed in their private theater, the whole pit of which had been filled with roses. After a supper on a terrace, lit by tall candelabra, the guests watched a dazzling display of fireworks.[22]

After the grandeur of the Russian coronation, Elizabeth and Serge traveled to England the following year to witness a display of the British Empire's might. Early in June 1897 they arrived at Windsor Castle a few days before Queen Victoria's diamond jubilee. For Elizabeth, it was like returning to her old home. She could remember running along the corridors of the castle as a girl of seven while the queen had tried to work in her study. All her playmates of that time were here now, except Eddy, the duke of Clarence. She was reunited with the queen, who had often dispensed a mother's advice during her stays there as a young woman. On June 20, Elizabeth and Irene breakfasted with their grandmother, as they had done many years before. All the family joined the queen in a service at St. George's Chapel, and at the end they kissed her in a private congratulation of her sixty years on the throne.[23]

The following day they left for London to see the celebrations of the greatest empire the world had ever known. Kings and princes had come from all Europe and Asia to pay their respects to the queen in a ceremony at Buckingham Palace. Among the many opulent gifts from visitors was "a beautiful diamond pendant with sapphires, and the date with Slavonic characters on it" from Elizabeth and Serge. On June 22, the foreign princess took part in the procession to St. Paul's Cathedral. Crowds from all over the British Empire thronged the streets. They gave deafening cheers to the symbol of their unity, who had dedicated her life to acting as their sovereign. "A never-to-be-forgotten day," the queen wrote in her diary. "No-one ever, I believe, has met with such an ovation as was given to me. . . ."[24]

Elizabeth could honor her grandmother's triumph, and respected her all the more for the loyalty she commanded by her devotion to her duties. But when the time came for parting from her, she feared that the queen would not live much longer. They both felt that they would not meet again.[25]

## Notes to Chapter 13

*He did so by tradition, as head of the Orthodox Church and autocrat, by divine right, of Russia, The Orthodox Church had no single head (on earth) equivalent to a pope, but was a collection of independent national units; in Russia the tsar was head of both church and state. Until the reign of Peter the Great there had been a chief ecclesiastical figure in the patriarch of Moscow; thereafter the three metropolitans of Moscow, St. Petersburg, and Kiev were preeminent, ranking higher than archbishops and bishops.

†The partial cause of the tragedy was a dispute between the Moscow administration and the Ministry of the Imperial Court, headed by Count I. I. Vorontsov-Dashkov, over the management of the coronation festivities. Opponents of Count Vorontsov-Dashkov, such as General Kireev, argued that the ministry had shown great inefficiency, and tactlessly insisted on taking over the supervision of the entire coronation. Grand Duke Alexander Mikhailovich, on the other hand, asserted that Serge had never troubled to take any crowd-control precautions.

Exactly who was to blame will never be known. Certainly more foresight from both parties in crowd control could have prevented the catastrophe. A warning had come from the previous coronation, when thirty-two people had been crushed to death at the same place. It was ignored to the extent that only sixty men were present to control the crowd of some half-million that gathered on the plain. It was clear that both Count Vorontsov-Dashkov, and especially Grand Duke Serge, were arrogant, tactless personalities who were so convinced of their own superiority that they took little trouble over the arrangements. Serge's contemptuous attitude toward the common Muscovites probably contributed much toward his negligence. As Count von der Pahlen, who headed the investigation into the tragedy, sadly concluded, "whenever a Grand Duke was given a responsible post there was sure to be trouble."

‡Thank God Serge has nothing to do with all this!

# Chapter 14

⌒

*The Karenins, husband and wife, continued living in the same house, and met every day, but they were wholly estranged.*

—TOLSTOY, *ANNA KARENINA*

As Queen Victoria's reign was coming to a close, Elizabeth and Serge befriended the new generation that was coming of age in Russia. Every summer they would invite Dmitri and Marie, the children of Serge's brother, Grand Duke Paul, to stay at Ilinskoe. Since the death of their mother Alexandra after giving birth to Dmitri, they had felt an obligation to the two children, who at the ages of six and seven were just emerging from infancy. A play-room and bedrooms were set aside for the children's use, who had begun to feel that Ilinskoe was their second home, and the servants regarded them as children of the house.

Early in the summer the children would arrive in a gleeful holiday mood. Serge would take them in his arms, and they would run to Elizabeth and kiss her hands as she leaned to embrace them. Each morning Serge would take them on a tour of the farm. Elizabeth would join them for coffee after her morning stroll. After their lessons the children would race down to the river to bathe. They would rejoin their uncle and aunt for lunch. If they failed to make polite conversation to a guest, Serge would scold them severely. In the afternoon, while Serge took his nap and Elizabeth painted or read in the shade of the garden, the children would drive about the estate in their carriage hauled by ponies or mules.[1]

But while Serge loved them wholeheartedly, Elizabeth felt a barrier of reserve between her and the children. Once when Marie complimented her on a fine dress, she reproved the nanny for allowing her niece to make personal remarks. On another occasion Marie saw her in full court dress and kissed her devotedly on the back of the neck. "She said nothing," Marie later wrote, "but I could see her eyes, and the cold hard look in them chilled me to the heart." Marie remembered only once seeing her aunt show her direct affection and concern. During a severe attack of diphtheria, Marie

> looked between half-opened lids and saw my aunt bend over me. Her expression astonished me; she was watching me with mingled curiosity and anxiety. It was the first time in my life that I had seen her face relaxed and natural. It was as if I had penetrated indiscreetly into the interior of her soul.[2]

The cause for Elizabeth's emotional rigidity was partly her English upbringing, which made expressing feelings difficult. To compound matters, Serge gave the children complete affection, which he could never show her. For by now their relations had cooled to a strained fondness. Serge's recent display of callousness during the Khodinsky Field disaster had driven them further apart. Serge was beginning to sneer at the refuge she found in religion. As Marie later recalled, he

> regarded with anxiety his wife's increasing absorption in things spiritual, and ended by regarding it as immoderate.
>
> He treated her rather as if she were a child. I believe that she was hurt by his attitude and longed to be better understood, but it was as if she were being driven deeper and deeper within herself for refuge. She and my uncle seemed never

very intimate. They met for the most part only at
meals and by day avoided being alone together.[3]

For Elizabeth, this fragile relationship could only be made
more painful by the intrusion of the two children. Their presence in the house also reminded her acutely that she was childless.

She loved children, as one young visitor wrote: "It is a pity she
has no children of her own—when once you have seen her at a
children's party, you know what a mother she would have made."[4]
As if to make up for her loss she held many children's parties at
Ilinskoe. The sons of Elizabeth's friend Princess Zenaide
Youssoupova, Felix and Nicholas, visited from Archangelskoe,
and Felix became a close friend of Dmitri. John and
Constantine,* the sons of the Grand Duke Constantine, joined in
their games. Their infant brother Igor might be there to one side,
still learning to walk.[5] Anna Tanayeva, the daughter of a gifted
court composer, used to come from her family's nearby estate.

Elizabeth spoiled and petted all her young guests. After a lavish tea, she would let them run around the house searching for
toys which she had hidden. Or they would hunt for mushrooms
in the endless woods. All but Marie doted on Elizabeth. "I can
hardly remember a time I did not know and love the Grand
Duchess Elizabeth," Anna was to write. She was awed by her first
sight of Empress Alexandra, whom she was later to know well, at
one of these parties. "My childish impression of her was of a tall,
slender, graceful woman, with a wealth of golden hair and eyes
like stars, the very picture of what an Empress should be."[6]

The young Felix Youssoupov was also attached to the grand
duchess. Her and Serge's visits to his family's estate of Rakitnoe
near Kursk were to become an indelible memory of his childhood. In the late summer they came to the estate for the excel-
lent shooting. The shooting party would travel deep into the forest in enormous carriages, called *lineiki*. On the way Serge would
compel Felix to sing his favorite Italian song, *Eyes Filled with Tears,*

so often that Felix grew to detest it. He never liked Serge, finding his strange manners and his habit of staring at him discon-
certing. He would get his revenge by fingering at Serge's bone
corsets in curiosity, to Serge's intense annoyance. Among the
shooting guests was the shortsighted General Bernov, who often
mistook a cow for a deer. Prince Youssoupov was obliged to take
away his gun after he shot at and wounded a beater. In the
evening, Felix was sent to bed after supper while the guests
remained downstairs playing cards, but could not sleep until
Elizabeth had come to say good night. "She blessed me and
kissed me, and I was filled with a pleasant peace and went quietly to sleep." From his earliest childhood, he recalled, he loved
and revered her as a second mother.[7]

It seemed that Elizabeth's own and the older generation of
European royalty were dying off. In 1899, Elizabeth and Serge
witnessed a small tragedy while on one of their periodic visits to
Germany. They stayed at the Gotha Castle near Coburg, the
home of the ancestors of Elizabeth's grandfather, Prince Albert;
surrounding it were the woods in which Albert had loved to
roam as a boy. Here lived Elizabeth's uncle Alfred, duke of Saxe-
Coburg and Gotha, who as a child had wept at Princess Alice's
wedding, and his wife. Their son, Alfred, lay upstairs, pale and
gravely ill from consumption. Soon his condition had deteriorated to the point that he had to be sent away for a cure. His
death came as a shock to the entire company. As his coffin was
brought back to Gotha, they heard the peal of church bells and
the muffled tones of a funeral march. The duchess, always
devout, "sank to her knees, crossing herself, and burst into
tears."[8]

From all over Europe, news came of other deaths. The duke of
Saxe-Coburg died from cancer. Elizabeth's aunt Vicky, the
empress Frederick of Germany, was thrown from her horse.
Consulting a doctor, she was told she had cancer, and ended her

sad life with two years of agonizing pain. King Humbert of Italy was assassinated. Empress Elizabeth of Austria was stabbed in the back at Geneva. She struggled onto a lake steamer with the knife still in place, and died. Her sister burned to death in a fire at a charity bazaar in Paris. On January 13, 1901, Queen Victoria made her last entry in her diary.

The old queen died at Osborne on January 22. Many of her children and grandchildren were gathered at her bedside. Elizabeth's sister Victoria and Louis of Battenberg were present, and Emperor William had hurried from Germany in a special train, driving the engine himself.† After the sun had gone down, while William was supporting the pillow with his good hand, and Alexandra, princess of Wales, kneeling in prayer, was holding the queen's hand, she took her last breath.[9]

For Elizabeth, it felt as though she had lost a second mother. Many years earlier she had written to the queen:[10] "It is such a happiness to know that you care for us like your children and we have felt your great kindness to us all very much—If dear Mama was living how happy it would make her to see all your kindness to us. . . ." Over the years, despite their disagreements, the queen had poured out advice to Elizabeth in a continual stream of letters and done much to shape her sense of duty and strength of character. She had lost the last link with her parents' generation that had guided her in her faraway childhood scenes of Darmstadt, Windsor, and Balmoral.

It also seemed to Elizabeth that her generation of royalty had lost the custodian of the strict morality that Queen Victoria had come to personify. Soon Elizabeth came to hear of divorces that would have been inconceivable in her grandmother's lifetime. The first happened to her brother Ernest, whose failing marriage had been apparent for some time. He and Victoria Melita, "Ducky," had been unsuited for each other from the beginning. She had been conspicuously friendly with Grand Duke Cyril during the coronation festivities in Moscow. The queen had forbidden them a divorce, but months after her death Ducky wrote to her husband asking for one. They parted in December 1901, leaving Ernest with the frail seven-year-old daughter, Elizabeth. In 1907 Ducky would marry Cyril, and they would be banished from Russia; not until 1909 would the emperor allow them to return, which caused Elizabeth much sorrow. Even though she sympathized with her brother, she regarded marriage as an irrevocable tie and a sacrament of the church.[11] Her own pains and disappointment had in no way lessened her conviction.

She was therefore shocked to hear of another scandal. In August 1902 it emerged that Serge's brother Paul was in a dilemma over whether to marry his mistress, a beautiful divorcée called Mme. Pistolkors, and legitimize their infant son, Volodya. When Elizabeth and Serge visited Tsarskoe, they found him distraught and irritable. Over a family dinner with Paul's children, Dmitri and Marie, he and Serge had a heated argument. As they rose, Serge assumed a forced smile and said, "My boy, you are simply in a very bad mood; you ought to take better care of yourself." Elizabeth cast an anxious look at Paul's children.

A few days later Paul fled abroad.[12] Some months afterward Elizabeth and Serge learned with shock that he had secretly married his mistress in Rome. Traveling again to Tsarskoe Selo, they found the emperor and empress in a state of indignation. Nicholas feared that soon a whole colony of decadent grand dukes and their mistresses would be living in Paris. To Alexandra, Paul was committing a veiled form of adultery. It was decided that he must be exiled from Russia and deprived of his official revenues. Elizabeth and Serge also saw his two children, now aged eleven and twelve. Elizabeth in particular was sad and downcast at the thought that they would barely see their father again. She and Serge left for Rome, where Serge formally told his brother of his banishment. Henceforth he and Elizabeth, it was agreed, were to bring up Marie and Dmitri.

Back in Russia, it fell to them to inform the children. They were both, Marie later recalled, "overcome with sorrow; they cried over us for a long time." Over an untouched tea, they told them that in the spring they would move permanently to Moscow. Serge, however, could not conceal his glee at having the children to himself. "It is I who am now your father," he repeated to them, "and you are my children!" Dmitri and Marie stared blankly at him, and said nothing.[13]

The new family spent a subdued Christmas at Neskuchnoe. The mood was no more cheerful when Elizabeth and Serge settled into life with their new foster children. Despite the children's obvious sense of loss, Elizabeth was unable to relax her awkward reserve in their presence. Serge's open affection for Marie and Dmitri could only emphasize the aloof condescension he expressed to her. The children, equally resenting Serge's proprietorial attitude, still yearned to see their father. Almost a year would pass before Serge grudgingly allowed a reunion with Grand Duke Paul in Germany. The children's delight at meeting him caused Serge much annoyance. He loudly reminded his brother that he had full rights over them as their guardian.[14]

If adopting a new family was one source of concern for Elizabeth, another was her sister's growing reclusiveness and her involvement with eccentric, self-appointed religious mystics. For by now the imperial couple were coming to regard the grand court ceremonies with distaste. Their inexperience and Alexandra's shyness made the events an ordeal, and they both preferred their private family world at Tsarskoe Selo in their two vast palaces set in an eight-hundred-acre park. There they were isolated by fifteen miles from the malicious gossip and social whirl of St. Petersburg. In this seclusion Alexandra had become increasingly absorbed in religion; the intense religiosity she had inherited from her mother had begun to emerge. On taking the momentous step of converting to Orthodoxy, she had embraced her new faith with complete devotion, hoping thereby to immerse herself in the true spirit of Russia. Along with the peasantry and the benevolent rule of an autocratic tsar, she regarded the Orthodox religion as all that was noblest in her new country. She was receptive to the mysticism then fashionable in St. Petersburg, and believed certain "holy fools" to be divinely inspired. A monk, Koliaba, prone to epileptic fits, was rumored to have had visions. She had taken him seriously after his prophecy that she would bear a son.[15]

But on June 18, 1901, Koliaba's prediction was proved false by the birth of yet another girl. After the birth of Olga, Tatiana, and Marie, Nicholas and Alexandra still had hopes of producing another heir. The arrival of Anastasia seemed to defeat them. Elizabeth and the dowager Empress Marie were present when Nicholas heard the news. Saying nothing, the emperor turned about and started on a long and solitary walk through the park at Tsarskoe Selo.[16]

When Alexandra began to receive M. Philippe, a Frenchman who was fond of occult medicine, Elizabeth became aware of the dangers in her sister's credulity. For all her fervent devotion to Orthodoxy, Elizabeth retained a shrewd judgment of character. She became suspicious of the secrecy that surrounded Philippe's visits to Tsarskoe Selo, and feared his malign influence. Knowing well Alexis's obstinacy in religious matters, she decided to broach the subject with Nicholas. During a carriage ride around the park at Tsarskoe, she abandoned her affectionate tone and resorted to forthright questioning. She had heard many unfavorable rumors that Philippe was not to be trusted, she said, and she wanted to get at the truth. The whole affair had been veiled in secrecy; did he and Alix see him often? She thought it strange that a foreigner should exercise a spiritual influence over the governor of the Russian Church and his wife. Nicholas replied with evasive platitudes, but Elizabeth's searching questions struck home. Soon afterward Philippe returned to France.[17]

This was not the end of Alexandra's religiosity. In 1902, she had visited the shrine of a hermit called Seraphim at Sarovo in the province of Tambov. In the early nineteenth century Seraphim had spent his last years under a vow of silence in the wilderness, and experienced many spiritual visions. Alexandra, not doubting his holiness, did all she could to get him canonized, and inquiries were set in motion by the Holy Synod. On the opening of his tomb the corpse was found to have rotted away like any other mortal's,[18] but still, the process went ahead. In July 1903, on the way to the canonization ceremony, the imperial train drew into Arzamas, two hundred miles east of Moscow. With the imperial couple were Serge and Elizabeth. For Elizabeth the ceremonies were to be a landmark in her religious life.

At the station the imperial party boarded some troikas for the six-hour journey to Sarovo. With only a Cossack escort for protection, they passed thousands of pilgrims from all over Russia walking in the heat and dust. At each village the emperor disembarked to receive the blessing of the parish priest. A vast crowd of peasant pilgrims surrounded him, all struggling to kiss his hand, his sleeve, or his shoulder. He was truly a father-tsar in the midst of his people. It was an identity he cherished, which moved Elizabeth and all who saw it.

The night was spent at a monastery deep in the pine woods. The next day the emperor, Grand Duke Serge, and some cousins bore the remains of Seraphim on their shoulders from a humble grave in the abbey cemetery. It was taken in procession to the new golden-domed shrine. Constant prayers, litanies, and psalms were sung over the tomb.[19]

The High Mass of the canonization lasted four hours; darkness had fallen by its end. Some 300,000 pilgrims, every one bearing a lighted candle, had gathered outside. As the imperial party left the church, they saw the monastery grounds filled to the limit by a silent multitude standing or kneeling in prayer. As they left the grounds, there was an even greater throng with a vast array of lighted candles stretching into the distance. "Chanting voices arose from various places, but the singers could not be seen, and the voices seemed to come from heaven itself. . . ." The singing could be heard throughout the night.[20]

Elizabeth was caught up in this heady atmosphere of faith and spiritual exultation. She saw the thousands of pilgrims, many sick and crippled, bathing in the river nearby in hope of being cured. "Oh what misery and what illnesses we saw, and what faith!" she wrote to her sister Victoria. "It seemed as if we were living in Christ's time. . . . Oh how they prayed, how they cried, those poor mothers with sick children. . . ."[21] She saw what seemed to be miracles. A dumb girl suddenly found the gift of speech as her mother prayed with passion. A paralyzed girl was dipped in the waters, and then walked up the bank. A doctor affirmed her cure to be genuine.[22]

All this left a deep mark on Elizabeth. Her piety was strengthened by a profound faith. She had long believed fervently in the supernatural elements of Christianity, and now they seemed to be confirmed before her own eyes. The experience was the capstone on a belief that she had built up since her childhood. She was prevented only by her marriage and her duties from dedicating herself to a life of Christian self-abnegation. A few years later she was to write to Emperor Nicholas: ". . . and always more and more it grew in me, only being in a position where our *duty* was to receive, to see heaps of people, to give receptions, dinners, balls and . . . it could not fill *entirely* my life, *other* duties *having to go before.*"[23]

Despite her obligations, Elizabeth began to display to her family and friends a reinforced compassion and a greater sense of humility. In the fall of 1903 she heard that her brother Ernest's daughter Elizabeth had died of typhoid. Heartbroken, Ernest laid her small corpse in the Rosenhöhe alongside his mother Alice, Grand Duke Louis, and his sister May.[24] In sympathy Elizabeth wrote a letter:

> My darling boy,
>
> My whole heart and soul are with you. . . . Each time I draw nearer to you and it seems to me in you I can find much that I feel myself—I have been spared those awful moral sorrows which come alas into your life; yet the foundation of our

characters has something alike—but you stand on
the higher steps of the ladder to heaven and I am
still below, I am trying hard to get up but seem
always to slip down again and it did me good to see
how you have slowly and finally got all—sorrow
has purified your soul and heart which were thank
God always childlike but have got more perfect.
Keep that, dear Boy, it is that which Christ says we
must have. . . .[25]

Yet few outside Elizabeth's immediate circle could perceive the
renewed strength of her faith. On her occasional visits to St.
Petersburg she still appeared to the beau monde as the radiant
princess that had captured their attention two decades before.
Now in her late thirties, she had retained her looks, which she
had shown them at their most magnificent early in 1903, when
she and Serge attended a costume ball at the Winter Palace. It
was one of the most spectacular festivities ever staged there. The
several hundred guests were dressed in seventeenth-century costume, most of them representing their own ancestors, and wore
priceless jewels inherited from the appropriate period. The
emperor, dressed as Tsar Alexei, wore his ancestor's headdress,
usually stored in the Kremlin. The empress, at the height of her
beauty, was dressed as Alexei's consort, in "gold brocade with silver design," and a jewel-studded, miter-shaped headdress.[26]
Grand Duke Alexander Mikhailovich, dressed as a court falcon-
er, danced almost every one of the old Russian dances with
Princess Zenaide Youssoupova, the old flame of his youth whom
he thought one of the two most beautiful women present.[27] The
other was of course Elizabeth. All considered her the finest of all
in a brilliant dress fashioned by a modern designer.

In the fall of 1903 Elizabeth made an appearance before an
even grander audience. With Serge she traveled to Darmstadt,
where her sister Victoria was proudly presiding over the marriage
of her daughter, Princess Alice, to Prince Andrew of Greece.‡ It

was an opportunity for a reunion with relatives from all over Europe. The Russian emperor and empress came from Tsarskoe Selo, Queen Alexandra, representing her husband Bertie, King Edward VII, from England, Elizabeth's sister Irene and her husband, Prince Henry, from Kiel, Emperor William from Berlin, and King George and Queen Marie of Greece arrived with a large contingent. The preliminaries included a gala performance at the theater. Here the queens and princesses could display their beauty at its most splendid. Queen Alexandra looked as lovely as ever underneath a brilliant tiara. But her attendant, Lord Gosford, thought that Elizabeth and Empress Alexandra had stolen the show. Staring up at their box, he said that he was looking at the two most beautiful creatures in the world.[28]

Even while she reveled in this attention, Elizabeth may have sensed that this would be the last great European royal wedding at which she would shine. Already she could feel the approach of a storm that would sweep away the dynasties whose members were gathered there. Since the turn of the century she had been aware of a seditious spirit and a brooding disquiet in Russia. Revolutionary politics had begun to infect the universities. In February 1901 a student had killed Bogolepov, the minister of education; a year later another had killed Sipyagin, the interior minister.[29] The countryside had begun to stir after years of quiescence. In 1898, famine had again struck, and the peasantry, overcrowded on their land,§ desperately poor from the primitive agriculture they practiced, taxed to the hilt, had begun to be restive. In 1902, believing that their tsar had ordered the land to be given to them, they had gone on a rampage, burning manor houses, stealing the landlords' grain and sometimes their land.[30]

The situation had appeared to be so chaotic that Elizabeth was compelled to make a rare political intervention. Despite the liberal principles she had inherited from Alice, she sensed that only a rigorous, even ruthless enforcement of the law could prevent anarchy. Nicholas was vacillating over a new interior minister to replace the murdered Sipyagin. Out of an affectionate concern

for her nephew and fear for her country, Elizabeth urged a ruthless punishment for terrorists and suggested a new minister. In
Serge's absence, she wrote a hasty and excited letter:

> Darling Boy—dearest child—let me call you so
> and let an *old heart* pour out its *prayers* before you.
> . . .
>
> Sergei does not know of this letter, it will proba-
> bly be unlogical and overfeminine, but I have
> *picked other brains* and kept my *ears* open and as we
> hear much and through clever, devoted people
> with experience and love for *their sovereign* and
> country I thought who knows *even* a woman can be
> of use in heavy times.
>
> Nicky dear, for heaven's sake be energetic now,
> more deaths may be in store . . . put an end to
> this time of terror—forgive if I write *straight out*
> without phrases and as if I were dictating, I don't
> expect your doing what I say. I only put it so in
> case these ideas might be of use to you. I would
> have *directly* named your new minister, every day
> your looks will do harm—why not Pleve [sic] who
> has experience and is honest. Don't be so gen-
> tle—*all* think you are *wavering and weak,* they *no
> more* speak of you as *kind* and it makes my heart
> ache so bitterly.
>
> I fear I must be cruel and say more . . . a *firm
> decision counterordered* is worse than none at all, it
> becomes *fatal* and now this new sorrow—oh, is it
> really not possible to *judge* such brutes with a
> drum-head court? And let all Russia know that
> such *crimes* are punishable by *death*. . . .[31]

Yet Elizabeth had only a weak grasp of politics, a subject Serge
never discussed with her. Her recommendation of Plehve to
Nicholas proved to be an ill-informed error. Plehve's ineptitude
only exacerbated the situation. In the summer of 1903 much of

southern Russia was paralyzed by a wave of strikes; some 160,000 troops were called in to suppress the strikers' demonstrations.[32]

Regretting her rash advice, Elizabeth spent Christmas of 1903 with Serge and the imperial couple at Tsarskoe Selo. The festivities were dampened by Alexandra's ill health; she had contracted influenza, and was unable to participate in the social whirl of the new year's "season." The mood was not helped by the tense atmosphere of unrest that could still be felt in Russia. Elizabeth could recall with unease a visit she and Serge had made at Sarovo in the summer. According to a story still told by the Romanov family, they walked deep into the woods to meet an elderly hermit who told Serge: "You will be killed, and your head will be crushed to atoms."[33]

Unbeknownst to Elizabeth or Serge, this prediction began to be fulfilled as the underground revolutionary movement gathered strength. The Russian Social Democratic Party, an outlawed organization based on the doctrines of Karl Marx, held a conference in London in an attempt to heal its divisions. A vote was taken on a technicality, and was won by the adherents of an intransigent revolutionary policy. The faction came to be known as the "men of the majority," or "Bolsheviks"; their leader was Vladimir Ulyanov, who called himself Lenin.[34]

Lenin's aim was to turn the party into a tightly disciplined clique of full-time revolutionaries, composed of middle-class intellectuals such as himself. He had no time for the workers, and believed that efforts to improve their living conditions would only allay their discontent. During the famine of 1891 he had dissuaded his friends from following Elizabeth's example in raising money for its victims. Hunger, he said, "forms a progressive function"; it would "cause the peasants to reflect on the fundamental facts of capitalist society."[35] Christian charity was alien to Lenin, unlike his mother, a doctor's daughter, and his father, a school inspector, who were both devoutly Orthodox. He later declared that he had been an atheist since the age of sixteen; in that year, 1886, he saw his father die in front of him from a stroke. The following year his idealistic elder brother Alexander was hanged for taking part in an assassination attempt on the tsar.

A little later, Lenin embraced Marxism with the fervor of a religious convert. Having studied law, he joined a firm in St. Petersburg, and soon became a prominent figure in the Social Democratic Party. In 1895 he was arrested for importing subversive literature, imprisoned for fifteen months, and exiled for three years to Siberia, where he lived like a leisured country gentleman, reading and shooting duck. His sentence ended, he migrated abroad, and worked for the Social Democratic Party as an underground organizer and writer of revolutionary pamphlets.[36] He was to remain in exile until 1917, apart from a brief spell in Russia in 1905. His Bolshevik followers were soon to be fomenting revolutionary discontent among the Moscow proletariat.

Another underground party, the Socialist Revolutionaries, were agitating among the peasants. Their program was revolutionary terrorism by assassination.

## Notes to Chapter 14

*Grand Duke Constantine Constantinovich, son of Grand Duke Constantine Nikolayevich, who was the brother of Emperor Alexander II.

†William was not the royal figure to insist on taking charge of a train. King Boris of Bulgaria, a lifelong railway enthusiast, often drove locomotives. A cousin of King Alfonso XIII of Spain would personally drive the royal locomotive on state visits abroad. Once, when the king was bidding a protracted farewell to the French president, his cousin's grimy figure appeared at the locomotive window and said, "Get a move on, Alfonso, we're late already."

‡Parents of H.R.H. Prince Philip, duke of Edinburgh.

§Few peasants had left their native villages after the abolition of serfdom in 1861. Some had drifted to the industrial towns, forming a very small urban proletariat, some had taken to trade, but for the majority there was little chance of social advancement. It was very rare for a peasant to rise to the rank of "gentleman" (dvoryanin), a privileged position granting, among other things, exemption from military service and the right to own landed estates. For this it was necessary to hold a high rank in the government bureaucracy, which only a minority of literate and hard-working peasants could attain. Entry into the aristocracy was only achieved by a handful of individuals who enjoyed the emperor's favor or rendered him some outstanding service.

# Chapter 15

*How on earth can one be a revolutionary, and not be a terrorist?*

—KALYAYEV

In February 1904, the Japanese ambassador made an unusually low bow to Emperor Nicholas as he left the Hermitage Theatre. Some diplomats who were present had an uneasy sense that he was making his farewell. Two days later, without a declaration of war, the Japanese Navy launched a surprise attack on the Russian base at Port Arthur on the Northern Chinese coast.

The war had been expected for some time, even if the sudden assault was a shock. Some years before, the Russians had secured Port Arthur, a coveted prize which, unlike Vladivostok further north, was free of ice. They had occupied Manchuria after a war against China, and hoped to enlarge their empire and gain prestige in the world by extending their hold on the northern Pacific coast. They had turned acquisitive eyes on the Korean peninsula, a tributary state of the decaying Chinese empire. The Japanese, regarding Korea as vital for their own security, had grown hostile, and sent a distinguished statesman, Count Ito, to negotiate. The Russians prevaricated for so long that eventually he gave up, and his government embarked on war.

The war against the Chinese had convinced the senior military figures in Russia that they could defeat any Asian enemy, and they imagined that a quick victory would serve to unite the country in a wave of patriotic fervor. The prestige of the army would be enhanced, the revolutionaries would lose ground, and the emperor would emerge from the conflict in a blaze of glory, his people's loyalty redoubled.

When war was declared, Elizabeth, Serge, Dmitri, and Marie attended a service in the Cathedral of the Assumption, where Emperor Nicholas and his predecessors had been crowned tsar. The packed congregation heard the archdeacon read out the manifesto of war in a deep and trembling voice. In the surge of patriotic emotion, no one present had any idea of the terrible events to come.

Elizabeth saw signs of the patriotic fervor on which the generals had counted. Every afternoon, her niece recalled, a crowd bearing flags and portraits of the imperial couple gathered outside the governor's palace, bared their heads, and loudly sung *God Save the Tsar*. Their enthusiasm grew each day, and they stayed longer and longer. Serge saw these patriotic demonstrations as the true voice of the people, and was reluctant to quell them. Soon, however, the crowd, delighted at this unexpected freedom of assembly, refused to disperse and leave the square. After a few weeks their demonstrations degenerated, in true Russian fashion, into raucous drunken revels. The last ended with broken bottles and stones thrown at the palace windows; Elizabeth could hear the drunken roars and murmurs that carried on through most of the night.[1]

As the governor's wife, Elizabeth was head of all the Red Cross organizations in Moscow. Another grand duchess might have treated it as an honorary title, but for Elizabeth it was a call to take on heavy duties. She organized a fleet of ambulance trains to carry home the wounded from Manchuria on the Trans-Siberian Railway. She busied herself with organizing workshops in the Kremlin. There she and her thirteen-year-old niece, Marie, joined women of all classes in preparing bandages and linen for the hospitals. Their task was so large that it came to occupy all the palace halls. When the wounded began to arrive from the front, she toured the hospitals, and gave words of comfort to each new arrival.[2]

She was indefatigable, and encouraged the women in the Kremlin by example, overcoming obstacles with a smiling patience and tact. Yet at every stage her orders were negligently obeyed, or not at all. She designed a uniform for the hospital nurses. One day her lady-in-waiting admiringly showed it to a government official: "Look! Her Imperial Highness has drawn the design for a uniform for the sisters. It is to her that we owe these practical clothes; we copied her designs exactly." The official hesitantly pointed out that the design had been copied wrongly.

He recalled, "This lady and the others, astonished at my remarks, protested, but the grand duchess was silent.

"Never shall I forget the look she gave me—so sweet, so penetrating and so certain. I understood that she was exactly of my opinion, but she did not want to contradict the other ladies."[3]

The slipshod incompetence Elizabeth encountered everywhere was repeated on an immense scale in the running of the war. The troops marched off to war, not with the revered icon of St. Nicholas which had seen the army through three hundred years of fighting, but that of St. Seraphim, whose corpse, recently uncovered for his canonization, had proved to be thoroughly rotten. "As an inspiration for the troops," Grand Duke Alexander wrote, "he proved a total failure."[4]

The Russians, completely unprepared, rushed their troops to Manchuria on the single-track Trans-Siberian Railway. At Lake Baikal, the ferry that should have transported them was frozen fast. Rails were laid over the ice; as the first train crossed, the engine sank into the water with a loud crack. The travel-weary troops arrived to face a fresh, highly trained Japanese army who outnumbered them three to one. They had little choice but to retreat.

At Port Arthur the Far Eastern Fleet, unnerved by the sudden Japanese attack, was in no state to mount an assault. The Japanese surrounded the port with mines, and the fleet stayed safely in the harbor. In April, the one truly competent Russian admiral, Makarov, led out a sortie as a preliminary to a full-scale offensive; he was drowned after a mine sunk his flagship. His successors did not have the nerve to carry on the action. On one occasion two of the six Japanese battleships struck mines off Port Arthur and sank. Instead of challenging the enemy fleet, an action which might have won the war in a day, the Russian admirals stayed put. It was then decided that the Baltic Fleet should be sent to the Far East as a reinforcement. It began an epic voyage which was to take it around the Cape of Good Hope. In the North Sea, secret Japanese torpedo attacks were expected, and the fleet outraged the British public by firing on some Newcastle trawlers.[5]

The population had been expecting a succession of easy victories. The defeats at the front and the obvious ineptitude of the commanders came as a severe blow to national morale. The war became ever more unpopular, and discontent with the government spread. The peasantry felt that the nobles' land was by right their own. The urban proletariat, enduring wretched living conditions, began to strike. The student population, poor and severely harassed by the government, took to demonstrating in the streets. The revolutionaries were quick to exploit their grievances.

The government had taken many countermeasures of their own. The secret police, an amazingly complicated organization, penetrated everywhere; in addition to the Okhrana, the main body, every ministry, even the Holy Synod, had its own spies. All high officials, as well as the imperial family, were closely shadowed to forestall any potential assassins. Thousands of letters were furtively examined and resealed, even, it was rumored, the emperor's own correspondence.[6]

To contain the militancy of the workers, Colonel Zubatov, formerly a Socialist, had organized trade unions which were secretly run by the police. In St. Petersburg, a workers' movement with a membership of thousands was led by a secret agent and Socialist priest called Father Gapon. It was found that the loyalty of the workers could only be assured if these unions fomented strikes. Zubatov also infiltrated agents provocateurs into the revolutionary movements.[7]

The most successsful of them was Evno Azev, the son of a Jewish tailor. While a desperately poor student, he had accepted money from the government for informing on revolutionary fellow students. He gradually infiltrated the Socialist Revolutionary Party, the dangerous terrorist movement which included many members of the self-styled "Will of the People" that had assassinated Alexander II. He won the confidence of Gershuni, the head of the party's Terrorist Brigade, who named him as his successor in the event of his being arrested. Azev informed on Gershuni, and took over the Terrorist Brigade after his arrest.

At Easter 1903, a horrific pogrom took place in Kishinev, not far from Azev's birthplace. For two days gangs of hooligans, primed with vodka, beat up and raped the Jewish inhabitants and destroyed and looted their property. The police stood by and arrested only the Jews who tried to defend themselves. Possibly some of the victims were Azev's relatives. From then on he held Plehve, the minister of the interior and head of his department, to be responsible. He turned traitor and planned Plehve's assassination, bluffing both the police and the terrorists.[8]

Azev enrolled a number of discontented university students for this purpose. Two of them, Savinkov and Kalyayev, were from Warsaw. Savinkov was a cynical adventurer who loved the thrill and danger of terrorism. He had little taste for ideology, and was prepared to work for anyone.* Kalyayev was a poet, a romantic who believed in the revolutionary ideas with a fanatical, almost religious fervor. To him, the idea of dying during an assassination attempt or of being executed for his beliefs was a heroic martyrdom.

After several failed attempts on Pehve's life, Azev met Savinkov, Kalyayev, and other conspirators in Moscow early in July 1904. It was decided that four men, including Kalyayev, should be the bomb throwers, and Savinkov should be in command. On July 28, they lay in wait for Plehve near the main Police Department building in St. Petersburg, barely a hundred yards from Elizabeth's palace on the Nevsky Prospect. The bomb was thrown; Plehve was instantly killed and dismembered. The bloodstained horses bolted with the shattered remnants of his carriage. Azev, waiting in Warsaw to cover his involvement from his government paymasters, read of the murder in a newspaper. His hands trembled, and he nearly fainted from relief.

The terrorists then made their way abroad, and in Paris Azev presided over a clandestine conference. New murders were decided on, and bombs were prepared in a secret factory. Azev, it seemed, had not forgotten the expulsion of the Jews from Moscow in 1891. He directed Savinkov and Kalyayev to go to that city and assassinate Grand Duke Serge.[9]

On August 12, 1904, while the conspirators were discussing their murderous plans abroad, Alexandra gave birth to a son. A number of ill omens, little noted at the time, surrounded this event. It occurred exactly a year after the beginning of the canonization of St. Seraphim, whose decomposed body should have barred him from sainthood. The entire Russian Army, which had found Seraphim's icon so uninspiring, stood sponsor for the child. The name his parents chose, Alexis, had been avoided by the imperial family ever since Peter the Great had had his son of that name murdered for opposing his reforms. It was said that the dying Alexis had cried out a curse on the entire Romanov dynasty.[10]

Elizabeth, Serge, Dmitri, and Marie all attended the christening at Peterhof. A gilded coach bore the infant tsarevich to the chapel; they followed behind, their coach drawn by plumed horses. By tradition the imperial couple were absent from the ceremony and appeared afterward. Old Princess Golitsyna held the baby. The Prince of Wales and the Emperor William were the baby's godfathers.[11]

Not long after their return to Ilinskoe, an air of melancholy set in. When the boy bled from his navel, it was discovered that the tsarevich had hemophilia. "From that moment," Marie recalled, "troubled and apprehensive, the empress's character underwent a change, and her health, physical as well as moral, altered."[12]

Throughout the hot summer and autumn, Elizabeth could sense a mood of gathering unrest. The continued reverses the army suffered at the front aggravated the discontent among the population. After the first snows had fallen, her haven of secure tranquility at Ilinskoe was disturbed. Thieves broke in and stole a quantity of silver. They had been so bold and insolent as to stop to eat and smoke cigarettes.

In November, while Savinkov and Kalyayev were traveling to Moscow, Elizabeth and her family returned to the governor's house on Tverskaya Street. Strikes and student riots were now widespread. Serge, after searching his conscience, decided to resign from the post of governor of Moscow. The new interior minister, Sviatopolk-Mirsky, had proposed a wide program of liberal reforms, including civil rights and religious toleration. Serge, on the other hand, felt that only a policy of severe repression could keep order in Russia. Indeed, by his own reactionary standards, he had been too lenient in his treatment of the disorders and in some measure responsible for them. He felt that he had little choice but to quit.[13]

On January 1, 1905, Port Arthur surrendered to the Japanese. It could have been defended for several weeks to come, but the commanding officer, Stoessel, "a man of breath-taking incompetence,"[14] decided to give up the fight. As the news reached Moscow, several regiments mutinied, and strikes and disorders grew worse. When Elizabeth and Serge took the children to Neskuchnoe for the Christmas holidays, a squadron of cavalry was camped in the palace yard. They hardly dared venture outside the palace gates. The working-class suburbs surrounding Neskuchnoe were a hotbed of agitation, and at any moment a general uprising was expected.[15]

In St. Petersburg, the tension was mounting. The police agent Father Gapon, an excitable man, fond of drink, persuaded himself that he had a mission to save the workers from their hardship and oppression. He organized a strike at the Putilov factory, which was soon joined by all thirteen thousand workers. He decided to arrange a grand march to the Winter Palace to present to the emperor a petition for redress of the workers' grievances.† Over the next few days he toured the factories and harangued the workers. His handsome, bearded face, his reputation as a holy man, his rich baritone voice and his splendid oratory so aroused them that thousands joined him. "His passionate, burning speeches," an eyewitness wrote, "electrified the crowds and in reverential ecstacy they repeated after him: 'To the Tsar!' . . . Many people wept, stamped their feet, banged their chairs, beat their fists on the walls, and raising their hands high, swore to stand firm to the end."[16]

Sunday, January 22, dawned a clear and icy day. Father Gapon had informed the interior minister of the march, stressing its peaceful nature and pleading for the emperor to receive the petition. The minister, however, had brought in troops to the capital. From several points more than 100,000 people converged on the Winter Palace. Bearing icons and portraits of the emperor, they sang hymns and *God Save the Tsar*. At the head of one throng Father Gapon marched with another priest beside him. At the entrances to the Palace Square the cossack cavalry were lined up. They ordered the crowd to disperse, and warned that they would be fired on. But Father Gapon had told them that the emperor would be there to receive them, and they marched on. The troops opened fire. The crowd ran in panic, pursued by the Cossacks. More than a thousand were killed, many of them women and children. In the afternoon the corpses were lifted from the blood-stained snow and driven away on sleighs.

On the evening of this "Bloody Sunday," Emperor Nicholas wrote in his diary: "Lord, it is so painful and hard!" He had been told that the march was an attempt on his life.

Father Gapon made a final speech to his followers:

"Blood brothers, innocent blood has been shed! The bullets of the tsar's soldiers have riddled our portraits of the tsar and killed our faith in him. We must take revenge for our brothers on the tsar cursed by the people and on all his wicked breed, the ministers, and all the plunderers of the unhappy Russian land. Death to them. . . ."[17]

Before fleeing abroad he wrote in a manifesto to the emperor:

> The innocent blood of workers, their wives and children lies forever between thee, O soul-destroying tsar, and the Russian people. Now is the time for bombs and dynamite, terror by individuals, terror by the masses, and this must be, and so it shall absolutely come about. An immense sea of blood shall be shed. . . .[18]

The Kremlin was now felt to be the only secure place in Moscow for the imperial family. One night, not long after Christmas, Elizabeth, Serge, Dmitri, and Marie furtively entered a carriage and sped by a roundabout route to the Kremlin. No one spoke as they drove, curtains drawn, an escort following behind, through the silent snowy streets. When they arrived, the Nicholas Palace was damp and chilly from long disuse; dust sheets covered the furniture. Tea was made, and the family slept in improvised beds under piles of blankets.

For the next few days, Elizabeth rarely left the Kremlin, and only her closest friends came to visit her.[19] Serge, however, showed a complete indifference to danger. He despised the revolutionaries, and thought it beneath him to take precautions for his safety. Despite Elizabeth's fears, he went alone to his office each afternoon to sort out his papers and prepare for his successor. His coach, with its grand ducal crest and green lamps, was easily recognized.

Serge may have noticed a cab driver wearing a heavy fur coat with a red silk belt.[20] Kalyayev, disguised as a prosperous coachman, was following his movements to decide on the place and time for his assassination. Savinkov learned from the newspapers that Serge would attend a war benefit performance at the Opera House on February 15. He decided that Kalyayev would throw a bomb at Serge on his way to the theater.

A storm gathered throughout the afternoon of the 15th. By the evening the wind was whipping the walls of the Kremlin and driving flurries of snow into its corners. At eight Serge, Elizabeth, Dmitri, and Marie entered Serge's roomy, old-fashioned carriage and sat down on its silk cushions. They drove out through the Nicholas Gate into Red Square, and turned left to pass down the slope between the looming bulk of the Historical Museum and the Kremlin wall into the square beyond. The moon shone to reveal the area deserted, apart from a few peasants wandering to the Kremlin. Savinkov was waiting in the Alexander Gardens on the left; Kalyayev, the bomb in his hand, was standing in the shadow of a building to the right. He decided that if Elizabeth was with Serge, she would have to die. Kalyayev recognized the coach and the driver, Rudinkin. Whispering, "The time has come," he ran forward and raised his arm above his head.

At that moment he caught sight of Dmitri and Marie. The thought of murdering a pair of innocent children made him hesitate. Rudinkin cried out and whipped up the horses, and the four of them arrived safely at the theater. They knew nothing of Kalyayev's attempt and enjoyed the spectacle of Chaliapin at the height of his powers, amid a sea of jewels and uniforms.

Savinkov and Kalyayev hastily conferred, and decided to kill Serge if he left the theater alone. All four of the family returned together, and once more Serge's life was saved.

On February 17, 1905, two days later,[21] at three in the afternoon, the setting sun lit up the gilded cupolas of the Kremlin and the thick snow in a brilliant orange haze. The muffled sounds from the city outside did little to disturb the peaceful atmosphere. As Kalyayev, dressed as a peasant, strolled beside the Nicholas Gate, the family rose from lunch. Serge kissed Elizabeth and the children good-bye. He was in a cheerful mood; Emperor Nicholas had sent him a gold-leaved miniature portrait of Emperor Alexander III. Elizabeth prepared to visit her Red Cross workshop nearby; her sleigh was waiting outside the palace. All morning she had felt a vague sense of unease; she had just dissuaded Serge from making a dangerous trip to St. Petersburg.[22] The children left for their lessons. Marie was anxious to hear the result of a request General Laiming, Dmitri's tutor, was making of Serge for permission to buy her a mandolin. Having discussed the matter, Serge entered his carriage, and Rudinkin whipped up the horses and drove away.

A thunderous explosion shook the palace windows. The idea of some dire accident flashed through Elizabeth's mind. "It's Serge," she cried.[23] From her window, she could see people running toward the Nicholas Gate. She threw a cloak over her shoulders and called Mlle. Hélène. They ran, hatless, to the sleigh and drove at full speed around the corner of the square. The driver forced a path through the gathering crowd. Directly in front of the gateway stood Kalyayev. As two policemen dragged him away he shouted: "Down with the damned tsar! Down with the accursed government!"[24] Beside him, a hand, a severed leg, and an arm still clinging to its shoulder were the only remains of Serge amid the bloody morass of snow.

## Notes to Chapter 15

*He later served under Kerensky in the Provisional Russian Government, and afterward greatly impressed Winston Churchill as the leader of the anti-Communist conspiracy in Russia.

†The petition also pleaded for a constituent assembly, universal suffrage, universal education, the separation of church and state, and an amnesty for all political prisoners.

# Chapter 16

*THE GRAND DUCHESS. And to whom should I speak
of the crime, if not to the murderer?
KALYAYEV. What crime? I only recall an act of justice.*

—ALBERT CAMUS, *LES JUSTES**

Elizabeth never lost her calm for a moment. Her one
thought, she later told her sister, was, "Hurry, hurry, Serge so
hated mess and blood."[1] She brushed aside two peasant women
who tried to prevent her from alighting from the sleigh.
Deathly pale, she gave directions in an unbroken voice. A sleigh
was hastily summoned, and Rudinkin's badly mauled body was
driven away to the hospital. Seeing that many among the gap-
ing crowd still wore their hats, she ordered them to bare their
heads. On her knees, her dress now covered with blood, she
helped to gather up the unrecognizable fragments of her husband's corpse. These were laid on an army stretcher brought
from her workshop. The small pile was covered with a soldier's
overcoat. Elizabeth clutched very tightly in her hand the
medals Serge had worn on a string around his neck.

At a quarter past three, a detachment of soldiers roped off
the site of the murder and formed a guard of honor. They bore
the stretcher on their shoulders past the stunned and motion-
less crowd to the Monastery of the Miracle by Nicholas Palace.
In the church the litter was placed beside the altar steps. At one
end a single boot protruded, and a pool of blood formed

beneath the body. A bell in the monastery tower began a solemn knell.

Elizabeth knelt beside the litter, her blue, bloodstained dress a grotesque contrast with the surrounding gloom. Mlle. Hélène brought in Dmitri and Marie, and the church was thronged with kneeling and weeping mourners. Some lighted candles were held in the semidarkness. A frightened priest intoned the service in a trembling voice, and the congregation whispered the responses. At the end Elizabeth, leaning on the arm of the vice-governor, General Dzhunkovsky, advanced toward Dmitri and Marie, her face white and stricken rigid. Marie was never to forget that expression of infinite sadness. She held out her arms, the children ran to her, and she embraced them, pressing their heads against her. "He loved you so, he loved you," she endlessly repeated.

The children slowly drew her away from the prying glances of the mourners into the quiet of her rooms. "She let herself fall weakly into an armchair. Her eyes dry and with the same peculiar fixity of gaze, she looked straight into space, and said nothing." After a while, in need of distracting activity, she rose and demanded paper. With an unchanged expression she set about writing telegrams to all her relatives. To the imperial couple at Tsarskoe Selo she wrote that they need not come as the risk was too great. She rose again, paced the room tensely and sat down again. At the visitors who came and went she looked without seeming to see them.

As the evening approached, the palace remained unlit. Servants shuffled about in the gloom and spoke in whispers. Elizabeth decided to see Rudinkin. Her repeated inquiries had revealed that he lay dying in the hospital. Still wearing the same bloodstained dress, she drove there with Dzhunkovsky and was admitted to his bedside. "How is the grand duke?" he asked. "Why, it was he who sent me to see you," she replied. Rudinkin died peacefully that night.

Elizabeth found strength to join the children for their dinner. She could eat nothing, and they felt ashamed to eat on seeing her ashen face. Afterward she asked them to say their prayers in front of her, and all three knelt down together. She could not face the night alone, and joined Marie in her room. For a long time they talked of her husband. She slowly softened and abandoned her rigid self-control, and wept.

The next morning, the three of them joined a service of prayer around Serge's remains, now in an open coffin and covered in brocade, a sentinel at each corner. Every morning and evening until the funeral, they would return to the church.

That afternoon, Elizabeth took an extraordinary step for a grand duchess. She drove in a carriage covered in black crepe to the Taganka prison to see Kalyayev alone. She knew that Serge had felt a great distress for those who died unrepentant and unconfessed. In his memory she decided to do what would have been his wish, to awaken a feeling of repentance in Kalyayev for his deed, and so help his soul.[2] This unprecedented act threw the officials into confusion, but they had no choice but to obey a grand duchess.

From Kalyayev's own account,†[3] and the memoirs of Elizabeth's sister Victoria and her brother Ernest, it is possible to reconstruct their conversation.

As she entered the cell in slow, shuffling steps, pale beneath her black veil, Kalyayev failed to recognize her. "Who are you?" he asked.

"I am the wife of the man whom you have killed," she replied.

"It is useless for you to come," he said.

After a brief silence, she began, "You must have suffered so much to have committed this terrible act."

The mention of suffering stirred up Kalyayev's revolutionary fanaticism. He launched into a tirade, waving his arms in his excitement: "What does it matter whether I have suffered or not? Yes, I have suffered! But I suffered with millions of other people. Altogether too much blood has been spilled, and we have no other means of protesting against a tyrannical government and a terrible war. Why do they come and talk to me only after I have committed the crime? Listen! When I was a boy, I thought about all the tears that are shed in the world, and all the lies that are told, and sometimes it seemed to me that if I could, I would shed enough tears for everyone, and then the evil would be destroyed! But what could I do? If I went to the grand duke and showed him all the evil he had done, the misery of the people, why, he would have sent me to a madhouse or (and this is likely) thrown me into prison, like thousands of others who have suffered for their convictions. Why didn't they let the people speak?"

She answered, "I am sorry you did not come to us, then we would have known you earlier."

"So you think it is easy to go to you?" he continued. "Look what happened on January 9, when they tried to see the tsar. Do you really believe such things could go unpunished? Then there is this terrible war which the people hate so violently. Well, you have declared war on the people, and we have accepted the challenge! As for myself, I would give a thousand lives, not one, if only Russia could be free!"

At this Elizabeth remarked that in war men fought each other face to face, but he had murdered from behind. That was not war, but cowardice. She reminded him that her family also had their burdens to carry: "You think that you are the only ones to suffer. I assure you we also suffer, and we wish only good for the people."

The idea that the imperial family might be benevolent and suffering human beings went against the grain of all Kalyayev's convictions. He bitterly remarked: "Yes, you are suffering now, but as for giving good things to the people, you give with one hand and take it back with a knife."

At that point, Kalyayev recalled, they were both silent for a while, and the grand duchess became absorbed in memories of her husband. Having respectfully remained standing throughout while she had been seated, he now sat down as well. She told him that Grand Duke Serge had not deserved death, as he was powerless and no longer governor when he died. He was good to everyone.

Clearly stung once more by the idea that Serge might have shown kindness, Kalyayev begged her not to discuss him. "I have absolutely no desire to talk about him. Everything I have to say will be said at the trial. I killed him with a full sense of responsibility. He was a man who played a powerful role and knew exactly what he was doing."

"My husband never spoke about politics," Elizabeth replied. It was now clear that Kalyayev was showing no sign of repentance, and she prepared to end their conversation. "I came to tell you that he forgives you," she went on, and, rising to her feet, produced a small icon which she left on the table. "I beg you to accept this little icon in his memory. I shall pray for you."

Kalyayev accepted the gift, but refused to show any remorse. "My conscience is clear. I am sorry I have caused you so great a sorrow. I acted with a deep sense of my responsibility, and if I had a thousand lives, I would give them all, not only one. And now again I will say how sorry I am for you, but I still did my duty, and I will do so again to the very end, whatever the result. Good-bye."

She gave away nothing that evening when the children tried to question her about the interview.

Over the next few days Elizabeth "gave proof of an almost incomprehensible heroism," Marie later wrote, "no one could understand whence came the strength so to bear her misfortune." She could neither sleep nor touch a morsel of food. She spoke seldom to her family, "and seemed lost in a kind of dolorous dream," spending hours in prayer by the grand duke's bier. At the end of the daily services there she sometimes remained fixed to the same spot without seeing her surroundings. Marie would try gently to take her by the arm. "At this she would wince as if from a blow, and fix upon me a blind look tragic in its tormented simplicity."[4]

She took over the running of the household and arranged all the details of the funeral, including a free meal for the Moscow poor. These unfamiliar tasks took an immense effort of concentration. The political tension had deterred all but a few of the family from attending. Grand Dukes Paul and Constantine and Ernest and his wife came, as well as Victoria with the news that the Emperor William, meeting her en route at the Berlin station, had shown grave concern for Elizabeth. Her courage and rigid self-control amazed them all. "Her calmness," wrote Grand Duke Constantine, "her goodness, her submission to the will of God and her lack of anger are striking and deeply moving."[5] Yet, seeing her ashen face and wide-open staring eyes, all feared that she might not escape a nervous breakdown.

On February 23, the funeral was celebrated with great solemnity. Officers with drawn swords stood at the corners of the bier, around which a mass of wreaths and flowers was piled. Amid a packed congregation the archbishop and high clergy of Moscow held an exhaustingly long service. Marie almost fainted and had to be taken out, but Elizabeth endured it to the end. The coffin was taken to a chapel in the monastery, and every evening for forty days the three of them attended a service there.[6]

The rest of the family slowly departed. Before he left, Ernest saw his sister smile for the first time. It appeared that the warder at the Tanganka prison had told her that Kalyayev had placed the icon she had given him beside his pillow.[7] Her pleasure now consisted of carrying out small acts of Christian charity. Just as Princess Alice had become profoundly absorbed in religion after her father's death, so her daughter now founded her life on Christian self-abnegation after her husband's murder.

The cause was not only the shock of bereavement. The conversation with Kalyayev had had a profound effect. It was probably the first time that she grasped how much misery her husband's rule had caused, and how little freedom there was for the people in Russia. Serge, she had truthfully told Kalyayev, had never discussed politics with her. Her life and knowledge had been limited to court circles and her family. Some inkling of her husband's cruelty and contempt for the common Muscovites had come in the disaster at Khodinskoe Pole and the expulsion of the Jews, but she probably never knew of the vast powers he had had to expel subversives from Moscow, to censor the press, or dismiss radical students. She had never seen inside the grimy, over-crowded barracks in Serge's domain, where factory workers would return from twelve-hour shifts, sleeping in beds vacated by others who had just left for work. That an educated man should think it his duty to kill him was a double shock.

The meeting with a man made miserable by Serge's callousness could only throw his other failings into sharp relief. The conde-scension he had shown her, his growing indifference to her reli-gious strivings, his sexual inadequacies as a husband were brought vividly to her mind. Yet her life had been built around her marriage to him, insubstantial as it had been. She could not admit that their twenty years together had been in vain. She began to idealize him as a deeply religious man, sensitive beneath his haughty exterior, kind to her during her conversion, who loved children but was incapable of siring them. She would idolize him as a paragon of Christian virtue, just as Queen Victoria had idolized Prince Albert. "I hope God may give me strength," she would write, "that never one can say I was unwor-thy of having been in olden times guided by such a true noble husband and true Christian."[8] Partly to atone for the misdeeds of the grand duke she had once loved, and to erase them from her memory, she dedicated herself to pious good works.

Yet the impulse also seemed to come to her as a mystic revela-tion and fulfilment of her life's desires. "I took it up not as a cross," she was to write, "but as a road full of light God showed me after Serge's death and which years and years *before* had begun in my soul . . . it *little* by *little* grew and took form and many, many who followed all my life and knew me well here, were not astonished, taking it only as a continuation of what *before* had begun. . . ."[9] Released from from the bounds of her

213

marriage, she gave way to the impulses of the faith that had developed in her. The desire for worldly pleasure and grandeur was gone forever. In its place came an intense urge to ease the sufferings of the world.

Elizabeth withdrew entirely from her social life. She could never again eat meat, for it brought the memory of the bloody fragments of Serge's corpse.[10] She relaxed her reserve toward Marie and Dmitri and strove to understand them and act as a conscientious mother. The barrier of jealousy that had come up between them in Serge's presence had now disappeared. The children were both afraid that they might have to live abroad with their father, Grand Duke Paul, and his wife, whom they disliked. "Dmitri simply sobs and clings to me," Elizabeth wrote. "His intense fright was the idea of having to leave me. He decided he must watch over me as Uncle is no more and clings to me to such a degree that the arrival of his father was more an anguish than a pleasure, the intense fear he would take him."[11] She sought the two children out at every moment of the day and kept them near her. They had many long talks, full of an unknown intimacy. She admitted to Marie that she had been unfair to them and now tried to make amends.[12]

Although the grand duchess had ordered her visit to Kalyayev to be kept secret, it had become public, and wildly distorted rumors were now circulating. It was said that she had asked the emperor for clemency, that Kalyayev had refused a pardon when offered it, that he had been forcibly restrained by the guards from attacking her, and that he had begged her pardon on his knees with tears in his eyes.[13] Hearing of this Kalyayev wrote her three letters, full of spite and demanding an apology. In the third he went to an excess of violent malice:

> Grand Duchess!
> . . . You came to me with your sorrow and your
> tears, and I did not refuse you, I did not expel this

*Hessian Grand Ducal children, early 1878.*
LEFT TO RIGHT: *Alix, Ernest, Elizabeth, Victoria, Irene and* (IN FRONT OF IRENE) *May.*

LEFT TO RIGHT:

*Princess Victoria of Hesse,*
*Queen Victoria, Princess Alix and*
(BEHIND ALIX)
*Princess Elizabeth of Hesse.*

*Prince Emils garden, Darmstadt*

LEFT TO RIGHT: *Grand Duke Serge of Russia, Princess Elizabeth of Hesse, Prince Luis of Battenberg, Princess Victoria of Hesse, Grand Duke Louis IV of Hesse and the Rhine, Darmstadt, 1884.*

*Princess Alix being dressed for her first ball, assisted by her old governess, Mrs. Orchard, and her sister Grand Duchess Elizabeth, autumn 1888.*

Grand Duchess Marie
and Grand Duke Dmitri,
children of
Grand Duke Paul of Russia,
c. 1892.

The Castle
in the center of Darmstadt.

*Elizabeth, Grand Duchess Serge of Russia, 1894.*

*Grand Duke Serge of Russia, 1898.*

The Kremlin, Moscow,
from the south-west,
c. 1901.

Tsarevitch Nicholas of Russia and
Princess Alix of Hesse, Coburg,
1894.

STANDING, LEFT TO RIGHT:

*Emperor Nicholas II, Empress Alexandra, Princess Victoria of Battenberg,*
*Grand Duke Ernest of Hesse and the Rhine.*

SEATED:

*Nona Kerr* (LADY-IN-WAITING TO PRINCESS VICTORIA),
*Grand Duchess Elizabeth, Grand Duchess Victoria "Ducky,"*
*Grand Duke Serge, c. 1900.*

*Grand Duchess Elizabeth and family with wounded soldiers at Ilinskoe, 1905.*

STANDING:
*Grand Duchess Elizabeth, Grand Duchess Marie Pavlovna* (SECOND FROM RIGHT)
*Prince Christopher of Greece* (THIRD LEFT)*, Grand Duke Dmitri Pavlovich.*

SEATED:
*Princess Victoria of Battenberg* (SECOND FROM LEFT)*.*

*The cross where*
*Grand Duke Serge was murdered,*
*Moscow, June 1908.*

*The palace of*
*Grand Duke Serge of Russia,*
*St. Petersburg,*
*c. 1880s–1890s.*

*Grand Duke Serge's house in Ilinskoye, Russia, seen from the garden, 1901.*

*Grand Duchess Elizabeth and her sister Princess Victoria of Battenberg at Wolfsgarten, 1910.*

*Schloss Heiligenberg, home of Prince Alexander of Hesse.*

*The New Palace in Darmstadt*

(DESTROYED BY RAF BOMBING DURING WORLD WAR II).

*Scholss Wolfsgarten, seen from the air.*

*The church of SS Martha and Mary in Elizabeth's convent. In front of the gateway to Great Ordinka Street. On the horizon in the extreme right is the Cathedral of Christ the Saviour, built to commemorate Russia's victory in 1812 over Napoleon's army.*

*Elizabeth, Grand Duchess Serge of Russia, c. 1914.*

visitor from the enemy's camp. . . . For the first
time a member of the royal dynasty has bowed her
head before the vengeance of the people and
acknowledged the crimes of the imperial family. . . .
I should not have sympathized with you and I
should have refused to speak to you. I behaved
with kindness, momentarily suppressing the natural hatred I felt for you. I have revealed the
motives which moved me: you have proved unwor-
thy of my generosity. I cannot believe otherwise
than that you are yourself the source of the slan-
ders which have been published about me. . . .[14]

None of the letters ever reached the grand duchess. Kalyayev
was tried in a closed court, and at the end made a long speech,
declaring that Grand Duke Serge had amassed a heap of crimes
and made himself liable to revolutionary punishment. The wave
of unrest in Russia was the judgment of history on the tsarist
regime. "It is a wave of new life arising out of the gathering
storm—the death-throes of the autocracy." Kalyayev predicted
that within ten years the revolutionary forces would overthrow
the dynasty, "and not with secret weapons, but openly." He was
sentenced to death, and declared that his execution was a
supreme sacrifice in a world of blood and tears.

He was taken to the Schlusselburg fortress near St. Petersburg
and told that he would be hanged before dawn. At two in the
morning, the executioner entered and tied his hands behind his
back. He was led out into the cold courtyard and onto the black
gallows, barely visible in the surrounding gloom. A noose was
placed over his head, and the guards beat their drums as the platform was kicked away. His body remained suspended for thirty
minutes before it was buried outside the fortress walls just as the
sun rose.[15]

Azev eventually fled the country and died during the First
World War in a German prison camp. That both he and Father

Gapon were police agents invites theories of conspiracy. To this day in Russia a suspicion remains of a court intrigue behind the murders of Serge and Plehve and "Bloody Sunday." It is thought that a reactionary clique at court were disquieted by the new liberal tendencies of the emperor. They intended to stir unrest in the country to serve as a pretext for a wave of repression. Nicholas would be forced to abdicate, and Grand Duke Nicholas Nikolayevich, the tall, imposing commander of the St. Petersburg garrison, would become emperor.[16] A few years later, it was even thought that the extreme right wished to place Grand Duke Dmitri on the throne and appoint Grand Duchess Elizabeth as regent.‡[17,18]

For Easter the grand duchess, dressed in her mourning clothes, took the children to the emperor and empress at Tsarskoe Selo. Alexandra, full of sympathy, tried her best to comfort and console her sister. The festival, which should have been filled with the joy of the Resurrection, was the saddest that any of them had ever known. Shortly before the Easter service, two terrorists dressed as choristers were unmasked. They had planned to enter the cathedral and throw a bomb at the assembled imperial family.[19]

For the imperial couple this attempt and the death of Serge were yet more burdens piled on a growing heap. Alexandra found little peace from her anxiety for her husband and her son's disturbing illness. Nicholas was increasingly incapable of dealing with political turmoil and the gathering defeats at the front. Worse, news had come of fresh outbreaks of rioting in the countryside. Many of the marchers in Father Gapon's procession had fled there and told of the tsar's troops firing on a loyal demonstration. It seemed that the peasantry's age-old belief in the tsar as their father and protector was shaken to the point that they were prepared to rise up against their hated landlords.

On May 27 came the anniversary of the emperor's coronation.

On the day that should have been a time of rejoicing, he heard that his navy had suffered a crushing defeat. At the narrow strait of Tsushima between Japan and Korea, the Baltic Fleet ended its voyage around the globe in battle with the Japanese Navy. Within forty-five minutes, eight Russian battleships, seven cruisers, and six destroyers were lost.

In the Black Sea Fleet, all that remained of Russia's navy, the defeat stirred the men from sullen resentment at their diet of rotten meat to open mutiny. The crew of the battleship *Potemkin* killed many of their officers and raised the red flag. So close were the other ships to mutiny that their commanders dared not open fire on the rebels. The *Potemkin* steamed past unscathed, and bombarded Odessa; only a lack of fuel obliged it to dock in a Romanian port. The emperor now had little choice but to pursue peace.

Meanwhile, the grand duchess took Marie and Dmitri, now aged fifteen and fourteen, to Ilinskoe for the summer.[20] With them were a guard of soldiers and a motor car ready for a speedy flight. Yet in the bright sunshine and the peaceful woods the turmoil outside seemed remote. At last the three were able to relax their mourning stiffness. Elizabeth now lifted herself out of her doleful state and showed an initiative that had been denied her during her husband's lifetime. She established a hospital for wounded soldiers on the estate, and busied herself with its management, down to the smallest details. Here she would sit and talk to the soldiers and console as best as she knew. She found an outlet for her long-suppressed maternal instinct. "They are my big babies," she wrote to her brother, "who are so warmly thankful to me for my care."[21]

Marie at first accompanied her, but soon longed to escape and ride on horseback with Dmitri or join the game of their playmates. Her chance came when Queen Olga of Greece, their maternal grandmother, arrived with her young son, Prince Christopher. Her cheerfulness brightened the holiday, and she treated the children as her own. With pious fervor she joined

Elizabeth in working at the hospital, leaving the children, led on by her unruly son, free to make boisterous pranks. Elizabeth now treated them with more patience and trust, and watched their antics with amusement. Dmitri's charm softened her; he was growing into a high-spirited, fun-loving boy. Marie, however, had come to the end of her childhood; beneath her bright exterior she had a melancholy, pensive mind. At the age of fifteen, she was gawky and long-legged, with a solid, thick-set face. To add to the shock of bereavement, she was facing the disruption of adolescence, which the events to come did little to alleviate.

In the fall the grand duchess and the children returned to the Kremlin. Moscow was in a ferment of revolutionary agitation.[22] The war had ended, and the government had gone halfway to meeting the people's demand for a parliament, but the populace was still restive. The tension mounted as strikes gathered pace and fighting broke out in the streets. The gates of the Kremlin were closed, and only those with a pass were admitted. In mid-October, the railwaymen struck, and Moscow was cut off from the rest of the empire. The Bolsheviks spread leaflets among the workmen calling for an armed insurrection: "Lay down your tools and take up arms. Long live the armed uprising of the exhausted people!" One day the water supply turned brackish, and a panicked rumor spread through the city that it was poisoned. Food began to run short; there was no milk, and the price of meat doubled. On October 24, more than 2,000 railwaymen descended on the central telegraph exchange, barely five hundred yards from the Kremlin, and tried to close it down. Elizabeth could hear the shouts and the thunder of hooves as the cossack cavalry chased them away with whips.

Over the next few days almost all of Moscow went on strike. The post, telegraph, and telephone were forced to close. Elizabeth and the children were stranded in the Kremlin, running short of food and water, without communication with the outside world. Rumors spread of a threat to kidnap the children, and of a night assault on the Kremlin. The electrical workers struck, and Moscow was plunged into darkness. The Kremlin had an electric plant of its own, but the servants dared not attract attention by lighting up in the evening. The only illumination came from lamps placed under the tables.

All through October 28, the family heard rioting outside the Kremlin walls. In the morning, a demonstration tried to force its way into the city council building; the dragoons arrived, drew their swords, and chased the crowd away or trampled them underfoot. In the afternoon an angry student mob threw stones at the nearby shops that stayed open during the strike. The Cossacks fell on the students with whips and swords.

The grand duchess remained calm throughout. She quietly arranged for the children to be safely hidden away. She stayed true to the aim she had set herself of leading a life of Christian self-abnegation. Her bedroom was arranged entirely in white, like a nun's cell, and hung with icons and pictures of the saints. She gathered up the remains of the clothes Serge had worn on his last day and placed them in a large hollow wooden cross in a corner of the room. Every day she went to church. She rented a nearby house which she turned into a hospital for her fifteen wounded soldiers, and made frequent visits there, even at the height of the rioting, to the consternation of the police. One evening she felt obliged to assist at an urgent operation. She went out after dark, on foot, as a carriage might have attracted attention.

By chance the children heard of her visit. Marie was fraught with anxiety and gave vent to the anger and concern that had been building up in her. She told her aunt that her infatuation with the sick had not only become ridiculous but was now very dangerous. Serge, she added, would have strongly disapproved. "To my astonishment," Marie recalled, "my aunt listened meekly, without replying, to all I had to say. When I uttered my uncle's name she lowered her head and began to cry. Her tears melted my anger; immediately, I was sorry for all I had said; I stood silent."[23]

In a mild voice Elizabeth replied that Marie was perhaps right, that she had been too preoccupied with the wounded, and that Serge would have criticized her attitude. "But she found herself so lonely, so desolate, that she had to do something, to forget her grief at the sight of others' suffering."[24]

Order was only restored when the government gave ground and Emperor Nicholas, with great reluctance, signed a manifesto granting freedom of speech and assembly, civil rights, and an elected parliament.

Toward the beginning of December, however, the threat of an armed uprising arose once more in Moscow. The government's authority was still weak. As a result of the freedom of speech and assembly that the emperor had granted, large crowds gathered to listen to orators demanding a Socialist republic and the division of land among the peasants. A council of workmen's representatives, or Soviet, had appeared in St. Petersburg, headed by Leon Bronstein, a fiery orator and Menshevik§ revolutionary who called himself Trotsky. Now another Soviet appeared in Moscow and began to provoke more strikes. The post ceased again, and in the evenings it was still unsafe to venture out.

Elizabeth kept calm and continued her work among the sick. She dismissed suggestions to leave Moscow. A Russian aristocrat and family friend, "Masha," Maria Vassilshikova, arrived from her home in Hungary and helped her arrange her rooms. On December 2 she left for Vienna, bearing a letter from the grand duchess to her brother Ernest in Hesse. In it Elizabeth revealed her state of mind:

> All is going from worse to worse; one must not
> make oneself any illusions of better times coming
> for months. We are in the revolution—What turn
> all will take, nobody knows, as the government is
> so weak as, sooner to say, does not seem to exist.
> We feel physically very well and have good nerves,
> and don't think of moving—nothing will make me
> leave this place. Of course if the worst of worst

happens, I can always have Paul's children safely
sent off, but I will live or die here. . . .[25]

It was very fortunate that Elizabeth decided to take Dmitri and
Marie to Tsarskoe Selo in time to celebrate the emperor's nameday on December 19.

Just as she was leaving, the Moscow Soviet called for a general
strike. The workers again walked out, and the trains stopped.
The streets were thronged with crowds, and orators urged them
to take up arms. The insurgents built up barricades and fought
pitched battles with the troops. Order was only restored after a
regiment of the guards had come and shelled a factory district.
"It was such chance my having taken Marie and Dmitri for
Nicky's nameday to Tsarskoe; thank God they were away during
that sad time," she wrote to her brother. "The revolutionaries'
plan was to catch the Governor-General, kill the authorities and
. . . take the Kremlin with the arsenal and, in hopes that the
troops would join, hold Moscow, a month later go to Tsarskoe
and you can guess the end."[26]

## Notes to Chapter 16

*The conversation between the Grand Duchess and Kalyayev formed a key pas-
sage in Albert Camus' drama *Les Justes*, which explored the moral dilemmas of the
terrorists.

†In his cell Kalyayev described the conversation in a letter to Savinkov, who relat-
ed it in his memoirs. Elizabeth described the conversation to her brother and sister shortly afterward.

‡If genuine, these conspiracies followed a long tradition in Russia that sovereigns
came to power by palace coups d'etat. It dated back to the edict of Peter the Great
that empowered every monarch to choose his successor. "From Peter's death until
the accession of Paul I in 1796, Russia's rulers were chosen by high-ranking officials
in collusion with officers of Guards regiments." The "Decembrist" conspiracy to
place Grand Duke Constantine on the throne was another such attempt.

The practice persisted up to the 1917 revolution and beyond; the enforced abdication of Emperor Nicholas in favor of his brother was well within the tradition.
Felix Youssoupov, who had killed Rasputin, claimed that in mid-1917 he had been
offered the throne by several political figures, including Admiral Kolchak and
Grand Duke Nicholas Mikhailovich, who said, "The throne of Russia is neither

hereditary nor elective: it is usurpatory." At the same time similar offers were made to Grand Duke Dmitri. The accession of Stalin and Brezhnev involved similar furtive factional conspiracies.

§The "Mensheviks" or "men of the minority" were the faction of the Russian Social Democratic Party that had split away from Lenin's Bolsheviks in 1903. Bronstein used the alias "Trotsky" partly to conceal himself from the police, and partly to hide his Jewish origins.

# Chapter 17

SKOURATOV. *The grand duchess is Christian. You see,*
*the soul is her specialty.*

—CAMUS, *LES JUSTES*

"I feel entirely at peace—truly it is so; I never have one moment
of despair or loneliness," the grand duchess wrote to her brother in the new year of 1906. She had left the children behind in
the safety of Tsarskoe Selo and returned to Moscow. Order was
in some measure restored in the city. The Kremlin was quiet, and
only one gate was open to visitors from outside. Elizabeth was
now busy all day long. She would receive friends in her drawing
room and officials, one of whom, Vladimir Dzhunkovsky, the
vice-governor of Moscow, who had shielded her in the aftermath
of Serge's death, was to become a trusted friend.[1] She was reor-
ganizing the Orthodox Palestine Society for the purpose for
which it was intended. Serge had grossly mismanaged the society,
diverting the charitable donations into his own pocket, but she
made sure that they went toward helping Orthodox pilgrims to
travel to the Holy Land.[2] Every day she was at her hospital, organizing, talking and reading to the inmates, and assisting with
their supper. The warm gratitude they showed made it an intense
pleasure. She was building a chapel in Byzantine style for her
husband's relics, and on the site of his death she put up a cross
with the inscription, "Father, forgive them, for they know not

what they do."[3] Twice daily she prayed beside his coffin, and felt herself near to him in her faith that his soul lived in another world. "Shall I tell you why I feel calm alone?" she wrote to her brother. "Because the living and the dead are equally near me and I don't realize the entire earthly separation."

She faced the anniversary of her husband's death without anxiety. "I don't admit anniversaries," she wrote, "every day has its remembrances and one year as a day doesn't change anything."[4] Marie and Dmitri joined her for that day, but she had no need of their company. Her almost mystical frame of mind kept her from the nervous collapse that all around her had predicted. For the rest of her life, wrote Archpriest Michael Polsky, "in her face, especially in her eyes, she exuded a hidden melancholy, the mark of a lofty soul languishing in this world."[5] She coped with the enormous mental strain of the past few months only by devoting herself to acts of charity. In so doing she put herself at a great distance from everyday practical affairs. Some of the imperial family could hardly recognize her former self, the capable organizer of war work or the accomplished dancer at court balls. It would be some time before she resumed her grasp on practical details.

She still managed to think of Marie, who at sixteen was about to come out into society. Together with the imperial couple she arranged for a grand ball in the spring to mark the occasion. She took charge of her niece's appearance, and had a dress specially made. Elizabeth stayed away from the ball, which was too much a part of the old life she had abandoned. It was held in the marble palace of Grand Duke Constantine in St. Petersburg, and Marie found the very long evening an immense delight. She returned home exhausted, the hem of her dress in shreds, but dreamed only of beginning it over again. Dmitri, who had accompanied her, was still too young and declared that he spent a very dull evening.[6]

Russia was now experiencing a novelty which its inhabitants
had thought unimaginable a few years before. For the first time
in centuries it had a constitution which laid down clearly the relations between the government and its subjects, and an elected
parliament whose members could speak out freely without fear
of arrest. Emperor Nicholas had agreed to this step when it
seemed that the alternative was anarchy or revolution. His uncle,
Grand Duke Nicholas Nikolayevich, it is said, had threatened to
put a bullet through his own head if Nicholas did not go ahead
with the reforms.[7] Even so, the new parliament, the Duma, mod-
eled on the German Reichstag, had few powers. The emperor
still ruled and chose his own ministers without heeding the opinion of the Duma. He could dissolve the assembly, declare a state
of emergency, and rule by decree. The constitution stipulated
that no law could take effect without the consent of the Duma,
but this provision could easily be circumvented if the emperor
made laws when the Duma, having been dissolved, was not in session. In effect Nicholas continued to be, as he still signed himself, "Emperor and Autocrat of all the Russias."

Nicholas appointed as prime minister Peter Stolypin, a nobleman of energy, integrity, ability, and willpower, who became the
greatest of all the emperor's ministers. Over the next few years
he was to turn the fractious Duma into a workable institution,
and set into motion a highly complex land reform that would
erode Russia's anachronistic agricultural practices and partially
satisfy the peasants' hunger for land. First, however, the anarchy
in the countryside must be quelled. In the summer of 1906,
some six hundred terrorists* were sentenced to death by hanging by special field courts-martial.

Before these hangings, "Stolypin's neckties," could take
effect, Elizabeth and the children saw the signs of peasant rioting firsthand at Ilinskoe. At night the horizon glowed from the
flames of burning manor houses, and the smell of fire was in
the air. Her sister Victoria came on a visit from London, and
hardly recognized the place as the sunny holiday home of the

recent past.[8] All over Russia, the peasants were still on a rampage, burning down the landlords' houses and helping themselves to their land. The police were powerless to halt this widespread anarchy. Revolutionary agitators inflamed the peasants' centuries-old belief that the land was their own by right. "The peasants listen to the lies and pamphlets in which the revolutionaries tell them the Emperor allows them to take whatever they like," Elizabeth wrote.†[9]

That summer, Elizabeth learned of another disturbing event. On one August day, Prime Minister Stolypin was writing at a desk in his weekend retreat outside the capital. Three terrorists entered and threw a bomb, shouting, "Long live the Revolution!" The explosion demolished a wall of the house and tore up the trees outside by the roots. Stolypin was unharmed and resumed his duties the next day, but thirty-two people, visitors and servants, were killed, and his daughter was maimed.[10] The doctors thought she would die within hours. Yet she recovered after a "man of God" with wide staring eyes and a strange hypnotic power had prayed at her bedside.[11]

In Russian tradition the "holy man" (starets) was a venerated figure, a semiliterate, eternal wanderer, living in poverty. Throughout Russian history, hundreds of these men had roamed the countryside, surviving from the charity of monasteries and villagers. Some walked barefoot or fastened chains to their legs as a sign of asceticism. Others preached, or claimed to possess powers of healing. Their poverty and renunciation of worldly desires made them objects of reverence among the peasantry and earned the respect of educated Russians. They were regarded as mentors and men of great spirituality; many were canonized.

The "holy man" who had prayed for Stolypin's daughter was a bearded, lecherous, unwashed peasant from Siberia called Gregory Yefimovich Novykh. He appeared to have sinned and sincerely repented. In his rakish youth he had made free with Siberian girls, achieving his conquests by the direct method of grappling with the girls' clothing. His perseverance alone ensured a large number of prizes. Having married, he suddenly convinced himself that he had seen a vision requiring him to roam Russia as a pilgrim. Leaving his family, he walked two thousand miles to the monastery at Mount Athos in Greece. He returned with an aura of holiness, renounced his drinking and womanizing, prayed at length and began to kneel in supplication at the bedside of sick peasants. His fellow villagers were soon saying that he was a man close to God, and he arrived in 1903 in St. Petersburg with a reputation for saintliness and extraordinary powers. He freely admitted to his rakish past, but justified it with the sophistry that it is better and humbler to sin and repent than never to have sinned at all. As a mark of humility he bore his nickname of "debauchee," or "Rasputin."[12]

Having convinced the leading men of the church of his saintliness, Rasputin was introduced to Nicholas and Alexandra late in 1905. They were both in a mood to treat him well. The peasant rioting deeply shocked the emperor, for it struck at the core of his cherished belief in the union of the tsar and his people as the foundation of the autocracy. Alexandra revered the peasants as the idealized decent, loyal, and long-suffering tillers of the soil depicted in Tolstoy's novels. When Rasputin appeared, respectful but addressing them as "father" and "mother" with typical peasant directness, they welcomed him as the voice of the people. The miraculous cure of Stolypin's daughter gave Alexandra hope that he might help her son.[13]

But Elizabeth had few illusions about the Russian peasantry. She knew that their loyalty to their tsar, their good nature, and generosity were only one side of their character. The other aspect was their greed, cunning, and low regard for truth. She had seen firsthand their tendency to violent anarchy and wrote to Alexandra urging her to be cautious. Elizabeth did not doubt the curing of Stolypin's daughter, but it was not proved that Rasputin's penitence was sincere. She begged her to wait until it was certain that he was a man of God. The letter irritated Alexandra, and she ignored it.[14]

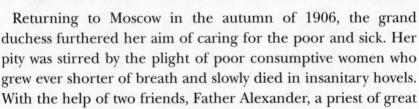

Returning to Moscow in the autumn of 1906, the grand duchess furthered her aim of caring for the poor and sick. Her pity was stirred by the plight of poor consumptive women who grew ever shorter of breath and slowly died in insanitary hovels. With the help of two friends, Father Alexander, a priest of great courage and integrity, and Mme. Uslova, the kindly widow of a victim of the Moscow riots, she planned another hospital. She bought land on the Great Ordinka, the street leading south from Red Square over the Moscow River. Here she carefully supervised all the arrangements, including a home where the women might live the rest of their lives in comfort.[15]

Dmitri and Marie stayed with her in the Kremlin. They both returned to their lessons after a year of disruption. Elizabeth, remembering her own irksome and unproductive school days, thought that Marie would achieve little by further study. She allowed her to visit the theater and widen her social experience. This seemed a more useful pursuit for a girl whose only vocation was marriage.[16]

Early in 1907 Elizabeth's sister, Irene, wrote from Berlin asking for photographs of Marie to be sent to Stockholm without delay. The crown princess of Sweden was looking for a bride for her second son, Prince William. As the crown princess was an old friend of them both, Elizabeth obliged. Plans were now set in motion to advance the engagement. Emperor Nicholas, who had become the guardian of Marie and Dmitri after their uncle's death, gave his approval. Diplomatic politics may have influenced his decision. The anarchy in the Russian countryside had aroused fears that Germany, under the impetuous emperor William,‡ might even invade the Baltic provinces. As Sweden bordered on the Russian Empire, it would be an advantage to secure her friendship by a marriage tie.

For some obscure reasons Elizabeth connived at this marriage of a schoolgirl who had only attended a single ball in her life. Perhaps it was true that as a Russian grand duchess, Marie was denied by diplomacy the choice of husband that Elizabeth had been granted as the daughter of a minor German prince. Possibly Elizabeth, like her grandmother, Queen Victoria, relished the idea of arranging another marriage after she had encouraged Alix's engagement. Most probably, she was so absorbed in her religious mission that she failed to understand the effect of marriage on a girl who was in effect an orphan. She had still not recovered from the anguish of abandonment, and so came to make the greatest mistake in her life.

For Easter she took the children to Tsarskoe Selo, where she arranged the details with the emperor and empress. It was decided that Prince William would come to Moscow soon after Easter, and that his courtship was to be compressed into a few days. Immediately after the ceremonies, Elizabeth took the children back to Moscow and took on the role of matchmaker. On the appointed afternoon William arrived for tea. Elizabeth and Marie were in the drawing room when he entered, a very tall, gangly young man. The grand duchess introduced him to Marie and kept up a polite conversation with him. Marie, calm and collected, remained silent for the most part. As he left, Elizabeth asked him to dinner, then asked Marie for her impression of him and received an evasive reply. That evening, she seated Marie next to the prince and watched in approval as they talked easily together. Afterward, Prince William, acting on cue, told the grand duchess in private that he wished to ask for Marie's hand during his few remaining days in Moscow.

The following morning, Elizabeth steeled herself to prepare Marie. She summoned her niece to the drawing room, and Marie kissed her hand and sat down. She held a handkerchief, Marie later recalled, and crumpled it nervously in her hand as she spoke. "Listen to me. I must speak to you of a very serious matter and I want you to think carefully before answering." She continued with an anxious, flushed face. "Prince William came here to make your acquaintance. He likes you, and wants to know whether you would consent to marry him."

To hear of a proposal from a man she had known for less than a day was a shock. In her stupefaction Marie said nothing. Elizabeth took her hand and told her that she must think it over.

That evening, at dinner in the presence of the prince, Marie fell ill and made her way unsteadily to bed. Over the next few days she developed a fever, diagnosed as sinusitis, and it was feared that an operation would be necessary. Elizabeth sat by her bedside and went in and out of the drawing room to inform Prince William of her progress. It was fortunate that Princess Victoria came at that time on another visit. She relieved her sister at Marie's bedside, and the patient recovered enough to be able to sit on a sofa. Marie now felt that her life as an orphan in the gilded cage of the Kremlin was not worth continuing. She told Elizabeth that she was prepared to accept the proposal.

The next day, Elizabeth, Victoria, and William joined her for tea. The two elder women took a hasty meal, and left the pair alone. The proposal was made, and they returned to congratulate Marie. Prince William left a few days later. It was agreed that the wedding should not take place until after Marie's eighteenth birthday.

In June the prince joined the grand duchess and the children for the announcement of the engagement at Peterhof. The four then stayed at Ilinskoe, and Elizabeth worked out the financial details of the marriage with the prince. She watched the engaged couple playing cheerful games with Dmitri, and it seemed to her that Marie was happy enough.

There was another young person in whose life Elizabeth took a close interest. It happened that Princess Zenaide Youssoupova's son, Nicholas, had died in a duel. He had become entangled with a nobly born girl, Countess Marina Heyden, who was engaged to a guardsman called Baron Arvid Manteufel. On the eve of the wedding the family had barely prevented him from yielding to her entreaties and eloping with her on the spot. On some pretext Nicholas had pursued the couple to Paris on their honeymoon. His brother, Felix, was sent with him in the role of chaperone. In Paris, it emerged that Nicholas had resumed his affair, and the husband was now pressing for a divorce. Felix consulted two clairvoyants. One told him that a member of his family was in danger of dying from a duel. The other said that he would one day carry out a political assassination, involving him in a terrible ordeal.

Returning to St. Petersburg, Felix heard rumors that the aggrieved husband had challenged Nicholas to a duel. A tradition in the Youssoupov family held that all the heirs but one would die before the age of twenty-six. The two other brothers had died, and Nicholas was within days of his twenty-sixth birthday. It was with immense relief that Felix heard that the duel was off, and arranged to dine with his brother at Constant's, a fashionable restaurant.

Nicholas never arrived. Felix searched for him throughout the city and returned home, unsuccessful, to a fitful sleep. He descended the next morning to find his father standing before his brother's corpse on a stretcher.

In Moscow, Elizabeth joined the family for the funeral procession to Archangelskoe. She stayed on at the vast estate for some time. The family was in a state of numb despair. The elder Prince Youssoupov§ concealed his grief behind his habitual reserve, but the death had borne heavily on him. Princess Youssoupova was in a state of nervous exhaustion. Her spirits gradually rose, but she never quite recovered from the loss of the son she loved. Felix burned with a desire for revenge. Elizabeth's kind presence comforted them all, especially the princess. She restrained Felix from committing some desperate act and made him promise to see her and talk of his future once his mother's health had improved.[17]

The youth of twenty who called at the Nicholas Palace was a neurotic, spoiled, self-indulgent character, on the edge of a nervous breakdown. Felix was the youngest of the family, and as a child had been his mother's pet. He had been a sickly, spindly boy, and his father's efforts to impose a character-building regimen of cold showers and spartan discipline had been abandoned when Felix broke down in tears and let out piercing screams. At fourteen, handsome and with long eyelashes, he was encouraged by his brother to stroll around St. Petersburg dressed as a woman and dine with Guards officers. Subsequent biographers and historians have taken these escapades as evidence of homosexuality.[||] Thereafter he followed a life of pleasure, following his tutor out of curiosity into a Neapolitan brothel, entering into a liaison with a Parisian girl, and taking opium. He tried in vain to strengthen his will by occult meditation, and after his brother's death his mind was close to collapse.

In a state of nervous despair he called on Elizabeth at the Nicholas Palace. In his memoirs he left the following account of their conversation:

> I was at once shown into the Grand Duchess's presence and found her seated at her desk. I broke down completely and threw myself at her feet. She gently stroked my hair and waited till I had calmed down. When I had recovered my self-control, I confided all my troubles to her: my spiritual turmoil and the conflicting emotions that were torturing me. To confess was in itself a relief. The Grand Duchess listened most attentively: "You were right to come to me," she said; "with God's aid I am certain I can help you. No matter what trials He sends us, if we have faith in Him and confidence in our prayers, He will give us the strength to bear them. When doubt assails you, do not despair; kneel before an icon of the Saviour and pray; you will feel better at once. The tears you

have just shed came from your heart. Always be
guided by your heart rather than your head, and
your life will be transformed. Happiness does not
consist in living in a palace or enjoying a large fortune. True happiness is something that neither
men nor women nor events can take from you.
You will find it in Faith, in Hope and in Charity.
Try to make those around you happy, and you will
be happy yourself."[18]

He found that her sympathy extended to his past misde-
meanors, which he felt obliged to confess to her. She heard him
in silence,

and when I had finished she kissed me.

"Don't worry," she said, "I know more about you
than you think. That is why I am so much interested in you. Anyone who is capable of doing so much
evil is also capable of doing much good, if he sets
about it in the right way. No matter how serious the
offence, it is redeemed by sincere repentance.
Remember, the only thing that defiles the soul is
spiritual sin; it can remain pure despite the weakness of the flesh. It is your soul that I am thinking
of, and I want to lay it open to you. Fate has given
you everything that a man could wish; you have
received much, and much will be asked of you. Do
not forget your responsibilities; you must set an
example and earn the respect of others. The trials
you are going through will teach you that life is not
just a pastime. Think of all the good you can do!
And all the evil! I have prayed much for you, and
believe that our Lord will hear me and help you."

These words, Youssoupov recalled, gave him renewed strength
and hope. Elizabeth advised him to look after his mother as he

was now her only son. At Elizabeth's suggestion, he began visiting the tubercular women in her new hospital, and took up charitable work among the poor of the Moscow slums. He determined to abandon occultism for the consolations of the faith he was taught as a child.[19] His cousin, Prince Serge Obolensky, considered that, after listening to her advice, he "went through a profound religious conversion."[20]

Felix now decided to make a firm effort to do something with his life. He planned to turn Archangelskoe into an art center with an academy, a school of music, and houses for artists. The family's houses in Moscow and St. Petersburg, unused for some time, were to become hospitals, clinics, and old people's homes. The land was to be given away to the peasants, and the factories turned into joint stock companies. He told the grand duchess of these plans, and she understood and approved. Yet in the face of the resolute opposition of his mother, from whose family the property had come, they had to be abandoned.[21]

At the end of April 1908, before leaving for her niece's wedding, the grand duchess took Marie and Dmitri to the completed chapel of Grand Duke Serge. The children knelt in prayer on the marble floor, and it seemed to Marie that she was asking for her uncle's blessing on her last visit to his tomb. She clasped her brother's hand in the knowledge that soon she would no longer be near him. Then Elizabeth, feeling moved herself, reminded them that it was time to leave for Tsarskoe Selo.

The wedding day was cold, and wet snow fell in the park. Elizabeth, dressed in her widow's bonnet, gave Marie her blessing, shook hands with her father, Grand Duke Paul, and kissed him. Paul had been allowed out of exile for the wedding, and on this day Elizabeth overcame her abhorrence at his morganatic marriage, treating him in a conciliatory manner. She then left for the chapel and took her place in the congregation along with Alexandra and the king and queen of Sweden. Marie, looking pale, entered on the arm of the emperor, who was acting as her guardian. She was wearing the jewels from the reign of Catherine the Great that Elizabeth had worn on her own wedding day.

After the service and the lengthy congratulations, Elizabeth took Marie aside to a private apartment. They rested and took tea while replying to the many congratulatory telegrams. Marie was relieved of the crown and robe of ermine and velvet; they were never to be used again.[#22] At the banquet that followed, Elizabeth felt herself out of place in the world of luxurious grandeur that she had renounced. She soon left for Sergievskaya Palace in St. Petersburg, where she later that evening welcomed the bride and groom with gifts of bread and salt. A few days afterward she bid them farewell at the station, leaving Marie with her unloved husband to face a life in a foreign country for which was ill prepared.

As Elizabeth unknowingly set the seal on her niece's future unhappiness, she had another matter on her mind. Her sister Alexandra had now accepted two new friends into her family circle. One was Anna Vyrubova, who as Anna Tanayeva had played childish games with Dmitri and Marie at Ilinskoe some years ago. In 1907 she had suffered an unhappy marriage with a naval officer, Vyrubov. His nerves had been shattered by the war with Japan, and he was unable to consummate the marriage. Now separated, Anna had become Alexandra's bosom friend, and lived in a cottage in the park at Tsarskoe Selo. She was an unusual royal favorite, a fat, plain, unintelligent and sentimental woman. Anna may well have encouraged Alexandra's friendship with Rasputin, whom she revered wholeheartedly and who had been an intimate of the imperial family since the previous year.

At the wedding, Elizabeth had also noticed Alexandra's tired and worn appearance. She was in a desperate worry over the health of her son. Some days earlier the tsarevitch had knocked his ankle against a footstool, and the resultant swelling had caused him so much pain that he had sometimes lost consciousness. Alexandra had moved her bed into his room, and spent hours by his side, clasping his hot hand as he begged her to take away the pain.

In desperation she had telegraphed Rasputin, then in Siberia. He replied that he would pray for Alexi. As soon as the wedding ceremonies were over, she rushed back to her son's bedside to find him fast asleep. His temperature, the nurse said, had fallen at around eight o'clock. A telegram from Siberia, it seemed, informed her that Rasputin would say a special prayer at eight that evening. The empress's faith in her holy man was redoubled.[23] It is unlikely that Elizabeth knew of this apparent miracle, but she had seen enough of her sister's dependence on Rasputin to cause her disquiet. She may well have heard the dark rumors about the Siberian peasant that were beginning to spread in high society. It was said that he had once been a horse thief, and a member of the Khlisti, an outlawed religious sect practicing free intercourse and occasional sexual orgies.[24] Clearly it would not be long before a scandal further undermined the shaky foundations of the Russian throne.

Back in Moscow, Elizabeth resumed work at her hospital. Her sister Victoria came again to stay, bringing her son Louis (who later became a naval hero and received the title Earl Mountbatten of Burma). They traveled to St. Petersburg, and Dmitri enrolled in the cavalry school to prepare for a career in the Horse Guards. On her doctor's orders Elizabeth took a holiday with her sister on the Baltic coast. Afterward Victoria stayed on with her son at the nearby port of Reval for the meeting between King Edward VII and Emperor Nicholas, an event which sealed the entente between Britain, France, and Russia.

Felix Youssoupov, meanwhile, after a tour of his many estates, decided to study at Oxford University. He told Elizabeth, and she at first tried to dissuade him, but ultimately gave way and promised to obtain his parents' consent. This proved to be a long and difficult task, and it was some months before he was able to go to England with an introduction from her to Princess Victoria. Victoria, he recalled, was anxious about Rasputin's ascendency over Alexandra, and questioned him very closely.[25]

## Notes to Chapter 17

*This number was insignificant compared to the sixteen hundred officials killed by the terrorists.

†This belief that the tsar was their friend and protector goes some way toward explaining the volatile, anarchic character of the Russian peasantry, as well as the urban proletariat. The peasants regarded the tsar as a semidivine fairy-tale figure who would dispense justice, which they saw as protecting their interests. In no sense did this conception correspond with a respect for the law or for the tsar's agents, the nobility, government officials, policemen, and justices of the peace. Rather the peasants considered them as corrupt and self-seeking individuals who were frustrating and concealing the tsar's benevolent intentions. They therefore felt perfectly entitled to riot and seize the land when they got the chance.

To a lesser extent this idea pervaded the urban proletariat. Although many had been influenced by Socialist propaganda demanding the tsar's overthrow, most believed that Nicholas approved of their strikes and rioting. The thousands who followed Father Gapon to the Winter Palace clearly imagined that he would grant their requests. Such was the veneration of the common people for the office of the tsar that in the revolution of February 1917 the Petrograd Soviet initially demanded, not a republic, but a new tsar to take the place of Nicholas.

‡In 1904, William, hoping to disrupt the Franco-Russian alliance, had persuaded Nicholas to sign a treaty of alliance between their countries. The treaty had collapsed as soon as Russian officials had had time to read it, and diplomats in European capitals were becoming wary of German designs. The pretext for a possible German invasion would have been the need to protect the German-speaking inhabitants of the Baltic provinces.

§He bore the same Christian name as his son, Felix.

‖On the other hand, there is a letter written by a fellow Oxford undergraduate, Seton Gordon:

"I knew Felix Youssoupov very well at Oxford and travelled with him to Russia afterwards. I shared rooms with him at Oxford in 1912 and met many of his friends.

"Under these conditions one gets to know a person and I saw nothing abnormal in his character at any time—indeed he was a delightful person and very popular, with an admirable character."

#In 1927, Prince Christopher of Greece was in the New York office of the jeweler Pierre Cartier. With the words, "I have something here I want to show you," Cartier opened his safe and produced the imperial wedding crown, saying that he had found it by accident in a Paris antique shop. He refused to sell any of the stones: "I am keeping the crown intact until the restoration of the imperial house, and then I shall present it myself to the emperor." Recalling the incident, Prince Christopher wrote: "Alas, that was ten years ago, and the crown is still reposing in his safe!"

# Chapter 18

*Jesus said unto him, If thou wilt be perfect, go and sell that thou hast, and give to the poor, and thou shalt have treasure in heaven: and come and follow me.*

—MATTHEW 19:21

Grand Duchess Elizabeth's duties to her niece and nephew were now fulfilled. She was able to dedicate herself to the task she had set herself: to care for the poor and sick and follow the life ordained by Christ. It was the culmination of a desire that stretched back from her earliest memories of charity in Darmstadt, and the religious yearnings that had begun with her voyage to Jerusalem and her conversion to Orthodoxy. With feelings of awe, exultation, and deep gratitude she had found her life's mission. She sensed a union with a divine purpose. Her mood was almost akin to the ecstatic mysticism experienced by some of the early saints of the church. She described it a little later to Emperor Nicholas:

> One can't believe that *I alone, without any outer influence* decided this step—which to many seems an unbearable cross I have taken up. And which I will either regret one day, throw over or break down under. . . .
>
> . . . life and time will show and certainly I am not worthy of the unboundless [sic] joy of God letting me work this way—but I will try and He who is all

love will forgive me my mistakes, as He sees the wish I have of serving Him and His [sic]. In my life I had *so much joy*—in my *sorrows* so much *unboundless* [sic] *comfort,* that I *long to give a little of that to others.* . . . Oh, this is not a *new feeling,* this is an *old one* which *always* was in me. *God has been so kind to me.* . . .

 *I don't for one minute think I have taken up a "nodvig"* [heroic deed], it is a *joy,* I don't *see my crosses* nor *feel* them because the unboundless [sic] kindness of God I have always felt—*I long to thank Him.*[1]

She remembered the story of St. Elizabeth of Hungary, the ancestress after whom she was named. Her mother's acts of welfare in Darmstadt came to mind. It was probably the example of these two women that inspired her most.

Like St. Elizabeth, she rid herself of her wealth and used it for the benefit of the poor. After her husband's death she had been the richest grand duchess. Now she sold her priceless jewels down to her wedding ring.[2] Her palaces she gave to her niece and nephew. She was probably the only person of her rank in modern times to follow literally Christ's commandment, "Sell that thou hast and give to the poor." There was one other wealthy Russian who had tried to do likewise. Leo Tolstoy had made over his estate and income to his wife in an attempt to live in Christian poverty. But he still lived in his manor house, waited on at table by liveried servants even while he wore peasant costume; he did little active charity.

Elizabeth embraced religious life wholeheartedly. She disbanded her court in the Kremlin, pensioned off the servants, and shut up the rooms in Nicholas Palace. She abandoned the world of glittering dances and spectacles that had been her entire social life, and moved into rooms by her hospital on the Great Ordinka, the street leading due south from Red Square over the Moscow River.

Here she began the work of founding a sisterhood of nuns dedicated to nursing and charity. She learned from the spiritual masters at the ancient Zossima Hermitage and two metropolitans, to whom she looked for guidance. "I find an immense and touching help in three of the 'igumena' [Fathers superior]," she wrote, "they consider me belonging to them. . . . There are the Metropolitans Tryphon and Anastasius who are now my masters whom I see and who have serious talks with me."[3] She traveled widely among the convents and monasteries of Russia. Yet the Basilian rule of Russian convents could teach her little in achieving her daring innovation. In Russia, as E. M. Almedingen has written,

> Nuns neither taught nor nursed. They led a strictly contemplative life, and they never left their enclosure except in those cases when the extreme straits of a house made it essential for the community to beg for alms. A few sisters carefully chosen by the superior would be sent out, but each such such excursion must first be sanctioned by the bishop of the diocese. Cloistered life was very severe. Most rigorous fasts were kept; meat never appeared at all and even fish was not served every day. . . . The nuns . . . rose about an hour or so after midnight for the lengthy Orthodox matins. . . . They had to stand for hours.[4]

Instead Elizabeth looked to the active good works of the order of deaconesses of early Christendom. She studied the German deaconess houses and pilgrims' homes, and with the help of her sister Victoria she learned about the Little Sisters of the Poor in London, whose ideals she admired. With little intellectual training, she pored over books on monastic rules throughout the centuries, just as her mother had read theological works during her spiritual crisis.

From 1908 on, she oversaw the building of her convent on the Great Orkinka. She planned a church dedicated to the Virgin Mary using the gifted Schussev as architect and the artist Nesterov as designer of the austerely beautiful interior. There was a Chapel of SS. Martha and Mary, after whom the convent was to be named. The robes of her new order were a pearl gray habit of white wool, a lawn wimple framing the face, and a white woolen veil which fell over the breast in long classical folds. It was her own artistic inspiration of simplicity and beauty.[5]

Like St. Elizabeth, the grand duchess found her ideas sneered at by the court and society. According to Felix Youssoupov, Alexandra at first considered they demeaned the dignity of the imperial family.[6] Her views were echoed by her attendants. Aristocratic St. Petersburg hostesses began to jeer that Elizabeth's mind had become unhinged by her husband's death. She was undaunted, and wrote in a tone of sincere humility to Nicholas:

> . . . I fear so *you think* I am *proud and self-satisfied,* that I interiorly *puff myself* up with *satisfaction of creating* something *grand.* Oh, I *wish you knew me better.* I know Alix imagines I allow people to call me a Saint—she said so to my Countess O[lsufieva]. I—good gracious—what am I, no better and probably worse than others. If people may have said foolish exaggerated things is it my fault, but they don't say it to my face, they know I *hate flattery* as a *dangerous poison.* I can't help people loving me, but then you see I love them and they feel it. . . . I try to do my best for them and people can be grateful although one must never expect it.
>
> . . . *Forgive* me, *both of you.* I know and feel alas, *I worry you* and perhaps you don't quite understand me, please forgive and be *patient* with me, forgive my mistakes, forgive my *living differently* than *you* would *have wished, forgive* that I *can't often* come to

see you because of my *duties here.* Simply with your good hearts *forgive,* and with your large christian souls *pray* for me and my work.[7]

Elizabeth's innovations upset the church when she submitted her plans to the Holy Synod. In a fierce debate, Bishop Hermogen of Saratov and the conservative St. Petersburg prelates drowned out the support of Metropolitan Vladimir of Moscow and his deputies. Her ideas were dismissed as un-ortho-dox novelties, too Protestant for Russian tastes.

Undeterred, she altered the rules and tried again. At about this time Dmitri came from St. Petersburg, and Marie from Sweden, to pray dutifully beside her in the convent.[8] Once again the Synod took umbrage, particularly at the idea of her sisters venturing into the outside world to do good works. But she had an ally in Emperor Nicholas. Himself piously Orthodox, he had earlier warned her of the spiritual pitfalls of being enticed into hubris by a *dukh prelest,* an evil spirit of enchantment.[9] But he now sympa-thized with the aims she had described to him in a series of impas-sioned letters. He cut through the synod's vacillations and estab-lished her convent by imperial decree in March 1910.

With trepidation she looked forward to taking her veil, and wrote to Nicholas with a plea for moral support:

> I am as if *bidding* goodbye *to the past its faults and sins and with the hope of a higher goal and purer exis-tence. Pray for me deary.* . . . my taking of vows is even *more serious than if a young girl marries. I am espous-ing Christ and His cause, I am giving all I can to Him and our neighbors,* I am *going deeper into our Orthodox Church and becoming like a missionary of Christian faith and charity work and Oh dear I am so so unwor-thy* of it all and I *do* so want *blessings and prayers.*[10]

On April 15 her mission was realized. She said to her assem-bled Sisters, "I am about to leave the brilliant world in which it fell to me to occupy such a splendid position, but together with you I am about to enter a much greater world: that of the poor and afflicted." Sisters from all social levels, knelt down in front of Archbishop Triphonius. Among them were Mme. Uzlova, her companion who became her assistant, and her faithful maid Varia, who as Sister Barbara was to follow her to her death. The archbishop gave them their veil, saying, "This veil will hide you from the world, and the world will be hidden from you, but it will be at the same time a witness of your work of charity which will resound before the Lord to His glory."[11]

Their charitable work resounded before the people of Moscow. The city had few charitable institutions, and the plight of the poor was accepted as a law of nature. Like her mother, Elizabeth was to effect a radical innovation in welfare in her adopted country; and like Princess Alice, the sisters took food from the convent's kitchen to the homes of the poor, and stayed there to scrub their floors. A cluster of new institutions slowly grew up around the convent. To add to the home for consumptive women, the grand duchess set up a hospital and recruited the best available doctors. There followed a women's hostel and homes for cripples, expectant mothers, and old people. There was an orphanage, but, unusually, she tried to give its inmates a hopeful start in life by employing them as messenger boys in another organization she set up. Over the years, the nuns traveled to other cities and founded similar institutions. This unprecedented movement spread to every large Russian city.[12]

The convent was a cheerful community in which every Sister had her rightful place and felt herself valued. To give them strength for their active charity, all except the foundress were allowed a relaxed form of fasting and a fortnight's annual holiday. Elizabeth taught them the charitable and menial tasks her mother had taught her many years before. Every morning she gave them her blessing, and her door was open to any Sister in low spirits. One Sister, Princess Marie Obolenskaya, recalled that she was like a mother to them all, an example of humility and self-abnegation.

Elizabeth lived by prayer, which gave her the willpower for her tasks. Her only holidays were pilgrimages to monasteries in the depths of Russia. She might use a carriage for traveling to the outer regions of Moscow, but her daily life was spartan in its austerity. She kept rigidly to a vegetarian diet, from which her Sisters were excused. In her whitewashed cell with only an icon given by some respectful devotees for ornament, she would lay her head on the hard pillow and fall asleep with ease on her bare wooden bed. However late the hour, she would never turn away any visitors. She often managed with only two or three hours of sleep, rising at midnight to pray alone in the silent chapel and then make the rounds of the hospital. Or she would attend an all-night service in the Kremlin or some modest church, returning contented as the first streaks of dawn appeared over Moscow.[13]

By day she looked after the sick. She would take on the most responsible tasks of assisting in operations and changing bandages. Twice a week she visited her home for incurable consumptive women. If patients were dying she made sure that they were told and well prepared for a peaceful end. She took part in the reading of the psalms over a coffin, a continuous ceremony required by Orthodoxy until the funeral proper. At her request she was always told if a patient was near her death, and she would sit beside her. Often a mother would confide to her: "My children are no longer mine, but yours, for they have no one in the world but you," and she would find a place for them in her orphanages.[14] Once she was at a dying woman's bedside when the patient's hastily summoned husband joined her. They each held the woman's hand for her last moments. The man, a Communist, was astonished, and said his political opinions would have to change if all the imperial family were like her.

She saw every patient in the hospital each day, knowing the power of faith to help cure them; some would describe her as a healing force. Sometimes she took the gravest or most disturbed cases to a special service. Felix Youssoupov, back from Oxford during a vacation, joined her for a service in the Kremlin in which her patients took an active part. It was the glorification of the relics of a Russian holy man, Blessed Yossaff:

> A vast crowd filled the cathedral. The shrine containing the remains of Blessed Yossaf was placed in front of the chancel and sick people carried on stretchers, or in the arms of relatives, were brought to kiss the relics. Cases of people "possessed by the Devil" were particularly gruesome; the inhuman screams and contortions of the victims grew more and more violent as they approached the shrine, and it sometimes took several people to hold them. Their shrieks drowned the magnificent religious chants as though Satan himself were blaspheming through their mouths; but their cries calmed down the moment they were made to touch the shrine. I saw several miraculous cures.[15]

Such was the reputation of her hospital that the municipal bodies sent their worst cases to her. One was a woman burnt by the oil from an upset stove, which had set her clothes on fire. Gangrene had set in, and the doctors despaired of saving her. Twice a day the grand duchess changed her bandages. Several nurses fainted at the overpowering stench, which so impregnated Elizabeth's own clothes that she had to change them afterward. The woman recovered within a few weeks, and the doctors thought it a miracle.[16]

Her greatest altruism, however, lay in her work outside the convent. To the east, on the site of a damp, fetid swamp beside the Yausa River, lay the Khitrovka. It was a market for stolen goods, illicit vodka, and very plain food. Narrow alleys of filth and decrepit hovels led out of it; around it were barrack shelters which housed several families to a room. In this tight space, surrounded by stench and disease, lived some twenty thousand people, prostitutes, pimps, beggars, thieves, and escaped convicts. Law and order never prevailed. Whenever the police made one of their occasional raids, word would pass around to the suspects long before their arrival. The many children born there were kept hungry so that their wailing would induce the public to give more alms. Few among them reached maturity, and few girls remained virgins beyond the age of ten. Leo Tolstoy had visited it some years earlier, and was so appalled that afterward he was unable to bear the thought of a meal served at table by liveried servants.

The horror of a childhood in this city of dreadful night had haunted the grand duchess for some time, and she determined to give some of the infants the hope of a new life in her homes in Moscow. With her faithful Sister Barbara she often went among these social outcasts and prostitutes. Barely understanding their language, she asked if any would give up their children into her care. In the squalid tenements where space was measured by inches and the foul air took an effort to breathe, she risked catching the disease that had killed her mother. Yet she braved the danger, concerned only about following the example set long ago by Princess Alice. The police despaired for her safety and begged her to give up her visits. She thanked them, and said she was in God's hands. As she showed no disdain for their grimy existence, the people respected and never harmed her. Once an old woman saw her sneeze, and offered her a dirty rag, which she accepted with gratitude. To her they were all made in God's image, the blessed poor and meek who would inherit the earth.[17]

For this, the grand duchess was now widely loved by the people of Moscow. She gained a charisma equal to that of Mother Teresa in modern Calcutta. They revered her as a saint, and called her *matiushka,* their holy mother. In the streets, crowds would fall on their knees and cross themselves as she passed. As she alighted from her carriage, they would kiss her hand or her nun's habit.[18] One ardent convert, pleading to be allowed to help in the convent, said to her: "Once admitted, I would feel as though I were presented at the court of heaven."[19]

# Chapter 19

*The holy man is he who takes your soul and will and makes them his. When you choose your holy man, you surrender your will. You give it to him in utter submission, in full renunciation.*

—DOSTOEVSKY, *THE BROTHERS KARAMAZOV*

On October 17, 1910, Grand Duchess Elizabeth took leave of her Sisters and boarded her train en route for Germany. She arrived at Wolfsgarten for a cheerful reunion with the rest of her surviving family. Alexandra and Nicholas had come from Tsarskoe Selo with their children, Louis and Victoria from England, Irene and Henry of Prussia from Kiel. Ernest welcomed them all with his new wife. It was like another summer of their childhood. The four sisters were staying in the main block of the house, and there was ample opportunity to wander into each other's room for an intimate talk. Emperor William dropped in on an unexpected visit, much as he had done while studying at Bonn University and courting his Ella. On October 30, Princess Marie of Battenberg, Elizabeth's cousin, arrived for lunch. At the meal Emperor Nicholas, she noted, seemed as happy as a schoolboy on holiday as he enthusiastically talked of plans for a "Peace Palace" at The Hague.[1]

Alexandra, however, was absent, lying on her bed in her room upstairs. She had developed sciatica, a disease of the nerves that caused her great pain in the legs and made walking a severe trial. Her heart had troubled her for some years. A few months earlier she had reluctantly gone with Nicholas to Nauheim for a cure. It seemed to have done little good, and now she was obliged to spend her time lying down or being wheeled about in a bath chair.[2]

Her ill health was aggravated by the mounting anxiety she felt for her son. From the first signs of severe bleeding six weeks after his birth she had never been sure that Alexis would be free from pain. A bruise or a nosebleed was enough to cause a swelling from the rush of blood which only clotted very slowly. If a joint was hit, blood would pour into the affected space, corrode the bone and tissue, and give intense unrelenting pain as it entrapped the nerves; for months the tsarevich would be unable to walk. The endless vigil Alexandra kept over him produced a strain akin to battle fatigue in soldiers, but for her there was no chance of withdrawing from the front.[3]

At Wolfsgarten, Irene could show her sympathy, for she too had given birth to a hemophiliac boy,* who had died six years before. Yet Alexandra's plight was far worse. While Irene had two other healthy sons, Alexandra's sole son was the heir to the Russian throne, and on his health the future progress of a great nation depended. The severe pain she had endured in the births of her five children, aggravated by her sciatica, meant that she could not face that ordeal again. In vain had she made a painstaking search for a medical cure, and now she spent many hours in prayer in hope of a miraculous one. It seemed as if the curse of the Coburgs, which had struck at many of Prince Albert's relatives, had descended on his granddaughter.

The appearance of Rasputin had seemed to Alexandra little short of a godsend. By praying at the foot of the tsarevitch's bed, or even from his home in Siberia, he seemed able to effect a slow recovery or a release of pain. There is a plausible medical explanation of this apparently supernatural ability. Rasputin had both a strong hypnotic power and an uplifting psychological effect on his patient. In 1909, Felix Youssoupov had met Rasputin, and experienced the full glare of his wide staring eyes that seemed to penetrate his mind. He recalled in his memoirs that he was so mesmerized that he could not speak. Some medical authorities affirm that this hypnotic power could play a part in reducing the tsarevich's bleeding by reducing emotional stress and causing the arteries to contract.

More importantly, both the empress and her son held the Orthodox belief in the power of prayer and spiritual healing. As they had confidence in Rasputin as a holy man with extraordinary powers, the knowledge that he was praying for Alexis gave them mental strength and eased their fears. The reduced tension may well have caused Alexis's bleeding to cease. The tsarevitch would probably have recovered without Rasputin's intervention. Robert Massie, writing from direct experience as the father of a hemophiliac boy, affirms: "It is one of the mysteries of the disease that the recuperative powers of the victims, especially when they are children, are extraordinary. A child who has been totally disabled and in great pain can be quickly restored."[4]

Whatever the extent of Rasputin's powers, the empress was convinced that he was a saintly man with great spiritual powers. She knew of his rakish youth, but thought he had sincerely repented, and called to mind several "holy fools" of the Russian Church who had also given way to the temptations of the flesh.[5] Like her grandmother, Queen Victoria, and her mother, Princess Alice, she needed a man to guide and support her. Nicholas, a diffident, indecisive character, could never fill this role; it was she who was dominant in their marriage and bolstered his self-confidence. Instead Alexandra slowly came to depend on the Siberian peasant. The emperor was reluctant to interfere in an arrangement which calmed her nerves.

From Moscow, Elizabeth had observed this mounting dependence with dismay. For all her ecstatic mysticism, she still retained a sound common sense and a clear judgment of character. She knew all about Rasputin's true nature, and she had none of her sister's naive credulity. Soon after his acceptance by the imperial couple, rumors began to spread in St. Petersburg society that Rasputin had been a member of the Khlisti.[6] Senior figures in the church investigated Rasputin's habits, and the facts passed through ecclesiastical circles to her. It transpired that Rasputin rarely prayed or went to church. He spent much of his time in bathhouses with loose women, and his evenings carousing in cabarets or brothels, or alone in his St. Petersburg flat with prostitutes. To Elizabeth it seemed monstrous that such a man should be an intimate of the revered imperial family, for whom prayers were said in church every Sunday. The emperor's authority rested on the belief that he was divinely appointed to rule Russia; as head of the Russian Orthodox Church he, and the empress, must live with exemplary virtue. For Elizabeth it was a source of great sorrow that her much-loved sister should have caused this disgrace.

Several times Elizabeth warned Alexandra that the "holy man" was a fraud and a lecherous drunkard. Alexandra would flatly refuse to believe her, maintaining that saintly men were always pursued by slanderous rumors. She still remained the obstinate "Sunny" of their childhood, the youngest sister who would persist in having her own way. After a heated argument she would be as obdurate as before, but Elizabeth would often undergo agonies of self-reproach. After one such acrimonious meeting at Tsarskoe Selo she wrote a contrite reply to Emperor Nicholas, making a guarded mention of Rasputin:

> ... *please please forgive me now and forgive me the past (I of course never will forgive myself* and there is hardly a confess I don't again repeat that why was I too rough then when perhaps with *profound gentle* love I might have *helped you really and not lost your confidence for ever).* Perhaps if all that had been managed by me otherwise you would have seen the real truth and no more looked for helpers who hidden from others *bring you their particular religion in seeming not to break you from the true Orthodox Church.* "Du choc des opinions jaillit la verite"† and perhaps we

all would have quietly talked and examined and come to the conclusion *that we can be mistaken and that not all who seem holy are. Perhaps they are sincere* it may be so, although *it seems otherwise,* but let us say they are sincere alas the devil has caught them— "prelest" [enchantment], and *the more we try to mount, the more we take nodvigi* [heroic deeds] *upon ourselves the more the devil is at work, to blind us to the truth, the higher we mount the oftener we fall,* we must *advance so slowly* that we have the feeling of not advancing at all. . . .[7]

The senior churchmen and many other members of the imperial family endorsed Elizabeth's warnings. Those who had been Rasputin's supporters, Grand Duke Nicholas and the Montenegrin princesses,‡ now turned against him. Alexandra, having found that any friend of hers soon became the object of intrigues and malicious slander, ignored them.

By the beginning of 1911, Rasputin's presence at court had become an open scandal in St. Petersburg. Women, many from high society, flocked to his flat, and found his earthy peasant voice and penetrating eyes a new and exotic diversion. He enthralled them with his religious talk of humility. His idea that salvation came only through sin and repentance, that virtue was an expression of sinful pride, made his lechery seem innocent. He spoke constantly of "love," making no distinction between its carnal and spiritual varieties. Those who saw him in his home could not imagine that he behaved at Tsarskoe Selo as a meek and devoutly Christian peasant. Many believed that he must be carrying his lecherous ways with him into the palace.

The prime minister, Stolypin,§ who loathed Rasputin, feared greatly for the sanctity of the monarchy. He ordered an investigation into his excesses and presented it to the emperor. Nicholas read it and did nothing, and Alexandra refused to believe it. Rasputin, however, felt the atmosphere in the capital was becoming too heated for him. In March, he fled to Jerusalem, ostensibly on a pilgrimage.[8]

Elizabeth heard the news with some relief. It seemed as though the reputation of the imperial couple would now be safe. At the beginning of the summer, she traveled in a cheerful mood to see them at Tsarskoe Selo. There is no record of their conversation.[||,9] No doubt she warned her sister of the harm Rasputin had caused her and her family. The riots in Moscow in 1905 had taught Elizabeth that the imperial family must be above suspicion and present an impeccable face to the world.

She made no impression on Alexandra. In June Rasputin was back in St. Petersburg, and on the seventeenth he called again at Tsarskoe Selo.[10]

Worse news was to follow. On September 14, 1911, the emperor, the empress, and their two elder daughters attended an opera performance while on a visit to Kiev. In the first row of the orchestra sat the prime minister, Stolypin. During the second interval, the imperial family left their box to take some air. Hearing two pistol shots, the emperor ran back into the auditorium. "Women shrieked," he later wrote to his mother, "and right in front of me stood Stolypin in the stalls. Slowly he turned his face towards us and made the sign of the cross in the air. Only at this point did I notice that he was very pale and that his right hand and uniform were stained with blood. He sat down quietly and started to unbutton his tunic."

Stolypin died a few days later. His assassin, Bogrov, was a police agent; most probably cajoled into committing the killing by the revolutionaries whom he was supposed to infiltrate. Rumors circulated that he was a tool of right-wing figures determined to put an end to Stolypin's reforms. It is also said that Rasputin was in Kiev that day, had seen Stolypin drive past in a procession, and shouted: "Death is after him! Death is driving behind him!" Prince Felix Youssoupov and a few others were convinced that his followers were behind the assassination.[11]

It was true that Rasputin was now beginning to acquire an influence in state affairs. People petitioned him for favors from the bureaucracy, and he wrote notes in his semiliterate scrawl asking officials to grant them. The officials, anxious to placate a court favorite, duly complied. A courtier, General Bogdanovich, thought Rasputin's influence extended far wider, and glumly wrote:

> A more ignominious time could not be lived through. The tsar does not govern Russia, but that scoundrel, Rasputin, who loudly declares that the tsarina does not need him, but rather he, Nicholas. Is this not horrific![12]

Rasputin was surrounded by a growing clique of highly placed devotees, including Anna Vyrubova, the plain, unintelligent woman who was the empress's closest companion. Elizabeth had her own group of friends in Moscow, who came to follow her lead in opposing Rasputin's power. She encouraged their resistance, and her high status served to protect them from Alexandra's wrath. A rift slowly developed between the two circles.

Elizabeth and her friends came to loathe Rasputin when he began to use the empress's influence and meddle in Church appointments. To her it was an abomination to find a lecherous drunkard interfering in the Orthodox Church that she ardently revered. Late in 1911, they were outraged to hear that a friend of Rasputin, "an illiterate, obscene and debauched peasant"[13] called Father Varnava, was made bishop of Kargopol. Elizabeth encouraged her friends Samarin and Count Sheremetiev, and Novoselov, Druzhinin, and Vasnetsov, all defenders of traditional Orthodoxy, to make a public protest. Michael Novoselov, who was a lecturer at the Moscow theological academy, went further. An expert on Russian religious sects, he prepared a pamphlet in January 1912 showing evidence that Rasputin had been a member of the Khlisti.# Elizabeth may have connived in this; she read the pamphlet and hoped its publication would cause Rasputin to flee St. Petersburg. Much to her annoyance, the police confiscated the printed copies, broke up the type, and destroyed the manuscript.[14]

A bishop and a monk, Iliodor, who had harangued Rasputin and made him swear never again to see the imperial family, were banished from St. Petersburg.[15]

Now, other events widened the antipathy between Elizabeth and her sister. Elizabeth's close friend Princess Youssoupova tried to warn Alexandra of the dangers of Rasputin's influence, and was soon barred from her circle.[16] Another old friend, Sophia Tyuteva, whom Elizabeth had recommended to Alexandra for the post of governess to her children, met with a similar fate. She was shocked at Rasputin's free and easy way of treating her charges. He would hang about the young girls' bedrooms after they had changed into their nightgowns on the pretext of joining in their prayers. Mlle. Tyuteva protested to the emperor, and he asked Rasputin to avoid his daughters' rooms. But Alexandra was indignant, and she later dismissed her. Mlle Tyuteva returned to her family in Moscow and spread about the story** of Rasputin's improper behavior.[17] She went to the convent, told it to Elizabeth, and begged her to speak plainly to Alexandra.

Elizabeth continued to warn her sister of the harm caused by the false holy man, but Alexandra began to show her an increasing hostility. She may well also have felt a slight jealousy of the fond sympathy that Nicholas bore toward his Aunt Ella.[18] Gradually the warm affection between the sisters dwindled to the point of coldness. Elizabeth had no wish to abandon Alexandra when she suffered so greatly for her son's health. She visited her as often as before, but the empress began to feel oppressed by her presence.

Pressure was growing on the imperial couple from other directions as well. By 1912, the press was attacking Rasputin, and openly described him as a sinister manipulator who controlled church appointments and had the ear of the empress. Newspapers printed the accusations of the female victims of his seductions and the anguished cries of their mothers. From Moscow, the newspaper *Golos Moskvy* thundered against "that cunning conspirator against our Holy Church, that fornicator of human souls and bodies—Gregory Rasputin." Soon it was being said that Elizabeth was refusing to visit Tsarskoe Selo. By the October Manifesto, freedom of the press was guaranteed, and Nicholas was powerless to prevent these attacks. He tried to forbid any mention of Rasputin on pain of a fine, but the saucy stories were so profitable that the editors gladly paid it.[19]

An even worse rumor spread around St. Petersburg to the effect that Rasputin was the empress's lover. It even appeared to be given confirmation by the monk Iliodor, who had made Rasputin swear to leave the capital. He had obtained letters supposedly written to Rasputin by the empress. Some of these, no doubt counterfeited, contained expressions of intimate devotion which were readily misconstrued. An ambitious politician, Guchkov, the leader of the liberal "Octobrist" party, had obtained these letters and circulated them in St. Petersburg. He and many on the left now made strident speeches against Rasputin in the Duma, intending by discrediting the imperial family to force them to yield up their share of power.[20] The new prime minister, Kokovstev, warned the emperor again of the scandal Rasputin was bringing to the throne. He was authorized to investigate the man's habits, but soon aroused the empress's hostility. Once again Rasputin, feeling threatened by the hostile atmosphere in the capital, fled to his native Siberia.[21]

Both Ernest and Victoria were now concerned about the strained relationship between their sisters and the scandal of Rasputin. Ernest wrote to Victoria about Alexandra: ". . . through ruining the position of her friends she is ruining her own future, that I am sure she would not like."[22] They both came and tried to reconcile the sisters and persuade Alexandra that she must abandon the Siberian peasant for good. In April 1912, Ernest joined Nicholas and Alexandra at Livadia. He found it difficult to harp on about Rasputin for fear of hurting Alexandra, and he sadly concluded that she was blind to his true nature. "The Emperor is a saint and an angel, but he does not know how to deal with her," he told the foreign minister.[23]

In July, Victoria came to see Elizabeth before going on to Peterhof. In the midst of a very hot summer, the meeting was a delight for Elizabeth. Her sister stayed in her austere quarters at the convent, and they spent many hours together. During that time, a stream of friends and fellow abbesses called in, and Victoria, with her limited Russian, was often at a loss whenever Ella left the room.[24] Elizabeth briefed her on Alexandra's state of mind, and she left for St. Petersburg.

Victoria's visit, it seemed, had some steadying effect on Alexandra. Rasputin remained in Siberia, and soon afterward Elizabeth was able to meet her in a harmonious atmosphere. In August she traveled to the gilded statues and tall fountains of Peterhof.[25]

There was another matter on her mind. In a month's time Moscow was due to celebrate the centenary of the battle of Borodino. The memory of the time when all Russians had stood together and repulsed a foreign invader should have been an occasion of great patriotic rejoicing. Yet the ministry of the court, fearing for the emperor's security, had planned that the main event of his visit to the city was to be a trivial tour of the Land Handicrafts Museum. The suffragan bishop of Moscow, Anastasius, thought that a public Te Deum in Red Square would give the people a chance to see their tsar. He had called on the grand duchess, who agreed with him. She knew how well a public appearance would restore the much-needed prestige to the throne, and managed to persuade the imperial couple to accept the idea.[26]

Elizabeth was proved right. In September 1912, Nicholas braved the risk and entered Red Square surrounded by a vast guard of Cossacks. A solemn and moving service followed, and the Muscovites' reverence for their emperor was much enhanced. Everywhere he was met by cheering crowds and great expressions of loyalty. He also unveiled a monument to his father in the Kremlin; on the way he knelt in prayer on the spot where Serge had been assassinated. It was a reminder of the fate he was courting. A British diplomat, Robert Bruce Lockhart, wrote: ". . . as far as Moscow was concerned, everyone breathed a sigh of relief when the suspense was over and the Imperial train had left the city."[27]

The imperial couple and their children took leave of Elizabeth and left for Spala, the ancient hunting lodge of the kings of Poland, set in a vast forest south of Warsaw. There Alexis fell prey to a severe bout of bleeding in his groin. He cried ceaselessly, and as his strength faded he gave way to muted wailing and could eat nothing. "When I am dead, it will not hurt anymore, will it?" he asked his mother. Bulletins were issued asking for the people's prayers, and the finest doctors available warned that there seemed to be no hope. In agony the empress telegraphed to Rasputin in Siberia. He replied promising his prayers, and from that date a slow recovery began. Henceforth, the empress was convinced that Rasputin was a saint.[28] He was back in favor, and soon returned to St. Petersburg for good.

### Notes to Chapter 19

*Prince Henry (1900–1904).

†Disagreements produce the truth.

‡Grand Duchess Militisia and Grand Duchess Anastasia, daughters of King Nicholas I of Montenegro, who had both married into the Russian imperial family.

§Stolypin had no great regard for Empress Alexandra, but admired Grand Duchess Elizabeth. He told his daughter: "There is such a difference between Alexandra Feodorovna and Grand Duchess Elizabeth Feodorovna. The latter is not only holy, but a woman of remarkable energy, logical thought and ability, who carries matters to their conclusion. . . . There is a woman before whose example it is possible to bow."

|The only record of the grand duchess's visit is in a letter from the empress to her old governess, Miss Margaret Jackson: "Ella spent a week at Zarskoe with us, looked well, pink and cheery." However, given that the tsarevitch's hemophilia was a closely guarded state secret, the empress would have undoubtedly avoided any mention of matters connected with it, including Rasputin. Almost every chronicler of this period, including the grand duchess's niece, affirms that she made repeated warnings to her sister.

#Some members of the heretical Khlisti ("flagellants") were imprisoned in a Siberian monastery which Rasputin had visited in his youth. Although at the time it was widely rumored that he had been a member of this sect, and membership would have been in keeping with his lustful character, modern historians think it improbable.

**Baroness Buxhoeveden and Anna Vyrubova maintain that Mlle. Tyuteva was inventing these stories of Rasputin's behavior. They are, however, confirmed by the emperor's sister Grand Duchess Olga, who recalled meeting Rasputin in the company of the imperial children in their nightdresses.

# Chapter 20

*There is only one truth, so only one nation can have the true God, even though other nations may have their own great gods. The Russian people is the only "God-bearing" nation.*

—DOSTOEVSKY, *THE POSSESSED*

In spite of Rasputin's continued presence at court, the year 1913 was marked by enthusiastic demonstrations of loyalty as the emperor and empress celebrated the tercentenary of the Romanov dynasty.\* In February Elizabeth, dressed in her white habit with a plain wooden cross, was present at a special service in the Cathedral of Our Lady of Kazan in St. Petersburg. She and the rest of the imperial family saw vast crowds, cheering wildly, as they drove down the Nevsky Prospect from the Winter Palace to the cathedral. During the service she and the others noticed a beautiful omen: two doves of peace circled about the immense dome of the cathedral.[1] To Emperor Nicholas it signified that his country would remain for years under the sway of his dynasty. Russia's stability seemed assured on a wave of unprecedented prosperity. The economy was growing faster than any other in Europe; harvests were at record levels thanks to fine summers and Stolypin's land reforms. The growth of a law-abiding middle class, liberal and constitutional in politics, promised to strengthen the social fabric. The revolutionary tide was on the ebb; the exiled Lenin, unsuccessfully treating his baldness with hair oil, despaired of creating a workers' uprising in Russia. When

Elizabeth saw the imperial couple again at celebrations in Moscow, the cheering crowds everywhere reinforced this impression of a secure and confident dynasty.

It was a contented year for Elizabeth in other ways as well. Late in the summer of 1913, she was able to spend time away from her work in nursing and charity, and take a pilgrimage to a monastery on Solovetz Island, far to the north in the White Sea.[2] She asked Felix Youssoupov, who had now finished his degree course at Oxford University, to accompany her. The three years at Oxford had changed him from a nervous, neurotic, and effeminate youth into a boisterous man-about-town and a keen sportsman and fox hunter. He had become engaged to Irene, daughter of Grand Duke Alexander Mikhailovich, defeating Elizabeth's nephew, Dmitri, a rival suitor. Elizabeth, hoping perhaps to sober him with religious influences, was keen for him to come with her to the monastery.

She stopped several times to visit churches on the way to the port of Archangel, where she had arranged to meet Youssoupov. Youssoupov, characteristically, had lost count of the time while strolling around the town, and she boarded the ferry without him. He hired a launch and only managed to catch up with her, looking sheepish, as she landed on the island.

The entire community was present to greet her. As she made her way to the monastery, she was overwhelmed by a swarm of monks, dressed in black, with long hair and beards, all staring at her in intense curiosity. The monastery, one of the greatest in Russia, was surrounded by crenellated fifteenth-century walls made of pink and gray blocks of granite, on which many bell towers rested. Her cell was a clean whitewashed room adorned with many icons. The diet at the monastery consisted of bread and tea.

Elizabeth attended all the services, sometimes with Prince Youssoupov. At one, four hermits appeared in the congregation, wearing black cowls which almost completely obscured their emaciated faces; on their chests were gruesome embroidered representations of a skull and crossbones. With Felix she went to visit one of these hermits. They traveled past some of the hundreds of lakes linked by canals that were dotted around the island, to a cave deep in the forest of fir trees. They crawled through a tight underground passage to a bare stone cavern. The only ornaments were an icon lit up by a flat candle, and a slab of rock on which the hermit slept. Without uttering a word he gave them his blessing, and they left.

In the far northern latitude the sun barely set. In the long evening twilight the moving sound of the deep-voiced chants of the monks echoed over the lakes and woods. Elizabeth and Felix would join a few monks with whom they had made friends, and talk deep into the night. Away from her burdens and anxieties, Elizabeth no doubt felt a peace and contentment she had not known for some years. Prince Youssoupov felt likewise, and began to wonder if the monastic life was not the only true one. He asked Elizabeth, and she unhesitantly replied that he must marry the grand duchess Irene, whom he loved and who loved him:

"You will remain in the world and of the world, and wherever you go must always try to love and help your neighbor. Let yourself be guided by the only true teaching, that of Christ. It answers to all that is best in the heart of man and kindles that flame of charity which is love."

"The whole of my life," Youssoupov wrote, "has been brighter for the radiance cast over it by this remarkable woman, whom I have regarded as a saint since my early youth."

At the end of this idyllic fortnight, the grand duchess's return to the mundane routine of duty was enlivened by a highly comic incident. At Archangel, she visited some churches and a convent, and arranged to meet Prince Youssoupov on board the train. She was taking tea with some ecclesiastical dignitaries in her salon when he arrived. Outside, furious grunts were suddenly heard, and a crowd gathered on the station platform. The churchmen exchanged anxious glances, and only Elizabeth remained calm.

It turned out that Youssoupov, strolling around Archangel, had seen a poster advertising the auction of a white bear. On a whim, he had bought the bear and arranged for it to be put in a cattle truck, which was then attached to the train. Elizabeth was convulsed with laughter. "You are quite mad," she told him, in English, "What will these poor bishops think?" The bishops, giving the prince sour looks, took leave of the grand duchess in an icy manner. As the train moved off, the crowd outside burst into cheers. The passengers slept fitfully that night, being awakened at each stop by blood-curdling snarls.

At St. Petersburg station, several court officials and civic dignitaries were assembled for a solemn reception. They stared in stupefaction as the grand duchess emerged with a growling Russian bear.

Not long after parting with Felix Youssoupov, Elizabeth heard news of the unhappiness of another young friend of hers. In September 1913, a Swedish doctor with white hair, a small beard, and thick blue spectacles called on her at the convent. Dr. Axel Munthe was a famous physician who lived on the Island of Capri in the Tyrrhenian Sea. There he had arranged that her niece, Marie, should spend the winter months away from the harsh climate of Sweden. His opinion was that the cold would prove dangerous to her health.[3]

Marie's marriage at the age of eighteen to Prince William of Sweden had proved to be unhappy. She had felt rootless and homesick in her strange new country, and the private life of its court was far more formal and stilted than in Russia. She had never come to love her husband, a good-natured, decent but dull naval officer. The birth of a son had not brought them closer together or filled the emptiness that she felt in her life. Shortly before Christmas 1912, her mother-in-law, the queen of Sweden, an invalid, had summoned her to Dr. Munthe's† villa where she habitually spent the winter months. The doctor had taken Marie into his confidence, and she had trusted him as a mentor who might resolve her predicament. He had deduced that her nervous anxieties were the result of a kidney disorder, aggravated by the cold Swedish climate. He had persuaded the king of Sweden that she should spend the winters at his villa.

He had also asked for the approval of a member of Marie's family. Elizabeth had gone over to Sweden early in 1913. Marie recalled:

> I was genuinely glad to see her again. She brought to me in my confusion a breath of ordered activity and normal life. I so envied her serenity and the satisfaction she took in her work that her convent seemed, for the moment, a refuge where I also might find work, usefulness and peace. I begged her to take me with her, to initiate me into her Order. She smiled sadly at my outbursts and gave me no other answer.

Elizabeth knew that her niece's worldly frame of mind would never be calmed in the cloistered air of her convent. She also believed that Marie must regard her marriage as irrevocable and accept the pains that went with it, as she had done. She had spent hours in private talks with the doctor, and his sympathetic and intelligent manner had convinced her that Marie was in good hands.[5]

Now, however, on meeting Dr. Munthe again, her opinions changed abruptly. He had come to seek her firm approval for his plans to take Marie away and dictate the course of her life; it seemed that she had become reluctant to go with him and be parted from her son for months. He spoke more harshly of his patient, attributing to her a frivolity which Elizabeth knew she did not possess. He appeared to regard her as a child who needed correcting, and was determined to repress what remained of her youthful vitality. He had one sinister characteristic: although he claimed to be almost blind, underneath his thick blue spectacles he had a penetrating stare.

Elizabeth's suspicions were aroused. She prepared to write to her niece and warn her. At that point news reached her that Marie had fled to her father, Grand Duke Paul, in Paris, with the secret connivance of her brother Dmitri. She persuaded her father that there was no chance of retrieving her marriage.

It became clear to Elizabeth how unhappy her niece had been in Sweden. With great regret she discovered her error some years before in contriving Marie's marriage so hastily. She still knew nothing of Marie's last-minute efforts to break it off, but the thought that she had been partly to blame was hard to bear. She made no objection when her niece sought to have her marriage annulled. After much persuasion by Grand Duke Paul and two diplomats who had come into contact with the Swedish doctor, the emperor made the decree of annulment to the Holy Synod.[6]

In January 1914, Elizabeth was in St. Petersburg on a visit to Alexandra when she met Marie again. She told her of her last meeting with the doctor, and uttered no criticism of her niece's divorce. "My aunt was," Marie later wrote, "in a word, both understanding and sympathetic; she reproached me with nothing and went so far as to deplore the haste she had shown to see me married. From this time on we were intimates and got on wonderfully together."[7]

A few months after her reconciliation with her niece, Elizabeth was glad to be able to travel on a long pilgrimage with her favorite sister. On 21 July 1914 she left Moscow for Nizhni-Novgorod with Princess Victoria, and Victoria's daughter, Louise.‡ They then transferred to a yacht for a cruise down the Volga and its tributary, the Kama. It was an idyllic journey. They ate freshly caught sterlet and watched the distant tree-lined banks[8] flow quietly by. Elizabeth stopped several times to visit convents, and the villagers would turn out in their best clothes to receive her. At one place Victoria was delighted by the scent of a wood of limes in full bloom. As in their childhood, the two sisters would part to pursue their own interests. At Kazan, Elizabeth visited the churches while Victoria and her daughter looked at the walled fortress and the

Tartar population in gaudy oriental dress. From Perm they traveled on by land, and Elizabeth left the others to see more convents further north.

She journeyed into the Urals, through a virgin forest of birch and pine to an area of mineral workings and industrial railways. She came to Alapayevsk, a mining town of grubby one-storied buildings and unpaved rutted streets. The population were eager converts to socialism from their grimy and arduous lives in a harsh climate, and they received her with cold indifference. At the edge of the town she was welcomed at the convent and the adjacent monastery. The prior of the monastery was an old friend called Father Seraphim, the son of a rich merchant. He held her in great reverence.

Victoria and Louise, meanwhile, went on to Yekaterinburg, another industrial town a hundred miles further south. It lay just east of the edge of Europe. They found the same indifference in the population, who showed little enthusiasm for an evening entertainment of fireworks. Several times Victoria drove past a comfortable house in a square not far from the center; she was told it belonged to a rich merchant, Captain Nicholas Ipatiev. Nicholas and Alexandra were to end their lives there.

At that time Elizabeth's brothers-in-law were caught up in the mounting international crisis. Irene's husband, Prince Henry of Prussia, was hurrying back to Germany from England to take charge of the battle fleet. Victoria's husband, Prince Louis of Battenberg, canceled the demobilization of the fleets of the Royal Navy. He made urgent arrangements for the return of Victoria and Louise.[9]

At Alapayevsk Elizabeth received a telegram from the empress. Having read it, recalled Father Seraphim,

> Her Highness turned pale and could say nothing for several minutes. To my question, what had happened? she replied: "My sister has asked me to

pray to God to prevent war, for Russia's enemies want war and want her to be destroyed." Tears began to flow from her eyes.[10]

Elizabeth rejoined Victoria and Louise, and on the train they heard that Germany and Russia were at war.

## Notes to Chapter 20

*In 1613, after a long period of fighting between rival claimants to the Russian throne, a Land Assembly of nobles, priests, and peasants had declared Mikhail Romanov to be tsar of Russia. Mikhail, the great-nephew by marriage of Tsar Ivan IV ("the Terrible"), had no blood connection with the dynasty of Rurik Sviatoslavich that had ruled since the ninth century, but was the only candidate on whom all parties could agree.

†In Marie's memoirs, *Education of a Princess,* from which this account is taken, the Swedish physician is known only as "Dr. M." Undoubtedly he was Dr. Axel Munthe, the queen of Sweden's personal doctor during the last years of her life. Prince Christopher of Greece remembered him as "that baffling and dynamic Swede. . . . Whenever you mention his name you will find conflicting opinions as to his character. . . . whether people like him or dislike him they do it intensely. He seems to have exercised an extraordinary fascination for women all his life." His memoirs, *The Story of San Michele,* describing horrific diseases and vivid adventures with sardonic humor, are still widely read.

‡In 1923 she married Crown Prince Gustav of Sweden, and on his accession to the throne in 1950 became queen of Sweden.

# Chapter 21

*Just think of the responsibility you're advising me to assume! Remember it's a question of sending thousands and thousands of men to their death!*

—Nicholas II, on being asked to mobilize the Russian Army, July 30, 1914

Elizabeth and Victoria were not the only ones to be unprepared for the sudden onset of war. Few had appreciated the consequences of the shooting of Archduke Franz Ferdinand in Sarajevo on 28 June 1914; yet the assassination of the Austrian emperor's nephew by a Serbian nationalist, seemed only of local importance, and almost no one thought that it presaged a catastrophic war. When Austria delivered an ultimatum to Serbia on July 23, the abject reply acceded to so many of the extreme concessions demanded that the Austrians looked unlikely to engage in the hostilities which they had threatened. The Germans, in particular Emperor William, thought that by resolute firmness in defense of their Austrian allies, they might cow Russia, France, and Great Britain into not taking up arms on Serbia's behalf.

Yet as a result of the Kaiser's blundering diplomacy, abetted by his generals and other advisors, especially Admiral Alfred von Tirpitz, Germany had made firm enemies of three powers of the entente. By now the stability underpinned by the network of royal marriages that Queen Victoria had arranged* had disintegrated. On the accession of her son, Edward VII, Serge had remarked to Elizabeth: "Thank heaven your Uncle Bertie is king of England. Willie will never dare plunge into anything; he is mortally afraid of his uncle."[1] But Edward's condescension toward his nephew had infuriated William and deepened his inferiority complex toward the British Empire; he had responded with a program of aggressive naval expansion. Believing that he possessed some diplomatic flair, William convinced himself that Germany must be the sole arbiter of war and peace on the continent.[2] The chancellor, Bethmann Hollweg, gloomily summed up the folly of his swaggering diplomacy: ". . . a Turkish policy against Russia, Morocco against France, fleet against England, all at the same time—challenge everybody, get in everyone's way, and actually, in the course of all this, weaken nobody. Basic cause: lack of planning, craving for petty prestige victories. . . ."[3] Now the powers of the entente were in no mood to bow down before the Kaiser's bluster.

In Russia, Emperor Nicholas felt honor-bound to protect the Serbs who were, like the Russians, both Slavic and Orthodox. Furthermore, in 1908 Austria had humiliated the Serbs by annexing the province of Bosnia-Herzegovina, which they regarded as Serbian. His army was by no means ready for war, and he knew how easily it could destroy the country's prosperity, the greatest ever in Russia, and the fragile parliamentary system. But when Austria had invaded Serbia, he felt that hostilities were inevitable, and mobilized his army. On the evening of August 1, he and Alexandra knelt down in the church at Tsarskoe Selo, and prayed earnestly for peace. At the same moment, the German ambassador handed his country's declaration of hostilities to the foreign minister.[4] Soon afterward, the French felt obliged to take up arms on behalf of their Russian ally, and the British for the sake of the Belgian neutrality that Germany had violated.

Elizabeth and Victoria, hastening westward from the Urals, were soon caught up in the grim excitement of war. Their train was repeatedly shunted aside to make way for troops hurrying to the front. To add to their discomfort, Victoria's lady-in-waiting and her daughter Louise had both caught tonsilitis. Elizabeth, using her nursing experience, tried to soothe their pain and high fever. She could do little, and the doctors summoned by telegraph to the larger stations were not of much greater use.[5]

On August 4, they reached St. Petersburg. From the railway station, they were rushed to the Winter Palace, where two days before the emperor had solemnly declared war and seen a vast crowd in the square outside, kneeling and singing *God Save the Tsar*. They were reunited with Alexandra, and Elizabeth's differences with her sister were forgotten. Rasputin was fortuitously absent in Siberia, recovering from a stab wound inflicted by a demented prostitute.[6] Alexandra's mind was intent only on the tasks she faced in helping the war effort. She and Elizabeth made their farewells to Victoria, who faced a difficult journey through Scandinavia and across the North Sea, where a German naval blockade was feared. She had to leave her family jewels behind her.[7] None of the sisters had any idea that these jewels would not return to England, or that the three of them would never meet again.

St. Petersburg believed that the war would last a few months; the soldiers in the streets, cheered on by exultant crowds, hoped to be in Berlin by Christmas. Outside the home of Grand Duke Constantine, where Elizabeth was staying, there was a throng of people loudly rejoicing at the news that all six of his sons were about to leave for the front. Inside, Elizabeth took tea with the young men, who were already in uniform. The family was very close to her, in particular the eldest son, John, a deeply religious man. In these gatherings of her relatives, Elizabeth would normally have been taciturn. This time the thought of the young soldiers facing bloodshed and death made her eloquent, and she talked with animation about the Russian Church.[8]

At Tsarskoe Selo Elizabeth held some earnest discussions with Alexandra about hospitals, ambulance trains, supply depots, and field chapels. She then hurried to Moscow. The city, showing a determined purpose, was in a frenzy of activity. In the convent, several of her Sisters felt it their duty to nurse at the front. She and Father Mitrophan agreed, and they left with her blessing. Elizabeth soon set about implementing the plans made at Tsarskoe Selo. "She has any amount to do," Alexandra wrote to Victoria, "is energetic, here, there and everywhere."[9] In an effort to cut through the administrative chaos, she made plans to centralize all donations for the wounded. Without neglecting her homes, her orphanage or her consumptive patients, she prepared her hospitals to receive the many expected injured soldiers. She spent hours arranging the dispatch of supply trains to the front. Everywhere she met with appalling incompetence; on one occasion a train of urgent surgical materials for the western front was sent to the southeast. She abandoned her Christian meekness and berated the officials with undisguised fury.[10]

On August 17, the emperor, the empress, and their children arrived in Moscow. Nicholas was to carry out the tradition of announcing to his people from the Kremlin that war had been declared.[11] It was to be a great demonstration of loyalty to him from the people of Moscow. Not since the War of 1812 against Napoleon, in which the Kremlin itself had taken such a prominent part, had the citizens been so united in a patriotic cause.

The following day, Elizabeth joined them as they drove through a vast crowd in the Red Square that greeted them with deafening cheers. On the stroke of eleven they entered the St. George's Hall of the Kremlin, where the nobility, high officials, and the allied ambassadors were gathered. In a deep and firm voice, Nicholas addressed his people. He proclaimed that, by the tradition of his ancestors, he sought the moral support he needed from the holy relics of the Kremlin. A heroic national impulse was sweeping through all the nations and races of Russia. "From this place, the very heart of Russia, I send my soul's greeting to my valiant troops and to my noble allies. God is with us!" He was answered by a prolonged burst of cheering.

The imperial party passed the St. Vladimir Room, the Sacred Gallery and the Red Staircase into the square outside. Here Elizabeth saw an immense crowd, bareheaded and cheering exultantly, that filled the Kremlin to the limit. They entered the Cathedral of the Assumption, where Nicholas and all his predecessors had been crowned tsar. The fateful moment of the coronation when he had dropped a chain was entirely forgotten. Ahead of them stood the three metropolitans and twelve archbishops of Russia; to the right were more than a hundred bishops, archimandrites and abbots. At times the church seemed to glow with a supernatural light from the diamonds, sapphires, and amethysts that sparkled on their miters and chasubles. After a long service, the imperial family knelt in turn at the sacred relics and tombs of the patriarchs. When Elizabeth's turn came, the French ambassador, Maurice Paléologue, admired her graceful bearing: "To kiss the figure of the Virgin of Vladimir which is set in the iconostasis she had to place her knee on a rather high marble seat. The Tsaritsa and the young grand duchesses who preceded her had had to make two attempts—and clumsy attempts—before reaching the celebrated icon. She managed it in one supple, easy and queenly movement."

Again they emerged to face the overwhelming cheers of the crowd. The empress was in a state of inspired patriotic fervor. The emperor called over Paléologue and the British ambassador, George Buchanan, to his side as representatives of Russia's allies. Elizabeth came to join in their conversation. "Her face in the frame of her long white woollen veil was alive with spirituality," Paléologue wrote. "Her delicate features and white skin, the deep, far-away look in her eyes, the low, soft tone of her voice and the luminous glow around her brows all betrayed a being in close and constant contact with the ineffable and the divine."

It was not only an intense religious faith that animated Elizabeth. She now combined it with the wave of patriotic enthusiasm in which she and her sister had joined. Having renounced any German patriotism she might have held in her youth, she considered herself entirely Russian. From her close knowledge of his character, she blamed Emperor William for secretly sowing among enmity the peoples of Europe.[12] To her the war was just, a great Orthodox crusade by the Russian people; it seemed that all the saints of Russia stood behind them. With the power of their faith and prayer, the people would surmount all their obstacles to attain victory. That evening, she and Alexandra, both intent on their common purpose, sat into the night talking of their war work. "I feel so strong and well," Alexandra told her.[13]

A few days later, they witnessed another sign of the powerful religious and patriotic strength of Russia. With the emperor they visited the St. Serge Monastery, forty miles outside Moscow. It was a fantastic assembly of gleaming blue-and-golden cupolas over cathedrals that formed one of the oldest citadels of Russian Orthodoxy. The abbot blessed them and gave the emperor an ancient icon that the tsars had always taken on their campaigns. Alexandra departed with the emperor for Tsarskoe Selo, and each sister resumed her tasks with added zeal and feverish energy.[14]

Not long afterward, Elizabeth traveled to St. Petersburg to bid farewell to her niece, Grand Duchess Marie. Returning to Russia after the annulment of her marriage, Marie had enrolled as a nurse and was now about to leave for the front. On August 29, Elizabeth took her to pray before a celebrated icon in the house where Peter the Great had lived. Marie, wearing her nurse's uniform for the first time, was feeling self-conscious. News of their presence had leaked out, and an emotional crowd surrounded them as they left the house. Many of the women were in tears; seeing Marie's uniform, they bent to touch her dress and kiss her hands. A sobbing old woman cried, "Our dear one, you too are going to war. God bless you!" Others joined in with good wishes: "God help you! God save and protect you!" Another old woman repeatedly asked Elizabeth to try and find out about her son.

They were both deeply moved as they stepped into the carriage.

That evening, Elizabeth and Volodya Paley, Marie's half-brother,† accompanied her to the station. The platform was crowded with piles of stores and friends making emotional farewells. Marie embraced both her relatives, and Elizabeth, with tears in her eyes, fervently blessed her with a wide sign of the cross over her forehead. She waved for a long time as the train pulled out.[15]

Elizabeth went on to Tsarskoe, which was now completely turned over to the serious bustle of war. The palace of Catherine the Great, the site of state ceremonies, had become an officers' hospital. Alexandra was training hard with her two elder daughters to receive a nurse's diploma, steeling herself to face the sight of blood and death. In her spare moments she tied religious images onto strings, one for each of the millions of Russian soldiers.‡[16] On the day the grand duchess left for Moscow, the emperor signed a decree renaming St. Petersburg with the truly Russian-sounding title of Petrograd.[17]

By October, requiem services for the dead soldiers were being held daily in the Moscow churches. It was not long before one of the grand duchess's own relatives was included in their number. Late in October, she learned that Oleg, one of the sons of Grand Duke Constantine, with whom she had taken tea at the outbreak of war, had died of wounds at Vilno.§ His father had personally closed the boy's eyes. Elizabeth felt that she must give what comfort she could to the grand duke's family, who ranked high in her affections. She left to others the management of supplies and the care of the wounded soldiers and her patients, and set out for a few days for Ostashevo, the family estate near Moscow where the funeral was to be held.

She stayed on after the service, and late in the evening, entered the room of Oleg's sister, Tatiana. She told her that she would often pray for her and her husband, Prince Bagration-Mukhransky, then serving at the front. At the mention of the prince's name, Tatiana said that she was deeply afraid of losing him as well as her much-loved brother. Casting aside her tiredness, Elizabeth sat talking to her deep into the night. To distract her, she knitted her a black-and-white hood.[18]

This was by no means the only act of charity for which Elizabeth found time in the midst of her war work. Later in the war, hearing that her niece, Grand Duchess Marie, was in charge of the twenty-five nurses in a military hospital near Pskov, she remembered an old priest, a man of great learning and lofty spirituality. The archimandrite Michael had been paralyzed from the waist down after a deranged theological student had shot him in the back during the 1905 revolution. He was now living with Father Gabriel, her confessor, in a house she had built for him in the grounds of a monastery near Pskov. He was struck down with erysipelas, a disease involving inflammation of the skin. She ordered that he be received into Marie's hospital, although the nature of his disease would normally have ruled this out. For the sake of her aunt, Marie began to visit him and, as he recovered, the two became close friends.[19]

Late in November 1914, the grand duchess saw the line of battle for the first time. She traveled south to the newly captured areas of the Carpathians to inspect Alexandra's field hospitals and depots. At Lemberg[||] she met once again her nursing sister who had gone to war, Princess Marie Obelenskaya. The weather was bitterly cold, and snow had already fallen. Elizabeth saw some of the numerous wounded and dying soldiers that represented the cost of the advance into Austria. Yet morale was still high, and the empress's facilities seemed well run. She was able to visit Tsarskoe and give her sister a reassuring report. In Catherine Palace, she met a soldier whom she had seen in the hospital in 1905.[20]

Back in Moscow, however, as the first snows of winter fell, a mood of pessimism was sweeping the city. A few days earlier, an immense German offensive had succeeded in reversing the Russian advance on the Polish front.[21] The Russian soldiers, who had advanced so well with cavalry and bayonet charges, were now being mown down by machine guns and artillery. More than half a million men had been lost, and Lodz had fallen. An alarming shortage of ammunition was becoming apparent. Russia could not make up the deficiency, and could only import new supplies by the Trans-Siberian Railway or the port of Archangel, ice-bound in winter. With grim determination and a fierce hatred of Germany, Moscow resigned itself to several more years of war.

The city's anti-German spirit showed itself not only in the occasional looting of German-owned shops but in a wave of rumors. It was said that the empress herself, being of German birth, was carrying on a secret correspondence with the enemy. The suspicion extended to Grand Duchess Elizabeth. Worse, Rasputin was now back in Petrograd, and had been received at Tsarskoe Selo.[22] From her many friends in government and the church, Elizabeth heard a vast range of rumors about his political influence. Several high officials were among his friends. He was said to be strongly against the war, and word spread that he was passing on secrets to the Germans. Elizabeth, acutely aware of public opinion from her visits to the Moscow poor, feared greater dangers from her sister's association in the tense climate of war.

They had a chilly encounter when Alexandra visited Elizabeth's Moscow hospitals early in December.[23] At the station Elizabeth and the executive of her convent, Mme. Gordieva, met the empress. With her were her two elder daughters and her inseparable companion Anna Vyrubova, a fat, plain, unintelligent woman whom Elizabeth had treated with cold distance since she became a fervent disciple of Rasputin. In the empress's entourage was General Vladimir Dzhunkovsky, the head of the secret police and an old friend of Elizabeth.

Alexandra's health had begun to fail, and her spirits were low. She had ordered that her visit be private and that no notice be taken of her. As a result, the streets were almost empty, and the imperial party was virtually ignored. The same reception met them when Alexandra, who never made the best impression on the wounded, toured Elizabeth's hospitals.[24] On these occasions few people recognized her in her nurse's uniform; in the eyes of the patients it robbed her of her dignity as empress. As she spoke to them, they appeared anxious and embarrassed, and she failed to communicate the sympathy she sincerely felt.

Alexandra was hurt at this cold reception, and irrationally felt that Dzhunkovsky and the Moscow officials had contrived it. One evening her palace commandant gave General Dzhunkovsky a severe dressing-down in front of the whole company. To Elizabeth it seemed unfair that her friend, a capable and honest official, should be blamed for obeying orders. During the rest of the visit she had some unfriendly exchanges with Alexandra. She asked her sister about Rasputin's political influence; Alexandra denied there was any such thing, which Elizabeth showed a cold refusal to believe. Alexandra, and especially Anna Vyrubova, imagined there must be some conspiracy against herself and Rasputin. She was showing signs of the paranoia which was later to control her. Henceforth, she regarded Dzhunkovsky as her enemy and Moscow as a hotbed of intrigues. On every occasion, Elizabeth was to urge her to banish Rasputin.

In the new year of 1915, Moscow's morale sunk further as more defeats were suffered at the front. Even while the southern armies were advancing in the Carpathians and the Caucasus, the western armies steadily retreated before the Germans. The shortages of ammunition meant that the army had little choice but to retire in good order before the well-equipped Germans. The strategy recalled the campaign of 1812, which had ended with Moscow in the hands of Napoleon's invading army, its wooden buildings burned to the ground. The grossly mismanaged railway system exacerbated food shortages.

The city, always more determined on winning the war than

Petrograd,‖ bore a sullen resentment toward the government and court. The liberal politicians, of whom Moscow was the center, believed that they must have a greater share in government to relieve the chaos created by the imperial bureaucracy.[25] More rumors circulated about the empress, now called "the German woman," sympathizing with her native land; Rasputin was thought to be in the pay of the Germans.[26] Although Grand Duchess Elizabeth never believed the wildest rumors, the city's mood was one which she fully shared with her friends in government and the church.

Her suspicions of Rasputin's disloyalty were confirmed in a startling manner. Early in April 1915, he arrived in Moscow on the pretext of fulfilling a vow to pray at the Cathedral of the Ascension in the Kremlin.[27] That he should defile a sacred shrine of Orthodoxy with a false show of piety was bad enough, but that evening he held a scandalous debauch at the fashionable restaurant Yar. Arriving at the restaurant already drunk, he ordered a meal in a private room and hired a band of female Gypsy singers. He made the singers dance suggestively, and invited them to spend the night with him. Then he took it on himself to slur the name of the empress, saying that the "old girl" had sewn his caftan herself. "Imagine," he asked his guests, "how annoyed she would be to see me now."[28] After a while the party, a British diplomat in a nearby room recalled, degenerated into bedlam: "there was a violent fracas in one of the neighbouring 'cabinets.' Wild shrieks of women, a man's curses, broken glass and the banging of doors raised a discordant pandemonium. Head waiters rushed upstairs. . . . The cause of the disturbance was Rasputin—drunk and lecherous, and neither police nor management dared evict him."[29]

A journalist had been one of Rasputin's guests that night; soon the whole of Moscow was talking of the scandal.[30] It was said that Rasputin had exposed his body to the singers; the empress was openly declared to be Rasputin's lover. Elizabeth and her circle were outraged. General Adrianov, the prefect of the Moscow police, "a man of courage and conscience," according to Paléologue,[31] drew up a report on Rasputin's orgy and tried to obtain an audience to present it to the emperor. He was refused admittance by the palace commandant, General Voekov.

Elizabeth wrote directly to Alexandra, begging her to throw off Rasputin for good. She had no effect on her. Alexandra's faith in her "holy man" had been reinforced when he had helped Anna Vyrubova recover from a motor accident; she was convinced that Moscow was engaged in evil intrigues against him and herself. She reputedly replied: "God's saints have been known to fall, and they repented and overcame the devil."[32]

As if this were not enough, a communication from Germany added to the people's suspicions about the empress. At the beginning of May, her brother Ernest, Grand Duke of Hesse, sent her a secret letter via the queen of Sweden. His lifelong fear of death had combined with the traditional Hessian distrust of the swaggering diplomacy of Prussia to make the present war repellent to him. He suggested to Alexandra that Russia should pursue peace.

Alexandra had replied that peace was out of the question, and sent their brother's letter on to Elizabeth.[33] It is not known if Elizabeth read the letter or threw it away unopened; she made no reply. But the damage had been done. Reports of this supposedly top-secret missive leaked out. It was now said that the empress had a secret telephone line to Berlin. Worse, rumor had it that Elizabeth was giving help to German prisoners of war whom she was hiding in her convent. The convent was supposedly a "den of spies."[34]

Ernest's letter, though it reflected his own feelings, was part of a German strategy to knock Russia out of the war. It preceded a massive offensive on the hundreds of miles of front from the Carpathians to the Baltic. The Russians, desperately short of ammunition, lost thousands of men. "The army is drowning in its own blood," a general reported. The soldiers could only begin a slow retreat.[35]

In Moscow, refugees poured in and overtaxed the food and housing. Bread riots broke out, and the Socialists began agitating in the factories, protesting against the war as well as the government. On June 3, news came that the Austrian fortress of Przemysl, captured with the loss of thousands of Russian soldiers, had fallen.[36] It now seemed that the way to the acquisition of Constantinople, the holy city of Orthodoxy, was barred forever. There the Orthodox faith had been born and nurtured centuries before its arrival in Russia; Russians had dreamed of restoring the city to the rule of a Christian tsar ever since its fall to the infidel Turks in the fifteenth century. The loss of this objective was another grievous blow to morale.

The enraged citizens of Moscow took to the streets. For three days from June 10, they sacked and burned any shops and factories with a German connection. The mob, maddened from looted drink, killed a German-speaking factory manager and ransacked the leading piano store, barely a mile from the convent. "Bechsteins, Blüthners, grand pianos, baby grands and uprights, were hurled one by one from the various stories to the ground, where a high bonfire completed the work of destruction," the British consul, a witness to the mayhem, later recalled. "The crash of falling woodwork, the cruel tongues of flame, and the raucous yelling of the mob swelled into a terrifying discord, which even the troops, who had been called out, were unable to quell."[37] In the evening, the sky glowed from the many fires that had broken out; had there been a wind, a disaster on the scale of 1812 might have occurred.

As the fever rose, a mob gathered on Red Square. There were shouts of "Treason!" and demands that Rasputin be hanged and the empress, "the German whore," shut away in a nunnery. The emperor must be deposed in favor of Grand Duke Nicholas Nikolayevich, the commander of the Army: "Long live Tsar Nicholas III!"[38]

Then the mob remembered Grand Duchess Elizabeth, and with true Russian fickleness, entirely forgot all her good works in the city. They surged down the Ordinka to the convent. Believing that Ernest was hiding there, they demanded that "the accursed German" be given up to them. After a while, Elizabeth, dressed in her gray habit, came out onto the porch and told them he was not there. They refused to believe her. As they began to throw stones at the convent, her Sisters persuaded her to retreat inside. Just in time the troops arrived, and were met by a hail of stones. They opened fire, and killed and wounded some of the rioters. The victims were looked after in the convent.

At the same time, another crowd was gathering in Red Square. Some ringleaders shouted that they would storm the Kremlin and its arsenal and set up their own government. Once more the military was called out, and Elizabeth could hear the shots from the fierce battle that followed. Order was only restored after the stones in the square had been stained with blood.[39]

A few days later, Elizabeth saw further signs of the people's rebellious spirit. She traveled to Petrograd for the funeral of Grand Duke Constantine, the poet, who had died at Pavlovsk while grieving for his son Oleg. Everywhere she could sense an atmosphere of nervous tension. An extremely tight security surrounded the service, the last burial of a grand duke at the Fortress of SS. Peter and Paul for many decades.[#] It was known only at the last moment that the imperial couple would attend. When they did, Nicholas appeared a changed man; his hair was graying, and his face was thinner, with a solemn and distant look in his eyes. Alexandra had lost all the energy and strength of purpose that had animated her at the beginning of the war. She was highly nervous, Paléologue recalled: "her face was veined like marble and every now and then she turned deathly pale."[40] She was suffering from heart trouble, which caused her constant pain, a feeling of suffocation and chronic facial neuralgia.[41] It is doubtful if she spoke much to Elizabeth.

When Elizabeth returned to Moscow, an angry rabble surrounded her car and spat at her. They threw stones, smashing the windscreen and injuring her driver. She alighted at the convent, her expression calm but her face drained of all color.[42]

Absorbed in her religious mission as she was, Elizabeth understood the reality of the situation. She was the only member of the imperial family or official circles to venture into the slums of Moscow and experience the public's restive mood firsthand. Though politically naive, she was well briefed by her friends, the Youssoupovs, Dzhunkovsky, and Samarin. In her turn, she knew her sister better than anyone else in Moscow, and could let them know her state of mind. It had become clear to them all that a crisis was at hand. Alexandra, weak, wracked with pain and nerves, was beginning to show an irrational hostility to those who disagreed with her. She was becoming blindly convinced that Rasputin's opinions were automatically right. The continued visits of Rasputin to Tsarkoe Selo had sullied the name of the dynasty. The emperor must summon the Duma and appoint a ministry acceptable to its members to allievate the anger caused by the growing food shortages and military defeats. Otherwise a revolt against the autocracy seemed likely. As the most important figure in her circle, Elizabeth was decisive in stirring them to action. She now accepted that she could have no influence on her obstinate younger sister, so she spurred on her friends to try their utmost to make the emperor change his course.

The first was General Vladimir Dzhunkovsky, the assistant minister of the interior and head of the secret police. He was an unusual man for such an appointment. Elizabeth respected her old friend as a capable and honest man.** From his police work he knew all about Rasputin's seamy life. The emperor, shocked at Elizabeth's treatment by the Moscow mobs, sent him to make a report on the riots. Returning to Tsarskoe Selo, he risked his career and showed the emperor a report on Rasputin's debauch at the Yar. Nicholas, who liked Dzhunkovsky, was shaken by his revelations, but did nothing. The empress and Rasputin now regarded Dzhunkovsky with a still greater enmity.[43]

Late in June 1915, Nicholas traveled to the army headquarters on the western front, and there, away from his wife's influence, he began to be receptive to Elizabeth's Moscow circle. On June 29 her friend Prince Youssoupov, the governor of Moscow and husband of Princess Zenaide, attended a conference in the emperor's presence. Prince Youssoupov expressed his views vehemently about the causes of the Moscow riots, became heated, shook his fists, and banged them on the table.[44] At the same time Grand Duke Nicholas Nicholayevich, commander of the army, angrily denounced the infamies of Rasputin. In this atmosphere, also influenced by his ministers, the emperor agreed to replace the procurator of the Holy Synod, or governor of the Church. Sabler, a pliant creature without the strength to oppose Rasputin, was removed. His replacement came from Elizabeth's circle: Samarin, the marshal of the nobility in Moscow and a man of integrity and patriotism.[45]

Alexandra, however, feared some conspiracy against her, and wrote a series of frantic letters to her husband:

> Yes Lovey, about Samarin I am much more than sad, simply in despair; just one of Ella's not good very bigoted clique. . . . I hope heart and soul Samarin won't accept. If he does it means Ella's influence, and worries from morning to night. He is against us, against Gregory [Rasputin]. . . & now the Moscow set will become a spider's net around us, our Friend's enemies are ours. . . . I feel so wretched ever since I heard it & can't get calm. . . . Tell him severely, with strong and decided voice, that you forbid any intrigues against our Friend or talks about him or the slightest persecution, otherwise you will not keep him. . . .[46]

Rasputin, hearing of Samarin's appointment, again fled to Siberia.[47] His repeated exits from Petrograd were becoming farcical interludes in a somber political tragedy.

Elizabeth could rejoice at his departure. It seemed that the church that she deeply revered, now in the hands of a trusted friend, was rid of Rasputin's malign influence. His absence from Tsarskoe Selo would remove the slurs of treason attached to the imperial family. Her friends, now able to influence the emperor, might ensure that he would not return.

Moreover, the emperor had been persuaded to summon the Duma, and it seemed that, given a voice, its members might become less restive. He had also appointed some capable new ministers to rectify the bureaucratic incompetence. Together with Samarin and Dzhunkovsky, who were both popular in Moscow, the ministry almost satisfied popular opinion; a few more changes would give it the confidence of the Duma.[48] A munitions council of Duma and Zemstvo members had been set up to reduce the appalling shortage of ammunition.[49] It seemed at last that Russia's divisions were healed, and the country could wage war in unity and determination.

Elizabeth's hopes were short-lived. In the middle of August Rasputin returned to Petrograd. He had conceived a great hatred of Elizabeth, and angrily declared to his friends that she had no right to ask the empress to banish him from the capital.[50] It is said that, on seeing her photograph, he tore it up, jumped and spat on it, and called her a dangerous enemy.[51]

On August 17, he was received at Tsarskoe Selo.[52] It was not long before Alexandra began to put pressure on her husband, now back from the front. She soon persuaded him to unravel the spider's net of "Ella's not good very bigoted clique." Dzhunkovsky was dismissed and sent to the battlefield.[53] Prince Youssoupov ceased to be governor of Moscow,†† and retired with Princess Zenaide to his estate near Kursk. Samarin, waging an energetic campaign in the Holy Synod against Rasputin's protégé Bishop Varnava, aroused her fury and weakened his own position.

She also turned against Grand Duke Nicholas Nicholayevich, whom she loathed for opposing Rasputin and believed to be plotting to seize the throne for himself. She urged Nicholas to dismiss the grand duke and take over command of the army himself. Partly to calm his wife, partly because he believed that Grand Duke Nicholas was responsible for the army's defeats, partly because he thought the presence of the tsar on the battlefield would raise the army's morale, Nicholas agreed. The grand duke was sent to command at the Persian front. Nicholas's ministers, the foreign ambassadors, and many in the court were horrified; in vain they pleaded with him to reconsider his decision. Nicholas left for headquarters, leaving the government largely in the hands of Alexandra.

Elizabeth, equally shocked, was now virtually the only firm opponent of Rasputin left who might influence the imperial couple. Dowager Empress Marie, who had often argued with her son on the subject, had retired permanently to Kiev. Elizabeth could never be dismissed from her post or removed from her convent, nor could Alexandra bar her elder sister from Tsarskoe Selo while the emperor still held her in high regard.

## Notes to Chapter 21

*Her children and grandchildren married into the ruling dynasties of Prussia, Russia, Hesse-Darmstadt, Spain, Denmark, Greece, Romania, and Sweden.

†Son of Marie's father, Grand Duke Paul, by his second, morganatic, marriage.

‡Virtually none of the soldiers who received these gifts knew who had made them. The empress's exhausting effort, carried on throughout the war, was never appreciated.

§Now Vilnius.

‖Now Lviv, the city was called Lvov during the Communist era.

#Until the funeral of Grand Duke Vladimir Kirilovich in 1992.

**In their memoirs, both the French ambassador, Paléologue, and the British consul in Moscow, Robert Bruce Lockhart, affirm that Dzhunkovsky was a man of high character. It might well be asked, however, how such a man came to be head of the secret police. One answer is that in the twentieth century the tsarist political police forces, the Department of Police and the Corps of Gendarmes, had very little in common with their Soviet successors, the Cheka and the K.G.B. They concentrated not on political dissent but on subversion; since the October Manifesto of 1905, Russians had, in general, been allowed to express their political opinions. The secret police had enormous powers but used them with great leniency. In 1901, for example, only 4,113 people were in exile in Siberia for political offenses; of these only 180 were in labor camps, the rest being free men as long as they stayed in their allotted region in Siberia. Torture, concentration camps, and the imprisonment of dissidents in psychiatric hospitals were unknown.

Another answer is that a man of integrity such as Dzhunkovsky did not fit in well with the slothful, dishonest, and repressive nature of the secret police. As we shall see, Dzhunkovsky did not last long.

††It is possible that the antagonism of Alexandra and Rasputin was not the only reason for Youssoupov's dismissal. He may have been to blame for allowing the riots in Moscow in June to get out of hand.

# Chapter 22

*It's at the top, the head, that we must strike first. The emperor could be maintained on his throne, for though he's weak-willed, he's patriotic enough at heart. But the empress and her sister, the Grand Duchess Elizabeth, Abbess of Moscow, must be shut up in some convent in the Urals; that's what one of our great tsars would have done with them.*

—BRANCHANINOV, LEADER OF THE NATIONAL LIBERAL PARTY IN THE DUMA, SPEAKING TO THE FRENCH AMBASSADOR

One hundred miles south of Moscow, hidden in a wood by a river's bank, lay the great Optina Monastery. Many pilgrims came here in search of spiritual solace here. In his novels, Fyodor Dostoevsky had praised it in glowing terms, and Leo Tolstoy had knocked on its door five years earlier. Family quarrels and a futile attempt at a life of Christian poverty had driven Tolstoy half mad, and within a week he was dead. In September 1915, Elizabeth turned up at its gates in the hope of finding a few days' respite from the turmoil outside.[1] Her dream was one day to retire from the world to such a place as this.

Alone with her thoughts and prayers, Elizabeth was filled with anxiety about the future. The fate of Russia, her monarchy, and the church all seemed in doubt. The defeats at the front had left the army in a sorry state. With Nicholas absent from the capital, there was no one to recall Alexandra to her senses. Rasputin was securely entrenched. He was now able to persuade her to dismiss anyone with the strength to oppose him, and to replace them with his allies. Elizabeth's friend Dzhunkovsky had left, and so had Grand Duke Nicholas Nikolayevich, another firm opponent. So also had the elder Prince Youssoupov. Samarin's position as procurator of the Holy Synod looked insecure. The government seemed destined to fall into the hands of flatterers and mediocrities, and if he went, the church would follow suit.

In a despondent mood she returned to her convent and resumed her work in Moscow. A few months before, she had received a copy of a favorite poem by Theodor Körner, "A Prayer in the Midst of Battle," from a sympathetic admirer, a retired schoolmistress called Wilhelmina Oelzen. Fräulein Oelzen had spent weeks preparing the manuscript in beautiful illuminated script.[2] Now the lines "Father, do thou lead me, / Lead me to victory, bear me on to death"* gave Elizabeth inspiration as she sought strength for the troubled times ahead.

She read in the newspapers that Prince Youssoupov had been "officially suspended" from the governorship of Moscow. A retiring official would normally be announced as leaving in accordance with his requests. This seemed a discourtesy to a loyal servant of the emperor. She wrote to Alexandra expressing her disquiet. Nicholas sent a telegram promising to investigate the matter, which Alexandra passed on to Elizabeth. "It will quieten her," she wrote to Nicholas.[3]

In October, Samarin was dismissed and returned to Moscow to receive a hero's welcome at a meeting of the nobility.[4] It was not long before Rasputin's influence over the new procurator of the Holy Synod, Volzhin, began to make itself felt. Her friend, Metropolitan Vladimir of Petrograd, who as metropolitan of Moscow had staunchly supported her plans for the convent, was moved to Kiev. Monsignor Pitirim, a great intriguer and an old crony of Rasputin, was installed in his place. The maneuver was performed quickly to forestall Elizabeth's opposition. "It would be good you did it as soon as you come," Alexandra wrote to Nicholas, "to prevent talks and beggings from Ella."[5] This appointment, the French ambassador wrote in his diary, had "made Rasputin the absolute master of the Church."[6]

Nor was this all. In December, a meeting occurred which could lay Alexandra open to accusations of treason. After the failure of Ernest's peace offer in April, the German High Command was still convinced that it could negotiate a separate peace treaty with Russia. Its spies had kept it well informed about the severe food shortages, the unpopularity of the imperial family, the war weariness of the population, and the lack of supplies and ammunition at the front. The numerical superiority of the allies and the economic hardship caused by their blockade had convinced the Germans that an honorable victory could only be obtained by a separate peace with Russia. The departure of Grand Duke Nicholas, whom the Germans considered a great soldier and strategist, seemed a gesture of resignation.[7] In September they had approached a Russian noblewoman, a former lady-in-waiting to Alexandra who had been living in her villa in Austria since the outbreak of the war.[8] Maria Vassilshikova, formerly a close friend of Elizabeth and her sisters, known to them as "Masha," was no stranger to intrigue. She had smuggled out Elizabeth's letter to her brother Ernest during the 1905 revolution. The Germans asked her to write to Elizabeth, the emperor, and some senior ministers to persuade them to arrange a peace treaty. She readily agreed and sent off the letters, but Elizabeth and the other recipients threw them away.

The Germans, however, were determined to try again. Mlle. Vassilshikova was summoned to Berlin and instructed by Emperor William to personally go to Petrograd. She then spent a month with Ernest in Darmstadt and, early in December, set out with letters from him to Elizabeth and Alexandra. Elizabeth was, no doubt, strongly tempted to read her much-loved brother's letter. Memories of her happy, faraway childhood years must have flooded through her mind. But knowing her duty to her adopted country she sent it back unopened, and ordered the secret police to bar Mlle. Vassilshikova from entering Moscow.[9]

Alexandra, it appeared, had been far more indiscreet. The emperor was away at the front, but someone from Tsarskoe Selo had arranged for a special messenger to escort Mlle. Vassilshikova from the Russian border to a luxurious hotel in Petrograd. The next day she was received at Tsarskoe. Nicholas, hearing of this, angrily banished Mlle. Vassilshikova to her sister's estates at Chernigov.

Elizabeth, too, was alarmed. There was no doubting Alexandra's patriotism, but this meeting seemed a deplorable folly. The rioting outside her convent in June had been a grave reminder of how easily communications with the enemy could leak out, and how dangerous distorted rumors could prove. In this frame of mind she set out on Christmas Day 1915 through the snowy streets of Moscow to board her train for Tsarskoe Selo.

She arrived the next day. It was more than a year since she had been to the palace. By now her visits there had become a source of great anxiety to the empress. Elizabeth's presence would bring out their latent disagreements. Alexandra felt that as empress she could have the last word; yet Elizabeth had the authority of an elder over a younger sister.[10]

There is no record of their conversations. There may have been heated arguments, or they may have politely skirted around any mention of Mlle. Vassilshikova, or Rasputin, or the incompetence of the government. In any case, they spent little time together. That evening they dined with Anna Vyrubova, who by now had become Elizabeth's enemy, and any intimate conversation was impossible. The next day Elizabeth was away in Petrograd for all but but three hours in the afternoon; she dined that evening at the Anichkov Palace in the city.[11]

Nonetheless, Elizabeth was still keen to give support and comfort to Alexandra. She had come to Petrograd to resolve another matter, and hoped that its solution would accord her some religious satisfaction. She found that it provided an opportunity for her enemies at court to blacken her name.

Some weeks earlier, a priest in her service and a Siberian bishop had given her a clue to the whereabouts of a missing sacred icon.[12] More than ten years before, the icon of the Holy Mother of Kazan had been stolen from the convent at Kazan. Revered throughout Russia, it had accompanied medieval tsars on their campaigns, and its loss had shocked Alexandra. The thief, Chaikin, had been imprisoned and testified that he had burned it, but a suspicion remained with the prosecutors that he had hidden it in the hope of selling it to the Old Believers.† It had emerged that a convict imprisoned in Kursk, one of his old partners in crime, knew its hiding place. Elizabeth had gone to Kursk and made inquiries. She felt, however, that it was beneath her dignity to interrogate a criminal, and she had arranged for Stephen Beletsky, head of the Okhrana, or secret police, to find an official to take over the investigation. Beletsky had replaced Dzhunkovsky as head of the Okhrana, and Elizabeth was obliged to deal with him rather than her friend. But while Dzhunkovsky had been an upright and loyal official, Beletsky was, as the French ambassador noted, "resourceful and astute, entirely unscrupulous, recognizing no principle but political expediency, and capable of anything to preserve the favor of his sovereign.[13] He was also a close friend of Rasputin. Anxious not to offend a grand duchess, he had appointed Prince Shirinsky-Shikhmatov, a religious man and an old friend of Elizabeth, to head the investigation, promising to keep the matter secret. He soon broke his promise, telling everything to the empress's keenly interested confidante Anna Vyrubova.

Prince Shirinsky soon suspected that the prisoner was a fraudulent trickster hoping to escape. The search seemed doomed to fail. Elizabeth, however, kept her faith in the prisoner's testimony, as he had sworn on the Cross to tell the truth. She felt that Prince Shirinsky, an old man in failing health, should be relieved of his task. She discussed the matter with her sister, and Alexandra gave her an icon of St. Nicholas to be presented as a reward for his efforts.[14]

Elizabeth also saw Beletsky in Petrograd, in her study at her palace‡ overlooking the Fontanka Canal. She thanked him for his help and told him that she thought Prince Shirinsky's suspicions of the prisoner were unjustified. She asked him to quiet her conscience and put an end to the inquiry by taking the prisoner to the place where, he said, the icon was to be found. Beletsky obsequiously assured her that her wishes would be carried out.

Taking her leave of Alexandra and returning to Moscow, Elizabeth was on the point of replacing Prince Shirinsky when she found that his fears had been proved right. After an exhaustive search, he found a piece of paper hidden about the prisoner's person containing a detailed description of the icon; he had used this knowledge to convince the authorities that he was familiar with it.

Alexandra's clique gloated over her failure. Beletsky described it in detail to Anna Vyrubova, to her delight. She added some slighting details to Shirinsky's final report to the empress. Rasputin, glad of an opportunity to malign Elizabeth, loudly declared that she "wanted to betray God." The gulf between the court and Elizabeth's Moscow circle had widened further still.

By 1916, food and fuel were becoming scarce in Moscow. Butter was unobtainable at any price, and an egg was now a rare luxury for Elizabeth. Twice the population, frustrated from endless lining up in the snow, looted carts from Ilinskoe bearing vegetables for her patients and the poor of the city. On one occasion they surrounded a truck bound for the convent, dragged out the driver, bound him hand and foot, and made off with the produce. Some vented their anger on the grand duchess and accused her of living in luxury.[15]

All over the empire, a wave of discontent was growing from shortages and rising prices. The railways, which should have brought in fresh supplies to the cities, were in a chaotic state. The drain of skilled workers into the army severely hampered maintenance and construction work.

This incompetence was paralleled in the higher reaches of the government. The ministers Alexandra appointed after her husband's departure for the front were supporters of Rasputin, for the most part mediocrities and flatterers. Alexis Khvostov, referred to by the empress as "my tail," was one of the first. He was made minister of the interior, apparently after Rasputin had admired his singing in a Petrograd cabaret;[16] three more ministers of the interior were to succeed him before 1917. In February 1916, Boris Sturmer, "worse than a mediocrity," according to Paléologue "—third rate intellect, mean spirit, low character, doubtful honesty, no experience and no idea of state business,"[17] was made prime minister on Pitirim's recommendation. Another minister was possibly guilty of treason. Alexander Protopopov, vice president of the Duma, had met a German industrialist, Stinnes, and later a banker, Warburg, and assured them both that Russia was ready for peace.[18] Soon afterward he was made minister of the interior.

The remaining competent ministers were weeded out. In July 1916 Sasonov, the highly respected foreign minister, was declared to be too ill to remain in office. Returning from a holiday, he found Sturmer in his place. Polivanov, whose energetic efforts as war minister had restored the army's war-readiness after the defeats of 1915, had long opposed Rasputin. After repeated pleadings from Alexandra to Nicholas, he too was dismissed.[19]

Rasputin's influence may even have prolonged the war by a year. He had been against the war from its outset, and the three million Russian soldiers killed, wounded, or taken prisoner since 1914 had shocked him. In June 1916, a meticulously planned offensive led by General Brussilov began an enormous advance into the Austrian Carpathians, promising to turn the tide of the war. The German armies were occupied in the siege of Verdun. The opportunity was open for the Russians to advance into Austria; further north a follow-up attack was planned toward Warsaw. Once the Germans had transferred troops to meet the the offensive, the French and British could begin a push from the west.[20]

But as the offensive continued, as Robert Massie has shown, Rasputin urged Alexandra to call a halt. On August 7 she wrote to Nicholas, "Our Friend finds better one should not advance too obstinately as the losses will be too great." She repeated the admonition a fortnight later. On October 5, Nicholas gave way: "I told Alexiev to order Brussilov to stop our hopeless attacks."[21] When the attacks were resumed with reinforcements, the Germans had had time to bring up more of their own troops, just as Brussilov had feared. As J. N. Westwood has written, "What might have been a war-winning triumph remained only a great victory." The offensive was halted, the end of the war deferred, and the coming revolution made more certain.

Alexandra knew little of the damage done to the monarchy's prestige[22] by Rasputin and his nominees. The new ministers, adroit flatterers, kept away all knowledge of the grievous economic situation and her own unpopularity. Sturmer, and later Protopopov, arranged for the Okhrana to write hundreds of fabricated letters, purportedly from the peasantry, assuring her of their devoted loyalty.[23] The church, under Rasputin's influence, presented her with a *gramota,* or letter of commendation, praising her work in glowing terms.[24] On Easter 1916, she had kissed Rasputin publicly, following the Russian custom, at the cathedral in Tsarskoe Selo.[25] Rumors that she was his lover, arising from his nocturnal visits to Tsarskoe, were given fresh credibility. The imperial family was now spoken of "with open animosity and contempt." In Moscow, the public was declaring that she was ruining Russia and must be shut up in a nunnery.

In Petrograd, bread riots were becoming common. In a secret conference the Socialists resolved to overthrow the monarchy. Revolutionary propaganda, aided by German money as part of a scheme to sow sedition in Russia, spread throughout the barracks and factories. The workers began to strike with ever greater frequency; in the Vyborg quarter the soldiers mutinied. In November the Duma reconvened, and the deputies stridently fulminated against the government. Miliukov, the leader of the moderate "Cadets," openly accused Sturmer and Protopopov of treason. He and many other deputies demanded a ministry accountable to the Duma.[26]

Warnings came from inside the imperial family. Grand Duke Nicholas Mikhailovich and the dowager empress both told Nicholas of the dangers facing him. In London, King George V, alerted to the dangers of revolution by the Easter Rising in Dublin, voiced his disquiet to the Russian ambassador, Grand Duke Michael Mikhailovich. The grand duke wrote to the emperor: "I have just returned from Buckingham Palace. Georgy is much grieved at the political situation in Russia. The agents of the intelligence service, who are usually very well informed, predict a revolution in Russia. I sincerely hope, Nicky, that you will find it possible to meet the just demands of the people before it is too late."[27]

Many now looked to Elizabeth to intervene with the imperial couple and avert a catastrophe. Count Sheremetiev and Monsignor Vladimir, defenders of Orthodoxy against Rasputin, hoped that she might rid the church of the fraudulent holy man. Her Moscow friends who had endured dismissal or hostility from the empress, Samarin, Dzhunkovsky, and the Youssoupovs, looked to her to remove the dark forces from the government. Elizabeth had urged Princess Zenaide Youssoupova to seek an audience with the empress and give a final warning. Alexandra had dismissed her with the words "I hope never to see you again." The princess had written a full account of the audience to Elizabeth. From Petrograd, Princess Eugenie Golitsyna voiced the conviction that "her prayers will one day save this country." All the Muscovite supporters of the throne fixed their hopes on her.[28]

Elizabeth, however, felt she could be of little use. She knew Alexandra's state of mind and had often spoken to Nicholas, but they had never had a serious conversation. Even while sympathizing with her opinion, the emperor had always cut short her pleas with some flippant remark.[29] She was well aware of the situation. The new governor of Moscow, General Klimovich, who knew her well and held her in great respect, kept her closely informed.[30] Rodzianko, the president of the Duma, had often spoken to her.[31] It was clear to Elizabeth and her Moscow friends that the time was fast approaching for coups d'état, conspiracies, and assassinations.

On November 16, 1916, a howling gale and a dense blizzard swept the streets of Moscow and drove the temperature to thirty degrees below zero. Felix Youssoupov drew up outside the convent. The weather was a shock to him; he had been to the Crimea to see his parents, and was now on his way to Petrograd.[32] At the outbreak of war he had, as an only son, been exempt from military service and took up work as a hospital orderly. After a year, he felt it his duty to serve his country and enrolled in the Corps of Pages, an elite officer training college in Petrograd. He often visited Tsarskoe Selo and soon became aware of the extent of Rasputin's influence. His father's dismissal and the snub his mother had received when trying to warn the empress had confirmed his fears. His active imagination led him to believe the wildest rumors about the Siberian peasant, and he became obsessed by the idea of killing him. "During November 1916," the Russian historian Alexander Bokhanov has written, "the plan of the killing took on a definite shape in Youssoupov's mind."[33] The French ambassador put the date as mid-November.[34] It was at this time that Felix met Elizabeth in her convent.

Elizabeth knew nothing of his plans as they talked together while the blizzard raged outside. She told him how little hope she had while her sister obstinately clung to Rasputin and allowed him to dictate the emperor's choice of ministers. She pinned her hopes on Rodzianko, the president of the Duma, a Russian patriot and staunch opponent of Rasputin, who had persuaded the emperor to set up the munitions council.[35]

It was about this time that Felix, bidding farewell to Elizabeth and taking the train to Petrograd, met Rodzianko.

Rodzianko's words, he recalled, made up his mind to carry out the killing himself: "The only solution is to kill the scoundrel, but there's not a man in Russia who has the guts to do it. If I weren't so old I would do it myself." Soon afterward Grand Duke Dmitri, Elizabeth's nephew and his friend since childhood, admitted to him that the idea of killing Rasputin had haunted him for months.[36]

Encouraged, Felix began to seek out Rasputin's company. He knew Maria Golovina, a lady-in-waiting to Alexandra, who had long felt a "strong romantic feeling" for him.[37] A naive devotee of Rasputin, she was ready to introduce him into his circle. Felix started to ingratiate himself with Rasputin, and was so successful in winning his confidence that, by his own account, Rasputin even offered to make him a minister and revealed his plan to depose the emperor and make Alexandra regent during the minority of Tsarevich Alexis.

Dmitri, however, was hesitant about joining Felix's conspiracy. He was well acquainted with Rasputin's grasp on the Russian monarchy. A frequent visitor to Tsarskoe Selo, he was a favorite of Alexandra, who was often amused by his jokes. At the outbreak of the war he had rejoined his regiment in the guards and won the St. George's Cross for carrying a wounded corporal to safety while under fire in a cavalry charge. He became the emperor's aide-de-camp at headquarters. After reading Dzhunkovsky's report on Rasputin's Moscow debauch,[38] he was horrified when Nicholas proposed to take over the supreme command. "We're lost," he told his father. "From now on it will be the empress and her camarilla§ who will command at headquarters."[39] In vain he urged Nicholas to change his mind. Thereafter, the palace commandant, General Voekov, seemed determined to keep him out of the emperor's presence. Yet Dmitri still wondered if Rasputin could be removed without resorting to murder. He decided to consult Elizabeth, and took the train to Moscow.

299

In Moscow, meanwhile, Elizabeth's fears were beginning to be confirmed. Rumors of Maria Vassilshikova's mission to Petrograd had spread in a wildly distorted form. It was said that Ernest himself had come to Russia on the Kaiser's orders and that it was Elizabeth and Alexandra, now dubbed "the Hessian witches," who had invited him. He had been seen in Petrograd, had stayed at Tsarskoe Selo, waited on by Alexandra and her daughters to prevent gossip by the servants, and was now hiding in Elizabeth's convent.[40]

A drunken mob had picked up this rumor. Egged on by a few Socialist agitators, they made their way down the snow-ridden Ordinka to the convent. Shouting curses on "the German woman," they poured through the gate and hurled stones and broken bottles at the windows. Some of the Sisters were hurt. As they made for the main door, the grand duchess appeared calmly before them, alone in a gray working dress. The mob was silent in its surprise at seeing her so plainly clad. Faced with her strong character, their courage evaporated. She asked in an unfaltering voice if they wanted to speak to her. Some muttered incoherently, and one shouted that they wanted her brother. She quietly told them that he was not there; they might search the convent as long as they did not disturb the sick people there. Her slight foreign accent revived their anger. They began to surge forward. At that moment a troop of cavalry rode through the gate, rounded on the mob, and beat the ringleaders with the flat of their swords. At this show of armed force, the rest ran away. Elizabeth ordered her Sisters to attend to the injured.

That evening, the governor of Moscow, General Klimovich, and the metropolitan, Macarius, called on Elizabeth. General Klimovich told her that she would receive greater protection from the police and asked her to avoid the slums of Moscow. Metropolitan Macarius, seconding the pleas of many in her Moscow circle, pleaded with her to intervene and persuade the imperial couple to change their course. With reluctance she agreed to write to Nicholas and, if that brought no result, to go in person to Tsarskoe Selo. She felt she would be of little use, however, and still hesitated before acting. Soon afterward, Dmitri called at the convent.

They had a long talk together. Elizabeth described her many vain attempts to bring Alexandra to her senses. She told Dmitri how Alexandra had refused to believe that Rasputin had ever been at the Yar restaurant, and had dismissed all the emperor's ministers from Moscow, believing them to be part of a bigoted clique headed by Elizabeth. Rasputin and all of Alexandra's circle were now her bitter enemies. The empress imagined that Elizabeth was involved in some enormous conspiracy against her, in league with Ducky, the grand duchess Cyril, who was close to the British ambassador, and plotting with the grand duchess Vladimir, Miliukov, and Rodzianko.[41] She convinced him that there was little chance that her sister could ever be persuaded to change her mind. Dmitri left her determined to join Felix in a last attempt to save the throne.[42]

Elizabeth had also made up her mind to intervene. One other event may have decided her: on December 2, Vladimir Mitrophanovich Purishkevich, an ardent defender of the autocracy and a member of the extreme right bloc in the Duma, rose to speak.

> It requires only the recommendation of Rasputin to raise the most abject citizen to high office. Today Rasputin is more dangerous than the false Dmitri in days of old. . . . If you are truly loyal, if the glory of Russia, her mighty future, which is closely bound up with the brightness of the name of the tsar, mean anything to you, then on your feet, you ministers. Be off to headquarters and throw yourselves at the feet of the tsar. Have the courage to tell him that the multitude is threatening in its wrath. Revolution threatens and an obscure *moujik* shall govern Russia no longer.[43]

Felix Youssoupov heard this speech. He had crept into the chamber in civilian clothes, hoping not to be noticed. At its end, he turned pale and trembled with uncontrollable emotion. The following day, he persuaded Purishkevich to join his conspiracy. The speech, widely reported in the press, inflamed opinion throughout Russia. "We are under the *overwhelming* effect of Purishkevich's speech," Princess Youssoupova wrote from the Crimea.[44] It seemed to Elizabeth that soon some parliamentary orator would progress from urging the removal of the emperor's associate to demanding the overthrow of the emperor himself. Clearly a last effort from her was imperative.

She sat down and wrote to Nicholas, urging him to come to an agreement with the Duma, set up a ministry accountable to it, observe the constitution of 1905, and banish Rasputin from Petrograd. Nicholas may never have received this letter; in reply Alexandra sent a short note asking her to come to Tsarskoe Selo. Without delay Elizabeth prepared for her journey.[45] She promised Felix Youssoupov that she would see him afterward.

On a very cold day in mid-December 1916, dressed in her gray monastic habit, she took leave of the consumptive patients in her wards and took the train for Petrograd. The snow-mantled park at Tsarskoe, the mounted Cossacks riding around its border, was now an unfamiliar world of past luxury. She strode through the endless corridors, past a giant Ethiopian footman, into Alexandra's mauve boudoir with its pictures of their mother, Princess Alice, and their grandmother, Queen Victoria. She came not as an abbess to an empress, but as Ella, the elder sister, to Alicky, the younger one. Alix curtly informed her that the emperor was preparing to leave for the front and must on no account be disturbed. Ella addressed her final appeal to her sister. She repeated her plea that Nicholas should behave as a constitutional monarch and begged her sister to exile Rasputin to Siberia for good.[46] Elizabeth's warning was stern: "Rasputin is exasperating society. He is compromising the imperial family and will lead the dynasty to ruin." Alix refused to listen:

"Rasputin is a great man of prayer. All these rumors are slander."[47] They both knew, she added, that saints had been maligned before, and asked Ella never to bring up the subject again.[48] But Elizabeth persisted. Noticing a portrait of Marie Antoinette, she reminded Alix of the fate of Louis XVI.[49] Alix cut short the conversation, and coldly asked her sister to leave.[50] With her two elder daughters she saw Ella off at the station. It was the last time they would meet.

Greatly depressed, Elizabeth drove straight to Felix Youssoupov and his relatives at the Alexander Palace as she had promised. She described her meeting with Alexandra in detail, adding, almost in tears: "She drove me away like a dog! Poor Nicky, poor Russia!" Sadly she returned to Moscow.[51]

Rasputin heard of her visit and said to Youssoupov: "Your mamma is hand in glove with Elizabeth, isn't she? And they both have but one thought: to send me away from here. They won't succeed. Indeed they won't; no one will listen to them. They're much too fond of me at Tsarskoe Selo."[52]

After the trials of the past winter, Elizabeth was in a state of nervous exhaustion. She longed to retreat and recollect her thoughts amid happy memories of the distant past, before all the troubles of war, revolution, and hemophilia had begun. Many years ago, she, Serge and the whole family had traveled to Sarovo for Seraphim's canonization. They had walked, in joyous faith and hope, through a vast crowd of peasant pilgrims, all struggling to kiss Nicholas's hand. Then he had truly been a father-tsar among his devoted people. Alix had prayed for a son and thought her prayers would be answered.

Elizabeth took the train to Arzamas, and drove for hours through the snow and pine woods to the golden-domed monastery at Sarovo.[53] She settled down for some days of prayer and meditation. It seemed almost as if her prayers were answered, for there she heard that in Petrograd Rasputin had been killed.

# Elizabeth

## Notes to Chapter 22

*In the original German, "Vater, du führe mich, / Führ' mich zum Siege, führ' mich zum Tode. . . ." Fräulein Oelzen was not a German but the daughter of a schoolmaster from Riga in Courland, then a part of the Russian Empire.

†The "Old Believers" were a sect that had broken away from the Russian Orthodox Church in the seventeenth century when they refused to accept the liturgical reforms of the patriarch Nikon. They were subjected to a double tax under Peter the Great, and persecuted under Nicholas I. A legend survived among them that they would attain complete freedom to confess their faith only when the icon of Our Lady of Kazan was in their hands.

‡Although the grand duchess had given away this as well as her other palaces to Dmitri and Marie, she still used it on her occasional visits to the capital.

§A Spanish word meaning "clique" or "cabal," originally used with reference to a group of influential intriguers at the court of King Ferdinand of Spain.

# Chapter 23

## The Ides of March

*All our world is being snipped into little bits, all that was gained in centuries is being demolished and by our own people, those I love from all my heart. Truly they are morally ill and blinded not to see where we are going. One's heart aches, but I have no bitterness—can you criticise a man in a delirium, a lunatic?*

—LETTER FROM GRAND DUCHESS ELIZABETH
TO HER SISTER VICTORIA, SPRING 1917

"I don't like your mother. I know she hates me; she's a friend of Elizabeth's. Both of them plot against me and spread slander about me. The tsarina herself has often told me that they are my worst enemies. Why, no earlier than this evening, Protopopov came to see me and made me swear not to go out for a few days. 'They'll kill you,' he declared, 'Your enemies are bent on mischief.'"

This, according to Youssoupov's account,[1] was what Rasputin said as he helped him on with his overcoat on the night of December 29, 1916. They left Rasputin's apartment by the back stairs to escape the secret police, who followed all his movements. Youssoupov drove Rasputin to his palace on the Moika Canal. His plans had been carefully laid. Dmitri and Purishkevich were waiting in an upstairs room of the palace, ready to assist if Youssoupov failed to kill Rasputin. A Polish doctor, Lasovert, the fourth conspirator in the plot, had laced several cakes and glasses of wine with cyanide. These had been placed in the basement, into which Youssoupov was to lure Rasputin on the pretext that his wife, a pretty woman who was away in the

305

Crimea, was upstairs entertaining a few guests. Rasputin was keen to meet Irene, and was told that she would be down after the guests had gone.

Once in the basement, Youssoupov plied Rasputin with conversation and induced him to take the poisoned cakes and wine. His guest suffered little more than a tickling in the throat from a dose supposedly sufficient to kill several men. For more than an hour Youssoupov sung to him and played on the guitar in a state of rising panic. At 2:30 A.M. he slipped upstairs, and told Dmitri and Purishkevich that Rasputin still lived. It was decided that Youssoupov should return and finish off the assassination. He descended holding a revolver behind him and directed Rasputin's attention to a silver crucifix, but Rasputin turned to examine an ebony cabinet. With the words, "Grigory Efimovich, you'd far better look at that crucifix and say a prayer," Youssoupov fired into his chest. Rasputin screamed and fell.

Youssoupov's friends rushed into the cellar, and Lasovert declared him dead. Purishkevich and Youssoupov stayed behind while the other conspirators drove off, one of them impersonating Rasputin to baffle the secret police. On an impulse Youssoupov, without his revolver, returned to the basement and shook the corpse. The left eyelid flickered, the eyes opened, and with a violent effort Rasputin rose. He clawed at Youssoupov in an attempt to grab his throat. With a struggle Youssoupov freed himself and fled. He and Purishkevich saw Rasputin climb the stairs to an outside door which Youssoupov thought was locked. Rasputin opened it and Purishkevich, bearing a revolver, pursued him into the courtyard. He fired and missed; fired again and missed. He bit his left hand in an effort of concentration, and shot Rasputin in the shoulder and head.

The others returned and wrapped the corpse in a blue carpet. They drove to the Neva and dropped it through a hole in the ice, but not before the shots had alerted the police. Dmitri and Youssoupov were placed under house arrest in Sergievskaya Palace.

Later on, Elizabeth was to hear Youssoupov describe the killing in his own words. For the moment she knew nothing of the gruesome details, and she reacted with joy. The man whom she loathed above all in Russia, whom she, according to her niece, regarded as the incarnation of evil, was no more. It seemed to her that his death was an act of Providence. On December 31 she returned to Moscow with deep gratitude. She sent a telegram of congratulation to Grand Duke Dmitri: "Prayed for you all. Please send letters with particulars. God grant Felix the necessary strength after the patriotic deed." She wired a message to the elder Prince Youssoupov and his wife at Kursk: "My prayers and thoughts are with you all. God bless your dear son for his patriotic act."[2]

Even after their final, heated conversation, she knew the anguish the empress must be feeling. In sympathy she sent her some treasured sacred icons from a shrine at Saratov. But Alexandra had heard from the secret police of her message to Dmitri; she no doubt concluded that Elizabeth had been an accomplice. Without glancing at the icons, the empress sent them back. This last communication between the two sisters was to effect a complete breach.[3]

It was now clear that the death of Rasputin had come too late to alter the empress's mind. Isolated from public opinion and most of her own family at Tsarskoe Selo, she still believed that her detractors were conspiring against her. She kept the same mediocrities in the government, and in countless letters sternly admonished her husband never to yield a shred of his autocratic power: "Be an Emperor. Be an Ivan the Terrible. . . . Send Miliukov, Guchkov and Polivanov to Siberia."[4] Nicholas, fatalistic and indecisive, was too preoccupied with the army and too weak to disagree. Elizabeth could sense that her sister's rigid obstinacy was making a rebellion inevitable, which she now awaited with sad resignation.

She made one final plea to the emperor for the welfare of his people and leniency toward the two assassins. She wrote Nicholas a confused, impassioned letter, clearly showing the strain of the past months:

> . . . Arrived here the news that Felix killed him, my little Felix I knew as a child, who all his life feared to kill, who did not wish to become military so as never to have the occasion to shed blood—and I imagine what he must have gone through to do this, and how moved by patriotism he decided to save his sovereign and country from what we all were suffering. I telegraphed to Dmitri not know-ing where the boy was—but got no answer and since then all is in a kind of silence. . . . crime remains crime, but this one being of a special kind, can be counted as a duel and it is considered a patriotic act and for these deeds the law I think is alternating [sic]. Maybe nobody has had the courage to tell you now, that in the street of the towns people kissed like at Easter week, sang the hymn in theatres and all moved by one feeling— at last the black wall between us and our Emperor is removed, at last we will see, hear, feel him as he is and a wave of pitying love for you moved all hearts. God grant that you may know of this love and feel it and not miss this great movement as the storm is still and thunder rolls afar. . . .
>
> Your heart must be so heavy in spite of your deep faith in God, yet your heart must ache and maybe a doubt of the truth of the position knocks at the door of your brain, don't shut the door, open it clearly and let the bright wisdom from above enter for the welfare of all. . . .[5]

The two assassins were never brought to trial. Sixteen other members of the imperial family had signed an appeal to the emperor for clemency.*[6] Irresolute as always, Nicholas was also fearful of publicly condemning two men who were now the people's heroes; instead, he ordered them to be exiled. Marie came to see Elizabeth with the news that Youssoupov had been sent to join his parents at Kursk. She had seen Dmitri off at the station on his journey to the Persian front. During Dmitri's arrest at Serge Palace, she had seen among the numerous sympathetic visitors some officers who had offered to start an uprising to put him on the throne. Yet he remained true to his oath of loyalty to the emperor.[7]

In Moscow, the citizens took pride in the killing, considering Dmitri as one of their own. As Elizabeth had written, the city was in a fever of nervous enthusiasm on hearing that the "dark forces" had been eliminated from the throne. News of her visit to Tsarskoe Selo leaked out. Once more she was considered their saintly *matiushka* and treated with reverence. She was able to resume her visits to the slums, and was greeted with smiles.[8]

Yet, pleased as they were to see her, Elizabeth sensed the hunger and suffering of the common people and their mood of sullen rebelliousness. The winter that year was one of the coldest on record, and the snow fell heavily in the beginning of 1917. Firewood could barely be obtained to heat the damp and unhygienic lodgings. Food became even scarcer after the snow had almost brought the railways to a halt. A few streets away from expensive restaurants serving luxurious food, men dressed in rags and garrulous women stood for hours in lines for bread.

In Petrograd, early in March, a group with sinister faces was seen that had waited all night outside a bakery in a temperature of thirty-five degrees below. Soon afterward, crowds were pouring onto the streets of the capital, led on by Bolshevik agitators. They shouted for "Bread and Peace!" bore the red flag and sang the revolutionary *Marseillaise.* By March 9, the troops were out on the streets; they were obliged to fire to disperse the crowds, and many were killed. The following day, most of the city was on strike; vast crowds filled the boulevards. On the eleventh, the Volkhynsky regiment refused to fire on the mob. That night they mutinied; the following morning they killed their commanding officer, and took to the streets. On the Nevsky Prospect that day a procession bearing red flags advanced toward a column of troops. As they met, the soldiers lifted their bayonets above their heads and, to loud applause, mixed freely with the rebels.[9]

The regime was clearly in dire peril if the army would not suppress its opponents. Rodzianko wired to the emperor at the front: "Anarchy in the capital, government paralyzed . . . shooting in the streets . . . supplies of food and fuel completely disrupted . . . universal dissatisfaction growing. . . ." He begged the emperor to appoint a responsible ministry. But Nicholas had heard reports of riots in Petrograd before. Misinformed and thinking Rodzianko was exaggerating, he instead dissolved the Duma.[10]

By now, revolutionary soldiers were putting up barricades and exchanging machine-gun fire with loyal troops. The law courts, police stations, and government ministries were on fire. The Fortress of St. Peter and St. Paul was under siege, and the Winter Palace was occupied. A "Soviet of Workers' and Soldiers' Deputies," hastily formed from the ever growing number of mutinous troops, was directing the revolution. Rodzianko and the other Duma members had no choice but to defy the emperor and set up a provisional government of their own.

On March 14, three crack regiments of the army marched in perfect order with red flags to the seat of the Duma and swore allegiance to the revolution. Furthermore, Grand Duke Cyril broke his oath of fealty to the emperor. Wearing a red cockade, he marched to the Duma with his regiment, the marine of the guard, and placed them at the service of the rebels. It was clear to the Duma committee that the monarchy could only be preserved if Nicholas abdicated. Two members, Guchkov and Shulgin, boarded a train for Pskov, where the emperor's train had been stopped on its way to Tsarskoe Selo.[11]

On March 15, Grand Duchess Marie was in Pskov, and heard

from a general a firsthand account of Nicholas's abdication, which she was to pass on to Elizabeth. The day before, General Ruzsky, the commander of the northern front, had, after much argument, convinced the emperor that he must appoint a responsible ministry. By then it was too late. General Alexeiev heard Rodzianko declare on the telephone that the emperor's abdication was essential. He agreed to ask the opinions of the other generals. Their replies arrived by telegram at Pskov on the morning of the fifteenth; everyone agreed with Rodzianko. Abandoned by his generals, the emperor had no alternative. Hearing from his physician, who was with him on his train, that his son would never lead a healthy life, he abdicated in favor of his younger brother, Grand Duke Michael. After the arrival of Guchkov and Shulgin from Petrograd, he signed the document. Then he left for the front to take leave of his troops.[12]

"Read a lot about Julius Caesar," he wrote in his diary as he traveled away from Pskov.[13] It was one of the many ominous coincidences of his reign that his downfall took place on the Ides of March. The vacillating and indecisive Nicholas made a feeble comparison with the Roman emperor and military genius who died on the same day almost two millennia earlier.† Ironically Julius Ceasar was claimed by Nicholas's predecessors to be one of their ancestors. It was even said that the empress had received a warning much like the one given to Caesar by the soothsayer. In December she had met a holy prophetess, 107 years old, in a convent, who greeted her with the words, "Here is the martyr Empress Alexandra." She added, the story tells, "Tell the tsar to beware the 1st of March."[14] March 1, the fourteenth in the western calendar, was the day he ceased to be an autocrat. In the Russian calendar it was also the anniversary of the assassination of his grandfather, Alexander II. The day of his abdication, the fifteenth, was the Ides of March.

In Petrograd, the Soviet was now firmly for a republic. Less than a day after receiving the crown from his brother, Grand Duke Michael was prevailed on to abdicate and place all authority in the provisional government. A deputy, Miliukov, pleaded with the British ambassador to ask King George V to offer asylum to the imperial couple in England. Sir George Buchanan complied, and on March 23 came the reply that the king was prepared to do so. The following day, the Soviet compelled the government to announce that the emperor and empress, now both in captivity at Tsarskoe, would stay in Russia.[15]

In Moscow, meanwhile, Elizabeth had heard of the coming revolution and resorted to prayer. Throughout that week, services had been held day and night at the convent, and the Sisters had kept up a constant vigil of prayer.

On March 15, a bitterly cold day, the new order made its appearance in her life. Two cars, decked with red flags and full of soldiers and newly released criminals, drew up in the snow outside. The men, bearing rifles and revolvers, many of them drunk, entered the convent. The grand duchess told her Sisters to leave, and faced them alone.

They said they had come to arrest her, and to remove the ammunition from the convent. "You are for the emperor?" they asked. Naturally she was for the emperor, she replied, but was ready to submit. She requested one favor, to go into the church and pray. They followed her, and she asked them to leave their weapons outside. To a soldier who refused to relinquish his revolver, she said: "Put the revolver into your pocket so as not to alarm the Sisters." Inside the church, the Sisters were still at their vigil of prayer that had begun the week before. Elizabeth knelt, and Father Mitrophan began a short service. The soldiers, bareheaded and slightly uneasy, joined in. At the end the Father held up the cross for the congregation to kiss. He asked the soldiers if they wished to do likewise. "Of course, Father, we are all Orthodox," they replied. One of them recognized him: "Look, it is our priest from Oryol."[16]

Their stiffness relaxed, the men began to feel awkward. The

grand duchess announced that she was ready, but had they a written order for her arrest? They had not, and looked confused. "How can you act without a written order?" she repeated. They searched in their minds for their reasons for coming. One remembered an old rumor and asked why she gave money to German prisoners? She replied that she had never been to a hospital for German prisoners. Finally the men sheepishly said that they had no idea what to do with her if they arrested her. They searched throughout the convent, found nothing, and left.

In the streets outside, there was no bloodshed. Moscow went peacefully over to the revolution. Crowds filled the streets, and a surging mob surrounded the town hall, the headquarters of the new regime. Inside, the corridors were thronged with officious soldiers, raucous, shouting students, and exultant revolutionaries, now freed from prison. Amidst the commotion the gray-bearded mayor of Moscow, Chelnokov, struggled to keep the city in order.[17]

One of Chelnokov's first acts was to post a sentry outside the convent to deter any further intruders. He also sent some officials to the grand duchess to offer her the safety of the Kremlin. She received them in her bare office with its four wicker chairs and a cheap pine table for furniture. She refused to abandon her Sisters; her fate was in God's hands.[18]

Posts and telegrams were in a chaotic state. Elizabeth wrote to all her relations without receiving any reply. She knew nothing of the fate of the captive imperial family at Tsarskoe Selo; the three telegrams she sent there were returned. In the face of such uncertainty, Elizabeth and her community carried on with calm resolution. Father Mitrophan kept the emperor's name in the liturgy as he sung the daily mass. When told that the emperor was no longer sovereign, he gave an angry retort: "Who would dare uncrown an anointed tsar?" Elizabeth busied herself with the sick, and rarely went out. She spent hours at the bedside of three dying women at her home for incurables.

She forbade her Sisters to show fear, and her fortitude inspired them. When a drunken, disheveled ex-convict found his way into her clinic and asked who she was now, as she was no longer an Imperial Highness, she replied, "I am your servant." The man hoarsely asked her to dress a wound in his groin. She removed his filthy, foul-smelling clothing and dressed the ulcer. She told him to return the next day and not to neglect the wound for fear of gangrene. He was stupefied, again asked who she was and received the same answer. As he left, his comrade muttered, "She is still a German; you can tell by her accent." This frightened the Sisters, but not the grand duchess, who rebuked them for such weakness.[19]

One visitor was greatly impressed by her inspiring presence in those troubled times. Two brothers of a crippled child in Elizabeth's orphanage, Volodya Crichton, came to see him a fortnight after the revolution. George Crichton recalled: "I remember an occasion, while we were in Volodya's room, she suddenly entered the room. She was calm, composed, and smiling. I cannot adequately describe the effect her sudden appearance made on me. Her presence could be felt as well as seen, and I believe that had I been blind, I would have known just as well that a holy person had entered the room."[20]

A few weeks later, Felix Youssoupov, now released from exile, called at the convent. She gave him her blessing, and listened closely as he described the killing of Rasputin. At the end, Youssoupov recalled, she commented: "You could not have acted otherwise. You made a supreme attempt to save your country and the dynasty. It is not your fault if the result is not what you hoped for. The fault lies with those who failed to do their duty. It was no crime to kill Rasputin; you destroyed a fiend who was the incarnation of evil. Nor is there any merit in what you did: you were destined to do it, just as anyone else might have been."

They talked about the parlous state of Russia. The grand duchess feared the worst, but as she was to do often during the following year, she put her trust in God and the church: "Poor Russia; what a terrible ordeal lies ahead of her! . . . But even though all the powers of hell may be let loose, Holy Russia and the Orthodox Church will remain unconquered. Some day, in this terrible struggle, virtue will triumph over evil. Those who keep their faith will see the powers of light vanquish the powers of darkness. God punishes and pardons."[21]

For Emperor William of Germany, the war had gone badly. To add to the gloom of the relentless Allied advance, he found that his generals saw fit to ignore him and take matters into their own hands. He confided to a dinner guest: "The general staff tells me nothing and never asks my advice. If people in Germany think I am the supreme commander, they are grossly mistaken. . . .The only one who is a bit kind to me is the chief of the field railway department, who tells me all he does. . . ." He was reduced to traveling constantly among his various estates, and dreaming of introducing motor racing to Berlin after the war and encouraging the nobility to build palaces there.[22]

In this mood of depression he remembered the Ella he had courted in his student days. He still felt a strong devotion to her. In April 1917, against the Kaiser's will,‡ General Ludendorff sent Lenin through Germany to Russia in a sealed train, and the Kaiser dreaded the consequences of Bolshevism. He feared that Elizabeth would be the victim of an assassination. Ever since the boy Cohen had shot at his grandfather, he had felt a horror of assassination, and the news of attempts would send him into paroxysms of rage. He sent an urgent message to his Ella through the Swedish minister, begging her to leave at once, offering her safe passage to Germany and refuge there.

For Elizabeth, Germany was little more than a distant memory. Her life was in Russia; her mission now was to serve the poor and sick. She knew that the people loved her, and thought that the government would not dare move her. The Swedish minister warned her of the coming Bolshevik coup d'etat. She told him that she could never leave her Sisters and must share the fate of her adopted country, which she considered her own. After letting her know that every effort was being made to get the emperor and empress out of the country, and receiving her warm thanks, he left.[23]

As spring gave way to a hot summer, the amenities of civilization steadily decayed. Bread, meat, potatoes, and grain were all in short supply. The lines grew longer, and fights broke out almost every day outside the bakeries. Criminals, released from prison, roamed the streets. The drains, damaged by the riots in March and never repaired, threatened to cause an outbreak of cholera. All drinking water, berries, and lettuce were boiled as precautions. Elizabeth fell prey to typhoid, and was forced to give up her visits and lie on a wicker lounge, knitting and embroidering.[24]

It was in this state that Marie found her while on a visit to Moscow. She described to her the abdication of the tsar, and they talked for a long time about the revolution and the state of Russia. Telling her of the life of the imperial family in captivity, Marie offered to deliver a letter to the empress.

> Her eyes turned hard and cold, her lips tightened. She replied somewhat sharply that she could not send a letter; she had nothing to say; she and her sister had long ago ceased to understand one another.[25]

While Elizabeth slowly recovered, the provisional government composed of Duma members was losing its power. In the countryside, its officials were unable to prevent a wave of anarchy. The abdication of the emperor had removed the sole source of authority that the peasants respected, and they now went on a rampage. They seized all the land and forests, and refused to hand over food to the government. In the army, discipline withered away when the soldiers refused to obey orders. An offensive on the southwestern front turned into a rout; officers trying to goad their men into battle were often shot. Thousands deserted, commandeered trains and fled to the countryside to stake their claim in the seizure of land. The army was ruined, and the Bolsheviks spread propaganda in favor of peace.

In July the government summoned a state conference in Moscow in an attempt to restore order. Guchkov, now minister of war, argued for a restoration of the monarchy, perhaps with Grand Duke Dmitri on the throne. The delegates dozed off or slowly absented themselves. Kornilov, an old imperial army general, demanded iron discipline, the liquidation of the Bolsheviks, and the hanging of their leaders. Despairing of having any effect, he led a counterrevolutionary putsch in Petrograd which soon collapsed in chaos. Thereafter the Bolsheviks were in the ascendant. In September they gained a majority on the Moscow Soviet, and in Petrograd they became the largest party. On September 13, Lenin demanded that they prepare for an armed seizure of power.[26]

As Moscow became ominously quiet, Elizabeth carried on with calm resolution. It was only in September that she heard that the ex-emperor Nicholas and his family had been removed to the Siberian town of Tobolsk. She was amazed that they had not been taken away to a safe haven. What animosity she still felt toward Alexandra now disappeared, and she redoubled her prayers for the imperial family. She wrote them many letters, only one of which they received.

A sign of the imminent Bolshevik coup was the scores of people with fearful, uncertain faces who filled the outpatient room. They came not for their health but for advice and reassurance. Many wanted letters written to relations whose whereabouts were unknown, and others wondered how they could survive in these uncertain times. Elizabeth helped as much she could, and many left with some of her courage in their hearts.[27]

Another sign was that those close to Elizabeth came to Moscow seeking a safe place for their valuables. Toward the end of October Felix Youssoupov, released from exile after the revolution, arrived to hide the family jewels in his palace. He called at the convent, where they had a long talk. Youssoupov left after making a short prayer in the chapel. They both feared that it would be their last meeting.[28] A few days later, Marie arrived to retrieve her jewels from a Moscow bank. She had remarried, this time to an officer called Putiatin. She and her husband stayed at the convent for a while. On October 30, they left to visit the state bank. The street outside seemed eerily deserted. The janitor remarked: "Something's wrong in the the town. It strikes me that the Bolsheviks are up to something today. Perhaps you shouldn't go out. It pays to be careful nowadays."[29]

Without having bid a proper farewell, Elizabeth was never to see Marie again. That day the Bolsheviks began their assault on Moscow.

## Notes to Chapter 23

*Grand Duchess Olga Alexandrovna (Nicholas's sister), the dowager empress Marie, Grand Duke Cyril and his wife Victoria Melita ("Ducky"), Grand Dukes Boris and Andrew (brothers of Cyril), Grand Duke Paul, Grand Duchess Marie (daughter of Paul), Grand Duchess Elizabeth (widow of Grand Duke Constantine), Princes John, Gabriel, Constantine, and Igor Constantinovich (sons of Grand Duke Constantine), Princess Helen (wife of Prince John), Grand Dukes Nicholas and Serge Mikhailovich (sons of Grand Duke Mikhail Nikolayevich, brother of Emperor Alexander II).

†Ivan III, the first Russian ruler to call himself "tsar" or "tsezar" (Caesar), married the niece of the last Byzantine emperor. His descendants traced their ancestry, spuriously, back to Emperor Augustus, nephew of Julius Caesar.

‡In 1911 he had declared to Prince Louis of Battenberg that if revolution threatened Russia, "the emperor of Austria and I would instantly march in shoulder to shoulder, and reinstate Emperor Nicholas."

# Chapter 24

*Weep, my holy Russia, weep! For thou art entering into darkness. Weep, my holy Russia, weep! For thou shalt shortly die.*

—RIMSKY-KORSAKOV, *BORIS GODUNOV*

Moscow rapidly became a battlefield. Soldiers gathered in groups, then in larger crowds, the younger ones bearing an inane expression of excitement which was soon to disappear. Shots were fired, and the government and Bolshevik forces were soon exchanging volleys. Corpses began to litter the streets, and crowds of people fled from the fighting. By noon, pitched battles were raging, and the Bolsheviks began shelling the city. Explosions could be heard, followed by a deafening roar as a building was destroyed.[1]

It was some days before the Bolsheviks captured the city. During that time a stream of wounded soldiers and civilians was borne on stretchers into the hospital. Father Mitrophan sung a Te Deum to give the inmates of the convent strength. Pale and thin after her illness, Elizabeth faced the situation with her usual courage. When a band of Communists came to search the convent, she coolly asked them to do so as quietly as they could lest they disturb the sick and aged. Having searched the premises thoroughly and noted with astonishment the grand duchess's austere living quarters, they left their leader behind, an earnest young student. He expounded his Socialist gospel at length, and

Elizabeth remarked that they both might be traveling to the same end by different roads. He replied that there were sixteen hundred churches in Moscow; the time was ripe for eradicating religion. The convent would, however, be given a breathing space. "Dear Sisters," Elizabeth told the assembled community afterward, "it looks as though we are not yet worthy to receive a martyr's crown."[2]

In the winter of 1917–18, law and order came close to collapse in Moscow. Food prices, already high, rose further and drove the workers into pilfering and to the black market. Thousands fled to the countryside. Worse, gangs of bandits overran the city and robbed the citizens at gunpoint. In masks they descended on the more elegant restaurants and, brandishing machine guns, made off with the patrons' jewels and wallets.* They lived a debauched life in the nobility's palaces with prostitutes and stolen champagne.[3] People ventured out at night only from necessity, never alone, and always walked in the middle of the street. Elizabeth forbade her Sisters to leave the convent.

In these precarious conditions popular support for the fragile Bolshevik regime withered away. The government could only avoid a popular discontent if it tolerated the grand duchess and her convent, for Elizabeth was the one member of the imperial family still respected by the Muscovites. The slum dwellers and all who had seen her charity continued to revere her as a saint. Her hospital was one of the very few places to which the sick could turn for help. Recognizing this, the authorities made regular deliveries of food and medicine, and the Red Guards patrolling the Ordinka allowed free access to the convent. The church was still filled to overflowing on Sundays.[4]

Yet it was clear that the regime's lenience was only temporary. Already it was gathering strength, and taking over the people's lives by a series of decrees. The first of these gave it control of the press, eradicating the freedom granted by the October Manifesto of 1905; within a fortnight most of the opposing newspapers were closed. Before the end of the year the state had taken control of all banking, industry, and church schools, organizations which the tsarist regime had left in private hands. As the novelist Ilya Ehrenburg later described it: "Every morning the inhabitants carefully studied the new decrees, still wet and crumpled, pasted on the walls: they wanted to know what was permitted and what was forbidden." In January an assembly elected to decide the fate of Russia met in Petrograd; among the 707 delegates the Bolsheviks were in a minority of 175. Lenin's henchman, Sverdlov, shoved aside from the tribune the oldest member, who was about to open proceedings, and took charge. The day after, Red Guards closed off the building, and fired on a peaceful protest demonstration outside.[5]

When the new government moved to Moscow in March, it began a ruthless suppression of all disobedience. The Cheka, or secret terrorist police, was set up in an office block near the Kremlin, the Lubianka. Within its walls an "inner prison" was built for political suspects; outside, the first concentration and labor camps were already in operation. Soon visitors to the convent were being questioned; a few patients were removed from the hospital and never seen again. Thousands of citizens were arrested, and many shot. By the end of the year, some 50,000 people had lost their lives; in the last years of Emperor Nicholas's reign an average of less than twenty had been executed. An entirely new principle pervaded these operations. Whereas the tsarist police had imprisoned people, albeit sometimes unfairly, for committing a crime, the Cheka arrested and shot people for their birth or occupation. As Lenin put it, there had to be "a purge from the Russian land of all vermin," among whom he included "the idle rich," "bureaucrats," "slovenly and hysterical intellectuals," and "priests."[6]

Lenin set to work on his purge of priestcraft when he arrived in the Kremlin. Within its walls, one of the holiest shrines in Russia, the icon of the Virgin at the Iversky Gate, was closed off. Lenin noticed the cross Elizabeth had put up on the site of Serge's murder, before which the emperor had knelt in prayer six years earlier. With the remark, "They still haven't pulled down this monstrosity," he fastened a noose and threw it over the cross. Other ropes were attached; Lenin, Sverdlov, and other men in the government took hold and pulled. The monument crashed onto the cobblestones.[7]

Lenin propagated his gospel of Marxism with jesuitical fervor, although religion was anathema to him. Above all he feared the saints of the church, the devoted clergy who might inspire the people by the example of their good works to resist the barbarism of his regime. "It was as though he recognized in the true man of God the same zeal and spirit which animated himself," Paul Johnson has written, "and wished to expropriate it and enlist it in his own cause."[8] The thought of a grand duchess living almost in sight of the Kremlin, dispensing charity, revered by all who knew her, no doubt infuriated him. "Crowned virtue is a greater danger to world revolution than a hundred tsars," he later reputedly said. His government was now determined to be rid of Elizabeth, but feared making her a martyr figure around which rebellious Muscovites might rally.

"Really, it is a miracle that we are still alive," the grand duchess wrote to an old friend who still remained in Petrograd. She knew her fate and was resigned to it as God's will. She lived on by the strength of her faith, offering thanks for His mercy in ensuring that her convent survived. In the same letter she wrote:

> We must turn all our thoughts to our marvelous country, to see all that is going on in it in a true light, and be able to say: "let it be Thy will," when our beloved Russia entirely collapses. Remember that the Holy Russian Orthodox Church—against which the forces of Hell cannot prevail—still all exists and will exist to the end of time. . . . I am sure that the God of Vengeance is also a Loving God. In recent times I have often been reading the Bible. If

we believe in the Supreme Sacrifice of God the
Father in sending His Son to death and resurrection for our salvation, then we feel at the same time
the presence of the Holy Spirit spread above our
path, and our joy will be eternal, even in our condition, if our imprisoned human hearts and minds
can pass through the vale of terrible suffering. . . .[9]

A man who owed her a debt of gratitude for nursing his family
offered to take her away. "You must escape, dear Mother, you are
so dear to all of us, the common people of Moscow. The
Bolsheviks are afraid of you; they are bound to do you harm some
day." She refused, as always, for she could never leave her
Sisters.[10]

The government now thought it had found a way to be rid of
her: to send her abroad. At Brest-Litovsk it had signed a peace
treaty with Germany, ceding large areas of the Ukraine and
Belorussia. When diplomatic relations were restored, Emperor
William, hoping again to see his Ella, ordered his ambassador,
Count Mirbach, to offer her asylum in Germany. The Bolsheviks
readily agreed to let her leave. Mirbach arrived in Moscow on 24
April 1918. One of his first acts was to try and meet the grand
duchess. He called twice at the convent, and both times she
refused to meet the agent of an enemy of Russia.†[11]

Her fate was now sealed. The Bolsheviks resorted to the traditional Russian method of dealing with recalcitrant princesses.
They decided to imprison her in a distant nunnery. Very soon
after Mirbach's failed mission, they sent a man to the convent
who suggested that she might like to join the emperor and
Alexandra in Siberia. She replied that she believed it her duty to
remain with her nuns but was ready to go wherever God willed.

A few days later, during Easter week, Elizabeth was leaving the
chapel after evening vespers. Two cars filled with armed

Bolsheviks drove into the convent yard. She was told that she must be removed from Moscow for her safety. She asked for two hours to make her farewells and collect her luggage. Only half an hour was allowed, and she gathered up her few possessions. She assembled her Sisters in the chapel and gave them her blessing. A short prayer was held, and she thanked Father Mitrophan for all his work. She remained calm and resolute, but the nuns wept as she left them. Two of them insisted on joining her: Catherine Yanisheva, and her faithful Barbara, who had knelt down beside her when she received the veil. The Bolsheviks yielded to her request to let them come.[12]

An Englishman, Gerard Shelley, witnessed their departure:

> As the cars drove away, the crowd was moved with a deep emotion and in heartfelt tones called down on the saintly Grand Duchess the protection of Heaven. Many raised their eyes to the black cross of the Chapel dome, crossed themselves, and sinking to their knees, beat their brows against the earth. . . . For many weeks desolation reigned among the Sisters and patients the Grand Duchess had left behind.[13]

Halfhoping that she might see Alexandra and her family, Elizabeth was hustled with her two Sisters onto a guarded train. For days on end, they stopped and started and crawled eastward through the endless Russian forest. Elizabeth could hardly recognize the Trans-Siberian line as the smooth, well-ordered railway on which she had hurried westward at the outbreak of war. The worn-out engines, fed on poor fuel, struggled to move on the dilapidated track. Their brakes would fail at critical moments, and the drivers would pray as they descended a steep incline. Soldiers, hurrying home from the western front, had clambered onto the roofs of overcrowded carriages or driven locomotives themselves at full throttle. The trackside was littered with overturned engines and the corpses of passengers thrown from the trains.[14]

It was a relief at last to see the pine-clad slopes and sparkling streams of the Urals. Possibly the scenery brought memories to Elizabeth of carefree holidays at Balmoral. Her destination, however, proved to be a bitter contrast. Yekaterinburg, the capital of the "Red Urals," was a fierce stronghold of Bolshevism, and its factory workers would show none of the reverence accorded her by the Moscow poor. Elizabeth and her Sisters were taken to the Novotikhvinsky convent, where life was a pale shadow of their recent existence. Armed guards controlled their daily routine; soon the Latvian guards who had shown them kindness were replaced by brutal Russians whom Elizabeth pitied. Twice a day she was fed a horseflesh stew; she could not make them understand that she was a strict vegetarian. She had to write to the Patriarch Tikhon to arrange for a diet of milk and turnips. None of the letters she sent to Moscow contained a word of complaint.[15]

Some of her relatives, also arrested by the Bolsheviks, were housed in the convent and the adjacent monastery. She saw her nephew, Vladimir ("Volodya") Paley, Grand Duke Paul's son by his second wife, and Grand Duke Serge Mikhailovich. With them were the three sons of Grand Duke Constantine, John, Igor, and Constantine, and John's wife, Princess Helen of Serbia. At the outbreak of war Elizabeth had taken tea with the three young soldiers in a far more cheerful mood.

She was never to see Alexandra again. A few days before, her sister, Nicholas, and one of their daughters, Marie, had been transferred from Tobolsk, and imprisoned a little over a mile away in the Ipatiev House, but Elizabeth could not visit them. The convent supplied the Ipatiev House with food, and she managed to send some gifts of coffee, Easter eggs, and chocolate.

Soon Alexandra's other children, Olga, Tatiana, Anastasia, and Alexis, would be joining their parents. The Bolsheviks feared the dangerous presence of "too many important guests at once in Yekaterinburg during the days of the great struggle with counterrevolution."[16] On May 20, in the dead of night,

Elizabeth and her fellow prisoners were moved to Alapayevsk one hundred miles further north.

The small mining town had changed little in the four years since Elizabeth's last visit. The streets were still muddy, and the houses no less shabby than before. The local school, a one-storied brick building in an unkempt yard, was now their prison, which was barred off from the street by a high wall. Inside they slept on plain iron beds with stiff mattresses. A cook would serve their meager meals at a bare wooden table. Elizabeth would eat in the bedroom she shared with her two Sisters. From another room the guards would keep a continuous watch.

The treatment was less harsh than before. On Sundays they could attend church in the nearby monastery, and Elizabeth often met the strong, bearded prior, her friend Father Seraphim. He became her confessor, and her fortitude in adversity filled him with a great reverence. In the green meadows outside the town they could wander unescorted, and the clear air and spring flowers lifted their spirits. In the schoolyard Elizabeth planned out a kitchen garden, and she and the others dug and sowed vegetables. It soon became a cozy place where they could talk, read, and drink tea. There Volodya Paley, a gifted dramatist and poet, worked on his play on the life of Lermontov. Serge Mikhailovich, normally a morose and taciturn old soldier who complained of rheumatism, helped him out with details of Caucasian life.[17]

Just as Elizabeth had cared for her convent Sisters, she now gave her affection to her companions. She drew closer to her nephew Volodya, who had once been a distant figure during the exile of his father, Grand Duke Paul. In a secret letter to his mother, Volodya wrote of "Aunt Ella and her great kindness to me."[18] She had known Grand Duke Constantine's three young sons Igor, John, and Constantine, since they were infants. Now she gave them the support in adversity that she had shown at the funerals of their brother and father. John's wife, Princess Helen of Serbia, would sit and sew beside her in her room, and he would join them both for evening prayers.

As spring advanced and the garden became greener, it seemed that they were in little danger. Their spartan existence was familiar enough to Elizabeth, and the peaceful atmosphere allowed her to spend hours in private. In this remote place, it was as if she had found the life of prayer and quiet contemplation for which she had often longed.

In the world outside, the Bolshevik regime was meeting with resistance. In May 1918, a legion of Czech troops‡ in Siberia suddenly turned against their Red Guards and began to revolt against the Communist regime. Soon they had seized the Trans-Siberian Railway and were advancing west to the Urals. Early in June they captured Chelyabinsk to the south, and mutinous riots broke out in Yekaterinburg. Russia's erstwhile allies, assured of victory over the Germans, sent troops in support of the rebels. To the north a British army had landed at Archangel. In the Volga region and the southern Urals a White army of Cossacks was gaining ground. The Civil War had begun, and the Bolsheviks began to feel threatened.

Slowly they turned on their royal captives. At Perm Grand Duke Michael was clandestinely taken away to a dark forest and shot. The rumor was spread that he had escaped, and on this pretext a harsher regime was imposed at Alapayevsk. Three times a group of Magyar Red Guards subjected the prisoners to pointless searches of their rooms late at night. Serge Mikhailovich protested in vain at these intrusions. The prisoners' property and money were confiscated, they were left only the clothes and shoes they wore, and they slept on bare beds. No longer could they walk outside the school or attend church. Finally, on June 21, they were put under a prison regime, and confined to their rooms. Elizabeth and the others sweltered in the torrid summer heat, unable to open the padlocked windows and freshen their airless bedrooms.[19] They could guess what form Michael's "escape" had taken, and looked to the future with a vague dread.

While hope withered away, one hundred miles to the south a lone British diplomat was struggling to save the lives of the imperial family. Thomas Preston, British consul in Yekaterinburg, whose office was yards from the Ipatiev House, harangued the Bolshevik officials. On his own initiative and without support from London, he repeatedly visited the deputy head of the Soviet, Chutskayev, at the headquarters in the railway station. In a room piled high with rifles and stinking of stale tobacco and unwashed bodies, he demanded assurances that the emperor and all his relatives would be unharmed. Chutskayev equivocated, saying that they were in good health and no danger. Unconvinced, Preston demanded a firm guarantee. At length Chutskayev threatened to withdraw his diplomatic status, and Preston's efforts came to naught.

Meanwhile, plans were made for grim deeds in a building five doors away from the British consulate. A fabricated message, written in ungrammatical French, had been sent in a milk bottle to the Ipatiev House. It told of a plot by loyal officers to rescue the emperor and his family, and Nicholas had sent a reply in another bottle. Armed with this supposed proof of the emperor's treason, Philip Goloshchekin, military commissar of the Urals, left for Moscow early in July. In the Kremlin he met Lenin and his henchman Sverdlov. They agreed that Yekaterinburg could not hold out much longer against the Whites. Before the city fell, an end must be put to the prisoners there and at Alapayevsk.

By the evening of July 16, 1918, the guns of the advancing Whites could be heard in the streets of Yekaterinburg. After midnight, an order came via telegram from Moscow. At two in the morning, Yurovsky, a Cheka officer, awoke the imperial family and told them that there was unrest in the town, and they must move into the basement. In silence they descended: Nicholas carrying Alexis in his arms, Alexandra and her four daughters in plain dresses, bearing pillows. Chairs were brought in for Alexis, who had had an attack of hemophilia, and Alexandra, who could not stand for long. With grim humor Yurovsky told them that he needed their photograph, and lined them up against the wall. The emperor's family stood in the first row, the servants and a lady-in-waiting behind. A firing squad entered the crowded room, less than thirty yards square.

Yurovsky read out the death sentence. In disbelief Nicholas asked him to repeat it. As the policeman neared the end of the text, Nicholas said, "You know not what you do." At the last word, Alexandra and Olga began to cross themselves, and Yurovsky pulled out his revolver. A guard behind him was quicker off the mark and fired the first shot at the tsar. The assassins then fired shot after shot. They were so close-packed that the wrists of the men in front were burned by the fire from those behind.

In the gathering smoke the girls were still alive: the bullets had ricocheted off the diamonds sewn in their dresses. Marie and Anastasia, crouched against the wall, held up their arms to protect themselves. The maid, Anna Demidova, wailed and covered her head with a pillow, into which the guards continually fired. Alexis, lying on the ground, raised his arm with a strange vitality to shield his face. With a shaking hand a guard fired a whole clip of bullets into him, and he fell silent. In the din an order was shouted to finish off the job with bayonets. A guard tried to stab Anna Demidova, but his bayonet would not pierce her chest, as she grabbed the weapon and screamed. He resorted to the butt of his rifle. Then Alexis, gushing blood, stirred and moaned. Yurovsky advanced and shot him twice, point-blank. The doors were opened, and the smoke cleared to reveal eleven inert bodies.

The assassins returned with sheets to bear the corpses onto a truck outside. The last emperor of Russia was taken out first. The guards began to pick up one of his daughters. At this point, one of them recalled, the girl screamed and covered her face with her arm; the other three were also still alive. In horror a guard grabbed a bayonet and stabbed again and again.

The truck, laden with the remains of the imperial family, drove deep into the woods. Before finding a burial place, Yurovsky ordered the grand duchesses' dresses to be stripped of their jewels. As the sun rose on the morning of July 17, some Bolsheviks took them to an unnamed house in Alapayevsk. Safarov, the chairman of the Ural Soviet, headed there to fulfill his plans.

At midday, Elizabeth and her fellow prisoners were confined in their rooms, awaiting their meal in the stifling heat. Three days before, there had been a portent of the end. The guards had taken away Sister Catherine against her will. Volodya's Polish servant Krukovsky had gone with her, bearing a secret letter to Volodya's mother, Princess Paley. Before leaving, Krukovsky had given his master all his savings, and Volodya "had thanked him with tears in his eyes."[20] Princess Helen had left as well, for there is no further reference to her in the investigation subsequently carried out by the White authorities.§

Now the prisoners fully realized the fate in store for them. A Cheka policeman, Startsev, entered the schoolroom with a gang of Bolsheviks. He ordered the Red Guards to leave, and took away the prisoners' remaining money. That night, he told them, they would be taken to a mine shaft ten miles further north at Verkhne-Sinyachikha. For Elizabeth, the remaining hours could only be spent in prayer.

Their dinner was served, and they were given little time to eat: "Finish your meal quickly. At eleven we are going to Sinyachikha." They asked if they should take what remained of their luggage. "No."[21] They put a few trinkets in their pockets, and Elizabeth wore a plain wooden cross around her neck. As the last glimmers of the evening sun faded, they were hustled at gunpoint out of the brick schoolroom. For the first time in weeks they stood in the open air.

They were herded out of the town onto a dirt road. A line of wooden carts awaited them, and two prisoners were placed in each. In the gathering gloom they jolted through the empty pine woods. There were no cries, no conversation, and no appeals. They passed no one for two hours but some drunken peasants. They halted on a bare plain from which no light could be seen.

They were made to walk some hundred yards in the darkness, the rifles leveled at their backs. The only sound was the cracking of twigs at their feet. Elizabeth began to sing a hymn, *Hail, Gentle Light,* in which the others joined. The commander called a halt by the deep shaft of an abandoned mine. He told them that they had been sentenced to death, and would be thrown down the shaft. For some reason he chose Elizabeth as the first.[22]

In her gray dress, a white handkerchief around her neck and a veil over her head, she knelt at the edge. She asked one favor, to be allowed to say a short prayer. At that moment her instinct of compassion must have turned her thoughts to the souls of her assassins. She could remember that Serge had felt great pity for those who had died unrepentant and unconfessed. She had told Kalyayev that her husband had forgiven him. On the site of his murder, she had written the plea for forgiveness that Christ had made on the Cross. Now she repeated the words, aloud and in English: "Father, forgive them, for they know not what they do."

The butt of a rifle struck the left side of her head. Four hands grasped her unconscious body, and flung her, still breathing, into sixty feet of darkness.

In their turn, the others passed over the edge. The Constantine princes, once the people's heroes, now suffered the lot of common criminals. Sister Barbara, a very small woman, deeply pious, earned her martyr's crown. Volodya Paley, not yet twenty-one, was denied his artist's vocation. Serge Mikhailovich, protesting against this barbarity, was shot in the head.

Stones, planks, and sticks were gathered up and thrown on top of the living bodies. The blast of a hand grenade echoed in the summer night. The creaking carts were driven away, and a silence fell on the empty plain. The sentinels trudged about as a glimmer of dawn appeared in the east.

## Notes to Chapter 24

*The few British residents were usually spared this treatment. One young diplomat, Robert Bruce Lockhart, dining out in the company of British officers, was confronted by an armed gang and felt compelled to hand over his watch and wallet. The gang leader, however, noticing the British uniforms, saluted and handed them back. "You are English officers. We do not rob Englishmen. I apologize for the state of my country which forces me to adopt this manner of earning our living."

†Two months later, Mirbach was shot dead by a member of the left Socialist Revolutionary faction.

‡The Czech soldiers had allowed themselves to be taken prisoner by the Russians, and had then fought on the Allied side for an independent Czech state. After Russia had signed the peace treaty with Germany, they traveled home on the Trans-Siberian Railway via Vladivostok.

§According to a letter from Irene to Victoria, Princess Helen was allowed to leave for Petrograd to see her children. Arriving at Yekaterinburg, however, she was imprisoned on the pretext of being a Serbian spy, then sent to a prison in Perm. The Whites negotiated with the Bolsheviks for her release, and she managed to leave Russia via Sweden.

# Epilogue

*Siberian Cortège*

*Gott, der ergeb' ich mich!*
*Wenn mich die Donner des Todes begrüssen,*
*Wenn meine Adern geöffnet fliessen . . .*

*Lord, I yield to thee,*
*When death's loud thunders greet my shrinking ear,*
*When blood streams from my veins and death draws near . . .*

—THEODOR KÖRNER, "GEBET WÄHREND DEN SCHLACHT"
(A PRAYER IN THE MIDST OF BATTLE)

It is said that on that night one of the assassins went mad. He ran into the woods and arrived at his cottage raving. After a week of silence, he broke down in front of his wife, and confessed. When the White soldiers came, she told them where the murders had taken place.

But there is another story of how the mine shaft was found. It was told by Father Seraphim to a member of the British royal family. Later that night, the sound of exploding grenades was heard. In the early dawn, the townspeople saw a squad of Red Army troops move up in line toward the school building. The Bolsheviks pretended—though no one believed them—that the prisoners had escaped. Word spread to the monastery, which lay near the road to the mine shaft. Possibly one of the monks had seen the silent procession of carts; Father Seraphim soon guessed where they had gone.

Early in the morning he made his way along the dirt road through the forest. On the wide grassy plain he met the Red Sentinels. They were men from Alapayevsk, and they let him pass. Father Seraphim crept up to the shaft, and peered over the edge at the rubble from the exploded grenades. He was then given another proof of the courage in adversity that he had so admired in Grand Duchess Elizabeth. From the bottom of the shaft he could hear the faint singing of hymns.

Late in September, the Bolsheviks fled Alapayevsk in the face of the White advance. When order was established, Father Seraphim was allowed to excavate the mine shaft with the help of the White soldiers. Slowly they dug downward, and he beheld a scene that became ever more gruesome. All but Serge Mikhailovich had survived the fall; they had lain in the darkness and fallen unconscious as their strength failed them. On October 10, the soldiers reached the floor of the shaft. With a lantern Father Seraphim climbed down, and was overwhelmed by what he saw. Side by side lay the remains of Prince John and Elizabeth. The two who had prayed together in the evenings had joined together in singing their final hymns. A piece of Elizabeth's veil had been torn off and used to bandage his wounds, her last act before she died. The fingers of her right hand were stiffened in the sign of the cross; her body was raised to the surface, and seemed not to have decayed.

At this sight, Father Seraphim determined that the remains of the prisoners should rest in a chapel of God. He laid them in his church at Alapayevsk, but feared that they could not stay there long. After some months he heard warning that the Whites were retreating eastward. Possibly he knew of Elizabeth's wish to be buried in Jerusalem. In July 1919, accompanied by two followers, he began a long journey to the east.

Many years later, he told an extraordinary tale to the countess of Athlone.* His first destination was the convent at Tobolsk, and he loaded the coffins on a train. Suddenly, Lady Athlone recalled,

> . . . my "Sacred Lady" appeared and told him there
> was to be a railway accident and he must have the
> van detached from the train. The station-master
> demurred to do so, saying there was nothing like-

ly to happen; however he insisted and a train did crash into the train Father Seraphim would have been on.

They left for Tobolsk—were welcomed by the Mother Superior—but had hardly arrived when "my sacred lady" appeared and told him he must go on to Peking as the Bolsheviks were coming and would destroy the Convent. Once again the Mother Superior tried to persuade him to remain, as the Reds were so far away. However he insisted and later heard of the arrival of the Reds and the murder of the Mother and her nuns.[1]

With a pass from the Cossack chieftain Semyenov, Father Seraphim headed eastward on the Trans-Siberian Railway. The journey gradually became a battle of endurance. The brutal fighting of the civil war was reducing the area to chaos. Food became scarce; in places gangs of half-starved peasants terrorized the country. In the towns thousands fell prey to typhus among the swarm of refugees.[2] The railway, the lifeline of Siberia, was often blocked for miles ahead by trains bearing soldiers to the front. If the fighting was too close, Father Seraphim's wagon was uncoupled and forced to retrace the day's journey on another train.[3] Alongside the track were many refugees:

Always that steady stream of sleighs hauled by Siberian ponies, with their pathetic burdens, old and young, women and children, some starving, many of them ill, but somehow clinging on desperately to the top of the few possessions which they had managed to save. If anyone got ill they just fell down and died in the snow—there was nothing anyone could do about it.[4]

Somehow he reached the convent at Irkutsk. There he hid the coffins and lay low for some months. "The coffins," Elizabeth's sister Victoria later recalled, "were opened as this was necessary and our Ella's body was not decayed, only dried up. The nuns cleansed it and exchanged the grave cloth for a nun's dress. . . ."[5]

By the new year of 1920, it had become clear that Admiral Kolchak's forces could not hold Irkutsk. Father Seraphim pressed on toward Harbin along the Chinese Eastern Railway. In February, as he neared the Chinese border, his destination seemed almost in sight. But a band of Communists attacked his train, and the body of Prince John was lost. On April 3, 1920, he interred the remaining coffins at the Russian mission in Beijing. He stayed on, and kept watch.[6]

For a while in Moscow, there continued a reminder of Elizabeth's old presence at the convent. She had specifically asked the nuns to look after the crippled boy in her orphanage, Voldya Crichton. His brother later recalled:

> One of the nuns told me how amazed she was that the other children at the hospital loved to come and play in Volodya's room, and that he liked equally well to watch them at play, although he could not take part in their games. She also told me that the children never quarrelled there and never had she observed the slightest hint of bad temper. It seemed that the spirit of Elizabeth still endured in Volodya's room.[7]

Soon, however, the Bolsheviks set about undoing the good works of Elizabeth, and obliterating her memory. The convent was disbanded, and the countess who had taken it over, thrown into prison.[8] The nuns also suffered imprisonment or fled the city. Father Mitrophan was arrested; he was to spend the next seventeen years in labor camps in the far north of Russia.[9] The chapel was closed, and a functional hospital continued on the site.

Elizabeth's niece, Grand Duchess Marie, was deprived of the dream she had once cherished of succeeding her as abbess of the convent. After many trials she and her husband, Prince Serge Putiatin, settled down to a life in a cottage near Pavlovsk, growing vegetables in the garden. Early in July 1918 she gave birth to a boy. On the day of Elizabeth's death the child was christened, but died soon afterward. As the dangers grew, Marie, her husband and his brother fled for the German-occupied Ukraine. At every stop on the journey south, soldiers entered their train and examined the passengers' passports. But Marie and the Putiatin brothers had no Russian documents; the soldiers were only barred from their compartment by the ingenious excuses of the conductor, whom they had bribed. At the border, the agent who should have smuggled them out of Russia was unable to help. In desperation Marie approached a frontier guard and spun a story of relatives who had already crossed over with their documents. They had no money, she said, and her husband's brother would remain behind with their luggage. The ruse worked, and she and her husband, Prince Serge Putiatin found themselves opposite the German guards. Marie produced a document from the Swedish legation, which she had kept hidden in a cake of soap. It identified her as a Swedish princess, and the Germans helped her obtain the proper documents from the Bolshevik Ukrainian commissar. Only then could they retrieve her brother-in-law from the Russian side.[10]

Arriving in London, Marie met her brother Dmitiri. Exiled to the Persian front after the killing of Rasputin, he had joined the British Army and escaped the revolution. Their father, Grand Duke Paul, had been imprisoned in Petrograd and shot.

In England, Marie and her relatives harbored the hope that Elizabeth was still alive. In the summer of 1918, the retreating Bolsheviks had ostentatiously left behind a telegram which stated that the Whites had assaulted the schoolroom and Elizabeth and her fellow prisoners had escaped. The story had appeared in the press, and her sister Victoria was in an anxious state of uncertainty. In August 1919 she had written to her brother Ernest: "I dare not not give myself up to hope. . . . I can face the thought of their death as a release from suffering and entry into happy rest, though the ache of the loss is just one more burden which we have to bear. . . ."[11]

In the fall of 1920, her fears were confirmed. Princess Beatrice, Queen Victoria's youngest daughter, saw a photograph in the *Illustrated London News*. It showed an Orthodox chapel in Beijing; beneath it was written that this was the grave of the victims of the murders at Alapayevsk. Beatrice believed that this must be where Ella lay. She sent the photograph to Victoria, who made inquiries and discovered the truth.[12] Lady Milford Haven† then arranged for the coffins of Elizabeth and Sister Barbara to be sent to Shanghai and shipped to Port Said. Father Seraphim, always faithful to his revered grand duchess, traveled beside her.

At Port Said he took the coffins through the deserted, moonlit streets to the city's Greek church. At midnight, Victoria and her husband arrived from England. With them was Kitty Stroukov, the lady-in-waiting who had followed Elizabeth on her pilgrimage to Jerusalem many years before. In the dim, quiet chapel, a small candle burned at the coffin's head, illuminating Ella's likeness which was set into the wooden frame. In the old days, Ella had often met her sister after a long journey. Now Victoria gazed at her picture and knelt in prayer by her side.[13]

A railway van took the coffins to Jerusalem for burial in the Church of St. Mary Magdalene, whose foundation Elizabeth had witnessed thirty-two years earlier. The cortege passed many of the holy places that had inspired her to take up Orthodoxy. The coffins were unloaded by the Garden of Gethsemane, where Christ is said to have gathered with His followers. Beneath them, in the distance, stood the gleaming golden roof of the Dome of the Rock, on the site where Abraham had prepared to sacrifice Isaac. Above them rose the rocky mass of the Mount of Olives; from its summit Christ had ascended into Heaven. It was a scene of intense emotion for the mourners. Victoria's husband, Lord Milford Haven, recalled:

. . . the coffins were lifted out and carried up the
steep, stony, zig-zag path to the church. Most of
the carriers were Russian peasant women, stranded pilgrims, who staggered under the tremendous
load, sobbing and moaning all the time, and
almost fighting to get at some part of the coffin. I
clung to one of the handles, and once had to
climb over the body of one of the women who had
tripped over a stone and fallen full length. One
huge lay priest, with hair like a lion's mane, was
happily at the head end, but it was a relief when
we reached the church safely. A service was held at
once, the congregation overflowing through the
open doors.[14]

For Father Seraphim, it was the supreme moment of years of
devotion. After the ceremony, he told Louis and Victoria the
story of his arduous travels. He then made his home in a small
room beside the crypt. Until his death, he was to watch over the
mausoleum whose occupant he revered as a saint. Victoria wrote:
"Truly a faithful man."[15]

Victoria kept alive among her children the memory of the
saintly woman who had given her life to the poor and sick. Her
daughter, Princess Alice, suffered bereavements similar to
Elizabeth's. Her daughter Cecilia, her son-in-law, and her two
grandsons were killed in an air accident on November 16, 1937.
In war torn Athens Alice remembered Ella's example, and, undeterred by her deafness, took to nursing in crowded hospitals.
Respected and unharmed by the occupying Germans, she sheltered Jews and refugees from the SS. In 1944 she learned of her
husband's death from a heart attack. Soon after the marriage of
her son, Prince Philip, to Princess Elizabeth, she took inspiration
from her aunt's convent and founded the Sisterhood of Martha
and Mary in Athens. She expressed a wish, fulfilled many years
later, to be buried alongside Elizabeth in Jerusalem.

After Father Seraphim's death, the priests continued to look after the quiet chapel at the foot of the Mount of Olives. In 1982 they had cause to open the shrine once more. In a service in New York attended by thousands of believers, the Russian Orthodox Church in exile canonized Elizabeth and Sister Barbara among other martyrs of Communist persecution.[16] Such was their reverence for Elizabeth that they believed her body to remain uncorrupted:

> When the inner casket of the grand duchess's coffin was opened, the chapel was filled with a sweet fragrance, which was said to be like that of honey and jasmine. Although the chapel was open and well aired, this fragrance remained.
>
> The clothing of the martyrs was found to be damp, although the atmosphere at Gethsemane is very dry. The material was as if some liquid had been poured over it, so moist was it, although hitherto the coffins had been sealed.[17]

In May 1984, a service was held in a final act of devotion. In the presence of a bishop, three archbishops, and eight priests, the two coffins were removed from the crypt and taken in procession twice round the church. They were then laid in a shrine for the veneration of Orthodox pilgrims.[18]

A few years later the patriarch of Moscow also held a service of canonization for the martyr-saint Elizabeth. Some of his clergy now sought to make a memorial on the site of the mine shaft. They headed through the remote forest north of Yekaterinburg. A small copse of pine had grown up at the center of the grassy plain, and tall birch trees now lined the old road. Clearing away the scrub and bushes, they found a shallow pit. In reverence they put up a wooden cross; at its foot, wreaths of flowers would be placed. Beside it was built a brick chapel with a gleaming silver dome.

In 1992, another chapel was erected on the site of the Ipatiev House at the center of Yekaterinburg, a plain wooden building with a golden roof. Inside, the priests placed an icon of the beautiful woman dressed in a nun's habit to whom the chapel was dedicated. Today tourists and pilgrims from all over Russia enter and gaze at the face of Queen Victoria's granddaughter, Elizabeth, Princess and Martyr.

## Notes to Epilogue

*Princess Alice, Countess of Athlone, was the daughter of Prince Leopold, Duke of Albany, fourth son of Queen Victoria. In 1931 she met Father Seraphim while on a visit to Jerusalem.

†In 1914, Victoria's husband, Prince Louis of Battenberg, had renounced his German title and been made Marquis of Milford Haven. His surname, Battenberg, was anglicized to Mountbatten.

# Appendix 1

DOCUMENTARY EVIDENCE
OF THE LAST JOURNEY AND DEATH OF
GRAND DUCHESS ELIZABETH
AND THE REMOVAL OF HER REMAINS TO BEIJING

Several discrepancies arise in the varying accounts of the final months of the grand duchess's life, her death, and the subsequent events. A close examination of the evidence is necessary to establish what exactly happened.

The first point of uncertainty is the date of the grand duchess's removal from Moscow. E. M. Almedingen (*An Unbroken Unity*, p. 120) comments: "March, April and even May 1918 have been given in various sources." A clue is given by the visits of the German ambassador, Count Mirbach, to the convent. A note in the Broadlands Archives and an account given by Princess Paley (*Memories of Russia 1916–19*, pp. 204–205) affirm that Mirbach did make these calls. A British diplomat stationed in Moscow, Robert Bruce Lockhart, (*Memoirs of a British Agent*, p. 267), writes that Mirbach arrived in Moscow on 24 April 1918. Elizabeth's departure must, therefore, have occurred a few days afterwards at the earliest.

E. M. Almedingen writes that she arrived in Yekaterinburg on May 1: "That is proved by a statement of the then British consul at Yekaterinburg, Mr. T. H. Preston." In the Broadlands Archives there is a note from the British consulate, dated May 1, but this refers to the transfer of ex-Emperor Nicholas and his family from Tobolsk to Yekaterinburg. Given the ramshackle condition of the Trans-Siberian Railway, it would have been impossible for the grand duchess to travel to Yekaterinburg in so short a time. (It took ex-Emperor Nicholas and his family some five days to travel from Petrograd to the Urals in August 1917, when the railway was far better organized.)

Another reference is provided by Metropolitan Anastasius (*Svetloi Pamiati Velikoi Knyagini Elizabety Feodorovny*, reprinted in the magazine *Orthodox Life*), who states that she was taken from Moscow at Easter, 1918. (This endorsed by another source, M. Belevskaya-Zhukovskaya, in *Materialy k zhitiyu prepodobnomuchenit-si velikoi knyagini Yelizaveti*, p. 134.) As Anastasius was then bishop-suffragan of Moscow and a close friend of Elizabeth, his date is probably the most accurate. We can assume, then, that she left Moscow with her two Sisters at Easter, which by the Russian Orthodox calendar fell at the beginning of May.

The next area of uncertainty is whether the grand duchess and her Sisters were imprisoned at Perm en route, as E. M. Almedingen believes (*An Unbroken Unity*, p. 122). A flimsy piece of evidence provides the one confirmation (that I have been able to trace) of their stay there. In ex-Emperor Nicholas's diary (*Journal Intime de Nicholas II*, p. 202) there is an entry dated 16 May 1918: "This afternoon we received from Ella, from Perm, coffee, Easter eggs and chocolate." However, granted the chaotic state of the Trans-Siberian Railway at the time, and the greed of the average Bolshevik official, a parcel containing such useful commodities would have been unlikely to make the 170-mile journey from Perm with its contents intact. It is more probable that the Bolsheviks wanted to prevent any communication between Elizabeth and her sister's family and deliberately concealed her whereabouts from them. Moreover, Metropolitan Anastasius writes that the three Sisters were taken directly to Yekaterinburg.

At any rate, the sources agree that Elizabeth and her two Sisters were imprisoned in the Novotikhinsky convent in Yekaterinburg by the middle of May. For the remaining days of the grand duchess's life the chief source is the investigation carried out by Nicholas Sokolov during the White occupation of the Urals and published in the West as *Enquête judiciare sur l'assassinat de la famille impériale russe* (chapter 25). Sokolov interviewed a vast range of witnesses before drawing up an account of the life of the grand duchess and her fellow prisoners.

He states clearly that they were taken to Alapayevsk on May 20. The information about the daily life and increasingly severe treatment of the prisoners comes chiefly from the testimony of their cook, Krivovna, and the guards. Another source is the letter smuggled out by Prince Vladimir Paley's Polish valet to Vladimir's mother, Princess Paley.*

The story of the murders in the Ipatiev House comes from the exhaustive research in the Russian State Archives of the Russian playwright and historian Edvard Radzinsky, published in *The Last Tsar: The Life and Death of Nicholas II*. Radzinsky established that the murders were authorized by Lenin and his commissars in the Kremlin. The account of the slaughter in the basement comes from the testimonies of the assassins, though they differ in small details.

As for the murders at Alapayevsk, the story begins early on the morning of July 17 with a statement by Radzinsky from the Russian archives that the Red Guards took the jewels stripped from the grand duchesses' corpses to an unnamed house in Alapayevsk. Possibly these were the same men as the "several Bolshevik workers" that Sokolov records as entering the schoolroom at midday, led by the Cheka policeman, Piotr Startsev. Sokolov also tells us that Safarov, the chairman of the Ural Soviet, came personally to Alapayevsk to oversee the executions. Krivovna testifies that the Bolsheviks hurried the prisoners over dinner: "Finish your meal quickly. At eleven we are going to Sinyachikha."

At eleven P.M., therefore, not long after the midsummer sunset in this far northern latitude, the prisoners were hustled into a line of wooden carts. The mode of transport is affirmed by a group of peasants who met them on the road while returning from a drinking spree. One, Trushkov, testified in Sokolov's report: "There were no cries, no conversation, no songs, no groans; absolutely no sound I could hear. They all proceeded calmly and quietly."

Given the state of the average Russian unmetalled road,[†] with ruts three feet deep, the ten-mile journey with horse-drawn carts must have taken two hours. At around one A.M. on July 18, they neared the mine shaft. A White officer, Colonel Paul Rodzianko,[‡] arriving in the Urals a few months later, recalled meeting a nurse who told him that the prisoners were made to walk several hundred yards to the shaft. The old Alapayevsk road runs directly past the mine shaft, and Rodzianko's account is third- or fourth-hand, but his point is confirmed by Sokolov's assertion that the shaft was "without doubt" blown up with grenades after the executions had taken place. Had the cart-horses been any nearer to the shaft, they would undoubtedly have reared up or bolted with the carts on hearing the blast.

Rodzianko also tells us that the grand duchess sang a hymn as she walked.

That Elizabeth was the first victim is confirmed by the fact that her body, the furthest down in the shaft, was the last to be recovered by the White soldiers. Several historical accounts write of her last words as a prayer of forgiveness for her executioners.[§] However, as neither Sokolov nor the White generals mention them, they are difficult to confirm. The strongest evidence comes in a letter Elizabeth's sister Victoria, Lady Milford Haven, wrote to their brother, Grand Duke Ernest: "I have heard that it was told by one of those who was present at her death that she prayed 'Lord forgive for they know not what they do'—& I believe it for how should one not knowing her have thought of putting these words in her mouth."

We now come to the strangest part of the events of July 18, the continued survival of the victims at the bottom of the shaft. Lady Milford Haven wrote to her brother, "The autopsy on the bodies proved that life was extinct before they were thrown down into the pit so thank God the tales of further suffering are not true." However, Lady Milford Haven was most probably concealing the truth from Grand Duke Ernest, a highly sensitive man with a life-long fear of death, for the report of the autopsies published by Sokolov proves the opposite. Sokolov's report establishes that all except Serge Mikhailovich, who was shot in the head, were stunned by a blow to the head and thrown down alive. The writer Lord Lambton showed the report to a forensic expert, Professor Bowen of Charing Cross Hospital, London, and published the results in a factual appendix to his novel *Elizabeth and Alexandra* (pp. 410–412). Professor Bowen concluded that they gradually died of an accumulation of blood in the brain; in some cases, including that of Grand Duchess Elizabeth, they could have survived for hours.

An account by a White officer, General I. S. Smolin, *The Alapayevsk Tragedy,* confirms that all but Serge Mikhailovich were seized and thrown down alive (Broadlands Archives). It adds: "According to the Red Soldiers' testimony, sacred songs together with groans and moans were heard for some time from the shaft."

This gives credence to the tale told by Father Seraphim to Princess Alice, Countess of Athlone, (in the Broadlands Archives) that he "was allowed near the mine down which the Grand Duchess Elizabeth (Ella) and others had been thrown and he said he could still hear them singing hymns although he could not communicate with them." At first it appears strange that Father Seraphim could have reached the mine shaft within the few hours of life left to the victims. However, it seems that he was alerted soon after their disappearance from Alapayevsk. Sokolov reports that before three A.M. the Bolsheviks stage-managed a fictitious escape of the prisoners: "Late that night [July 17–18] grenade explosions and gunshots were heard near the school building. This caused consternation in the town." The whole of the small town, little more than an overgrown village, must have been awakened by the sudden racket in the summer night.

We know from the letters of Lady Milford Haven, who met Father Seraphim later on, that he was a deeply religious man who revered the grand duchess. Clearly he would have tried to find out what had happened to her. The fresh tracks of the carts (some ten or eleven in all, according to Sokolov) on the unpaved road outside his monastery would have given him an unmistakable clue. It would have been an easy matter for him to follow the tracks on horseback through the forest to the mine shaft, arriving there in the early hours of the morning. Sokolov tells us that the assassins were men from Alapayevsk and the surrounding area. Most probably the guards who had remained there as sentinels knew Father Seraphim, a prominent local figure, by sight, and let him up to the shaft. There is no evidence, therefore, to contradict what Father Seraphim told Lady Athlone.

Neither is there any evidence, on the other hand, to support the story told to Paul Rodzianko, that one of the assassins went mad after the killings.

Father Seraphim told Lady Athlone that he "was given permission to exhume their bodies, which he proceeded to do." Unfortunately, neither Sokolov nor General Smolin mention Father Seraphim's presence at the excavation of the mine shaft after the White armies had captured the area. However, it is the Russian Orthodox custom, which the Whites would most likely have respected, for a priest to be present when a corpse is exhumed. According to Sokolov, the local priest, Father Udintsev, had been murdered by Soloviev, a Bolshevik. Father Seraphim would have been the only clergyman for miles around. In addition, Lady Milford Haven wrote that the bodies were then interred in his monastery at Alapayevsk.

Father Seraphim also told Lady Athlone that the body of the grand duchess, "strange to say was not decomposed at all." Lady Milford Haven seemingly confirms this, in a passage already quoted in the Epilogue, that later on when he opened her coffin at the convent in Irkutsk, "our Ella's body was not decayed only dried up." (Hessian Grand Ducal Archives). Prince Nicholas Kudashev, the last envoy of imperial Russia to China, also happened to see her body at Harbin, where Father Seraphim stopped en route to Beijing. "The Grand Duchess," he wrote, "lay as if alive, completely unchanged since the day that I met her in Moscow on the way from Beijing, except that on one side of her face was a large bruise from a blow sustained in the fall into the mineshaft." (*Materialy k zhitiyu...*, p. 152). General Smolin tells us that her fingers "were stiffened in the sign of the cross."

According to Lady Milford Haven, Father Seraphim "started from Alapayevsk in July 1919 and after many vicissitudes reached Beijing in April 1920." (Hessian Grand Ducal Archives). Lady Athlone and Metropolitan Anastasius both affirm that he took the bodies of the other royal victims as well as those of the grand duchess and Sister Barbara. We have only his own description, as told to Lady Athlone, of his almost miraculous escape from a railway accident and from the murders at the convent of Tobolsk.

For his subsequent journey, we have the account he gave to Princess M. A. Putiatina some years afterward in Jerusalem (*Materialy k zhitiyu...*, pp. 153–5). Conditions on the Trans-Siberian Railway have been described by General Sir Brian Horrocks, then a British officer attached to the White armies, in *The Sunday Times* of 10 August 1958.

## Notes to Appendix 1

*Published in her memoirs, *Memories of Russia 1916–19*, pp. 205–07.

†While visiting Verkhne-Sinyachikha I tried to persuade my taxi driver to leave the the modern tarred highway and venture down the old road along which the prisoners had gone. The elderly peasant who was my guide said, "That is a poor road." The driver, fearing for the state of his vehicle, refused point-blank.

‡As retold in his memoirs, *Tattered Banners*, pp. 253–254.

§For example, E. M. Almedingen, op. cit., p. 128; Rodzianko, op. cit., p. 253; Radzinsky, op. cit., p. 354.

# Appendix 2

| WORLD EVENTS | YEAR | EVENTS OF GRAND DUCHESS ELIZABETH |
|---|---|---|
| Austro-Prussian occupation of Schleswig and Holstein | 1864 | Birth and christening of Princess Elizabeth of Hesse |
| Seven Weeks' War, Prussia defeats Austria | 1866 | Completion of New Palace at Darmstadt; birth of Elizabeth's sister, Princess Irene |
| | 1868 | Birth of Prince Ernest |
| | 1870 | Birth of Prince Frederick William |
| Franco-Prussian War; republic established in France | | |
| Unification of Germany | 1871 | |
| | 1872 | Birth of Princess Alix |
| | 1873 | Death of Frederick William |
| | 1874 | Birth of Princess Marie "May" |

| WORLD EVENTS | YEAR | EVENTS OF GRAND DUCHESS ELIZABETH |
|---|---|---|
| | 1877 | Deaths of Prince Charles of Hesse and Grand Duke Louis III |
| Creation of Bulgaria | 1878 | Death of Princess Alice and May |
| Prince Alexander of Battenberg ("Sandro") elected prince of Bulgaria | 1879 | Grand Duke Serge of Russia and Elizabeth meet |
| Death of Empress Marie of Russia; assassination of her husband Emperor Alexander II | 1880 | Elizabeth refuses Prince William's proposal of marriage |
| Alexander III imposes restrictions on the Jews in Russia | 1882 | Serge begins to court Elizabeth |
| | 1883 | Engagement of Victoria and Prince Louis of Battenberg; Elizabeth accepts Serge's proposal of marriage |
| | 1884 | Death of Prince Leopold; wedding of Victoria and Prince Louis of Battenberg; wedding of Elizabeth and Serge |
| "Sandro" abdicates the Bulgarian throne | 1886 | Grand Duke Louis and Irene visit Elizabeth in St. Petersburg |

| WORLD EVENTS | YEAR | EVENTS OF GRAND DUCHESS ELIZABETH |
|---|---|---|
| Students hanged for attempted assassination of Alexander III | 1887 | Elizabeth and Serge in London for Queen Victoria's golden jubilee |
| | 1888 | Death of Emperor William I of Germany; wedding of Irene and Prince Henry of Prussia; Frederick III becomes Emperor of Germany; death of Prince Alexander of Hesse |
| | 1889 | Wedding of Grand Duke Paul and Princess Alexandra of Greece |
| Failed harvest and severe famine in Russia | 1891 | Elizabeth converts to Russian Orthodoxy; Serge appointed governor of Moscow; death of Alexandra (Grand Duchess Paul) |
| | 1892 | Death of Grand Duke Louis |
| | 1894 | Wedding of Ernest and "Ducky," Princess Victoria of Coburg; engagement of Alix and Nicholas; death of Emperor Alexander III; wedding of Alix (now called Alexandra) and Emperor Nicholas II in St. Petersburg |
| | 1895 | Birth of Alexandra's first child, Olga |
| | 1896 | Coronation of Nicholas II |

| Year | Events of Grand Duchess Elizabeth | World Events |
| --- | --- | --- |
| 1898 | | Famine in Russia |
| 1899 | Death of Alfred, son of duke of Saxe-Coburg and Gotha | |
| 1901 | Death of Queen Victoria; divorce of Grand Duke Ernest and Ducky | Murder of Bogolepov, minister of education |
| 1902 | Secret marriage and exile of Paul and Mme. Pistolkors | Murder of interior minister, Sipyagin |
| 1903 | Canonization of St. Seraphim at Sarovo; wedding of Princess Alice of Battenberg to Prince Nicholas of Greece; death of Ernest's daughter Elizabeth | Russian Social Democratic Party splits into "Bolshevik" and "Menshevik" factions; Pogrom of Jews in Kishinev |
| 1905 | Serge assassinated | "Bloody Sunday" in St. Petersburg; mutiny on battleship *Potemkin*; treaty of Portsmouth ends war; 1905 "Revolution" |
| 1906 | Elizabeth warns Alexandra against Rasputin | First session at the Duma |
| 1908 | Wedding of Marie to Prince William of Sweden; Elizabeth begins building her convent | Beginning of Entente between Britain, France, and Russia; Bosnia-Herzegovina annexed by Austria |
| 1910 | The convent is established and Elizabeth takes the veil | |

| World Events | Year | Events of Grand Duchess Elizabeth |
| --- | --- | --- |
| Stolypin is assassinated; Rasputin's nominee, Father Varnava, is made Bishop of Kargopol | 1911 | |
| Romanov tercentenary celebrations | 1913 | |
| Assassination of Archduke Ferdinand in Sarajevo; Elizabeth nurses wounded soldiers; outbreak of First World War | 1914 | |
| Nicholas takes control of the Russian army; Alexandra runs Russia | 1915 | Elizabeth urges that Rasputin be banished; Maria Vassilshikova is received at Tsarskoe Selo with a German peace offer |
| Food shortages and rising prices foster discontent; strikes and revolutionary propaganda in Petrograd | 1916 | Rasputin assassinated |
| The "February Revolution"; Nicholas II abdicates; Lenin is returned to Russia by the Germans; Bolsheviks seize power in the "October Revolution" | 1917 | Elizabeth falls sick with typhoid; Nicholas, Alexandra, and their children are exiled to Tobolsk |
| The government moves to Moscow; peace signed with Germany at Brest Litovsk; the Civil War begins; Germany surrenders to the western allies | 1918 | Elizabeth is exiled and imprisoned; Nicholas, Alexandra, and their children are murdered; Elizabeth and her fellow prisoners are murdered |

| World Events | Year | Events of Grand Duchess Elizabeth |
|---|---|---|
| Treaty of Versailles is signed | 1919 | |
| | 1920 | Elizabeth is buried in Jerusalem |

# Appendix 3

## LIST OF CHARACTERS

**Albert**, prince consort, prince of Saxe-Coburg and Gotha, husband of Queen Victoria

**Albert Victor ("Eddy")**, prince, duke of Clarence, son of King Edward VII ("Bertie")

**Alexander II**, emperor of Russia, son of Emperor Nicholas I, husband of Princess Marie of Hesse and by the Rhine, father of Emperor Alexander III

**Alexander III**, emperor of Russia, son of Alexander II, husband of Princess Dagmar of Denmark (Empress Marie of Russia), father of Nicholas II

**Alexander (Mikhailovich)**, grand duke, son of Grand Duke Michael (brother of Emperor Alexander II), grandson of Emperor Nicholas I, husband of Grand Duchess Xenia, father of Grand Duchess Irene

**Alexander ("Sandro")**, prince of Battenberg, sovereign prince of Bulgaria, son of Prince Alexander of Hesse and Princess Julie of Battenberg

**Alexandra**, princess of Denmark, queen of Great Britain, sister of Empress Marie of Russia (wife of Emperor Alexander III), wife of King Edward VII

**Alexandra**, princess of Greece, sister of Princes Nicholas and Andrew of Greece, first wife of Grand Duke Paul, mother of Grand Duchess Marie (Pavlovna) and Grand Duke Dmitri

**Alexis**, tsarevich, son of Emperor Nicholas II and Princess Alix of Hesse

**Alice**, princess of Battenberg, daughter of Prince Louis of Battenberg and Princess Victoria of Hesse, wife of Prince Andrew of Greece, mother of Philip (prince of Greece, duke of Edinburgh)

**Alice**, princess, daughter of Queen Victoria, husband of Grand Duke Louis IV of Hesse and by the Rhine, mother of Grand Duchess Elizabeth

**Alix**, princess, Empress Alexandra of Russia, daughter of Grand Duke Louis IV of Hesse and by the Rhine and Princess Alice, sister of Grand Duchess Elizabeth, wife of Emperor Nicholas II of Russia

**Anastasia**, grand duchess, daughter of Emperor Nicholas II and Princess Alix of Hesse

**Andrew**, prince of Greece, brother of Princess Alexandra (Grand Duchess Paul), husband of Princess Alice of Battenberg

**Augusta**, princess of Sachsen Weimar, empress of Germany, wife of Emperor William I, mother of Emperor Frederick III

**Auguste Victoria**, princess of Schleswig-Holstein-Augustenburg, wife of Emperor William II of Germany

**Beatrice**, princess, daughter of Queen Victoria

**Catherine Dolgoruki**, princess, mistress, and, later, morganatic wife of Emperor Alexander II

**Charles**, prince of Hesse, brother of Grand Duke Louis III of Hesse and by the Rhine and Empress Marie of Russia (wife of Alexander II), father of Grand Duke Louis IV

**Constantine (Constantinovich)**, grand duke, son of Grand Duke Constantine Nikolayevich, grandson of Emperor Nicholas I of Russia, father of Princes Oleg, Igor, Constantine, and John Constantinovich

**Constantine**, prince, son of above, died with Grand Duchess Elizabeth at Verkhne-Sinyachikha

**Cyril**, grand duke, son of Grand Duke Vladimir, second husband of Princess Victoria Melita ("Ducky")

**Dmitri**, grand duke, son of Grand Duke Paul, assassin of Rasputin

**Edward VII ("Bertie")**, Prince of Wales, then king of Great Britain and Ireland, son of Queen Victoria, brother of Princess Alice, father of Albert Victor ("Eddy"), Duke of Clarence; King George V

**Elizabeth ("Ella")**, princess of Hesse, Grand Duchess Serge of Russia, wife of Grand Duke Serge of Russia, daughter of Grand Duke Louis IV and Princess Alice

**Elizabeth**, daughter of Grand Duke Ernest, died in infancy

**Elizabeth**, princess of Prussia, Princess Charles of Hesse, wife of Prince Charles of Hesse

**Ernest**, grand duke of Hesse and by the Rhine, son of Grand Duke Louis IV and Princess Alice, husband of Victoria Melita ("Ducky")

**Felix Youssoupov**, prince, Count Soumarkov-Elsten, husband of Princess Zenaide Youssoupova, father of Prince Felix (Felixovich) Youssoupov

**Felix (Felixovich) Youssoupov**, prince, son of above, husband of Grand Duchess Irene, assassin of Rasputin

**Frederick ("Frittie")**, son of Grand Duke Louis IV of Hesse and by the Rhine and Princess Alice, died in infancy

**Frederick III**, emperor of Germany, son of Emperor William I, husband of Princess Victoria ("Vicky") of Great Britain, father of Emperor William II and Prince Henry of Prussia

**George V**, king of Great Britain, son of King Edward VII, grandfather of Queen Elizabeth II

**Helen**, princess of Serbia, wife of Prince John Constantinovich

**Henry**, prince, son of Emperor Frederick III of Germany, brother of Emperor William II, husband of Princess Irene of Hesse

**Igor**, prince, son of Grand Duke Constantine Constantinovich, died with Grand Duchess Elizabeth at Verkhne-Sinyachikha

**Irene**, grand duchess, daughter of Grand Duke Alexander (Mikhailovich), wife of Prince Felix (Felixovich) Youssoupov

**Irene**, princess, daughter of Grand Duke Louis IV and Princess Alice, wife of Prince Henry of Prussia

**John**, prince, son of Grand Duke Constantine Constantinovich, husband of Princess Helen of Serbia, died with Grand Duchess Elizabeth at Verkhne-Sinyachikha

**Julie**, countess von Hauke, princess of Battenberg, morganatic wife of Prince Alexander of Hesse, mother of Princes Alexander ("Sandro"), Henry, and Princess Marie of Battenberg

**Louis III**, grand duke of Hesse and by the Rhine, brother of Prince Charles of Hesse and Empress Marie of Russia (wife of Alexander II)

**Louis IV**, grand duke of Hesse and by the Rhine, son of Prince Charles of Hesse, husband of Princess Alice of Great Britain, father of Grand Duchess Elizabeth

**Louis**, prince of Battenberg, son of Prince Alexander of Hesse and Princess Julie of Battenberg, husband of Princess Victoria of Hesse. Later 1st Marquis of Milford Haven

**Louis**, prince of Battenberg, son of Louis, prince of Battenberg. Later Earl Mountbatten of Burma

**Louise**, princess of Battenberg, queen of Sweden, daughter of Prince Louis of Battenberg and Princess Victoria of Hesse, wife of King Gustav VI of Sweden

**Marie**, empress of Russia, wife of Emperor Alexander II, sister of Grand Duke Louis III of Hesse and by the Rhine

**Marie**, empress of Russia, Princess Dagmar of Denmark, daughter of King Christian IX of Denmark, sister of Queen Alexandra of Great Britain, wife of Emperor Alexander III, mother of Emperor Nicholas II

**Marie (Alexandrovna)**, grand duchess, daughter of Emperor Alexander II, sister of Grand Duke Serge (Alexandrovich), wife of Prince Alfred, duke of Saxe-Coburg and Gotha

**Marie (Nikolayevna)**, grand duchess, daughter of Emperor Nicholas II and Princess Alix of Hesse

**Marie (Pavlovna)**, grand duchess, daughter of Grand Duke Paul, wife of Prince William of Sweden

**Marie ("May")**, daughter of Grand Duke Louis IV and Princess Alice, died in infancy of diphtheria

**Marie ("Missy")**, princess of Great Britain, queen of Romania, daughter of Prince Alfred (Duke of Saxe-Coburg and Gotha), wife of King Ferdinand of Romania

**Marie**, princess of Battenberg, daughter of Prince Alexander of Hesse and Princess Julie of Battenberg

**Marie ("Miechen")**, princess of Mecklenburg-Schwerin, wife of Grand Duke Vladimir, mother of Grand Duke Cyril

**Michael (Alexandrovich)**, grand duke, son of Emperor Alexander III, brother of Emperor Nicholas II

**Michael Mikhailovich**, grand duke, son of Grand Duke Michael

Nikolayevich (brother of Emperor Alexander II), grandson of Emperor Nicholas I

**Nicholas II**, emperor of Russia, son of Emperor Alexander III, husband of Princess Alix of Hesse, Empress Alexandra of Russia

**Nicholas (Nikolayevich)**, grand duke, grandson of Emperor Nicholas I

**Nicholas**, prince of Greece, brother of Princess Alexandra of Greece (Grand Duchess Paul)

**Oleg**, prince, son of Grand Duke Constantine Constantinovich

**Olga (Alexandrovna)**, grand duchess, daughter of Emperor Alexander III, sister of Emperor Nicholas II

**Olga (Nikolayevna)**, grand duchess, daughter of Emperor Nicholas II and Princess Alix of Hesse

**Paul**, grand duke, son of Alexander III, brother of Grand Duke Serge (Alexandrovich), married, first, Princess Alexandra of Greece with children: Grand Duchess Marie (Pavlovna) and Dmitri. Later married Mme. Pistolkhors (Princess Paley) with son, Prince Vladimir (Volodya) Paley

**Philip**, prince of Greece, duke of Edinburgh, son of Prince Andrew of Greece and Princess Alice of Battenberg, husband of Queen Elizabeth II

**Mme. Pistolkhors (Princess Paley)**, second, morganatic wife of Grand Duke Paul, mother of Prince Vladimir (Volodya) Paley

**Serge (Alexandrovich)**, grand duke, husband of Grand Duchess Elizabeth

**Serge (Mikhailovich)**, grand duke, son of Grand Duke Michael (brother of Emperor Alexander II), grandson of Emperor Nicholas I, died with Grand Duchess Elizabeth at Verkhne-Sinyachikha

**Tatiana**, grand duchess, daughter of Emperor Nicholas II and Princess Alix of Hesse

**Victoria ("Vicky")**, princess of Great Britain, empress of Germany, daughter of Queen Victoria, wife of Emperor Frederick III, mother of Emperor William II and Prince Henry of Prussia

**Victoria**, princess of Hesse, daughter of Grand Duke Louis IV and Princess Alice, sister of Grand Duchess Elizabeth, wife of Prince Louis of Battenberg, mother of Princess Alice of Battenberg (Prince Andrew of Greece) and Earl Mountbatten of Burma

**Victoria**, queen of Great Britain and Ireland, wife of Prince Albert of Saxe-Coburg and Gotha, mother of King Edward VII ("Bertie"); Victoria ("Vicky"), Empress of Germany; Princess Alice, Grand Duchess of Hesse and by the Rhine; Prince Alfred, Duke of Edinburgh and Duke of Saxe-Coburg and Gotha; Princess Beatrice

**Victoria Melita ("Ducky")**, princess, daughter of Prince Alfred (Duke of Saxe-Coburg and Gotha), wife of Grand Duke Ernest of Hesse, later wife of Grand Duke Cyril of Russia

**Vladimir**, grand duke, son of Alexander III, brother of Grand Duke Serge (Alexandrovich), husband of Marie ("Miechen,"

Princess of Mecklenburg-Schwerin), father of Grand Duke Cyril

**Vladimir (Volodya) Paley**, prince, son of Grand Duke Paul and Mme. Pistolkhors, died at Verkhne-Sinyachikha with Grand Duchess Elizabeth

**William I**, king of Prussia and later emperor of Germany, husband of Empress Augusta, father of Emperor Frederick III

**William II**, emperor of Germany, son of Emperor Frederick III, brother of Prince Henry of Prussia

**William**, prince of Sweden, husband of Grand Duchess Marie (Pavlovna)

**Xenia**, grand duchess, daughter of Emperor Alexander III, sister of Nicholas II, wife of Grand Duke Alexander (Mikhailovich), mother of Grand Duchess Irene

**Princess Zenaide Youssoupova**, wife of Prince Felix Youssoupov (Count Soumarkov-Elsten), mother of Prince Felix (Felixovich) Youssoupov

# Source References

Abbreviation: RA: Royal Archives, Windsor Castle, England (followed by the classification number of the letter).

## Chapter 1

1. Gerard Noel, *Princess Alice: Queen Victoria's Forgotten Daughter* (Norwich: 1992), pp. 75–76.
2. Ibid. pp. 76–77; David Duff, *Hessian Tapestry* (London: 1967), p. 69
3. Noel, *Princess Alice*, p. 77
4. Ibid. pp. 79–80
5. Duff, *Hessian Tapestry*, pp. 68–70, 77.
6. Noel, *Princess Alice*, p. 31; Duff, *Hessian Tapestry*, pp. 20–23.
7. Duff, *Hessian Tapestry*, p. 28.
8. Noel, *Princess Alice* (letters), p. 69.
9. Duff, *Albert and Victoria* (London: 1977), pp. 235, 254–256.
10. Louis's courtship of and engagement to Alice are described in Duff, *Hessian Tapestry*, pp. 38–43, 47–50.
11. Ibid. pp. 50–51.
12. E. C. Kenyon, *Scenes in the Life of Princess Alice*, p. 46; quoted in Noel, *Princess Alice*, p. 70.
13. Duff, *Albert and Victoria*, p. 250.
14. Ibid. p. 249.
15. Duff, *Hessian Tapestry*, pp. 63–66.
16. Duff, *Albert and Victoria*, pp. 41–43.
17. Duff, *Hessian Tapestry*, p. 172.
18. Ibid. pp. 77–81.

19. Noel, *Princess Alice*, pp. 91–96.
20. E. F. Benson, *The Daughters of Queen Victoria* (London: 1939), p. 76.
21. Noel, *Princess Alice*, pp. 106–107.
22. *Princess Alice* (letters), p. 36.
23. Duff, *Hessian Tapestry*, p. 96.
24. Greg King, *The Last Empress: The Life and Times of Alexandra Feodorovna, Tsarina of Russia* (London: 1995), p. 9.
25. Marie, Princess of Battenberg, *Reminiscences* (London: 1926), p. 29.
26. Meriel Buchanan, *Queen Victoria's Relations (London)*, p. 27.
27. Baroness Sophie Buxhoeveden, *The Life and Tragedy of Alexandra Feodorovna, Empress of Russia* (London: 1928), p. 7.
28. Duff, *Hessian Tapestry*, pp. 93–95.
29. *Princess Alice* (letters), p. 57.
30. Ibid. pp. 77–78.

**Chapter II**

1. *Princess Alice* (letters), pp. 78–79.
2. Ibid. pp. 85, 90–91, 102–103.
3. Ibid. pp. 97, 122.
4. Duff, *Hessian Tapestry*, pp. 15, 115.
5. Ibid. pp. 120–121.
6. Buxhoeveden, *Alexandra Feodorovna*, p. 5.
7. Richard Hough, *Louis and Victoria: The First Mountbattens* (London: 1974), pp. 29–30.
8. Marie, Princess of Battenberg, *Reminiscences*, p. 69.
9. Duff, *Hessian Tapestry*, p. 122.
10. Princess Alice (letters), pp. 147–186.
11. Marie, Princess of Battenberg, *Reminiscences*, pp. 69–70.
12. *Princess Alice* (letters), pp. 147, 186.
13. Duff, *Hessian Tapestry*, pp. 123–125.
14. E. M. Almedingen, *An Unbroken Unity: A Memoir of Grand Duchess Serge of Russia 1864–1918* (London: 1964), p. 15.

15. Noel, *Princess Alice* (letters), p. 242.
16. Ibid. pp. 188, 207.
17. Noel, *Princess Alice*, pp. 137–147.
18. *Princess Alice* (letters), p. 187.
19. Buxhoeveden, *Alexandra Feodorovna*, p. 7.
20. Buchanan, *Queen Victoria's Relations*, p. 92.
21. Marie, Princess of Battenberg, *Reminiscences*, p. 117.
22. *Princess Alice* (letters), p. 205.
23. Ibid. p. 210.
24. Ibid. pp. 210, 212.
25. Duff, *Albert and Victoria*, p. 256.
26. Hough, *Louis and Victoria*, pp. 30–31.
27. Giles MacDonagh, *Prussia: The Perversion of an Idea* (London: 1994), pp. 64–66.
28. Ibid. p. 29
29. *Princess Alice* (letters), p. 242.
30. Duff, *Hessian Tapestry*, pp. 147–151; Hough, *Louis and Victoria*, pp. 34–35.
31. *Princess Alice* (letters), p. 236.
32. Ibid. p. 256.
33. Ibid. p. 263.
34. Marie, Princess of Battenberg, *Reminiscences*, p. 143.

**Chapter III**
1. *Princess Alice* (letters), p. 265.
2. Hough, *Louis and Victoria*, p. 35; Duff, *Hessian Tapestry*, p. 152.
3. Hough, *Louis and Victoria*, p. 35; Noel, *Princess Alice* (letters), p. 265.
4. *Princess Alice* (letters), pp. 267–269.
5. Hough, *Louis and Victoria*, p. 44; Noel, *Princess Alice* (letters), p. 271.
6. *Princess Alice* (letters), p. 272.
7. Hough, *Louis and Victoria*, p. 42; Duff, *Hessian Tapestry*, p. 158.

8. Duff, *Hessian Tapestry*, pp. 159–162; *Alexandra: Princess and Queen* (London: 1980), pp. 106–111.
9. Duff, *Alexandra: Princess and Queen*, p. 112.
10. Noel, *Princess Alice*, p. 174.
11. Paléologue, *An Ambassador's Memoirs*, I (London: 1922), pp. 162–163.
12. Duff, *Hessian Tapestry*, pp. 166–167.
13. Ibid. p. 167.
14. *Materialy k Zhitiyu*, p. 21.
15. Buxhoeveden, *Alexandra Feodorovna*, p. 18.
16. Almedingen, *An Unbroken Unity*, pp. 14–15.
17. Duff, *Hessian Tapestry*, p. 168.
18. Noel, *Princess Alice*, pp. 209–210.
19. Duff, *Hessian Tapestry*, pp. 167–168.
20. Buchanan, *Queen Victoria's Relations*, p. 23.
21. *Princess Alice* (letters), pp. 385–386.
22. Noel, *Princess Alice*, p. 201.
23. Hough, *Louis and Victoria*, p. 43.
24. *Princess Alice* (letters), p. 282.
25. RA Z78/166, RA Z78/111.
26. Buxhoeveden, *Alexandra Feodorovna*, pp. 7–8.
27. RA Z78/132, RA Z79/44, RA Z79/89, RA Z79/95; Buxhoeveden, *Alexandra Feodorovna*, pp. 7–8.
28. *Princess Alice* (letters), p. 328.
29. Hough, *Louis and Victoria*, p. 46.
30. Duff, *Hessian Tapestry*, p. 95.
31. Buxhoeveden, *Alexandra Feodorovna*, p. 6.
32. Ibid; Hough, *Louis and Victoria*, pp. 30, 40–41.
33. Noel,*Princess Alice* (letters), pp. 353–355.
34. Ibid. pp. 357–358.
35. Hough, *Louis and Victoria*, p. 40.
36. Hessian Grand Ducal Archives
37. RA Z79/132.
38. Hough, *Louis and Victoria*, p. 40.
39. Ibid. p. 41; *Advice to a Grand-daughter: Lessons from Queen*

*Victoria to Princess Victoria of Hesse* (London: 1975), p. 181.
40. Buxhoeveden, *Alexandra Feodorovna*, p. 6; Hough, *Louis and Victoria*, p. 56.
41. Duff, *Hessian Tapestry*, p. 177.
42. Noel, *Princess Alice*, pp. 235–236; Duff, *Hessian Tapestry*, p. 178.

### Chapter IV
1. Alice's death and its aftermath are described in Duff, *Hessian Tapestry*, 178–183; Noel, *Princess Alice*, pp. 236–242.
2. Hessian Grand Ducal Archives
3. RA Z86/3.
4. Hough, *Louis and Victoria*, p. 49.
5. RA Z86/3.
6. Hessian Grand Ducal Archives.
7. RA Z86/10.
8. Buxhoeveden, *Alexandra Feodorovna*, p. 12.
9. RA Z86/13.
10. RA Z86/30.
11. Buchanan, *Queen Victoria's Relations*, p. 66.
12. Princess Marie Louise, *My Memories of Six Reigns* (London: 1956), p. 61.
13. Almedingen, *An Unbroken Unity*, p. 17.
14. RA Z86/12.
15. RA Z86/55.

### Chapter V
1. Grand Duchess Marie, *Education of a Princess* (New York: 1931), p. 19.
2. Queen Marie, *The Story of My Life,* I (London: 1935), p. 95.
3. Meriel Buchanan, *Victorian Gallery* (London: 1956), p. 33.
4. Gordon A. Craig, *Germany 1866–1945*, p. 287. Another participant in the shooting was the future German chancellor, Theobald von Bethmann Hollweg.
5. Virginia Cowles, *The Kaiser* (New York: 1963), p. 46.
6. Duff, *Hessian Tapestry*, p. 193.

7. MacDonagh, *Prussia*, p. 80.

8. Duff, *Hessian Tapestry*, pp. 192–193.

9. Buchanan, *Queen Victoria's Relations*, p. 94.

10. RA Z86/62, RA Z86/63.

11. Cowles, *The Kaiser*, p. 48.

12. Duff, *Hessian Tapestry*, p. 193.

13. Noel, *Princess Alice*, p. 197.

14. *Beloved Mama: Private Correspondence of Queen Victoria and the German Crown Princess 1878–1885* (London: 1975), p. 73.

15. RA Z86/70.

16. Grand Duchess Marie, *Education of a Princess*, p. 18, Queen Marie, *The Story of My Life*, I, p. 93.

17. RA Z86/73.

18. RA Z86/77.

19. RA Z86/78.

20. Hough, *Louis and Victoria*, p. 54.

21. RA Z87/5, Z87/6, Z87/19, Z87/20, Z87/77, Z87/110. Grand Duke Ernest Ludwig, *Erinnertes* (Darmstadt: 1983), p. 60.

22. RA Z87/12.

23. *Beloved Mama*, p. 82.

24. Hough, *Louis and Victoria*, pp. 95–96.

25. Buchanan, *Queen Victoria's Relations*, pp. 42–43.

26. Charles Lowe, *Alexander III of Russia* (London: 1895), pp. 45–47.

27. Grand Duke Alexander, *Once a Grand Duke* (London: 1932), p. 73.

28. Lowe, *Alexander III*, pp. 53–58.

29. Buchanan, *Queen Victoria's Relations*, p. 93.

30. Edvard Radzinsky, *The Last Tsar: The Life and Death of Nicholas II* (London: 1992), pp. 16–17.

31. Grand Duke Alexander, *Once a Grand Duke*, p. 159.

32. Prince Nicholas of Greece, *My Fifty Years* (London: 1926), p. 89.

33. RA Z87/115.

34. Lowe, *Alexander III*, pp. 208–215.
35. RA Z87/130.
36. RA Z87/138.
37. *Advice to a Grand-daughter*, p. 44.
38. Ibid.
39. Duff, *Hessian Tapestry*, p. 194.
40. *Advice to a Grand-daughter*, pp. 48, 57.
41. Ibid. p. 52.
42. Ibid. p. 55.
43. Ibid. p. 57.
44. The original letter has not survived, but a copy exists in the Hessian Grand Ducal Archives in Darmstadt

**Chapter VI**

1. *Advice to a Grand-daughter*, pp. 56–57.
2. *Beloved Mama*, pp. 152–153.
3. Grand Duke Ernest, *Erinnertes*, p. 97.
4. Duff, *Hessian Tapestry*, p. 202.
5. RA Z88/19.
6. RA Z88/36.
7. Hough, *Louis and Victoria*, p. 52.
8. Duff, *Hessian Tapestry*, pp. 196–197.
9. Hessian Grand Ducal Archives
10. Duff, *Hessian Tapestry*, p. 198.
11. Hough, *Louis and Victoria*, p. 115.
12. RA Z88/38.
13. Hough, *Louis and Victoria*, pp. 115–116.
14. Ibid. pp. 117–118.
15. Grand Duke Louis's secret wedding and its aftermath are described in Duff, *Hessian Tapestry*, pp. 198–200.
16. Marlene Eilers, *Queen Victoria's Descendants* (New York: 1987), p. 67.
17. Hough, *Louis and Victoria*, p. 123.
18. RA Z88/45.
19. RA Z88/46.

## Chapter VII

1. Duff, *Hessian Tapestry*, p. 202.
2. Almedingen, *An Unbroken Unity*, p. 21.
3. RA Z88/40.
4. Radzinsky, *The Last Tsar*, pp. 19–20.
5. Almedingen, *An Unbroken Unity*, pp. 22–23.
6. The wedding ceremonies are described ibid. pp. 22–24.
7. As described in Elizabeth's letters to Prince Ernest in the Hessian Grand Ducal Archives.
8. Hessian Grand Ducal Archives.
9. RA Z88/50.
10. *Advice to a Grand-daughter*, p. 66.
11. Christopher Andrew, *Secret Service: The Making of the British Intelligence Community* (London: 1986), pp. 136–137.
12. RA Z88/50.
13. Hessian Grand Ducal Archives.
14. For a description of Ilinskoe, *see* Grand Duchess Marie, *Education of a Princess*, pp. 22–25.
15. RA Z89/53.
16. As described in Elizabeth's letters to her brother and father, now in the Hessian Grand Ducal Archives.
17. Grand Duchess Marie, *Education of a Princess*, p. 18.
18. Hessian Grand Ducal Archives. The original letter was in German.
19. Letter to Prince Ernest. Hessian Grand Ducal Archives.
20. Almedingen, *An Unbroken Unity*, p. 27.
21. Ibid. pp. 27–28.
22. Hessian Grand Ducal Archives.
23. Robert K. Massie, *Nicholas and Alexandra* (London: 1968), pp. 394–395.
24. Prince Felix F. Youssoupov, *Lost Splendour* (London: 1953), p. 85.
25. Hessian Grand Ducal Archives. The original letter was in German.

## Chapter VIII

1. *Reminiscences of Lady Randolph Churchill* (London: 1953), p. 175.
2. Letter to Ernest. Hessian Grand Ducal Archives.
3. King, *The Last Empress*, p. 32.
4. Letter to Grand Duke Louis. Hessian Grand Ducal Archives.
5. Almedingen, *An Unbroken Unity*, p. 29.
6. *Memoirs of H.R.H. Prince Christopher of Greece* (London: 1938), p. 53.
7. Grand Duchess Marie, *Education of a Princess*, p. 51.
8. Grand Duke Alexander, *Once a Grand Duke*, p. 159.
9. Ibid. p. 160.
10. Hessian Grand Ducal Archives.
11. RA Z88/61.
12. *Beloved Mama*, p. 188.
13. RA Z88/73.
14. Almedingen, *An Unbroken Unity*, pp. 31–32.
15. Ibid. p. 31.
16. As described in letters to Prince Ernest. Hessian Grand Ducal Archives.
17. Almedingen, *An Unbroken Unity*, p. 30.
18. Letter to Prince Ernest. Hessian Grand Ducal Archives.
19. Duff, *Hessian Tapestry*, p. 216.
20. Letter to Prince Ernest. Hessian Grand Ducal Archives.
21. Duff, *Hessian Tapestry*, pp. 221–222.
22. This period of German history is described in Craig, *Germany 1866–1945*, Chapter 5.
23. Duff, *Hessian Tapestry*, p. 218.
24. Ibid. pp. 210–212.
25. Ibid. pp. 218–219, 223.
26. Hessian Grand Ducal Archives.
27. Ibid.
28. Almedingen, *An Unbroken Unity*, p. 26.
29. Sources for the journey to Jerusalem are Almedingen, *An Unbroken Unity*, pp. 32–33 and Elizabeth's letters to Prince Ernest, Grand Duke Louis (in the Hessian Grand Ducal

Archives), and Queen Victoria (in the Royal Archives, Windsor Castle).

30. RA Z89/54.

## Chapter IX

1. Duff, *Hessian Tapestry*, p. 227.
2. King, *The Last Empress*, pp. 44–45.
3. Hessian Grand Ducal Archives.
4. Marie, Princess of Battenberg, *Reminiscences*, pp. 252–253.
5. Radzinsky, *The Last Tsar*, p. 16.
6. Letter from Elizabeth to Grand Duke Louis IV. Hessian Grand Ducal Archives.
7. *Dnevnik V.N. Lamsdorfa*, I (Moscow: 1926), p. 110.
8. Ibid. I, p. 116.
9. Ibid. I, p. 129.
10. Hessian Grand Ducal Archives.
11. Andrei Maylunos and Sergei Mironenko, eds., *A Lifelong Passion; Nicholas and Alexandra—Their Own Story* (London: 1996), pp. 15–16.
12. Ibid. p. 16.
13. Buxhoeveden, *Alexandra Feodorovna*, p. 25.
14. Hessian Grand Ducal Archives.
15. Prince Nicholas of Greece, *My Fifty Years*, pp. 88–89.
16. Hessian Grand Ducal Archives.
17. Ibid.
18. *A Lifelong Passion*, p. 17.
19. Duff, *Hessian Tapestry*, pp. 227–228.
20. Hessian Grand Ducal Archives.
21. *Dnevnik Imperatora Nikolaya II* (Berlin: 1923), pp. 18–20; *Dnevnik V. N. Lamsdorfa*, I, p. 304.
22. *Advice to a Grand-daughter*, p. 106.
23. Ibid. p. 110.
24. Radzinsky, *The Last Tsar*, p. 21.
25. Buxhoeveden, *Alexandra Feodorovna*, p. 27.
26. *Advice to a Grand-daughter*, p. 108.

## Chapter X

1. Paléologue, *An Ambassador's Memoirs, I*, p. 321.
2. Hessian Grand Ducal Archives.
3. *Materialy k Zhitiyu*, p. 9.
4. Ibid. p. 21.
5. Hessian Grand Ducal Archives.
6. Ibid.
7. RA Z90/1.
8. Hessian Grand Ducal Archives.
9. Ibid. The original letters were in German.
10. Ibid.
11. Almedingen, *An Unbroken Unity*, p. 40.
12. *Dnevnik V. N. Lamsdorfa*, II, p. 81.
13. RA Z90/1.
14. Almedingen, *An Unbroken Unity*, p. 40.
15. Prince Nicholas, *My Fifty Years*, p. 90.
16. Almedingen, *An Unbroken Unity*, p. 41.
17. J. N. Westwood, *Endurance and Endeavour: Russian History 1812–1986* (Oxford: 1986), p. 122.
18. Alexander Ular, *Russia from Within*, (London: 1985), pp. 75–79.
19. Lionel Kochan, *Russia in Revolution: 1890–1918* (London: 1967), p. 67.
20. Youssoupov, *Lost Splendour*, p. 84.
21. Almedingen, *An Unbroken Unity*, p. 42.
22. *A Lifelong Passion*, pp. 265–266.
23. *Materialy k Zhitiyu*, p. 22.
24. Olga Novikov, *Russian Memories* (London: 1917), p. 297. Letter to Grand Duke Louis IV, Hessian Grand Ducal Archives.
25. Almedingen, *An Unbroken Unity*, p. 43.
26. Letter to Grand Duke Louis IV. Hessian Grand Ducal Archives.
27. Almedingen, *An Unbroken Unity*, pp. 43–44.
28. *Souvenirs d'Alexis Volkov* (Paris: 1928), p. 27.

29. Grand Duchess Marie, *Education of a Princess*, pp. 9–10.
30. Princess Nicholas, *My Fifty Years*, p. 91; Grand Duchess Marie, *Education of a Princess*, p. 9.
31. Queen Marie, *The Story of My Life*, p. 214.
32. Grand Duchess Marie, *Education of a Princess*, pp. 10, 18.
33. RA Z90/27.
34. Ibid.
35. Duff, *Alexandra: Princess and Queen*, pp. 183–184.

**Chapter XI**

1. RA Z174/24.
2. RA Z174/8.
3. Princess Marie of Battenberg, *Reminiscences*, p. 252.
4. RA Z174/21.
5. RA Z174/24.
6. Duff, *Hessian Tapestry*, p. 225.
7. Buxhoeveden, *Alexandra Feodorovna*, p. 29.
8. RA Z90/27.
9. Ibid.
10. Grand Duke Ernest, *Erinnertes*, p. 60.
11. Materialy k Zhitiyu, p. 13.
12. E. E. p. Tisdall, *The Dowager Empress* (London: 1957), p. 151.
13. *A Lifelong Passion*, pp. 30–31.
14. Ibid. pp. 32–33.
15. Hessian Grand Ducal Archives.
16. RA Z90/62.
17. RA Z90/65.
18. *A Lifelong Passion*, p. 45.
19. Radzinsky, *The Last Tsar*, p. 33.
20. Duff, *Hessian Tapestry*, pp. 233–234. S. E. Buckle, ed., *The Letters of Queen Victoria* (3rd series), III, pp. 393–394.
21. Arthur Gould Lee, ed., *The Empress Frederick Writes to Sophie, Her Daughter, Crown Princess and Later Queen of the Hellenes: Letters 1889–1901* (London), p. 170.

22. Radzinsky, *The Last Tsar*, p. 33.
23. Ibid. p. 34.
24. *The Letters of Queen Victoria* (3rd series), III, p. 394.
25. RA Z90/76.
26. Grand Duke Alexander, *Once a Grand Duke*, p. 153.
27. RA Z90/76.
28. Prince Nicholas, *My Fifty Years*, pp. 113–116.
29. Letter to Grand Duke Ernest. Hessian Grand Ducal Archives.
30. RA Z499/15.

**Chapter XII**
1. Prince Nicholas, *My Fifty Years*, p. 116.
2. Radzinsky, *The Last Tsar*, p. 37.
3. *Dnevnik Imperatora Nikolaya II*, p. 81.
4. RA Z499/28.
5. Princess Catherine Radziwill, *The Intimate Life of the Last Tsarina* (London: 1929), p. 33.
6. Buxhoeveden, *Alexandra Feodorovna*, p. 39.
7. Massie, *Nicholas and Alexandra*, p. 64.
8. Prince Nicholas, *My Fifty Years*, pp. 117–118.
9. RA Z499/96.
10. Grand Duke Alexander, *Once a Grand Duke*, p. 190.
11. Charles Lowe, *Alexander III of Russia* (London: 1895), p. 289.
12. RA Z274/55.
13. Lowe, *Alexander III*, pp. 290–299.
14. RA Z274/25.
15. Ibid.
16. Lowe, *Alexander III*, p. 301.
17. Hessian Grand Ducal Archives.
18. RA Z90/81.
19. Tisdall, *The Dowager Empress*, pp. 171–173.
20. Buxhoeveden, *Alexandra Feodorovna*, pp. 58–59.
21. Almedingen, *The Empress Alexandra*, pp. 43–44.

22. Hessian Grand Ducal Archives.
23. Radzinsky, *The Last Tsar*, p. 43.
24. RA Z90/83.
25. RA Z274/59.
26. Almedingen, *The Empress Alexandra*, pp. 53–54.
27. Grand Duke Alexander, *Once a Grand Duke*, p. 191.
28. Lili Dehn, *The Real Tsaritsa* (London: 1922), pp. 44–45.
29. A. A. Mosolov, *At The Court of the Last Tsar* (London: 1935), p. 80.
30. Dominic Lieven, *Nicholas II: Emperor of All the Russians* (London: 1993), p. 71.
31. *A Lifelong Passion*, p. 141.

**Chapter XIII**

1. Richard Hough, *Louis and Victoria: The First Mountbatten* (London: 1974) p. 180.
2. The coronation is described in Buxhoeveden, *Alexandra Feodorovna*, pp. 63–67; Almedingen, *The Empress Alexandra*, pp. 58–69; Massie, *Nicholas and Alexandra*, pp. 73–79.
3. Buxhoeveden, *Alexandra Feodorovna*, p. 64.
4. Hough, *Louis and Victoria*, pp. 180–181.
5. Buxhoeveden, *Alexandra Feodorovna*, p. 65.
6. Ibid.
7. Lieven, *Nicholas II*, p. 64.
8. RA Z90/86.
9. Massie, *Nicholas and Alexandra*, p. 78.
10. Buxhoeveden, *Alexandra Feodorovna*, p. 67.
11. Massie, *Nicholas and Alexandra*, pp. 78–79.
12. Hough, *Louis and Victoria*, pp. 182–183; Almedingen, *The Empress Alexandra*, pp. 59–60.
13. *Illustrated London News*, June 6, 1896.
14. Queen Marie, *The Story of My Life*, II (London: 1934), p. 73.
15. *The Memoirs of Grand Duchess Olga Alexandrovna* (London: 1964), p. 79. Buchanan, *Queen Victoria's Relations*, p. 102.
16. Radzinsky, *The Last Tsar*, p. 49.

17. Lieven, *Nicholas II*, pp. 66–67.

18. Almedingen, *The Empress Alexandra*, pp. 60–61.

19. *A Lifelong Passion*, p. 147.

20. Ibid. p. 149.

21. Queen Marie, *The Story of My Life*, II, pp. 75–79.

22. Ibid. Youssoupov, *Lost Splendour*, p. 42.

23. *The Letters of Queen Victoria* (3rd series), III, pp. 170–171.

24. Ibid. pp. 172–174.

25. Buchanan, *Queen Victoria's Relations*, p. 104.

## Chapter XIV

1. Grand Duchess Marie, *Education of a Princess*, pp. 25–28.

2. Ibid. p. 22.

3. Ibid. p. 17.

4. Almedingen, *An Unbroken Unity*, p. 44.

5. Radzinsky, *The Last Tsar*, p. 51.

6. Anna Vyrubova, *Memories of the Russian Court* (London: 1922),
   pp. 2–3.

7. Youssoupov, *Lost Splendour*, pp. 98–99.

8. Queen Marie, *The Story of My Life*, p. 83.

9. Duff, *Alexandra: Princess and Queen*, pp. 213–214.

10. RA Z88/35.

11. Almedingen, *An Unbroken Unity*, p. 77.

12. Grand Duchess Marie, *Education of a Princess*, pp. 46–47.

13. Ibid. pp. 49–50.

14. Ibid. p. 56.

15. Almedingen, *The Empress Alexandra*, pp. 69–70.

16. Tisdall, *The Dowager Empress*, p. 192.

17. *A Lifelong Passion*, pp. 216–217.

18. Paléologue, *An Ambassador's Memoirs*, I, p. 207.

19. *The Memoirs of Grand Duchess Olga Alexandrovna*,
    pp. 123–124.

20. Lieven, *Nicholas II*, p. 163.

21. Buxhoeveden, *Alexandra Feodorovna*, p. 93.

22. *The Memoirs of Grand Duchess Olga Alexandrovna*, p. 124.
23. *Materialy k Zhitiyu*, p. 21.
24. Hough, *Louis and Victoria*, p. 210.
25. Hessian Grand Ducal Archives.
26. Buxhoeveden, *Alexandra Feodorovna*, p. 98.
27. Grand Duke Alexander, *Once a Grand Duke*, p. 236.
28. Duff, *Hessian Tapestry*, pp. 273–274.
29. Radzinsky, *The Last Tsar*, p. 53.
30. Kochan, *Russia in Revolution*, pp. 32, 79.
31. *A Lifelong Passion*, pp. 213–214.
32. Kochan, *Russia in Revolution*, p. 80.
33. This was revealed by Prince Nicholas Romanov in a television documentary, *Nicholas and Alexandra*, first broadcast in October 1994.
34. Westwood, *Endurance and Endeavour*, pp. 151–152.
35. Johnson, *A History of the Modern World* (London: 1991), p. 50.
36. Massie, *Nicholas and Alexandra*, pp. 98–100.

**Chapter XV**

1. Grand Duchess Marie, *Education of a Princess*, pp. 59–60.
2. Ibid. p. 60.
3. A. N. Roussoff, *Memoirs of Alexander Wolkof-Mouromtsov* (London: 1928), pp. 389–390.
4. Grand Duke Alexander, *Once a Grand Duke*, pp. 243–244.
5. Westwood, *Endurance and Endeavour*, pp. 141–143.
6. According to the anonymous author of *The Fall of the Romanovs* (London: 1918), pp. 196–199.
7. Radzinsky, *The Last Tsar*, p. 66.
8. Boris Nicholaevsky, *Azev: The Russian Judas* (London: 1934), pp. 33, 41, 51, 72–74.
9. Robert Payne, *The Terrorists* (New York: 1963), pp. 288–296; Nicholaevsky, *Azev*, pp. 78–94, 102–103.
10. Radzinsky, *The Last Tsar*, p. 63.
11. Buxhoeveden, *Alexandra Feodorovna*, pp. 103–104.
12. Grand Duchess Marie, *Education of a Princess*, p. 61.

13. Ibid. pp. 62–63.
14. Westwood, *Endurance and Endeavour*, pp. 142–143.
15. Grand Duchess Marie, *Education of a Princess*, pp. 63–64.
16. Kochan, *Russia in Revolution*, pp. 90–91.
17. Ibid. 91–92. Radzinsky, *The Last Tsar*, pp. 66–68.
18. Payne, *The Terrorists*, p. 297.
19. Grand Duchess Marie, *Education of a Princess*, pp. 64–66.
20. The work of Savinkov and Kalyayev is described in Payne, *The Terrorists*, pp. 298–304.
21. The assassination of Grand Duke Serge and its aftermath are described chiefly in Grand Duchess Marie, *Education of a Princess*, pp. 66–72.
22. *A Lifelong Passion*, p. 263.
23. Massie, *Nicholas and Alexandra*, p. 127.
24. Payne, *The Terrorists*, p. 312.

## Chapter XVI

1. Almedingen, *An Unbroken Unity*, pp. 52–53.
2. Duff, *Hessian Tapestry*, pp. 279–280.
3. Kalyayev's account is retold in Payne, *The Terrorists*, pp. 319–322, and A Lifelong Passion, pp. 269–270. The accounts of Victoria (Duff, *Hessian Tapestry*, pp. 279–280, and Ernest, *Erinnertes*, p. 64) recall only a few sentences of the conversation. These agree with Kalyayev's account, with one exception. Ernest writes that Elizabeth said to Kalyayev that in war men fought face-to-face, but Kalyayev had murdered from behind; this was not war, but cowardice. Kalyayev's omission of this remark suggests that he may have portrayed himself as a more impressive figure than he appeared to Elizabeth. Ernest writes that the conversation took two hours, Victoria that Elizabeth spent only a short time with Kalyayev.
4. Grand Duchess Marie, *Education of a Princess*, pp. 72–73.
5. *A Lifelong Passion*, p. 264.
6. Grand Duchess Marie, *Education of a Princess*, pp. 74–75.

7. Grand Duke Ernest, *Erinnertes*, p. 64.

8. *Materialy k Zhitiyu*, pp. 49–50.

9. Ibid. pp. 21–22.

10. Almedingen, *An Unbroken Unity*, p. 57.

11. *Materialy k Zhitiyu*, p. 16

12. Grand Duchess Marie, *Education of a Princess*, pp. 73–76

13. Almedingen, *An Unbroken Unity*, p. 54

14. Payne, *The Terrorists*, pp. 325–327.

15. Ibid. pp. 329–338.

16. Radzinsky, *The Last Tsar*, pp. 74–75.

17. *The Memoirs of Count Witte*, (New York: 1990), p. 476.

18. Youssoupov, *Lost Splendour*, p. 254.

19. Grand Duchess Marie, *Education of a Princess*, pp. 76–77.

20. Ibid. pp. 78–81.

21. Hessian Grand Ducal Archives.

22. The 1905 revolution in Moscow is described in Grand Duchess Marie, *Education of a Princess*, pp. 81–83; Engelstein, *Moscow 1905*, (New York), pp. 105–127.

23. Grand Duchess Marie, *Education of a Princess*, p. 83.

24. Ibid.

25. Hessian Grand Ducal Archives.

26. Ibid.

## Chapter XVII

1. Hessian Grand Ducal Archives.

2. Archpriest Michael Polsky, *Noviye Mucheniki Rossiskiye* (Jordanville, New York: 1949), p. 277.

3. Ibid. p. 269.

4. Hessian Grand Ducal Archives.

5. Lyubov Miller, *Svyataya Muchenitsa*, p. 156.

6. Grand Duchess Marie, *Education of a Princess*, pp. 86–87.

7. Radzinsky, *The Last Tsar*, p. 77.

8. Hough, *Louis and Victoria*, p. 211.

9. Letter to Grand Duke Ernest. Hessian Grand Ducal Archives.

10. Radzinsky, *The Last Tsar*, pp. 81–82.

11. Massie, *Nicholas and Alexandra*, p. 240.

12. Ibid. pp. 219–220.

13. Almedingen, *The Empress Alexandra*, pp. 115–118.

14. Ibid. pp. 112–113.

15. Grand Duchess Marie, *Education of a Princess*, pp. 87–88.

16. Prince William's courtship of Marie is described in *Education of a Princess*, pp. 92–100.

17. Youssoupov, *Lost Splendour*, pp. 116–119.

18. Ibid. pp. 126–127.

19. Ibid. pp. 127–128.

20. Greg King, *The Murder of Rasputin*, (London: 1997), p. 95.

21. Youssoupov, *Lost Splendour*, pp. 128–129.

22. *Memoirs of H. R. H. Prince Christopher of Greece*, pp. 62–63.

23. Almedingen, *The Empress Alexandra*, pp. 121–122.

24. Alexander N. Bokhanov, *Sumerki Monarkhii* (Moscow: 1993), p. 108.

25. Youssoupov, *Lost Splendour*, p. 135.

### Chapter XVIII

1. *Materialy k zhityu*, pp. 21–23.

2. Almedingen, *An Unbroken Unity*, p. 58.

3. *Materialy k Zhitiyu*, p. 23.

4. Almedingen, *An Unbroken Unity*, p. 59. For a general description of the foundation and daily life of the convent, see *An Unbroken Unity*, pp. 59–75.

5. Youssoupov, *Lost Splendour*, p. 123.

6. Ibid. p. 125.

7. *Materialy k Zhitiyu*, pp. 23–25.

8. P. Semenmkov, ed., *Nikolai II i Velikiye Knyazya* (Moscow: 1925), p. 40.

9. *Materialy k Zhitiyu*, p. 21.

10. Ibid. p. 46.

11. Archpriest Polsky, *Noviye Mucheniki*, p. 276.

12. Youssoupov, *Lost Splendour*, p. 124.

13. Archpriest Polsky, *Noviye Mucheniki*, pp. 272–273.

14. Ibid. pp. 274–275.
15. Youssoupov, *Lost Splendour*, p. 156.
16. Ibid. p. 124.
17. Almedingen, *An Unbroken Unity*, pp. 64–67.
18. Youssoupov, *Lost Splendour*, p. 125.
19. Almedingen, *An Unbroken Unity*, p. 69.

## Chapter XIX

1. Marie, Princess of Battenberg, *Reminiscences,* pp. 358–359.
2. Buxhoeveden, *Alexandra Feodorovna*, pp. 126–128.
3. Massie, *Nicholas and Alexandra*, pp. 159–160, 176.
4. Ibid. pp. 223–226.
5. Radzinsky, *The Last Tsar*, p. 99.
6. Bokhanov, *Sumerki Monarkhii*, p. 108.
7. *Materialy k Zhitiyu*, p. 46.
8. Paléologue, *An Ambassador's Memoirs*, I, p. 44. Massie, *Nicholas and Alexandra*, p. 247; Bokhanov, *Sumerki Monarkhii*, pp. 108–109.
9. Buxhoeveden, *Alexandra Feodorovna*, pp. 128–129.
10. Bokhanov, *Sumerki Monarkhii*, p. 109.
11. Massie, *Nicholas and Alexandra*, pp. 249–251.
12. Bokhanov, *Sumerki Monarkhii*, p. 126.
13. Paléologue, *An Ambassador's Memoirs*, I, p. 145.
14. Joseph T. Fuhrman, *Rasputin: a Life* (New York: 1990), p. 85; *Out of My Past: Memoirs of Count Kokovtsov* (Stanford, California: 1935), p. 293n.
15. Paléologue, *An Ambassador's Memoirs*, I, pp. 145–146. Massie, *Nicholas and Alexandra*, p. 234.
16. Bokhanov, *Sumerki Monarkhii*, p. 129.
17. Buxhoeveden, *Alexandra Feodorovna*, 152; Anna Vyrubova, *Memories of the Russian Court*, p. 62.
18. Bokhanov, *Sumerki Monarkhii*, p. 82.
19. Massie, *Nicholas and Alexandra*, p. 253.
20. Bokhanov, *Sumerki Monarkhii*, pp. 119–127.

21. Paléologue, *An Ambassador's Memoirs*, I, pp. 146–147; Massie, *Nicholas and Alexandra*, pp. 255–256.
22. Letter, 12 March 1912 (Broadlands Archives). Quoted in Hough, *Louis and Victoria*, p. 264.
23. Massie, *Nicholas and Alexandra*, p. 255.
24. Hough, *Louis and Victoria*, pp. 261–262.
25. Buxhoeveden, *Alexandra Feodorovna*, p. 129.
26. Almedingen, *An Unbroken Unity*, pp. 75–76.
27. Sir Robert Bruce Lockhart, *Memoirs of a British Agent*, (London: 1932), pp. 73–74.
28. Buxhoeveden, *Alexandra Feodorovna*, pp. 131–133; Almedingen, *The Empress Alexandra*, 125–126.

**Chapter XX**

1. Radzinsky, *The Last Tsar*, p. 110. Almedingen, *An Unbroken Unity*, p. 76.
2. The pilgrimage is described in Youssoupov, *Lost Splendour*, pp. 161–164.
3. Grand Duchess Marie, *Education of a Princess*, p. 156.
4. *Memoirs of H. R. H. Prince Christopher of Greece*, p. 242.
5. Grand Duchess Marie, *Education of a Princess*, pp. 152–153.
6. Ibid. p. 156; Almedingen, *An Unbroken Unity*, p. 78; *A Lifelong Passion*, pp. 383–384.
7. Grand Duchess Marie, *Education of a Princess*, p. 158.
8. Hough, *Louis and Victoria*, pp. 287–288.
9. Ibid. pp. 280–283. Duff, *Hessian Tapestry*, pp. 295–296.
10. Miller, *Svyataya Muchenitsa*, p. 197.

**Chapter XXI**

1. Almedingen, *An Unbroken Unity*, p. 81.
2. Hough, *Louis and Victoria*, p. 242.
3. Craig, *Germany 1866–1945*, p. 337.
4. Lieven, *Nicholas II*, pp. 202–203.
5. Hough, *Louis and Victoria*, p. 288.

6. Bokhanov, *Sumerki Monarkhii*, pp. 144–146.

7. Hough, *Louis and Victoria*, p. 289.

8. Almedingen, *An Unbroken Unity*, pp. 80, 82–83.

9. Buxhoeveden, *Alexandra Feodorovna*, p. 191

10. Almedingen, *An Unbroken Unity*, pp. 84–85; *Pisma Imperatritsi Alexsandry Feodorovny k Nikolayu II* (Berlin: 1922), p. 414.

11. The ceremony is described in Paléologue, *An Ambassador's Memoirs*, I, pp. 89–95.

12. Miller, *Svyataya Muchenitsa*, p. 206.

13. Almedingen, *The Empress Alexandra*, p. 135.

14. Buxhoeveden, *Alexandra Feodorovna*, p. 190.

15. Grand Duchess Marie, *Education of a Princess*, pp. 167–168.

16. Buxhoeveden, *Alexandra Feodorovna*, pp. 190–191.

17. Paléologue, *An Ambassador's Memoirs*, I, p. 108.

18. Almedingen, *An Unbroken Unity*, pp. 87–89.

19. Grand Duchess Marie, *Education of a Princess*, pp. 241–242.

20. *Pisma Imperatritsi Alexsandry Feodorovny k Nikolayu II*, 389, 406–408; Buxhoeveden, *Alexandra Feodorovna*, p. 198.

21. Paléologue, *An Ambassador's Memoirs*, I, p. 215.

22. Ibid. pp. 119, 133, 168.

23. Described by Vyrubova, *Memories of the Russian Court*, pp. 112–113.

24. Buxhoeveden, *Alexandra Feodorovna*, p. 200.

25. Lockhart, *Memoirs of a British Agent*, p. 101.

26. Paléologue, *An Ambassador's Memoirs*, I, 238.

27. Ibid. p. 331.

28. Bokhanov, *Sumerki Monarkhii*, p. 218.

29. Lockhart, *Memoirs of a British Agent*, p. 128.

30. Radzinsky, *The Last Tsar*, pp. 97–98.

31. Paléologue, *An Ambassador's Memoirs*, I, pp. 332–333.

32. Almedingen, *The Empress Alexandra*, p. 139.

33. Alexandra's letter survives in the Hessian Grand Ducal Archives. In it she writes that she will pass on Ernest's letter to Elizabeth.

34. Bokhanov, *Sumerki Monarkhii,* p. 216.

35. Massie, *Nicholas and Alexandra,* pp. 335–337.

36. Paléologue, *An Ambassador's Memoirs,* II, p. 11.

37. Lockhart, *Memoirs of a British Agent,* p. 112.

38. Almedingen, *The Empress Alexandra,* pp. 142–143.

39. Ibid. Paléologue, *An Ambassador's Memoirs,* II, pp. 12–13.

40. Ibid. II. pp. 15–16.

41. Buxhoeveden, *Alexandra Feodorovna,* p. 197.

42. Almedingen, *An Unbroken Unity,* p. 92.

43. Bokhanov, *Sumerki Monarkhii,* pp. 216–218; Radzinsky, *The Last Tsar,* p. 131

44. Youssoupov, *Lost Splendour,* p. 185; *The Letters of the Tsar to the Tsaritsa* (London: 1929) p. 62.

45. Paléologue, *An Ambassador's Memoirs,* II, p. 33.

46. *Pisma Imperatritsi,* pp. 472–474.

47. Paléologue, *An Ambassador's Memoirs,* II, p. 35. Bokhanov, *Sumerki Monarkhii,* p. 192.

48. Lockhart, *Memoirs of a British Agent,* pp. 127–128.

49. Paléologue, *An Ambassador's Memoirs,* I, p. 347.

50. *Padeniye Tsarskovo Rezhima,* IV, p. 266.

51. Lady Jackson, *Diary,* Broadlands Archives.

52. Bokhanov, *Sumerki Monarkhii,* p. 195.

53. Ibid. p. 219.

54. Youssoupov, *Lost Splendour,* p. 185.

55. Almedingen, *The Empress Alexandra,* pp. 147–148.

**Chapter XXII**

1. Almedingen, *An Unbroken Unity,* p. 95.

2. Ibid. p. 93.

3. *The Letters of the Tsar to the Tsaritsa* (London: 1929), pp. 174, 178.

4. Frank Golden, ed., *Documents from Russian History* (New York: 1927), p. 98.

5. *The Letters of the Tsaritsa to the Tsar* (New York: 1927), p. 217.

6. Paléologue, *An Ambassador's Memoirs,* II, p. 193.

7. Craig, *Germany 1866–1945,* pp. 347–350; Massie, *Nicholas and Alexandra,* p. 345.

8. Mlle. Vassilshikova's maneuvers are described by M. V. Rodzianko in *Documents from Russian History,* pp. 103–104.

9. *Padeniye Tsarskovo Rezhima,* Vol. IV, p. 266.

10. *Pisma Imperatritsi,* I, p. 612. *Padeniye Tsarskovo Rezhima,* IV, p. 266.

11. *Pisma Imperatritsi,* I, p. 612.

12. The investigation is described in *Padeniye Tsarskovo Rezhima,* IV, pp. 267–272.

13. Paléologue, *An Ambassador's Memoirs,* II, p. 170.

14. *Pisma Imperatritsi,* I, p. 615.

15. Almedingen, *An Unbroken Unity,* pp. 94–95.

16. Massie, *Nicholas and Alexandra,* p. 366.

17. Paléologue, *An Ambassador's Memoirs,* II, p. 166.

18. Craig, *Germany 1866–1945,* p. 375.

19. Duff, *Hessian Tapestry,* p. 314.

20. Lieven, *Nicholas II,* p. 218.

21. Massie, *Nicholas and Alexandra,* pp. 382–383.

22. Westwood, *Endurance and Endeavour,* p. 210.

23. Paléologue, *An Ambassador's Memoirs,* III, pp. 158–159.

24. Buxhoeveden, *Alexandra Feodorovna,* p. 233.

25. Paléologue, *An Ambassador's Memoirs,* II, pp. 238–240.

26. Westwood, *Endurance and Endeavour,* p. 213; Paléologue, *An Ambassador's Memoirs,* III, pp. 80–81, 90–92.

27. Massie, *Nicholas and Alexandra,* pp. 384–385, 392; Bokhanov, *Sumerki Monarkhii,* p. 244.

28. King, *The Murder of Rasputin,* p. 120; Almedingen, *An Unbroken Unity,* p. 97.

29. Bokhanov, *Sumerki Monarkhii,* pp. 243–244.

30. *Padeniye Tsarskovo Rezhima,* I, p. 104.

31. C. E. Vulliamy, ed., *From the Red Archives* (London: 1934), p. 104.

32. Ibid.

33. Bokhanov, *Sumerki Monarkhii*, p. 247.

34. Paléologue, *An Ambassador's Memoirs*, III, p. 152.

35. Alexander Spiridovich, *Raspoutine 1863–1916* (Paris: 1935), p. 353.

36. Youssoupov's dealings with Rasputin are described in his memoirs, *Lost Splendour*, Chapter XXII.

37. Bokhanov, *Sumerki Monarkhii*, p. 247.

38. Grand Duchess Marie, *Education of a Princess*, pp. 180–181; Radzinsky, *The Last Tsar*, p. 131.

39. Paléologue, *An Ambassador's Memoirs*, II, p. 67.

40. Almedingen, *An Unbroken Unity*, pp. 97–99.

41. Princess Catherine Radziwill, *Nicholas II, Last of the Tsars* (London: 1931), p. 235; *Padeniye Tsarskovo Rezhima*, I, p. 104. Almedingen, *The Empress Alexandra*, pp. 168–169.

42. Grand Duchess Marie, *Education of a Princess*, p. 280.

43. Paléologue, *An Ambassador's Memoirs*, III, pp. 110–111.

44. Vulliamy, ed., *From the Red Archives* (London: 1934), p. 106.

45. Almedingen, *An Unbroken Unity*, pp. 100–101.

46. Buxhoeveden, *Alexandra Feodorovna*, p. 239.

47. Russian State Archives. Quoted in Bokhanov, *Sumerki Monarkhii*, p. 244.

48. Pierre Gilliard, *Thirteen Years at the Russian Court* (London: 1921), p. 181.

49. Countess Alexandra Olsoufiev, *H. I. H. The Grand Duchess Elizabeth Feodorovna of Russia*, p. 12, Broadlands Archives.

50. Grand Duchess Marie, Paléologue, Youssoupov, and Lady Jackson (*Diary*, Broadlands Archives) all affirm, independently of each other, that the empress asked her sister to leave. Their impressive unanimity belies Almedingen's assertion (*An Unbroken Unity*, p. 101) that "to imagine the Empress asking her sister to leave the palace is preposterous."

51. Youssoupov, *Lost Splendour*, p. 187.

52. Ibid. pp. 216–217.

53. Almedingen, *An Unbroken Unity*, p. 102.

## Chapter XXIII

1. Youssoupov, *Lost Splendour*, Chapter 23.
2. Ulick Loring, "The Grand Duchess Elizabeth Feodorovna 1864–1818," *The Monarchist,* January 1980, pp. 39–46.
3. Vyrubova, *Memories of the Russian Court*, p. 185.
4. Kochan, *Russia in Revolution*, p. 190.
5. King, *The Murder of Rasputin*, p. 120.
6. *A Lifelong Passion*, p. 517.
7. Grand Duchess Marie, *Education of a Princess*, pp. 262–274, 280–281.
8. Almedingen, *An Unbroken Unity*, pp. 102–103.
9. Paléologue, *An Ambassador's Memoirs*, III, pp. 213–222.
10. Kochan, *Russia in Revolution*, pp. 192–193.
11. Paléologue, *An Ambassador's Memoirs*, III, pp. 223–224.
12. Radzinsky, *The Last Tsar*, pp. 169–172.
13. Ibid. p. 172.
14. *The Fall of the Romanovs*, p. 131.
15. Paléologue, *An Ambassador'' Memoirs,* III, pp. 257–258, 263, 268.
16. Almedingen, *An Unbroken Unity*, pp. 108–110. Another sources is an account by Count S. D. Samarin in the Broadlands Archives.
17. Lockhart, *Memoirs of a British Agent*, pp. 169–170.
18. Almedingen, *An Unbroken Unity*, pp. 110–111.
19. Ibid. pp. 105–107.
20. Broadlands Archives
21. Youssoupov, *Lost Splendour*, pp. 253–254.
22. Craig, *Germany 1866–1945*, pp. 367–368.
23. Almedingen, *An Unbroken Unity*, pp. 111–112.
24. Ibid. pp. 113–114
25. *A Lifelong Passion*, p. 577.
26. Kochan, *Russia in Revolution*, pp. 201–204, 232–233, 257–260, 269–271.
27. Almedingen, *An Unbroken Unity*, pp. 114–115.
28. Youssoupov, *Lost Splendour*, p. 260.

29. Grand Duchess Marie, *Education of a Princess*, pp. 311–312.

**Chapter XXIV**

1. Grand Duchess Marie, *Education of a Princess*, p. 312.
2. Almedingen, *An Unbroken Unity*, pp. 115–116.
3. Lockhart, *Memoirs of a British Agent*, pp. 258–259, 262.
4. Almedingen, *An Unbroken Unity*, pp. 116–118.
5. Johnson, *A History of the Modern World*, pp. 64–65.
6. Ibid. pp. 67–71.
7. Radzinsky, *The Last Tsar*, pp. 302–303.
8. Johnson, *A History of the Modern World*, pp. 50–51.
9. Archpriest Polsky, *Noviye Mucheniki*, pp. 279–280; Almedingen, *An Unbroken Unity*, p. 118.
10. Almedingen, *An Unbroken Unity*, p. 119.
11. Princess Paley, *Memories of Russia, 1916–1919* (London: 1921), pp. 204–205. Archpriest Polsky, *Noviye Mucheniki*, p. 281.
12. Almedingen, *An Unbroken Unity*, 120–121. Archpriest Polsky, *Noviye Mucheniki*, p. 281.
13. Broadlands Archives. A detailed analysis of the sources of Elizabeth's imprisonment and execution is given in the appendix "Documentary Evidence of the Last Journey and Death of the Grand Duchess Elizabeth and the Removal of Her Remains to Beijing."
14. Emil Lengyel, *Secret Siberia* (London: 1947), pp. 146–147, 152.
15. Almedingen, *An Unbroken Unity*, pp. 121–122.
16. Sir Thomas Preston, *Before the Curtain* (London: 1950), p. 100.
17. Princess Paley, *Memories of Russia*, p. 206.
18. Almedingen, *An Unbroken Unity*, pp. 125–126.
19. Princess Paley, *Memories of Russia*, p. 207.
20. Ibid. p. 207.
21. Paul Rodzianko, *Tattered Banners* (London), p. 253.
22. Ibid. p. 253; Almedingen, *An Unbroken Unity*, p. 127.

## Epilogue

1. Broadlands Archives.
2. Lengyel, *Secret Siberia*, p. 165.
3. *Materialy k Zhitiyu*, pp. 153–154.
4. *The Sunday Times* (London), August 10, 1958.
5. Letter to Grand Duke Ernest. Hessian Grand Ducal Archives.
6. Ulick Loring, "The Grand Duchess Elizabeth Feodorovna 1864–1918," *The Monarchist* (January 1980), pp. 39–46.
7. Broadlands Archives.
8. Preston, *Before the Curtain*, p. 166.
9. *Materialy k Zhitiyu*, p. 144.
10. Grand Duchess Marie, *Education of a Princess*, pp. 325–328.
11. Hessian Grand Ducal Archives.
12. Account by Lady Jackson, Broadlands Archives.
13. Duff, *Hessian Tapestry*, pp. 325–326.
14. Mark Kerr, *Prince Louis of Battenberg* (London: 1934), p. 262.
15. Hessian Grand Ducal Archives.
16. Press release from the Russian Ecclesiastical Mission in Jerusalem, May 1984.
17. "The Shepherd" (pastoral letter of the Russian Orthodox Church in exile) January 3, 1982.
18. Press release from the Russian Ecclesiastical Mission in Jerusalem, May 1984.

# Bibliography

## RUSSIAN LANGUAGE SOURCES:

Ambrosii, Archbishop. *Svetloi Pamiati velikoi knyagini Elizavety Feodorovny.* Jerusalem; 1925.

Bokhanov, Alexander N. *Sumerki Monarkhii.* Moscow; 1993.

*Dnevnik Imperatora Nikolaya II.* Berlin; 1923.

*Dnevnik V. N. Lamsdorfa.* Moscow; 1926.

*Krasni Archiv.* Moscow; 1932.

*Materialy k Zhitiyu prepodobnomuchenitsi velikoi knyagini Yelizavety: Pis'ma, dnevniki, vospominaniya, dokumenty.* Moscow; 1995.

Miller, Lyubov. *Svyataya Muchenitsa Rossiiskaya Velikaya Knyagina Yelizaveta Feodorovna.*

*Padeniye Tsarskovo Rezhima.* Leningrad; 1924.

Polsky, Michael, Archpriest. *Noviye Mucheniki Rossiskiye.* Jordanville, New York; 1949.

Semennikov, P. ed. *Nikolai II i Velikiye Knyazye (rodstvenniye pis'ma k poslednomu tsaryu).* Moscow; 1925.

## LETTERS AND DIARIES:

*Advice to a Grand-daughter: Letters from Queen Victoria to Princess Victoria of Hesse.* London; 1975.

Princess Alice. *Biographical Sketch and Letters.* London; 1884.

*Beloved Mama: Private Correspondence of Queen Victoria and the German Crown Princess 1878–1885.* London; 1976.

Buckle, G. E., ed. *The Letters of Queen Victoria* (3rd Series). London; 1932.

*Journal Intime de Nicholas II.* Paris; 1934.

Lee, Arthur Gould, ed. *The Empress Frederick Writes to Sophie, Her Daughter, Crown Princess and Later Queen of the Hellenes: Letters 1889–1901.* London.

*The Letters of the Tsar to the Tsaritsa.* London; 1929.

Mary, Lady Monkswell. *A Victorian Diarist: Later Extracts 1895–1909.*

Maylunas, Andrei and Sergei Mironenko, eds. *A Lifelong Passion: Nicholas and Alexandra—Their Own Story.* London; 1996.

*Pis'ma Imperatritsi Aleksandry Feodorovny k Imperatoru Nikolayu II.* Berlin; 1922.

## BIOGRAPHIES AND BIOGRAPHICAL STUDIES:

Almedingen, E. M. *An Unbroken Unity: A Memoir of Grand Duchess Serge of Russia 1864–1918*. London; 1964. *The Empress Alexandra 1872–1918: A Study*. London; 1961.

Anonymous. *The Fall of the Romanovs*. London; 1918.

Arthur, Sir George. *Concerning Queen Victoria and Her Son*. London; 1943.

Benson, E. F. *The Daughters of Queen Victoria*. London; 1939.

Bolitho, Hector. *Victoria the Widow and her Son*. New York; 1954.

Buchanan, Meriel. *Queen Victoria's Relations*, London; 1954. *Victorian Gallery*. London; 1956.

Buxhoeveden, Baroness Sophie. *The Life and Tragedy of Alexandra Feodorovna, Empress of Russia*. London; 1928.

Cookridge, E. H. *From Battenberg to Mountbatten*. London; 1966.

Cowles, Virginia. *The Kaiser*. New York; 1963.

Duff, David. *Hessian Tapestry*. London; 1967. *Albert and Victoria*. London; 1972. *Alexandra: Princess and Queen*. London; 1980.

Caesar, Egon (Count Corti). *The English Empress*. London, 1957.

Epton, Nina. *Victoria and Her Daughters*. London; 1939.

Fuhrman, Joseph T. *Rasputin: A Life*. New York; 1990.

Hatch, Alden. *The Mountbattens*. London; 1966.

Heresch, Elisabeth. *Alexandra—Tragik und Ende der letzer Zarin.* Munich; 1993.

Hough, Richard. *Louis and Victoria: The First Mountbattens.* London, 1974.

Kerr, Mark. *Prince Louis of Battenberg.* London; 1934.

King, Greg. *The Last Empress: The Life and Times of Alexandra Feodorovna, Tsarina of Russia.* London; 1995. *The Murder of Rasputin: The truth about Prince Felix Youssoupov and the Mad Monk who helped bring down the Romanovs.* London; 1997.

Lieven, Dominic *Nicholas II: Emperor of All the Russias.* London; 1993.

Countess of Longford, *Victoria R. I.* London; 1964.

Lowe, Charles. *Alexander III of Russia.* London; 1895.

Massie, Robert K. *Nicholas and Alexandra.* London; 1968.

Minney, R. J. *Rasputin.* London; 1972.

Nicholayevsky, Boris. *Azev: The Russian Judas.* London; 1934.

Noel, Gerard. *Princess Alice: Queen Victoria's Forgotten Daughter.* Norwich; 1992.

Poliakov, Vladimir. *The Empress Marie of Russia and Her Times.* London; 1926.

Radzinsky, Edvard. *The Last Tsar: The Life and Death of Nicholas II.* London; 1992.

Radziwill, Princess Catherine. *The Intimate Life of the Last Tsarina.* London; 1929. *Nicholas II, Last of the Tsars.* London; 1931.

Spiridovich, Alexander. *Raspoutine 1863–1916.* Paris; 1935.

Tisdall, E. E. P. *The Dowager Empress.* London; 1957.


## REMINISCENCES AND MEMOIRS:

Abrikissov, Dmitri K. *Revelations of a Russian Diplomat.* Seattle; 1910.

Grand Duke Alexander of Russia. *Once a Grand Duke.* London, 1932.

Balsam, Consuelo Vanderbilt. *The Glitter and the Gold.* London; 1953.

Grand Duke Cyril of Russia. *My Life in Russia's Service.* London; 1939.

Dehn, Lili. *The Real Tsaritsa.* London; 1922.

Grand Duke Ernest Louis of Hesse and by the Rhine. *Erinnertes.* Darmstadt; 1983.

The Infanta Eulalia of Spain. *Court Life from Within.* London; 1915.

Grand Duchess George of Russia. *A Romanov Diary.* New York; 1988.

Gilliard, Pierre. *Thirteen Years at the Russian Court.* London; 1921.

Lockhart, Sir Robert Bruce. *Memoirs of a British Agent.* London; 1932.

Prince Louis of Battenberg. *Recollections 1854–1884* (unpublished).

Princess Marie Louise. *My Memories of Six Reigns.* London; 1956.

Marie, Princess of Battenberg. *Reminiscences.* London; 1926.

Queen Marie of Roumania. *The Story of My Life.* London; 1934.

Grand Duchess Marie of Russia, *Education of a Princess.* New York; 1931.

*The Memoirs of Count Witte.* New York; 1990.

*The Memoirs of Grand Duchess Olga Alexandrovna.* London; 1964.

*Memoirs of H. R. H. Prince Christopher of Greece.* London; 1938.

Mosolov, A. A. *At the Court of the Last Tsar.* London, 1935.

Prince Nicholas of Greece. *My Fifty Years.* London; 1926.

Novikov, Olga. *Russian Memories.* London; 1917.

*Out of My Past: The Memoirs of Count Kokovtsov.* Stanford, California; 1935.

Paléologue, Maurice. *An Ambassador's Memoirs.* London; 1922.

Princess Paley. *Memories of Russia 1916–1919.* London; 1921.

Preston, Sir Thomas. *Before the Curtain.* London; 1950.

Radziwill, Princess Catherine. *Memories of Forty Years*. London; 1914.

*Reminiscences of Lady Randolph Churchill*. London; 1908.

Rodzianko, Paul. *Tattered Banners*. London.

Roussoff, A. N. *Memoirs of Alexander Wolkoff-Mouromtzov*. London; 1928.

*Souvenirs d'Alexis Volkov*. Paris; 1928.

Volkonsky, Prince Serge. *My Reminiscences.*

von Bock, Maria. *Reminiscences of My Father, Peter A. Stolypin*. Metuchen, New Jersey; 1970.

Vyrubova, Anna. *Memories of the Russian Court*. London; 1922.

Kaiser Wilhelm II of Germany. *My Early Life*. London.

Youssoupov, Prince Felix F. *Lost Splendour*. London; 1953.


## HISTORICAL AND MISCELLANEOUS WORKS:

Cowles, Virginia. *The Romanovs*. London; 1957.

Craig, Gordon A. *Germany 1866–1945*. Oxford, 1982.

Eilers, Marlene A. *Queen Victoria's Descendants*. New York; 1987.

Engelstein, L. *Moscow 1905*. New York.

Golden, Frank, ed. *Documents from Russian History*. New York; 1927

Grenville, J. A. S. *Europe Reshaped 1848–1878*. London; 1976.

Johnson, Paul. *A History of the Modern World*. London; 1991.

Kochan, Lionel. *Russia in Revolution: 1890–1918*. London; 1967.

Lambton, Antony. *Elizabeth and Alexandra*. London; 1985

Lengyel, Emil. *Secret Siberia*. London; 1947.

MacDonogh, Giles. *Prussia: The Perversion of an Idea*. London; 1994.

Pares, Sir Bernard. *The Fall of the Russian Monarchy*. London; 1939.

Payne, Robert. *The Terrorists*. New York; 1963.

Pipes, Richard. *Russia Under the Old Regime*. London; 1974.

Radziwill, Princess Catherine. *The Royal Marriage Market of Europe*. London; 1915.

Sokolov, Nicholas. *Enquête judiciaire sur l'assassinat de la famille impérial russe*. Paris; 1926.

Ular, Alexander. *Russia from Within*. London; 1905.

Vulliamy, C. E., ed. *From the Red Archives*. London; 1934.

Westwood, J. N. *Endurance and Endeavour: Russian History 1812–1986*. Oxford; 1986.

# Index